SO-AAD-588

STRATEGIES IN RHETORIC
from thought to symbol

EDITED BY

TOM E. KAKONIS
wisconsin state university

JAMES C. WILCOX
boston university

HELEN M. SCHULTZ
south dakota state university

HARPER & ROW, PUBLISHERS
new york, evanston, san francisco, london

STRATEGIES IN RHETORIC: from thought to symbol

Copyright © 1971 by Tom E. Kakonis, James C. Wilcox,
and Helen M. Schultz.
Printed in the United States of America. All rights reserved. No part of this
book may be used or reproduced in any manner whatsoever without written
permission except in the case of brief quotations embodied in critical
articles and reviews. For information address Harper & Row, Publishers, Inc.,
49 East 33rd Street, New York, N.Y. 10016.

Standard Book Number: 06-043454-6

LIBRARY OF CONGRESS CATALOG CARD NUMBER: 79-13783

CONTENTS

PREFACE

STRATEGIES IN RHETORIC is designed to lead the novice writer from the conceptual stages of prewriting through the principal forms of exposition to an introduction to the mythic and symbolic bases of literature. This guiding concept for the book requires some elaboration. Traditionally, there are four steps in the prewriting process. The first requires a conscious and deliberate pedagogical commitment to the importance of prewriting. Next, the student must be shown that the process of putting writing topics into verbal structures is primarily a mental one. This done, he must be taught to recognize that much of his material will necessarily grow out of critical observation and analytical thinking. Finally, from these three non-writing steps, he must be led from an easy, natural transition into the actual process of composition, a process involving all the standard principles of the discipline of rhetoric.

In our text, we have incorporated these four steps. The commitment itself is implied by the inclusion of the first two chapters, which are devoted solely to prewriting. The first chapter consists of essays on the analysis of the process of thinking; the second consists of essays that consider problems of close reading and observation. Both are instructive in the sense that they provide methods and techniques for the mastery of basic prewriting skills.

The fourth step, the transition to writing, is the subject of the remainder of the text. We include five chapters built around the most common and useful topics of rhetoric: definition, analysis, cause and effect, analogy, and comparison and contrast. Our final chapter, "Myth and Symbol," strives to translate the rhetorical principles of expository writing into the forms of literary art and criticism. Each chapter is introduced by brief, explanatory text and is followed by a series of selections that demonstrate the particular principle at work in the hands of accomplished writers. These models are chosen from fiction, poetry, and the essay for the purpose of showing that certain discernible rhetorical patterns exist in *all* types of writing. In the second part of the book, each chapter is followed by a section that gives suggestions for discussion and writing material.

The outstanding feature of STRATEGIES IN RHETORIC is the representation of the prewriting and writing processes in one book. These processes are presented in a coherent pattern that is adaptable and fundamental for courses in composition.

T. E. K.
J. C. W.
H. M. S.

PREWRITING
thinking, reasoning, and the imagination

THINKING

Before one begins the actual process of writing—regardless of the subject—he must engage in the sort of mental preparation that some call prewriting. This preparation is, quite simply, the thinking that leads to both the conception of ideas and the organization of a plan or structure for their development. The five essays that follow proceed from this assumption and explore intellectually three elements of the prewriting process: thinking, reasoning, and the imagination. Not only do these essays offer the novice writer an insight into the workings of his own mind, they also provide patterns for the possible structural approaches that an essay may take once the idea has been conceived. Such patterns are based on the intention of the writer and are usually structured around an expository or argumentative framework. That is, the writer's intention is either to explain a particular process or to argue for it in some way.

In his essay "What Do We Mean by 'Thinking'?," Robert Thomson defines the nature of thinking by breaking it down (the expository process of analysis) into its several qualities: autism, remembrance, imagination, belief, and reason. Of these qualities two are directly pertinent to the writing process: reason and the imagination.

The next two essays should be read as a unit. In "The Necessity for Reason," Gilbert Highet argues that it is basic to man's nature to develop and use his power of reason, for it is this power that leads both individuals and nations to a greater sense of freedom. Narrowing the focus of the manner of reasoning to a specific quality, Byron Guyer and Ronald Bird, in "Thinking Based on Evidence," explain through the process of analysis a means to achieve reason based on the scientific method. They describe the scientific method as inductive, in that it relies on observation and sampling and consequently develops by moving from particulars to generalities.

Growing out of the reasoning process as thought is the rhetorical necessity for persuasion (Aristotle defined rhetoric in part as "the art of persuasion"). In the essay "Persuading," the author explores the use of language as a tool to elicit a desired response. He suggests that the writer whose purpose is persuasion must be fully aware of the connotative and metaphoric meanings of words, and, equally, of the ethical problems inherent in persuasion. No small part of the relationship between writer and reader is communicated through tone; consequently, the writer's tone must be both consistent and in keeping with whatever relationship he hopes to establish. Thus the transition from reasoning to persuasion is accomplished in part by the writer's greater attention to the needs, attributes, prejudices, and predispositions of his audience. Hopefully, it will also be accompanied by a sense of ethical responsibility which, when based on rational evidence, will serve as a buttress to responsible thought.

The last essay in this section is concerned with the role of the imagination in the thought process. In "The Reach of the Imagination," Jacob Bronowski describes the interrelationship of reason and the imagination, how they cooperate to give birth to the creative process—a process that can be scientific as well as literary.

It is an unfortunate fact that in the past the concept of prewriting has been sadly neglected. The novice writer chooses— or has thrust upon him—a topic, and he plunges into it blindly with predictably dire results. Careful study of these essays will repay the student interested in developing a coherent, rational pattern of thought on any subject and translating that pattern into a well-wrought essay.

what do we mean by "thinking"?

ROBERT THOMSON

Aristotle selected rationality, the capacity to think, as the defining attribute of Man. Descartes sought to distinguish mind from matter by characterizing the former as "that which thinks." It is not surprising that these two philosophers should seize upon one of the most distinctive human capacities in their definitions. It is true that many of the activities involved in human thinking are present lower down the evolutionary scale, particularly among vertebrate animals; but the human animal has developed these activities to such an extent that there is a huge gap between man and the next most intelligent living creature. Thought is not necessarily the most significant psychological function, but no understanding of human behaviour can be complete without some study of the fact that human beings have the capacity to think in ways which no other animal is able to achieve. No psychology can be complete without some attempt to describe and explain what a man does when he is described as "thinking"—however much certain psychologists emphasize the irrational and unconscious factors in human make-up.

But what is thinking? This might seem a pointless question, since everyone knows by acquaintance what thinking is from his own first-hand experience of doing it. We all think from time to time. Even if we are not philosophers or scientists we have at

Reprinted with permission of Penguin Books Ltd., from *The Psychology of Thinking*, by Robert Thomson.

least followed an argument put to us by a schoolmaster or preacher. We have sometimes been bright enough to spot a flaw in such an argument and have managed to formulate a cogent objection against it. We have been defeated by chess or bridge problems or have battled with such teasers until we have succeeded in reaching a solution. We know very well how some thinking sticks to the point and moves steadily towards its conclusion while other thinking runs round in circles or drifts off into blind alleys or gets bogged down! Some answers to problems come to us in a flash, while at other times we are confused and befuddled in spite of hard efforts. In brief, we know quite a lot about thinking from our own practical experience of thinking. Why should anybody want to discuss thinking and to ask what thinking is?

Very few people ever think about thinking. It is one thing to practise an activity and quite another thing to stand back and try to observe, describe, and account for that activity. It is one thing to realize that certain activities happen, but quite another thing to take special steps to show precisely what does happen and how it happens in the way it does. Those who have traditionally given descriptions of what a man does who thinks have been the philosophers. They have chiefly relied on their own personal experience as their data, and have usually undertaken the inquiry as part of a larger enterprise—that of understanding the world and Man's knowledge of it. It is only recently that psychologists have tried to find out what happens when we think and what conditions influence our performance by applying the methods of science to this human capacity. In neither philosophy nor psychology have the results of this abstract approach to thought been really successful. But, at least, they have shown that thinking is a much more complicated business than common-sense acquaintance with it might lead one to suppose. There are still plenty of facts to find out and many difficult problems to be faced if we want to understand the nature of thought.

We must begin, however, by sorting out the common-sense knowledge which we all have about thinking. This is the surest starting-point for any academic inquiry. Moreover, it is readily accessible, since much of it is embedded in our everyday speech, in the ordinary language we use to describe or refer to thinking.

When we describe a person as "thinking" it is evident that we are using a highly ambiguous concept. The word or its synonyms mean quite different activities according to the context and manner in which it is used. If you ask the old nursery question "A penny for your thoughts?" the answer might reveal anything from a wool-gathering day-dream to a complex cogitation concerned with a problem in mathematical analysis. The verb "to think" has such a wide application that, in its most general use, we never stop thinking throughout our waking moments and even indulge in snatches of thought during sleep. Nevertheless we can distinguish several more particular meanings of the concept. What different kinds of activity does the notion of "thinking" indicate according to conventional usage?

(1) Much of our thinking is what psychologists label "autistic" thinking: fantasies, day-dreams, the idle flitting from one half-formed notion to another. This sort of activity is regarded as the imaginative expression of underlying wishes, needs, or wants.

(2) In quite a different sense we sometimes use a phrase like "I am trying to think when I last used my season-ticket." Here "thinking" is synonymous with "remembering." The attempt to recall what we have perceived or learned in the past is totally different from the wishful-thinking of fantasy. It is prescribed by actual happenings in the past and involves an attempt to describe these accurately.

(3) Between the uncontrolled flow of autistic thoughts and the deliberate attempt at recall comes imaginative thinking. Imagination is distinguished from fantasy in that it is evoked primarily by external sources of stimulation, such as persons, things, and events actually perceived. When we fancy or suppose or imagine happenings (which are not actual events either past or present), our pseudo-happenings have a coherence which is modelled on, and derived from, observations of how things usually happen. Imagining what is possible or feasible is often an essential part in the solution of some real problem. Imagination is closely allied with reasoning.

(4) Sometimes we use the imperative phrase "Think what you are doing!" Here is a command to take heed or pay attention to the execution of a practical task. Some tasks can be done either carefully or in a slapdash manner: others cannot be done at all

unless a worker thinks what he is doing. As Professor Gilbert Ryle, the distinguished Oxford philosopher, has pointed out, "thinking what one is doing" when engaged in a practical task such as mountaineering does not involve muttering detailed instructions to oneself as one works. It is rather adopting an attitude or frame of mind. We say of a boxer "Joe lost the fight because he wasn't thinking what he was doing in the sixth round" and we condemn people for "thinking of nothing but pleasure." In each case we are not talking about a person's capacity to reason: instead we are referring to a manner or style of behaviour. We can say, in this use of the term, that a person is thinking when engaged in fighting or climbing.

(5) When a man tells us, in social discourse, "what he thinks" about politics or religion or the local football team or when he asks us "What do you think about it?" the word "think" usually means "believe."

Everyone holds a number of beliefs, opinions, or views on a wide variety of topics. Such beliefs are rather like habits; we acquire them like habits uncritically, slipping into them gradually and abandoning them just as easily through subtle social influences. Beliefs are induced in us, or broken down in us, by means of "propaganda" carried out in newspapers, advertisements, political agitators (professional and amateur), or the preachings and pleadings of our friends. Beliefs are picked up, like fashions, through the unconscious or half-conscious or deliberate imitation of the example set by some group of people. We are often unaware of what we really do believe until some crisis or argument forces us to formulate, acknowledge, and defend our beliefs. Basically, beliefs are tendencies to react, consciously or otherwise, in a consistent manner in specific situations. A statement of a belief expresses what the attitude or tendency is. "I don't believe in drinking when you're driving" expresses a tendency (*a*) to abstain when responsible for a vehicle, (*b*) to disapprove of other people who take alcoholic liquor when in charge of a car or motorcycle, etc. We usually hold our own particular beliefs because of certain experiences in the past: a man's most fixed beliefs carry the stamp of his personal history. They are the result of the constant process of adapting needs to the brute facts of the environment.

In spite of the fact that most beliefs are formed uncritically (and may therefore be dubbed "irrational") they can be regarded from a point of view which is strictly logical. Once formulated in words some beliefs may be looked at as claims: they profess to be true or, at least, probable. Not all beliefs, of course, are statements; some express moral judgments, or sentiments of loyalty, or aspirations. But those which are statements claim to be capable of rational support. Evidence is available for or against a particular belief and the producing and ordering of such evidence introduces a further meaning of the term "thinking." Thinking, in the sense of attacking or defending a belief, may take several forms. We may attempt to show that the statement expressing the belief follows without contradiction from certain premises which are accepted as true by all involved in the argument. Or we may collect empirical evidence—appealing to observed facts and generalizations derived from facts (viz. "75 per cent of this town voted Labour in 1945") in order to show that these data lead us to the statement as a consequence. Or we may simply quote some accepted authority—an expert opinion, a dogma, a custom, or an order from some official—as the ground of the belief stated. In other words, reasoning of some kind, however crude, is required in order to establish the validity or plausibility of a particular belief or opinion. Beliefs may be formed in us as habits are, but they can be tested by the application of external criteria; this testing is a variety of thought.

(6) With this mention of the testing of beliefs, we arrive at the concept of "thinking" in the sense of "reasoning," "reflecting," or "pondering"—with what the old writers used to call the "intellect." This meaning is itself somewhat ambiguous. We are thinking, in the sense of "reasoning," when we are going over a neat argument which has already been worked out and accepted on a previous occasion. Other thinking may involve some kind of work or effort, but there are many different kinds of task which thinkers undertake: mathematical analysis, translating Italian into English, composing music, planning a new department in an industrial firm, designing a hospital building, writing a sermon or metaphysical treatise—besides all the work involved in the physical sciences, history—or the ponderings and calculations of the young man wanting to buy a house for his family.

Some intellectual exercises involve the formation of hypotheses in terms of which a range of events can be explained. Other exercises merely require the re-formulation of a practical problem or the definition of a specific topic.

As Ryle has suggested, "thinking," even in this sixth sense, is highly ambiguous in meaning. The term is what he calls a "polymorphous" concept. Some concepts such as "digesting" or "counting" can be analysed in terms of ingredient processes which always recur in a regular pattern in any activity described by these concepts. But polymorphous concepts are different from these: "farming" is a polymorphous concept which stands for any one or any set of the quite different doings of farmers. Some farming involves buying and selling cattle: but there are some farmers who do not deal in cattle at all. Ploughing, reaping, hedging, ditching, and milking are all farm jobs; but A and B might both be farmers without having many tasks in common or might perform whatever tasks were common to both their farms in entirely different ways. (The ploughing of a peasant in India has something in common with ploughing on the cornlands of Kansas; anyone who wanted to find out how different the two situations of the Indian peasant and American farmer turn out to be could probably do so by working for a spell with each!) Now, according to Ryle, the term "thinking" is, like the term "farming," a polymorphous concept. Thinkers indulge in many different sorts of work, many different kinds of activity, which have little in common with each other. Two thinkers may live very different lives and have very different capacities, skills, interests, and projects (take the familiar case—the literary scholar as contrasted with the scientist). Furthermore, there need be nothing going on in one type of thinking such that it *must* be going on in any other sort of thinking. The conclusion to which this analysis of the term "thinking" leads is that if one wants to study what a man does who is described as thinking, in this sixth sense of the word, it is necessary to sort out typical cases and select some of these for special scrutiny. The psychologist in trying to study "reasoning" or "reflective thought" is not studying a straightforward process like "respiration" or "digestion" or "sleeping," but must select most or some of a number of different types or species of activity each of which is properly describable as "thinking" or "reasoning."

Yet, in spite of their differences, it is likely that there is some common attribute or set of attributes in virtue of which this particular activity or that may be called "thinking." It may be that "thought" is a disjunctive as well as a polymorphous concept. "x" is a disjunctive concept if any value has the attribute "a" OR the attribute "b" OR the attribute "c," etc., etc. So that x_1 has "a" and is therefore categorized as an "x"; x_2 has "b" and is therefore categorized as an "x"; x_3 has "c," x_4 has "d," etc. We can, at least, select a number of instances of the category and study each of them in turn.

When a person thinks reflectively he may do any one or any number of several different things in the course of his thought. Now whatever differences and diversities, among the recognizable parts of a thought process, may be sorted out by a philosopher, he will agree that there is one thing they all have in common. They are all activities—behaviour patterns which are either overt and publicly observable or else covert yet capable of being objectified under certain favourable conditions.

Consider the case of a thinker at work. How do we describe what he does as he works? We tell the story of his activities. He may work through a series of calculations (using a slide-rule or a calculating machine), discover errors in his formulae, and correct them. He may have an intuition that a particular conclusion is the one he is striving for and then construct a chain of inferences to deduce this conclusion from well-established premises. He may ask himself specific questions and give answers in the light of facts or theories known and remembered by him. He may argue a case—taking first one and then the opposite side in the issue; he may cross-question himself—playing the roles of "witness" and "counsel." During all this he may work it all out in his head, or he may utter his thoughts out aloud to himself or he may jot them down in writing. He may consult books, papers, and mathematical tables in order to complete an inference. Whether he thinks in his head or utters his thoughts aloud or has his thinking tracked by a horribly ingenious machine, a description of his moves and counter-moves and his characteristic intellectual operations can be supplied.

What would this description amount to if it could be obtained with perfect accuracy? Whatever the details, it would be different

for each individual thinker. As he "racked his brains" for the
right phrase or hypothesis, as he "weighed" evidence, as he
tussled with a thorny dilemma—we would recognize similarities
to other individual efforts, but might also notice highly personal
and idiosyncratic features of any particular thinking session.
However, two points may be made.

(1) In the first place, everything that went on would be
recognizable as an instance of some familiar kind of activity: calculating, comparing alternative hypotheses and applying various
operations in relation to them, asking questions, giving answers,
discriminating discrepancies, etc. From all of which thinking
might be characterized as a dispositional concept. It refers, in
abstract fashion, to a number of unspecified capacities or skills to
carry out certain performances in response to an appropriate
stimulus-situation. Thinking, as Professor Ryle has argued with
such ingenuity and vigour, is *not* some mysterious shadow-process
which goes on behind the overt performances and the strivings
of the thinker. "Thinking," in the sense of "reasoning" or "cogi-
tating," is essentially a performance or activity: something
which human beings do and which consists in the exercise of
capabilities and skills in a special way. What kind of performance precisely, involving what particular skills, and executed in
what manner or style, depends upon the context; each individual
working at a given time and place and within a particular situation will behave according to the factors involved.

Thought is a variety of dispositional behaviour: as Ryle puts
it, very much a matter of "drills and skills."

All such thinking is motivated towards a particular goal, and
is determined by previous learning and experience. Much of it
may be symbolic (using words, images, asking oneself questions
in silent soliloquy), but other parts of it are more clearly action
(scribbling notes, referring to books, working slide-rules, etc.).

(2) If we want to study the thinking of an individual and especially if we want to compare his thinking with that of other
people, we need not take note of everything he does. Ryle has a
good example of how this is so. He gives us the illustration of a
soldier being questioned about a battle. If the soldier is asked to
report on the battle in which he has been taking part, his ques-
tioners do not want to be told all the petty details of which the

battle and the battlefield actually happened to consist. Nobody wants to know that the sergeant had a quick smoke while consulting a map or that two butterflies flew over the field guns or that there were cowslips in the meadows over which the infantry advanced. Nor is it necessary to know how many bullets were used or how much the uniforms cost. What is wanted is an account which misses out the details but which gives the important moves and counter-moves, the tactics adopted by each side, and the way in which the battle went. How did it go and why did it go in that way? The account of a battle is an abstract account: it is told in terms which apply to *any* battle, but which when handled in a particular way show how *this* battle went.

Since thinking can be regarded as a disposition—a complex coordination and integration of specific activities—the description of a thought process may be likened to the account of a battle. What moves and counter-moves did the thinker make? What tactics did he adopt, and how did he modify them in the light of obstacles, contingencies, and requirements imposed upon him by the situation? What method of attack did he employ, and what were the results of his strivings?

Although no two individuals may behave in precisely the same way—just as no two battles may follow precisely the same course or include exactly similar incidents—nevertheless when one looks, not at the details, but at the general patterns and outcome, then it is possible to study human thinking abstractly.

the necessity for reason
GILBERT HIGHET

With all its limitations, with all its dangers, reason is still one of the essential powers of man. It is not his sole essence. He is not a thinking machine, nor should he try to become one. He is not a thinking animal. He is something much more, something greater and more complex. "How noble in reason!" says the greatest of poets, and goes on "how infinite in faculty!" before adding one more of his inimitable, unforgettable phrases, "this quintessence of dust." But thinking is one of the necessary activities that make him human. He must think.

Day and night, from childhood to old age, sick or well, asleep or awake, men and women think. The brain works like the heart, ceaselessly pulsing. In its three pounds' weight of tissue are recorded and stored billions upon billions of memories, habits, instincts, abilities, desires and hopes and fears, patterns and tinctures and sounds and inconceivably delicate calculations and brutishly crude urgencies, the sound of a whisper heard thirty years ago, the resolution impressed by daily practice for fifteen thousand days, the hatred cherished since childhood, the delight never experienced but incessantly imagined, the complex structure of stresses in a bridge, the exact pressure of a single finger on a single string, the development of ten thousand different games of chess, the precise curve of a lip, a hill, an equation,

Reprinted with permission of Columbia University Press, from *Man's Unconquerable Mind*, by Gilbert Highet.

or a flying ball, tones and shades and glooms and raptures, the faces of countless strangers, the scent of one garden, prayers, inventions, crimes, poems, jokes, tunes, sums, problems unsolved, victories long past, the fear of Hell and the love of God, the vision of a blade of grass and the vision of the sky filled with stars.

It is curious to be awake and watch a sleeper. Seldom, when he awakes, can he remember anything of his sleep. It is a dead part of his life. But watching him, we know he was alive, and part of his life was thought. His body moved. His eyelids fluttered, as his eyes saw moving visions in the darkness. His limbs sketched tiny motions, because his sleeping fancy was guiding him through a crowd, or making him imagine a race, a fight, a hunt, a dance. He smiled a little, or looked anxious, or turned angrily from one side to the other. Sometimes (like Lord Byron) he ground his teeth in rage, and still slept. Sometimes he spoke, in a scarcely articulate shout or a gentle murmur sounding strong in his mind. His heart beat fast with excitement, or slow with despair. He sweated. He felt the passage of time and was making himself ready for the morning with its light and noise. And all that time he was thinking—vaguely and emotionally if he was intellectually untrained, in symbols, animals, and divinities if he was a primitive man, often in memories, sometimes in anticipations of the future, and, far oftener than he himself would believe, forming intricate and firm decisions on difficult problems carried over from his waking life. He will say "I never dream, I only sleep"; but he arises with eight hours of thought written on the records of his brain as surely as another strain of grey has grown on his hair or a new firmness in the muscles of his shoulder. He may call the result a vision or a determination, a revelation or a whim, but it is a thought, worked out by his brain while he slept as surely as his heart was beating and his pancreas secreting digestive juices. Awake or asleep, man thinks. Sometimes it seems as though the chief distinction between powerful and ineffective men lay in the control and direction of their thoughts: the wise and energetic man contrives to use his mind even while his body sleeps, the stupid and helpless man dreams half his life away, even when his eyes are open. Almost every man of affairs acknowledges this when he says "That is a difficult decision: I'll sleep on it." Poincaré the mathematician knew it well. Just before going to sleep, he wrote down his hardest problems, and often woke with them solved, clarified during the night hours by his unsleeping brain.

Day and night, throughout their entire lives, men think. They think as naturally and inevitably as they breathe. It is a crime to deny them the best material for thought, as it is a crime to deprive them without just cause of health, liberty, and life. And it is one of their duties to themselves to think as copiously and richly as they can, to exercise and enjoy their minds as they exercise and enjoy their bodies, making them part of the total harmony which is their life.

Anthropologists sometimes seem to talk as though they believed it impossible to compare one society with another, calling one "superior" and another "inferior." Yet they would agree, like the rest of us, that a nation whose children died in infancy or grew up weak and sickly was inferior physically to a nation which kept its children alive and contrived for them a long and healthy life. In the same way, there can be no doubt that a superior nation is one which uses the minds of its people, giving them a constant flow of interesting ideas to think about, ensuring that no class or group is kept from acquiring knowledge because of sex, color, caste, religion, or poverty, stimulating the free fresh production of ideas, respecting those who record and transmit knowledge, keeping open many channels of communication within the frontiers of the country, and beyond them throughout the world, and not only across geographical distances but through the long ranges of historical time. There have been too few nations such as that. It is for that encouragement of knowledge, that fertility and interchange of ideas, that we admire republican Athens, Augustan Rome, Renaissance Italy, and the France, England, and Germany of the nineteenth century. It is sad, nevertheless, to think through history, and to see how many millions of men and women, in so many hundreds of societies, have lived and died ignorant and thought-benumbed, as though born deaf and blind.

> Knowledge to their eyes her ample page
>   Rich with the spoils of time did ne'er unroll;
> Chill penury repressed their noble rage
>   And froze the genial current of the soul.

It is sobering to think that we ourselves, our children or their children, might be thrust into the same numbness, imprisoned in the narrow limits of daily routine, or suffering, or (even worse) pleasure. Against such dangers we must constantly assert the right to knowledge, its free possession and use.

thinking based on evidence
BYRON GUYER AND DONALD A. BIRD

MOVING FROM PARTICULARS TO THE GENERAL

Of the many tools of thought available to educated man, one of the most useful is the scientific method, a method made up of several rather complex elements. It seems best to take up these elements one at a time so that we can develop a good working knowledge of the whole method instead of acquiring a superficial understanding of words which describe it. The first step in the scientific method is accumulating the particular observations on which a generalization can later be built. Since this process leads from particulars to the general, it is often called "inductive." That is, the direction of the thought is to the generality. We will find this pattern of thought useful in writing.

Let's begin with the relation of particular statements to a general statement. In the following series can you say which statements reflect ideas of a limited, restricted, specific scope, and which statement includes more ideas, or more time, or more space—more "territory"?

a) Rained on Tuesday at 5 p.m. b) Rained on Wednesday at 2 p.m. c) Strong south wind began blowing on Tuesday about 1

Reprinted with permission of Wadsworth Publishing Company, Inc., from *Patterns of Thinking and Writing: A Modern Approach to American English,* by Byron Guyer and Donald A. Bird. © 1959 by Wadsworth Publishing Company, Inc., Belmont, California.

p.m. d) Strong south wind started on Wednesday about 10 a.m.
e) On both Tuesday and Wednesday there were heavy, dark
clouds in the southern sky. f) Heavy, dark clouds in the southern
sky and strong south wind bring rain.

It seems clear that statement *f* covers more territory than the
others, which are limited to specific times and refer to more specific events than *f*. The last statement in the series is therefore
the generality, while *a* through *e* are the particulars leading
inductively to it.

In the series just glanced at, the particulars happened to be
those conditions causing rain, and so we moved not only from
particulars to general but also from causes to effect. If we wanted
to write up that material in a paragraph, it is obvious that the
relation of particular to general (and in this case of cause to
effect) would be appropriate and would make the ideas easily
understandable to a reader. Contrariwise, if we developed such
a paragraph by setting up statements *a*, *b* and *c*, then *f*, and finished with *d* and *e*, the order or pattern of the paragraph would
be confusing to a reader. A pattern of writing for a paragraph
is good when it suits the pattern of the ideas making up the
material and when the pattern is either evident to the reader or
easily discoverable. Without a pattern, the sentences indented
as a paragraph only look like one; they are then from the perspective of logic a random series of statements.

Here is a paragraph illustrative of a pattern made out of the
thought relationship of particulars to general. The writer is
discussing how people thought and felt in the United States in
the 1920's:

> Thinking people questioned accepted ideas and beliefs, they
> put forward new (and unorthodox) theories, the airplane lessened
> distances, physicists said that time and space were curved, tech-
> nologists poured marvels from their gleaming labs with the
> regularity of the milkman bringing the morning milk, social sci-
> entists, using new methods of investigation, came forth with
> startling views of the social body. The sphere of American poli-
> tics suddenly became the world instead of the nation. Literary
> men, sneering at the gentility of their Victorian grandparents,
> boldly entered territories once walled off by reticence. Their
> novels, their stories, and their poems spoke in loud plain print

of matters once not even whispered between man and wife in
the safety of their dark bed. Thinkers, writers, and talkers mined
the walls of custom and blew them sky-high. They created new
patterns to replace the old. The world of the intellectuals was
stirred by excitement.

The last sentence of this paragraph is quite clearly the generality
which the preceding sentences have led up to.

A generality is, of course, always relative to some set of particulars. Thus in the paragraph above, if the topic were larger,
the final sentence might be one among various other particulars
leading to a still larger generality:

> The intellectual world was astir with excitement. The reli-
> gious world sensed the inrush of startling new ideas. Political
> circles foresaw changes in the fabric of politics. Educational groups
> realized that both the methods and content of learning were
> about to change. Industrialists knew that they were on the hori-
> zon of a second revolution. The man in the street, without know-
> ing what was about to happen, felt that tremendous changes
> were imminent. The whole civilization saw itself rushing towards
> new ideas and new ways of living.

In this paragraph, the sentence beginning "The whole civilization . . ." is the most general, and the one beginning "The intellectual world . . ." has become one of the particulars leading
to it.

Here is one more example of the relativity of a generalization.
We must suppose that the catalog of State College defines an
above-normal program as one of more than 15 semester units.

a)   Student X in physical science at State College takes 23 units.
b)   Student Y in physical science at State College takes 23 units.
c)   Student Z in physical science at State College takes 23 units.
d)   Physical science students at State College take above-normal
     programs.

e)   Language arts students at State take 23 units.
f)   Social science students at State take 23 units.
g)   Students in various other divisions take 21 to 23 units.
h)   Many State students take above-normal programs.

In choosing the particulars and generality to make up a good pattern, we must also keep in mind treating our material at a level of generality appropriate to the subject, the medium, and the audience. A study to be published in a learned journal for an audience of professional colleagues might contain a good many long paragraphs filled with masses of particulars leading to a very cautiously limited generalization. The same material appearing in a magazine devoted to educated lay readers might contain briefer paragraphs, some of the details being omitted, with the generalizations expressed with less qualification. In a popular magazine with mass circulation, only those details with "human interest" are likely to remain, and generalizations may be expressed loosely, even sensationally. Here are some examples to illustrate this principle at work.

An essayist writing somewhat informally to many readers of good education contented himself with a single sentence containing particulars as illustration for his rather broad generality. He wrote:

> By far the most considerable change which has taken place in the world of letters, in our days, is that by which the wits of Queen Anne's time [the writers of the early 1700's] have been gradually brought down from the supremacy which they had enjoyed, without competition, for the best part of a century. When we were at our studies, some twenty-five years ago [the 1790's], we can perfectly remember that every young man was set to read Pope, Swift, and Addison, as regularly as Virgil, Cicero, and Horace.

On the other hand, a writer reporting on prison conditions and practices in the early 1800's, and writing to a smaller group of readers with a special interest in the subject, patiently accumulated detail. He wrote:

> In Chelmsford, for example, and in Newgate, all accused or convicted of felony [serious crime] are placed in irons. At Bury and at Norwich, all are without irons. At Abingdon those waiting for trial are not ironed. At Derby none but the untried are ironed. At Coldbath, none but the untried, and those sent back to prison to await re-examination, are put in irons. At Winchester, all are ironed before trial, and so are those sentenced to transportation after trial. At Chester, those alone of bad character

are ironed, whether tried or untried. Throughout the country the practice of putting prisoners in irons is capricious.

Here is a paragraph from a recent text for freshman English. The writers are discussing the function of "highbrow art" and the attitude of the "middle-brows" towards it. The subject, medium, and message are somewhat scholarly, and the writers are, of course, writing to college students. The first sentence gives the frame of reference. The next two, which are rather long, offer a good many particulars to illustrate and support the assertion of the first sentence. The last sentence states the generality —the point of the paragraph.

> The only difficulty with all this is that educated men and women—most of whom are only a generation or two from the less educated and hardworking general run of people—go for the second-rate in art, music, architecture, and literature as bees go for a field of clover, and get very high and mighty before first-class artistic productions. Like the housewife who passes up Roquefort cheese for domestic Blue, or the car buyer who prefers juke-box gaudiness to grace in a car, they like semiclassical music, "realistic" and sentimental painting, "modernistic" ranch houses, and television dramatizations of "'Twas the night before Christmas." They mutter "I don't know anything about art, but I know what I like and I don't like this," unaware that they are really saying, "I don't know anything about art and I like what I know—which is nothing." To take their proper place among the cultivated guardians of our civilized heritage, they need to learn to take good artistic creation straight.
>
> DONALD J. LLOYD and HARRY R. WARFEL
> *American English in Its Cultural Setting*
> (Alfred A. Knopf, Inc., 1956)

.   .   .

OBSERVATION

We have considered one element among those making up the process of thought called the scientific method—working from particulars to a suitable generality. Obviously, if the generality is to be sound, it will have to be drawn from particulars resting on accurate observation. Observation is commonly considered a simple matter of looking at whatever is the subject of attention. After all, seeing is believing, isn't it? Well, yes and no.

The systematic study of observation is rather recent (and thus incomplete) and on some points conjectural. Nevertheless, enough seems to be established to provide a few rules of thumb useful in the improvement of thinking.

First, it seems clear that observing something is not a passive state in which the observer allows outside objects to strike his attention. Everything outside himself registering on his senses might be called a "field." What he *notices* in that field is not so much dependent on merely turning the eye or bending the ear as it is upon his temperament, his learning, his habits, moods, and interests. There seems to be a principle of economy at work. Since any field is so complex and diverse that everything cannot be given attention, only those matters important to the observer are allowed to filter through to attention. For example, a young man might notice the bright eyes of his girl; a physician might observe the flush on her face as indication of a possible fever; a shoe salesman might be aware not of her prettily blooming cheeks but of her handmade French shoes and slim ankles. Professor Irving J. Lee reported the case of an elderly male office worker who read demotion into being placed with two elderly women (soon to retire from the firm) across the aisle from the younger workers in his department. Actually this placing was in recognition of the older man's tact and experience. But his preoccupation with getting older and edging nearer to retirement caused his separation from the younger men to demand all of his attention; he did not notice the evidence of increased responsibility. In extreme instances observation may grossly distort the field presented. Thus the paranoid may construe the casual call of a door-to-door salesman as the sinister ruse of his enemies to spy upon him. But the normal trickiness of observing is better represented by the familiar puzzle contest in which the observer tries to find all of the squirrels hidden away in the pictured tree, or by the cleverness of some animals in blending into their natural background. When objects blend with the background of the "field," only the trained observer can see them.

Second, what we observe and what we make of our observations seem to be heavily dependent upon our share of the general experience and knowledge available within the culture of our society. We observe everything outside ourselves through our share of this experience and knowledge; our knowledge and experience act as lenses through which we shape up our perceptions from outside. An analogy might help to clarify this rather subtle idea.

Imagine a Martian, whose experience included no games or sports, watching a baseball game on the day of his arrival upon the earth. Let us suppose further that by a special process the language he hears is automatically translated into his tongue and put to him through a special headset. And let us suppose that for centuries in his Martian culture social rank has been of supreme importance and that such rank has long been symbolized by the type of hat worn and by the way it is worn. Our Martian might quite unthinkingly give most significance to the catcher, for he is the only man to wear his baseball cap backwards. The Martian might find corroboration for this fact by noting also that only the catcher wears mask, chest protector, and heavy mitt. It might seem to the Martian that the point of the game is for the pitcher to throw the ball to the catcher and that when a batter hits the ball away, the batter is penalized by having to run around the bases. Confirmation for this interpretation rests upon the fact that when the batter fails to hit the ball (and thus has not interfered with the honorable catcher) he is rewarded by being allowed to sit down. In the Martian's construct of the territory of reality outside himself, the home run would be further confirmation since the punishment for knocking the ball out of the park is to have to run all the way around the bases without stopping for a rest. Finally, the Martian notes that when the punishment of a home run occurs, various people in the stands cheer as if they approve the batter's getting what he justly deserves. The Martian may discover the inconsistencies in his interpretation and note the inaccuracy of his earlier observation only in the light of further experience and critical awareness of how the new experience relates to his first interpretation. Gradually by this critical process he sharpens his observation and corrects his construction of the reality "out there."

Third, observation is easily influenced by strong feelings and by firm or rigid convictions—a commonplace, to be sure, but worth mention and remembrance. In one experiment, for example, social psychologists found that some people strongly believing in the inferiority and intransigence of Negroes projected their notions into the events observed. Into an unsuspecting psychology class burst one man brandishing a stick and chasing another man. Some startled observers later insisted that the pursuer was a Negro intent upon killing the pursued with a knife. A few of these witnesses were hard to convince of their perceptual errors even when the psychologist explained that the elements of his experiment demonstrated the very inaccuracies they were committing. Trial lawyers and judges are sadly familiar with the oddities of witnesses. The conviction that seeing is believing and that seeing automatically reveals what really happened "out there" leads to many errors.

Finally, language appears to be so tightly knit up with experience that the language itself may influence patterns of thinking and observing. Recent awareness of the possibilities of such influence has come from those who study exotic languages, such as African or Amerindian. Study has revealed that the old assumption that the language of a primitive people was very simple, lacking in the subtle complexities of highly developed western European languages, was quite wrong. To the contrary, primitive languages are sometimes more complicated than those of modern, technologically developed civilizations. Even more important was the discovery that these languages did not necessarily picture the world the way French or English does. For example, in one African language the color spectrum is divided into two bands with a merging middle ground between. That is to say, there are two words in the language for what these people see as two broadly distinguishable colors. Botanists of the western world cultures brought into their studies the many words for various colors from their languages, and for their own convenience had to invent two terms for *light* and *dark*—the two "colors" to which plants react. In another African language the color spectrum is divided into three major bands. It is apparent that the native speaker of each of these languages—Bassa of Liberia, English, and Shona of Rhodesia—will be encouraged by each color vocabulary to see the world outside in terms of that vocabulary. Until he has different experience through acquaintance with other languages, he will assume without knowing it that everybody sees color his way because he supposes his way simply reveals the "actual" color spectrum.

Another illustration of this concept may suffice to make it clear. Anyone long accustomed to using the terms *either . . . or* may easily allow these terms to slip into his speaking or writing as descriptions of situations that are more complicated than *either . . . or* can accurately describe. Thus the convenience of *either . . . or* may lead one to say of a Mercator projection of the world that it is accurate or it isn't. Any flat representation of a sphere, however, has various degrees of accuracy for various aspects of the sphere. Thus, sailing along the Great Circle route approximates the most direct course. Again, *either . . . or* tempts one to think, "Well, *either* School Board member Jones is valuable to the Board *or* he isn't." But he may be valuable to the Board on problems of finance, yet less effective on problems of educational policy. The more thoughtfully one considers, the less is *either . . . or* likely to seem accurate enough as a language map of some territory. Awareness of how the language acts as a lens through which experience comes to us may help us to understand the relation between a language map and the territory it is supposed to describe.

Probably the most important point for the writer to keep in mind is that, as these remarks on observation have strongly implied, observation is often mixed with interpretation or with the observer's unrelated feelings.

A related matter—statements of fact and statements of opinion—may offer a practical rule of thumb by which the writer can keep observation and interpretation pretty well separated. A statement of fact will yield to checking, that is to say, to a process of confirmation available to various observers, regardless of differences among them. Thus, whether you are a student at Moscow University or State University in Calibhama, you agree on certain statements: The earth's surface has curvature; the distance from Moscow to Hollywood by way of the polar air route is X number of miles; a typewriter of given make and model, when weighed on an accurate scale, is of a specified weight; men and women normally have two legs. These statements of report can be checked. In the final analysis they rest upon observation. If we disagree with a confirmed report we are both silly and irrelevant. Our feelings about what is important and worthwhile simply have nothing to do with matters of fact.

Some statements, however, differ from reports. Suppose instead of "Women have two legs" we have "Women are beautiful." We cannot directly observe something named "beauty"; we cannot agree about what constitutes beauty. One observer might say, "Yes, that woman is beautiful because she is of certain proportions, has brown eyes and brown hair, carries herself well, and has a pleasant expression on her face." Another observer says, "She's not beautiful at all; she's merely pretty. A beautiful woman is one who has a certain look of attractive intelligence and femininity in her face. Her proportions do not matter a bit. Beauty is an illusion some women can create. It's a charm some women radiate regardless of looks and physical measurements." None of these statements is like "Joanna is five foot two." Unless there is an error in our method of measuring or an error in the tape measure, she is or she isn't. But "Joanna is beautiful" is a statement of opinion. It is not a matter of fact but a matter of opinion—of interpretation, of inference or deduction, of feeling about what is important, or good, or beautiful, or right. Such statements are not expressions of observation but of interpretation, opinion, attitude, or feeling, and therefore are subject to a wide range of disagreement.

For some purposes writing which treats of the subject in terms of statements of report is more useful than writing which consists largely of statements of opinion. Notice the difference between these examples. "The boss is a fanatical perfectionist" and "On a number of occasions, Mr. John Q., manager of Hypothetical Products, Inc., has fired secretaries with at least ten years' experience when he discovered one typographical error in one of the letters making up a week's secretarial work." The first statement is one of *opinion,* may or may not be related to observation, encourages disagreement, makes the judgment, and is not subject to ready checking. The second series of statements, on the other hand, is one of *fact* or *report,* is related to observation (that of the writer or some other observer), gives information on the basis of which the reader can make his own judgment, is subject to reasonably ready checking, and is true or not true.

Especially in matters of moment—public controversies, affairs of state, election of government representatives, and so on—fewer statements of opinion and more statements of report would make the writing on such matters a good deal more useful. Since the college student may be expected to develop into a responsible citizen, better able than some others to make wise decisions, the habit of recognizing the difference between statements of report and of opinion is rather important to him, both as writer and reader.

Before we leave the subject of observation, it might be useful to examine a paragraph in which observation plays an important part. While doing so we may note, too, that the amount and extent of observation alluded to seems to be suited to the subject and audience. We may also note that the material is presented in an unobtrusive but clear pattern.

In *The Descent of Man*, Charles Darwin offers some support for his belief that man is similar in structure to the animals. Since his primary purpose is to convince a scientific audience, he gives prominence to the observations of the best-known specialists in the relevant field.

> 1) It is notorious [in Darwin's time this word merely meant well-known] that man is constructed on the same general type or model as other mammals. 2) All the bones in his skeleton can be compared with corresponding bones in a monkey, bat, or seal; so it is with his muscles, nerves, blood vessels, and internal viscera. 3) The brain, the most important of all the organs, follows the same law, as shown by Huxley and other anatomists. 4) Bischoff, who is a hostile witness, admits that every chief fissure and fold of the brain of man has its analogy on that of the orang. . . . 5) Vulpian remarks: "The real differences between the brain of man and that of the monkey are minor. 6) There is no need to be confused about the matter. 7) Man is certainly more like the anthropoid apes in the anatomical features of his brain than he is like the other mammals or even certain quadrumanous monkeys like the guenons and macaques." 8) But it would be superfluous here to give further details on the correspondence between man

and the higher mammals in the structure of the brain and all other parts of the body.

We can now sum up the whole section on observation. Good writing depends in part on good thinking, and this in turn rests in part upon intelligent observation. Hence, improvement in writing is related to understanding the nature of observation and to improvement in observing. Improvement in writing is also related to developing the ability to judge how many of the particulars of observation to offer one's audience. This decision must be made in terms of the needs and tastes of that audience and in terms of the subject written about.

SAMPLING

We have seen that two of the many elements making up the process of inductive thinking are (1) separating the particulars from a generality and (2) noting or collecting observations— these being the data from which we will reason to the generality. If our reasoning is to be reliable, we must be careful to hold our generality to the scope of the material we have observed. For instance, if we want to know how Republicans may vote, we sample the opinions not of Democrats but of Republicans. Party registration makes an obvious difference, and so there is little danger of generalizing beyond the class sampled, but of course it is by no means always so easy to note the difference. If we want a cross section of the town's opinion for and against a large school bond issue, where do we sample? In the new suburban tract development communities? In the downtown apartment sector? In the business section itself? If we sample only in the new suburbs where all the homes have three or four bedrooms with bath and three-quarters, our survey will be weighted toward those more likely to favor the bonds. For in these suburbs are most of the younger people with two or more children. If we sample only in the downtown apartment area, we have another weighting, this time probably of those opposed to the opinion. For in this sector we are likely to find a preponderance of older people whose children have grown up and moved away;

these people see no need for so many new school facilities. In this particular problem, then, our sampling must follow the proportions of interested groups if it is to yield a likely prediction. That is, if about two-thirds of the registered voters are the younger suburbanites and about a third are the older or childless apartment dwellers, then the sampling of say 100 voters should run about 65 suburbanites and about 35 apartment dwellers.

Another way to put this idea is to say that the class actually sampled must be representative and typical of the class to be investigated. Suppose, for example, we want to predict the vote for president and vice-president. We employ 50 telephone girls and secure the opinions of 5,000 people, whose names we take at random from 15 metropolitan directories for 15 large cities scattered around the United States. Is our class under investigation the same as the class we actually sample? No, because while we have obtained a cross section of metropolitan opinion, our use of metropolitan directories has shut us away from sampling the opinion of farmers, small town dwellers, and anyone without a telephone. Since a great many of these people may very well be registered voters, the class actually sampled was not the same as the class we were supposed to investigate.

When we are studying a problem, whether in physical science, social science, natural science, language, or literature, the mere fact that we have a problem means that there is a great deal we do not know. Hence, we take every reasonable precaution to keep down the effect of all of the unknowns. One of the means of doing this is to make sure that our sampling is within the class we intend to investigate and that it represents a random cross section of the typical members of that class.

Another way to make sure that our samples are representative and typical is to sample extensively. If we want to do a paper on the techniques of the digest magazines, we had better sample extensively among various magazines, not just in two that happen to be handy on the table. Of course, if this extensive sampling reveals that there are no essential differences, then we may choose samples on a more restricted basis. If we want to study the appearance of political bias in the news stories of the dailies we must take the same care to make the samples extensive. If at random we sample metropolitan and small town dailies for September, October, and November, we have undermined our study before taking a single note. Since fall is election time, the likelihood of political bias in news stories is greater during this season than in any other.

Another important reason for choosing samples extensively and at random is to avoid the subtle influence of unconscious bias in the mind of the investigator. A serious student puts as much of the truth into his serious writing as he can manage to reveal, and he thus willingly takes reasonable measures to keep out special interest. An investigator of sinus trouble considers all the medical literature, not just that suiting his own ideas on the subject. If the nature of his medical training causes him to discount explanations of sinus trouble in terms of poor circulation of the blood, he may overlook likely leads. But if his scientific training is strong enough, he will include careful consideration of such accounts. A student of the problems of language learning may by nature be a strong believer in self-discipline and therefore tend to ignore methods of language learning which give no emphasis to self-discipline. But if his study is to be sound, he must set aside his dislike of such methods and give them critical consideration. Obviously, if the investigator sticks to the determination to make his sampling extensive and random, he will have the best chance of avoiding the influence of such unconscious biases.

Some students always ask how many samples must be taken before it is safe to generalize about the class investigated. There is no fixed number of samples to take because the infinite number of subjects, fields, or problems to be investigated is of different levels of complexity. That is to say, the more complicated the subject, the greater the number of unknowns, and therefore the greater the care and extent of the sampling.

When there is good reason to believe that the subject of investigation is quite simple and uniform, even a single sample might suffice. Thus, a stack of books all bearing the same title can be generalized about on the examination of one copy. The likelihood of the assumption that all are the same on the evidence of having the same title is strong. In a rare instance only would such an assumption turn out to be wrong. But almost anything needing study is likely to be a good deal more complex and diverse. In the world of nature, long observation by generations of men has pretty well established that no two natural objects are exactly alike; hence the need for many samples. In the social sciences, it is extremely difficult to generalize because people—the class under investigation—even within a small, well-knit community may differ markedly from one another in respects which affect the problem being studied. If we want to study novels the field is diverse and complex. It takes a lifetime to become well enough acquainted with the world's novels to begin generalizing about them soundly. If a student wants to write a paper on the world's novels, he can safely do one of two things: he can write on the broad subject and acknowledge that his generalizations are really just guesses, or he can narrow the subject, restricting it in various ways. He might, for instance, limit himself to a dozen American novels from 1930 to 1940 and be content with smaller but probably sounder generalizations. Of course, the restricting of the subject must be thoughtfully done. If the student chooses only those American novels of the thirties still well-known today, he may be shifting the class sampled away from that under investigation. For the qualities making an American novel well-known today may be the very ones which make it untypical of novels of the thirties.

We have been considering some of the matters which relate to good sampling as part of the process of inductive thinking. Let's glance at some typical generalities in actual student writing. One student wrote:

> The traffic jams in today's cities are a threat to the nerves and drain on the nation's financial resources. The other day it took me over an hour to get from my house to the stadium.

The rest of the theme gave details of his being nerve-racked on the city's boulevards. He returned to his generalization, putting it in other words. No matter how acceptable his grammar, his word choice, his sentence structure, and his mechanics, this student failed in his thinking. No evidence supported his large claim; he flagrantly overgeneralized on one sample of his personal experience. His opening sentence led his readers to expect either a sober summary of studies of the effects of city traffic or a humanized account of these effects with his personal experience kept pretty much in the background.

A student began a speech in this way:

> The average voter is the victim of slick advertising tricks taken over from the hucksters by petty Hitlers masquerading in decent business suits. The other night on "Seat the People" I heard Senator Rumple say. . . .

He then summarized the Senator's remarks, pointing out propaganda tricks among them. He concluded with a warning to the American people. You should be able to make your own analysis of the weaknesses in the thought of the speech described. Obviously, if there is any truth in the claims made by either student, that truth is quite coincidental to their work.

SUMMARY

One of the most useful and creative tools of thought is the concept of inductive process: reaching a generalization on the basis of the relevant particulars. The pattern of writing in which particulars clearly lead to a generalization or clearly follow the statement of a generalization is related to the inductive process. If such writing is to be good, the pattern must grow out of the relationship among those ideas. The pattern cannot be arbitrarily forced upon the ideas. Furthermore, the number of the particulars in relation to the generality—the balance—varies with the audience and the subject. The thoughtful writer keeps this in mind. Finally, the writer's generalizing should directly or indirectly reflect his knowledge of the nature of observation—on which his particulars rest—and on the nature of sampling.

While the writer sees to it that his ideas for a paragraph follow some pattern either obvious to the reader or discoverable by examination, the pattern of his thought before he turned to setting down his ideas may be quite different from the pattern he finally gives to the completed writing. Darwin accumulated many observations (in a systematic and careful way appropriate to his subject and purpose) in his paragraph on the similarity between the structure of man and that of animals. In writing out these ideas it seemed best that the generality be stated first, the illustrative particulars next. Perhaps because he sought to convince skeptical scientists, he set up his citation from Vulpian in order to put last the repetition of that idea he had already put first in his own words. He then stated the idea for the third time, once again in his own words.

On the other hand, if the writer supposes that his readers may balk at his generality, he may set down all supporting and illustrative particulars first. The generalization may be more acceptable since he has gradually led up to it.

persuading

HAROLD C. MARTIN

For centuries students of language have speculated industriously about the relationship between words and concepts, between words and the "real" world, between words and the intentions of their users, between words and the effects they have upon their hearers or readers. In recent times, some have suggested that language originated in gesture and in unstructured sounds expressing emotional responses; others, that it arose from early magical and myth-making attempts to coerce and control the nonhuman world. One group of linguists, those called "mentalists," believes that words refer only to mental events, to occurrences in the mind which are completely nonphysical; another group, those called "mechanists," insists that no such mental events occur and that words are really no more than signs of complex bodily processes; both groups, it is apparent, think of language as primarily related to the speaker's or writer's experience and only secondarily, if at all, to the process known as "communication." In contrast, other investigators think that the real importance of language lies not in its power to define and realize the speaker-writer's situation or condition but in its function as a transmitter, as a device for conveying some state of mind from one person to another. That state of mind they con-

Reprinted with permission of Holt, Rinehart and Winston, Inc., from *The Logic and Rhetoric of Exposition,* by Harold C. Martin. © 1957, 1958 by Harold C. Martin.

strue to be composed of three elements: the concept represented by the words used, the speaker's or writer's intention in representing it as he does, and the consciousness of various ways in which that verbal representation may be interpreted by the hearer or reader. Even so complex a concept of language as this three-part one surely does not provide an adequate account of the nature of language itself. Yet the concept has a certain utility, and it is adopted here as a means of beginning the discussion of a fourth procedure in which language is very important. To that procedure we give the name *persuading*.

.   .   .

THE UBIQUITY OF PERSUASION

Now, in a broad sense of the term, all communication is persuasive, a fact which Kenneth Burke has compressed into the effective statement, "Style is ingratiation." The generalization does not mean, of course, that a writer is always consciously intent on cajoling or convincing. Yet the fact that a writer must choose among words and combinations of words does mean that there must be a ground of choice, and that ground is essentially their capacity to "persuade," in the sense indicated above. Although a communication may be apparently only explanatory or descriptive in purpose, it is at the same time an attempt to lead others to see or understand something as the writer sees or understands it. Strictly speaking, there is no such thing as "objective" writing. A writer's words refer to events, ideas, things, and their qualities, true enough, but it is to events, ideas, things, and qualities as they are known to the writer. His use is always one man's use (though not necessarily different from every man's use, for all that), and his communication is the act of getting others to accept that use, even if only temporarily.

The fundamental persuasiveness of the act of communicating is enhanced by the nature of words themselves, and since it is with words (with words-in-order, to be precise) that a writer conducts his communication, a treatment of persuasion may well begin from them.

THE SOURCES OF CONNOTATIVE MEANING

. . . First, it is important to remember that words are arbitrary, that—to use the words of John Locke—there is no "natural connection . . . between particular articulate sounds and certain ideas, for then there would be but one language amongst all men." Yet, though words are arbitrary, they are not all alike in their referential character, and since it is partly with the character of words that persuasion is concerned, some way must be found of distinguishing among words on that basis. In the first place, it is clear that the concepts to which some words refer are much broader than those to which others refer. The referent of "pay," for instance, is large enough to *include* the referents of "salary," "wages," and "stipend." It is the work of the definer to sort these referents into categories and subcategories even though, in ordinary discourse, we often use one word rather than another without very careful attention to the distinctions at which a good definer would arrive.

There is more to the matter than getting the definitions straight, however. We may be able to make absolutely airtight distinctions between the words "fat," "stout," and "obese" and still hesitate about which word to use in referring to a person who is overweight. The point of interest here is the ground on which a choice among those adjectives might be made. To speak of a "fat" bankroll is certainly to say nothing in dispraise of it, but to refer to a woman as "fat" may be very uncomplimentary indeed. In part, the difference is that fatness is generally thought, in our culture, to be a good characteristic of bankrolls and a bad one of persons. But if the fatness of the woman is a fact, and if the fact must be mentioned, we still may choose to avoid using the word "fat" about a woman and decide to substitute for it the word "stout," or even "plump."

In rhetoric, "stout" and "plump" are sometimes referred to as "euphemisms" for the word "fat," but to call them "euphemisms" is not to explain their character or to explain our choice. What is it that makes one word more or less palatable than another?

Now, for a few words in the English language, there does appear actually to be something in the character of the word itself that affects its meaning. Those words take on distinct coloration because they contain sounds which, for reasons not fully understood, generally occur in words of a particular connotative tendency. Thus, when William Faulkner named one of the families in his novels "Snopes," he helped to establish its unsavory character, even before he depicted it, by using the sound "sn-" in its name. The English language has a remarkably large number of sn- words having unpleasant associations—*snoop, sneak, snide, snort, snare, snag, snarl, snob, snout, snap, snitch*—and "Snopes" catches some of the unpleasantness by aural contagion.

The number of words that have such indigenous bias is not great, but its smallness should not obscure the fact that the *sound* of a word may be a part of its persuasive capacity. Indeed, those words which we call "onomatopœic" because they are attempts to reproduce "natural" sounds—"crunch," "murmur," "buzz," and so on—are effective largely because of their sound. Advertisers constantly play upon our responsiveness to the sound of words, and poets, of course, do so, too. But, except in single words or brief phrases, neither can rely primarily on sound to convey meaning, or even to stimulate feeling. Not until idea joins sound, as it soon comes to do even in onomatopœic words, is the persuasive capacity of the word fully realized.

Two much more important sources of the persuasive effect of words are (1) the context in which they are habitually used and (2) the total character of the concepts to which they refer. A word that is "borrowed" from one situation and applied to another carries over to the new situation some of the associations of the one it has left. Thus, the word "scientific" is frequently employed to provide the stamp of approval even though nothing that remotely resembles scientific study may be involved. That particular use of connotative effect, of course, is bad, and it may be dangerous. The indiscriminate labeling of things with terms used largely for their associated meanings is the practice of charlatans and demagogues. But the exploitation of associated meanings must not be condemned simply because it is abused.

To go back to an earlier example, we may choose the word "stout" rather than the word "fat" out of the best of motives, knowing almost without thinking about it that "fat" has accumulated associations which make it unflattering when it is used to describe a person and that "stout" is for some reason rather free of such associations.

Consider again, for example, some of the words which refer to money received in exchange for services rendered: *wages, pay, salary, fee, hire, stipend, emolument, remuneration, honorarium, pittance, screw, dole.* As noted above, "pay" is probably the broadest of the lot, and were "hire" in more common use today than it is, the two words might be treated as the class-words for this series. "Wages" are generally paid weekly or daily and therefore are considered to be the return for manual or mechanical and perhaps intermittent work, which is most often paid on that basis. "Salary," on the other hand, is a fixed sum frequently paid only once a month or once every two weeks; generally speaking it is (or used to be) a larger amount than wages, though a policeman's salary today will fall considerably below a mason's wages. The word is undoubtedly used in some instances to lend prestige to relatively low-paying work, though its origin (from *salario*, a sum of money given to Roman soldiers for the purchase of salt) offers no support for that usage. A "fee" is the sum received for special and usually professional services—an architect's pay for designing a building, a doctor's pay for treating a patient, a lawyer's pay for drawing a contract; or for services whose cost is set by law or tradition—a notary's fee, a bailiff's fee, and so on. "Fee," too, may suggest a certain dignity simply because it is associated with the work of officials and of specially trained people, groups which continue to have prestige whether or not the prestige is matched by financial returns. The prestige of the work rubs off on the words by which its pay is designated.

The clearly honorific words (*stipend, emolument, remuneration,* and *honorarium*) are both seriously and ironically used. Where seriously, they often seem to be self-conscious efforts to take the supposed crassness out of exchanging money for services rendered. Of the four, only "honorarium" is etymologically grounded in a sense of *noblesse oblige,* and it is different from the others in that it generally refers to an unusual service, the value of which is not at all to be measured by the amount of the sum paid. A "stipend" is the least inflated and pretentious of the terms, but its association with permanence (it is generally used of pay calculated by the month or year) lends it a dignity greater than that owned by "salary." "Emolument" and "remuneration" are both so Latinate and uncommon that their use for "pay" nearly always signifies prestige. A certain Micawberishness about them, and about others in this group as well, makes them quick subjects for irony and for mockery of false gentility. Thus a medical intern, scraping along on almost no pay at all, may refer to his salary as "emolument." Or to give the slender monthly sum something nearer its due, he may exaggerate in the opposite direction and use a pejorative term for it. Of the pejorative terms listed (*pittance, screw, dole*), one—"screw"—is used only in England; its derivation is uncertain, but its use is confined largely to workingmen and, even among them, it is slangy. Both "pittance" and "dole" are deprecatory when used in half-humorous or sardonic reference to pay, probably because both are associated with the charity dispensed to the sick, the infirm, and the unemployed. "Pittance" has the same etymology as "pity"; "dole" comes from the verb "to deal" and therefore suggests a general distribution of money or goods, not one reckoned according to services performed or according to worth.

Now it is hard to say whether the connotative "aura" of some of these words used to designate money received in exchange for services is the product of context or of what is called above "the total character of the things" to which the words refer. Perhaps it is the product of both. The connotations of such a word as "wages" do undoubtedly implicate the situations to which the word is relevant (daily or hourly rates for work that may be intermittent) and the attributes of the actual amounts paid (barely enough to live on; not much, considering the hours you have to stand on your feet to earn it; good enough while it lasts but you never know how long it will; and so on). In fact, the connotative, or suggestive, effect of the word will probably reach even to the attributes of the work performed for wages and of the people who perform it. This may seem to be a great deal to expect of a word, and indeed it is more than one should expect, though not more than one should be prepared to take into account in making a choice among several words that come to mind.

There are, of course, no rules by which one can determine the connotative aura of a particular word; one must simply know. Such knowing is chiefly the result of a broad experience with words, and wide reading is perhaps the surest avenue to such experience. It takes more than wide reading, however, to make a person aware of still another way in which single words may persuade, a way which is often summed up in the word "metaphor." For an appreciation of the power of metaphor, the reading must be not only wide but perceptive and thoughtful.

THE METAPHORICAL GROUND

Metaphor is one of the most fundamental of linguistic activities; some have even suggested that most language is, at bottom, metaphorical. However that may be, it is certainly true that all developed language is deeply indebted to metaphor and that all good writing reflects the writer's consciousness of the metaphorical vitality of the words he uses.

As defined in the early study of poetry, "metaphor" usually means "a comparison without the use of 'like' or 'as.'" "He fights like a lion in battle" is said to be a simile; "He is a lion in battle," a metaphor. As "metaphor" is used in the discussion of language, it is a broader term, comprising all those linguistic activities by which the attributes of one thing are imputed to a different thing. To take an example close at hand, the previous paragraph speaks of developed language as "deeply indebted to metaphor." A debt is something owed by one person to another; to say that language owes a debt to metaphor is to personify language and to speak metaphorically. More obvious metaphors (a child's observation, for instance, that the sun is "smily") are easy to detect and fairly easy to use; submerged metaphors like the one just examined are likely to conceal their very real persuasive effect under the bland façade of ordinariness.

The way in which overt and submerged metaphors do their
work becomes apparent if we consider carefully a passage of
prose which is written with both kinds in mind.

"The style is the man"; but the social and rhetorical influences
adulterate and debase it, until not one man in a thousand
achieves his birthright, or claims his second self. The fire of the
soul burns all too feeble, and warms itself by the reflected heat
from the society around it. We give back words of tepid greeting,
without improvement. We talk to our fellows in the phrases we
learn from them, which come to mean less and less as they grow
worn with use. Then we exaggerate and distort, heaping epithet
upon epithet in the endeavour to get a little warmth out of the
smouldering pile. The quiet cynicism of our everyday demeanour
is open and shameless, we callously anticipate objections founded
on the well-known vacuity of our seeming emotions, and assure
our friends that we are "truly" grieved or "sincerely" rejoiced at
their hap—as if joy or grief that really exists were some rare and
precious brand of joy or grief. In its trivial conversational uses so
simple and pure a thing as joy becomes a sandwich-man—humanity degraded to an advertisement. The poor dejected word
shuffles along through the mud in the service of the sleek trader
who employs it, and not until it meets with a poet is it rehabili-
tated and restored to dignity.

WALTER RALEIGH,
"Social and Rhetorical Corruptions," in *Style*

This passage is so heavily metaphorical that meaning is as often
obscured as revealed in it, but its dense figurativeness provides
ample illustration of the ways in which metaphors work to persuade, and for that reason it is valuable for our purposes here.
The *statement* of the passage is approximately this: "Conventional and unconsidered use of language destroys the capacity
of words to express a man's thoughts and feelings." The expression of that statement is developed, in large part, by two metaphorical procedures: (1) *reification*, the treatment of abstractions
as though they were things ("influences adulterate and debase"),
and (2) *personification*, the treatment of things as though they
were persons ("the poor dejected word shuffles along"). Two
strong metaphors dominate: men's thoughts and feelings as "the
fire of soul" which "burns . . . and warms," and joy as a "sand-

wich-man." Of these two, the first is continuously elaborated in other metaphorical expressions of slightly reduced intensity, the "smouldering pile" of epithets, the "tepid" greeting, and so on. Still further down on the scale of intensity, or of obviousness, other metaphors continue the transformation of abstract into concrete, of inanimate into animate: the "heaping" of epithets, the way in which we "callously" anticipate objections which are "founded" on the "vacuity" of our emotions, the progressive meaninglessness of words "worn" with use, the eventual "rehabilitation" and "restoration" of a word when it "meets with" a poet.

The overt metaphors strike eye and ear at once and, if they are fresh and apt, persuade us to consider their subject in a particular light. The submerged metaphors, though they make less noticeable impression on us, affect our consideration fully as much for the reason that we assent to them without thought or examination. An overt metaphor may induce us to accept a new way of looking at a matter, but it does so over a certain amount of resistance simply because the new way runs counter to habit. A good writer is likely, therefore, to be sparing in his use of strong figures of speech. And, because he knows that submerged metaphors have a persuasive effect out of proportion to their quiet presence, he will treat them with a great deal of respect.

Metaphor is, then, a very important instrument for directing the persuasive energy of language, probably the most effective single instrument when it comes to controlling the connotations of a particular word. It may seem that the associative aura of words is being treated here too much as though it had a demonic capacity to make effective communication almost impossible. Therefore it may be wise to point out that, in addition to the connotative spread already noted, there is another with which the writer must deal. Besides the indigenous bias of a few words (the sn- words mentioned above) and the general connotative aura of most words, there are "meanings" for words which are either entirely private or limited to a small number of people. Such specialized meanings . . . no writer can completely predict. The adjective "fat" annoys a large number of people; used as a verb, the word "contact" may raise the hackles of only a few beleaguered purists; and the noun "asparagus" may revolt only a neurotic John Doe, who once became violently ill after eating asparagus and cannot forget the experience. Even could he predict such connotations, the writer can do nothing directly about them. Indirectly, however, he can still manage to control such random associations by the way in which he makes sure that this word, and no other, is the one that serves his purpose at the moment. If the word, or the image, is exactly right for his purpose, its context will in large measure protect it from taking on associations other than those he desires it to evoke.

If individual words and phrases have persuasive effect, it is obvious that sentences do, too, and attention is paid to the effects of syntax in later parts of this book. At this point, it is enough to reiterate the statement that all language is persuasive and requires constant alertness in those who use it.

THE ETHICS OF PERSUASION

To insist on the persuasiveness of language is to raise an ethical problem which has always engaged the attention of writers and which has been one of the main preoccupations of modern semanticists, or students of the meaning of words. Although what has been said so far . . . may often seem to imply that words have an autonomous life, wielding power independent of their users, that proposition is itself more metaphorical than not. *People* use words, and it is their way of using them that is largely responsible for their persuasiveness.

The traditional term for the use of language to persuade is "rhetoric," and the fact that an ethical problem is associated with that use is apparent in the disrepute into which the term has often fallen. In the sixteenth century, Montaigne decried persuasive practices in these words:

> . . . Aristo wisely defines rhetoric as "a science to persuade the people"; Socrates and Plato as "the art of deceiving and flattering." And they who deny the general definition verify it throughout in their precepts.
>
> The Mohammedans forbade their children to be instructed in the art, on account of its uselessness.
>
> And the Athenians, having perceived how pernicious was the practice of it, though it was held in high esteem in their city,

ordained that the principal part, the appeal to the passions, should be abolished, together with the exordiums and perorations.

It is a tool invented for handling and stirring up a mob and an unruly community; and it is a tool that is only employed for sick states, like medicine. . . .

Of the Vanity of Words

Montaigne, of course, is speaking here of the abuse of language, of the deliberate attempt to use words so that they will stifle the reason rather than encourage it to exert itself. It is against rhetoric of that kind that popular books on semantics wage their chief battles, and nothing said so far . . . should lead the reader to think that the act of persuasion is automatically a good act or, conversely, that it is automatically a bad act, either. At the bottom of most popular semanticists' worry about "slanting" and "prejudicial language" there would seem to be a serious misconception about words. It is not the words that are bad or good but the intentions of those who use them. Once stated, the objection seems so obvious as not to need statement at all, but the misconception is too common to be entirely ignored. The ethical problem is a serious one, of course, but it should not be confused with description of language itself.

It would be possible to provide a more elaborate description of the persuasive effect of words . . . , but economy of space dictates that we turn to other considerations about that matter, considerations which have to do with a larger relationship of the writer to his reader and to his subject matter.

THE WRITER'S PRESENCE

. . . The writer's "presence" in what he writes is to be taken for granted. No matter how much he may wish to dissociate himself from his text, of course he cannot. He uses the meanings of words as they are known to him; he represents the world as his senses make it possible for him to conceive it. Even the most fantastic creature of his imagination or the character most unlike his own day-to-day self is material from his autobiography. A man can only express what he can conceive (and not all of that), and what he conceives is a part of himself.

Above this necessary sense in which the writer is present in his work, there is another which is sometimes identical with the necessary one and sometimes very different. Even in expository prose, where no deliberate activity of the creative imagination may be required, the writer more or less consciously stands revealed in his work. One reason is that he writes out of some feeling or conviction about his material; he has an attitude toward it, and the nature as well as the strength of that attitude will affect his choice of words, his syntax, his organization. Another reason is that he frequently assumes a certain audience for his work. That audience is the person or group of persons to whom or for whom he is writing and with whom he already has, or hopes to establish, a relationship stable enough so that the lines of communication can be kept clear. The most obvious situations in which the writer singles out his audience come quickly to mind: letters above all, public addresses and private conversations, pieces written for special occasions, pieces written for magazines with known predilections and clientele, and so on. But even for those writings whose audience is generalized or unknown, the skilled writer usually tries to have someone or some *kind* of person in mind with whom he wishes to ingratiate himself. One of the most noticeable characteristics of amateur writing is its apparent ignorance of or indifference to the reader. Such ignorance or indifference can be fatal to the persuasiveness of a piece of writing, and the competent writer is therefore always concerned to draw his reader into active participation with him in the examination of whatever subject matter he treats.

TONE

In the main, the writer establishes the character of his putative reader and his own relationship toward that reader by adopting a manner suitable to that relationship. The term commonly used to describe that maneuver is *tone*. In an eighteenth-century novel or essay the author frequently addressed the reader outright, but that literary convention is rarely used today. Instead, a writer today relies principally on choice of vocabulary, on selection of images and examples, and on syntax to indicate the kind of person he assumes his reader to be and the relationship he wants to have with him. And the relationship he has in mind will also serve him as a means of knowing how much he must explain and what he need not explain at all, where and how strongly he should place emphasis, by what means and how fully he should elaborate. Although it is not always easy to put one's finger on the devices by which a writer achieves tone, even the unskilled reader is generally able to detect the tone that is being used. Though perhaps unconsciously, he may resent being patronized or coddled, resist being bullied, or feel satisfaction at being treated as an equal. Such responses indicate that tone is not *entirely* a matter of calculation by the writer. Rather it is a reflection both of what the writer is, as a thinking and feeling person, and of the role he chooses to play in a particular piece of writing. Often tone does not so much announce itself as make itself felt in sentence after sentence through patterns of words, images, allusions, and epithets, patterns showing a consistent habit of speech and through it a consistent way of looking at the world and of letting the reader look at it, too.

How swiftly it is possible for an author to establish tone, a series of brief excerpts will show more quickly than further discussion.

> It is not to be avoided—a book on the Victorian novelists must begin with Dickens. Not that he needs praising. He is the one novelist of his school whose books have not grown at all dusty on the shelves, whose popularity has suffered no sensible decline. Nor that there is much new to be said about him; Mr. Santayana and Mr. Chesterton, to say nothing of lesser critics, have seen to that.
>
> DAVID CECIL, *Early Victorian Novelists*

> After a few hundred of the more pressing post-war problems have been solved, it might not be a bad idea to launch a movement to put the legal profession on Basic English. Even if it could be got back to just plain English that would be so much velvet.
>
> FRANK SULLIVAN, *A Rock in Every Snowball*

> It is an easy phrase, "the art of living," and one which, like a cliché, is rather of the tongue than of the mind, yet in a general way we know well enough what we mean to signify by it.
>
> JAMES TRUSLOW ADAMS, *Our Business Civilization*

> Listening to music is such a muddle that one scarcely knows how to start describing it. The first point to get clear in my own

case is that during the greater part of every performance I do
not attend. The nice sounds make me think of something else.

                              E. M. FORSTER, "Not Listening to Music"

I like a country where it's nobody's damned business what
magazines anyone reads, what he thinks, whom he had cocktails
with. I like a country where we do not have to stuff the chimneys
against listening ears and where what we say does not go into the
FBI files along with a note from S-17 that I may have another wife
in California.

                              BERNARD DE VOTO, "Due Notice to the FBI"

One Christmas was so much like another, in those years around
the sea-corner now and out of all sound except the distant speaking of the voices I sometimes hear a moment before sleep, that I
can never remember whether it snowed for six days and six nights
when I was twelve or whether it snowed for twelve days and
twelve nights when I was six.

                              DYLAN THOMAS, *A Child's Christmas in Wales*

By his tone, the writer establishes the grounds on which communication between him and his reader is to be conducted. In
most expository writing the tone will be that which the writer
unaffectedly holds toward his assumed reader or readers. There
will be occasions, however, which may require that the writer
adopt one tone rather than another, as when he is addressing an
audience of varied ages, varied educational backgrounds, varied
interests, and so on. Because his actual social relationship with
a mixed group varies from one member to another, his tone
would change were he to address each one separately. Since that
is precisely what he is not doing, he must adopt a tone which
will be appropriate for the group. In practice, this is very hard
to do, and public speakers and writers for "popular" periodicals
may perhaps be excused some of their flatulence on that account.
Compared with them, a student writing a critical paper is in a
favored position: he usually has an audience of one for his work
and a social situation—teacher-student—of fairly clear-cut proto-
col. Some feeling of rebellion against the confinement imposed
by so limited an audience and so formal a relationship is natural,
but the confinement is in fact no more repressive in this situation
than in another, though obviously of a different kind.

PERSPECTIVE

There is something of make-believe in tone, just as there is in all art, no matter how deeply it is concerned to display the truth of things. A second manifestation of this make-believe, and a second means the writer has of making his identity felt in his work, is apparent in the stance he takes before his subject matter itself. No matter what the real situation is, he can appear to be detached or intimately concerned, actually in contact with the things he describes, or removed from them by thousands of miles or by centuries. He may profess to see them as they appear to others or greatly distorted, as in the mirrors of an amusement arcade. They are essentially choices of *perspective.*

The simplest perspective is probably that of *direct confrontation.* The writer stands before his subject, walks around it, studies it. The tone he adopts when he is using such a perspective may be cordial and comradely, that of "Come and look with me" or perhaps rather distant or even patronizing, that of "Stay there and I'll tell you what there is to be seen." In unskilled writing, the first tone is likely to take the form of exhortation ("Let us look now at . . .") and the second, the form of passive and impersonal constructions ("The matter can be considered . . ."). Yet neither is a necessary consequence of the perspective and tone because the same effects can be achieved without awkwardness by the skilled writer simply through careful choice of language and careful management of structure.

Instead of looking at the subject directly and in the round, the author may chose to take an oblique view of it, as though he were standing to one side with an eye (and perhaps a mind) half closed. By this means he sees the subject, as it were, in relief, and perhaps in profile. Angularities which seemed a part of the general harmony when the object was viewed in the round now are stark and even incongruous. The purpose of such perspective, of course, is emphasis, and its ground is a conscious bias, in the radical sense of that word. The writer views the subject from an announced or implied vantage point in sensation or emotion or thought. By that oblique viewing he brings clearly into view some aspect of the object which has heretofore been hidden. It is clear that this procedure has to do with something more than the manipulation of words, though it is through words that it will necessarily achieve its end. What actually happens is that a writer transforms the properties of whatever he is discussing, either by actually misrepresenting them or by misrepresenting their relationship with each other: an idiosyncrasy is exaggerated, something detestable is praised or something praiseworthy is condemned, the inconsequential is made important and the important inconsequential. Through these deliberate distortions the writer realizes his purpose of persuading the reader to re-examine a subject under his direction.

To speak of a writer's "perspective" and of his "tone" as partly make-believe may be somewhat misleading. A better way to describe what is meant by those terms is perhaps to say that they are conscious and artful means of conveying insight and feeling. To "distort" an object and to "assume" a tone are, therefore, not falsifications but revelations.

The actual means by which perspective is accomplished are several, and each is different from the other not only in nature but in purpose. One very effective way of persuading a reader to disapprove of something is to make a parody of it. In essence, a *parody* is simply an exaggeration, though not all exaggerations are by any means parodies. Underneath this device there is the assumption that almost any human proceeding has a certain amount of absurdity at its core. By seizing upon distinctive characteristics of the proceeding and stretching them, the parodist attempts to make that absurdity evident, and through it, to discredit the proceeding itself. The schoolboy who entertains his fellows with an artful imitation of the manner and speech of his teacher is a parodist; so, too, in a hackneyed fashion, is the after-dinner speaker at the suburban country club who begins with the phrase, "Friends, Roamers, and Country Gentlemen. . . ." These examples suggest another requirement of parody: it must have as its subject something that is well known, or the exaggeration will not be apparent. In fiction, parody is common; in expository writing, its use is less frequent but not for that reason ineffective. It may, in fact, be the most economical means of presenting a criticism, as in this excerpt from a book review.

The new book which Mr. ——— has written about the Constitution is a very different kind of book. You can read it without
thinking. If you have got tired trying to read the other kind of
books, you will be glad of the nice restful book that Mr. ———
has written. It runs along like a story in a very interesting way.
Most of the story is about how the Constitution got made. This is
really history, but it is written in a very lively way like a novel,
with a great many characters, almost all male, and plenty of conversation and a very exciting plot. Many of the chapters have
names like those in a novel such as "The Opening of the Battle,"
"The Crisis," "The Dawn," "Nearing the End," "The Curtain
Falls," and others. Besides the story there are many quotations
from Shakespeare, Beethoven, Horace, Isaiah, Euripides, Beard,
and other famous men. Many of these quotations are quite old,
but some of them seem fairly new. They help to make the book
a real high-class book. There is not much more to say about the
part of the book that tells how the Constitution got made, except that it is fun and easy to read and seems pretty true to life.
    THOMAS REED POWELL, "Constitutional Metaphors"

Although the writer has not announced his intention to make
fun of the style and content of the book he is reviewing, it is
quickly apparent that he is doing so. The repetition of exces-
sively simple sentences, the patronizing colloquialisms, the patent
emptiness of much that is said—all of these are criticisms conveyed by parody.

A more elaborate device of persuasion than parody is *satire*.
Where parody is largely concerned with the manner of an action
(and, of course, with whatever that manner implies about the
actor), satire deals with the action itself. Through selection, exaggeration, and meaningful juxtaposition, it attempts to expose
and to bring into ridicule whatever is unnatural or unwise or
evil. It plays primarily upon the difference between the state of
something and its ideal condition and is therefore commonly
concerned to lay bare the hypocrisy of human action, as when
it shows the claim of service for the common good to be subter-
fuge for the satisfaction of private interest, or the assertion of
righteous indignation to be a public disguise for wounded vanity.

The satirist, of course, may be himself a literal hypocrite, in
the sense that he may pretend to approve what he actually de-
tests. When he gives such approval, however, he does it in such

a way that his detestation is apparent to all but the most obtuse.
One of his favorite devices is to shift the apparent time or place
of the action; another, to rename characters and places; a third,
to analogize from one action to another. Thus, George Orwell's
novel *1984* is really concerned with the political tendencies he
discerned as threatening in 1948; and Aldous Huxley's *Brave
New World*, another anti-Utopia, is really an account of a coming world "brave" only in its disregard of human values. Another
way to develop a satire is to create a series of situations parallel
to the ones to be criticized and then to present the created situations in such a fashion as to make their absurdity, or their
wrongness, obvious. When, in *A Modest Proposal*, Swift advo-
cated that babies be fattened for human consumption as a
means of alleviating the twin problems of overpopulation and
poverty in Ireland, he did so in most solemn and reasonable
vein, and some actually took him to mean what he said. Here
the satiric device is to treat matter-of-factly that which is horrible beyond imagining, an oblique way of presenting the callous
attitude of the English Parliament of the time toward the oppressed and famine-stricken Irish people who were subject to its
authority. Still another way is to pretend to ignorance about the
premises on which certain actions are based, a procedure much
more effective than might at first be imagined. If a bird, for
instance, were endowed with a highly developed power to reason
but were completely ignorant of human behavior, what would
it make of a tennis game? or of a church service? It would note
the actions as well as any other intelligent being, but the mean-
ingfulness and the relatedness of the actions it would have to
guess at or reach by continued observation and a laborious inductive process. Either means is certain to be full of errors and
false leads, and it is such errors and false leads that the satirist
relies on to reveal the oddities of those things with which the
reader has always thought himself perfectly well acquainted. And,
finally, the most obvious means of the satirist is direct contradiction: by what he does a character contradicts the precepts he
preaches; a situation belies what is predicted or postulated of it.

The writer of expository prose will find the devices of satire
most useful when his general intent is to encourage change, for
satire is essentially the vehicle of reform. By making faults ridicu-

lous, it seeks to provide enlightenment, to stimulate disapproval, and to make correction mandatory: in its commitment to reform, it is more clearly an instrument of social action than parody, which mocks as much in fun as in hope of improvement. Because reform is the goal of satire, the subject matter must be, either directly or by implication, the behavior of human beings. La Fontaine's fables, for instance, have animals as their evident subject matter, but the correspondence of the animals' actions and speech in the fables to the actions and speech of human beings is so patent that every adult reader knows that the fables are really criticisms of human behavior.

The peculiar power of satire to persuade lies in its manipulation of different, and often contradictory, emotions. Though the faults which it attacks may be, and generally are, faults which the reader commits or has committed, the fact that he is brought to laugh at them, and thus at himself, destroys some of his power to resist the attack and to refute the demand for reform. As with all rhetorical devices, miscalculation in the use of satire—too gross an exaggeration, too obvious a contradiction, too blatant an absurdity—destroys effectiveness. Such miscalculation, it might be noted, is not always simply an awkwardness in the handling of the device but often a symptom of some intellectual dishonesty—of an attempt to misrepresent the reality as well as the appearance of the object.

Both parody and satire are formal structures; or, to use the metaphor of perspective, they are distortions which result from presenting the object obliquely so that details become magnified or dislocated. *Irony* is not so much an arrangement of situations as an attitude toward them and a device for conveying meaning by saying the opposite of what is meant. There is another difference. Satire and parody work on materials which are well enough known so that the falsification of them is apparent to nearly everyone. Irony, on the other hand, is an exclusive practice: it assumes a fairly large audience which may take words to mean only what they say and a small audience, the one it is addressing, which will understand them to be only a façade for another meaning. Irony is subtle and often delicate; it compares with satire as the sting of a whiplash compares with the pain of a thorough drubbing. Moreover, its purpose is often less clearly therapeutic than is that of satire. Irony notes the discrepancy between what things are and what they appear to be, or between what they are and what they ought to be, and it displays the writer's acuity and his amusement or contempt, but it does not always make a demand for reform. There is a kind of Olympian irony which affects to look on most human action with an indulgent smile, and a tragic irony which has no smile at all but a degree of compassion for the futility of the human condition. Whatever the kind, the ironist must in a sense look down on his subject, see it in a broader relationship than that available to most men, and then communicate what he has seen by such slight alterations in his language as will lead the initiated reader to know that the words he reads are to be understood as though they were preceded by "not."

The master ironist of the English language is probably the historian Edward Gibbon, and it is fitting that this discussion of irony close with a few illustrations from his *Decline and Fall of the Roman Empire.* A thoroughgoing eighteenth-century rationalist, Gibbon found religious controversy especially distasteful, referring to it as "the exquisite rancour of theological hatred," just as he both hated and feared the claims of supernatural intervention in the affairs of man, to which he gave the name "holy romances." Of the miraculous acts of St. James, the apostle, he writes:

> The gravest historians have celebrated his exploits; the miraculous shrine of Compostella displayed his power; and the sword of a military order, assisted by the terrors of the Inquisition, was sufficient to remove every objection of profane criticism.

Though much of his irony is directed against religion, and against Christianity in particular, Gibbon hated what he believed to be fraud or base servility wherever he found it. He speaks, for instance, of Herod and his sycophants in these words:

> . . . the greatest part of his life was spent in philosophic retirement at Athens and his adjacent villas, perpetually surrounded by sophists, who acknowledged without reluctance the superiority of a rich and generous rival.

As these examples show, irony is a devastating instrument of persuasion, for its agreeable surface deflects the expostulations even of those whom its implications have wounded. It thus invites the reader to participation with the writer by guaranteeing him safety even as it offers him the flattery of being among the elect who discern the real intent of what is said.

To include all literary devices, all figurative forms of speech, and even the accidental encrustations on words as elements of persuasion may be to stretch the category until it is an *omnium gatherum* into which all leftovers may find a resting place. Yet such catholicity has one virtue, and it is a virtue especially important to the concept of persuasion: to realize that all use of language is persuasive is to recognize that no user can safely be indifferent to his choice of words, his syntax, or his literary demeanor. Even as expositor of the slightest matter, he employs an instrument which has effects, produces reactions. Though he cannot predict reactions with certainty, he can in large measure control them if he is aware of the many ways in which language moves readers and if he then trains himself to use language wisely and well.

To conclude . . . , it may be wise to raise again a caution hinted at previously. The formal processes of proof, inductive or deductive, are not for practical purposes the only ways of knowing something to be true or probably true. The ability of a man to arrive at certainty is a complicated psychological matter, and the analytic activities appropriate to proof are not adequate to describe or to document it. Into the judgments of an art critic facing a painting, of a chemist examining the account of an experiment, or of a writer reading the work of another writer there goes such a compound of past experience, intelligent perception, and conviction about premises that no analytic apparatus can dissolve the compound into all of its components. Much of what is referred to as "good taste" is exactly that sort of compound, and it is foolish always to expect neat proof in support of it and equally foolish to think that procedures of analysis or of proof can substitute completely for the experience and training that compose so large a part of the compound. On a particular matter within the general judgment, however, or in any instance where the general judgments of equally competent persons come into conflict, the processes of logic provide the only recourse for the expert and the inexpert alike. There may be arguments beyond the reaches of logical analysis entirely, but it is quite certain that *no* human means will prove one or another conclusion to the general satisfaction of all for whom such arguments are important. Yet, for all that, those arguments are not necessarily futile since the consequences of the different conclusions may be of such importance that it is vital to keep the arguments alive whether or not proof is achievable. Rational proof, in sum, is important as a buttress to responsible thought, even though it may not be the only way of arriving at truth of statement. It is simply the surest way man has thus far been able to develop with the means at his disposal.

the reach of imagination
JACOB BRONOWSKI

For three thousand years, poets have been enchanted and moved and perplexed by the power of their own imagination. In a short and summary essay I can hope at most to lift one small corner of that mystery; and yet it is a critical corner. I shall ask, What goes on in the mind when we imagine? You will hear from me that one answer to this question is fairly specific: which is to say, that we can describe the working of the imagination. And when we describe it as I shall do, it becomes plain that imagination is a specifically *human* gift. To imagine is the characteristic act, not of the poet's mind, or the painter's, or the scientist's, but of the mind of man.

My stress here on the word *human* implies that there is a clear difference in this between the actions of men and those of other animals. Let me then start with a classical experiment with animals and children which Walter Hunter thought out in Chicago about 1910. That was the time when scientists were agog with the success of Ivan Pavlov in forming and changing the reflex actions of dogs, which Pavlov had first announced in 1903. Pavlov had been given a Nobel prize the next year, in 1904; although in fairness I should say that the award did not cite his work on the conditioned reflex, but on the digestive gland.

Hunter duly trained some dogs and other animals on Pavlov's

Reprinted with permission of J. Bronowski and The American Academy of Arts and Letters.

lines. They were taught that when a light came on over one of three tunnels out of their cage, that tunnel would be open; they could escape down it, and were rewarded with food if they did. But once he had fixed that conditioned reflex, Hunter added to it a deeper idea: he gave the mechanical experiment a new dimension, literally—the dimension of time. Now he no longer let the dog go to the lighted tunnel at once; instead, he put out the light, and then kept the dog waiting a little while before he let him go. In this way Hunter timed how long an animal can remember where he has last seen the signal light to his escape route.

The results were and are staggering. A dog or a rat forgets which one of three tunnels has been lit up within a matter of seconds—in Hunter's experiment, ten seconds at most. If you want such an animal to do much better than this, you must make the task much simpler: you must face him with only two tunnels to chose from. Even so, the best that Hunter could do was to have a dog remember for five minutes which one of two tunnels had been lit up.

I am not quoting these times as if they were exact and universal: they surely are not. Hunter's experiment, more than fifty years old now, had many faults of detail. For example, there were too few animals, they were oddly picked, and they did not all behave consistently. It may be unfair to test a dog for what he *saw*, when he commonly follows his nose rather than his eyes. It may be unfair to test any animal in the unnatural setting of a laboratory cage. And there are higher animals, such as chimpanzees and other primates, which certainly have longer memories than the animals that Hunter tried.

Yet when all these provisos have been made (and met, by more modern experiments) the facts are still startling and characteristic. An animal cannot recall a signal from the past for even a short fraction of the time that a man can—for even a short fraction of the time that a child can. Hunter made comparable tests with six-year-old children, and found, of course, that they were incomparably better than the best of his animals. There is a striking and basic difference between a man's ability to imagine something that he saw or experienced, and an animal's failure. Animals make up for this by other and extraordinary gifts.

The salmon and the carrier pigeon can find their way home as we cannot; they have, as it were, a practical memory that man cannot match. But their actions always depend on some form of habit: on instinct or on learning, which reproduce by rote a train of known responses. They do not depend, as human memory does, on calling to mind the recollection of absent things.

Where is it that the animal falls short? We get a clue to the answer, I think, when Hunter tells us how the animals in his experiment tried to fix their recollection. They most often pointed themselves at the light before it went out, as some gun dogs point rigidly at the game they scent—and get the name *pointer* from the posture. The animal makes ready to act by building the signal into its action. There is a primitive imagery in its stance, it seems to me; it is as if the animal were trying to fix the light on its mind by fixing it in its body. And indeed, how else can a dog mark and (as it were) name one of three tunnels, when he has no such words as *left* and *right,* and no such numbers as *one, two, three?* The directed gesture of attention and readiness is perhaps the only symbolic device that the dog commands to hold on to the past, and thereby to guide himself into the future.

I used the verb *to imagine* a moment ago, and now I have some ground for giving it a meaning. *To imagine* means to make images and to move them about inside one's head in new arrangements. When you and I recall the past, we imagine it in this direct and homely sense. The tool that puts the human mind ahead of the animal is imagery. For us, memory does not demand the preoccupation that it demands in animals, and it lasts immensely longer, because we fix it in images or other substitute symbols. With the same symbolic vocabulary we spell out the future—not one but many futures, which we weigh one against another.

I am using the word *image* in a wide meaning, which does not restrict it to the mind's eye as a visual organ. An image in my usage is what Charles Peirce called a *sign,* without regard for its sensory quality. Peirce distinguished between different forms of signs, but there is no reason to make his distinction here, for the imagination works equally with them all, and that is why I call them all images.

Indeed, the most important images for human beings are

simply words, which are abstract symbols. Animals do not have words, in our sense: there is no specific center for language in the brain of any animal, as there is in the human being. In this respect at least we know that the human imagination depends on a configuration in the brain that has only evolved in the last one or two million years. In the same period, evolution has greatly enlarged the front lobes in the human brain, which govern the sense of the past and the future; and it is a fair guess that they are probably the seat of our other images. (Part of the evidence for this guess is that damage to the front lobes in primates reduces them to the state of Hunter's animals.) If the guess turns out to be right, we shall know why man has come to look like a highbrow or an egghead: because otherwise there would not be room in his head for his imagination.

The images play out for us events which are not present to our senses, and thereby guard the past and create the future—a future that does not yet exist, and may never come to exist in that form. By contrast, the lack of symbolic ideas, or their rudimentary poverty, cuts off an animal from the past and the future alike, and imprisons him in the present. Of all the distinctions between man and animal, the characteristic gift which makes us human is the power to work with symbolic images: the gift of imagination.

This is really a remarkable finding. When Philip Sidney in 1580 defended poets (and all unconventional thinkers) from the Puritan charge that they were liars, he said that a maker must imagine things that are not. Halfway between Sidney and us, William Blake said, "What is now proved was once only imagined." About the same time, in 1796, Samuel Taylor Coleridge for the first time distinguished between the passive fancy and the active imagination, "the living Power and prime Agent of all human Perception." Now we see that they were right, and precisely right: the human gift is the gift of imagination—and that is not just a literary phrase.

Nor is it just a literary gift; it is, I repeat, characteristically human. Almost everything that we do that is worth doing is done in the first place in the mind's eye. The richness of human life is that we have many lives; we live the events that do not happen (and some that cannot) as vividly as those that do; and if thereby we die a thousand deaths, that is the price we pay for

living a thousand lives. (A cat, of course, has only nine.) Literature is alive to us because we live its images, but so is any play
of the mind—so is chess: the lines of play that we foresee and
try in our heads and dismiss are as much a part of the game as
the moves that we make. John Keats said that the unheard melodies are sweeter, and all chess players sadly recall that the combinations that they planned and which never came to be played
were the best.

I make this point to remind you, insistently, that imagination
is the manipulation of images in one's head; and that the rational
manipulation belongs to that, as well as the literary and artistic
manipulation. When a child begins to play games with things
that stand for other things, with chairs or chessmen, he enters the
gateway to reason and imagination together. For the human
reason discovers new relations between things not by deduction,
but by that unpredictable blend of speculation and insight that
scientists call induction, which—like other forms of imagination
—cannot be formalized. We see it at work when Walter Hunter
inquires into a child's memory, as much as when Blake and Coleridge do. Only a restless and original mind would have asked
Hunter's questions and could have conceived his experiments,
in a science that was dominated by Pavlov's reflex arcs and was
heading toward the behaviorism of John Watson.

Let me find a spectacular example for you from history. What
is the most famous experiment that you had described to you as
a child? I will hazard that it is the experiment that Galileo is
said to have made in Sidney's age, in Pisa about 1590, by dropping two unequal balls from the Leaning Tower. There, we say,
is a man in the modern mold, a man after our own hearts: he
insisted on questioning the authority of Aristotle and St. Thomas
Aquinas, and seeing with his own eyes whether (as they said) the
heavy ball would reach the ground before the light one. Seeing
is believing.

Yet seeing is also imagining. Galileo did challenge the authority of Aristotle, and he did look at his mechanics. But the eye
that Galileo used was the mind's eye. He did not drop balls from
the Leaning Tower of Pisa—and if he had, he would have got a
very doubtful answer. Instead, Galileo made an imaginary experiment in his head, which I will describe as he did years later

in the book he wrote after the Holy Office silenced him: the
Discorsi . . . intorno a due nuove scienze, which was smuggled
out to be printed in the Netherlands in 1638.

Suppose, said Galileo, that you drop two unequal balls from
the tower at the same time. And suppose that Aristotle is right—
suppose that the heavy ball falls faster, so that it steadily gains
on the light ball, and hits the ground first. Very well. Now
imagine the same experiment done again, with only one difference: this time the two unequal balls are joined by a string
between them. The heavy ball will again move ahead, but now
the light ball holds it back and acts as a drag or brake. So the
light ball will be speeded up and the heavy ball will be
slowed down; they must reach the ground together because they
are tied together, but they cannot reach the ground as quickly
as the heavy ball alone. Yet the string between them has turned
the two balls into a single mass which is heavier than either ball
—and surely (according to Aristotle) this mass should therefore
move faster than either ball? Galileo's imaginary experiment has
uncovered a contradiction; he says trenchantly, "You see how,
from your assumption that a heavier body falls more rapidly than
a lighter one, I infer that a (still) heavier body falls more
slowly." There is only one way out of the contradiction: the
heavy ball and the light ball must fall at the same rate, so that
they go on falling at the same rate when they are tied together.

This argument is not conclusive, for nature might be more
subtle (when the two balls are joined) than Galileo has allowed.
And yet it is something more important: it is suggestive, it is
stimulating, it opens a new view—in a word, it is imaginative. It
cannot be settled without an actual experiment, because nothing
that we imagine can become knowlege until we have translated it
into, and backed it by, real experience. The test of imagination
is experience. But then, that is as true of literature and the arts
as it is of science. In science, the imaginary experiment is tested
by confronting it with physical experience; and in literature, the
imaginative conception is tested by confronting it with human
experience. The superficial speculation in science is dismissed
because it is found to falsify nature; and the shallow work of
art is discarded because it is found to be untrue to our own
nature. So when Ella Wheeler Wilcox died in 1919, more people
were reading her verses than Shakespeare's; yet in a few years

her work was dead. It had been buried by its poverty of emotion and its trivialness of thought: which is to say that it had
been proved to be as false to the nature of man as, say, Jean
Baptiste Lamarck and Trofim Lysenko[1] were false to the nature
of inheritance. The strength of the imagination, its enriching
power and excitement, lies in its interplay with reality—physical
and emotional.

I doubt if there is much to choose here between science and the
arts: the imagination is not much more free, and not much less
free, in one than in the other. All great scientists have used their
imagination freely, and let it ride them to outrageous conclusions
without crying "Halt!" Albert Einstein fiddled with imaginary
experiments from boyhood, and was wonderfully ignorant of the
facts that they were supposed to bear on. When he wrote the first
of his beautiful papers on the random movement of atoms, he did
not know that the Brownian motion which it predicted could be
seen in any laboratory. He was sixteen when he invented the paradox that he resolved ten years later, in 1905, in the theory of relativity, and it bulked much larger in his mind than the experiment of Albert Michelson and Edward Morley[2] which had upset
every other physicist since 1881. All his life Einstein loved to
make up teasing puzzles like Galileo's, about falling lifts and the
detection of gravity; and they carry the nub of the problems of
general relativity on which he was working.

Indeed, it could not be otherwise. The power that man has over
nature and himself, and that a dog lacks, lies in his command of
imaginary experience. He alone has the symbols which fix the past
and play with the future, possible and impossible. In the Renaissance, the symbolism of memory was thought to be mystical, and
devices that were invented as mnemonics (by Giordano Bruno,
for example, and by Robert Fludd) were interpreted as magic

[1]Lamarck was a French biologist (1744–1829) who held that characteristics
acquired by experience were biologically transmittable. Lysenko is a Russian
biologist (1898–   ) who has held that hereditary properties of organisms
could be changed by manipulating the environment.

[2]This was an experiment designed to measure the drag exerted on the
passage of light by a hypothetical stationary medium. Its negative results
eliminated the concept of a motionless, measurable ether and cleared the way
for the development of the theory of relativity.

signs. The symbol is the tool which gives man his power, and it is the same tool whether the symbols are images or words, mathematical signs or mesons. And the symbols have a reach and a roundness that goes beyond their literal and practical meaning. They are the rich concepts under which the mind gathers many particulars into one name, and many instances into one general induction. When a man says *left* and *right*, he is outdistancing the dog not only in looking for a light; he is setting in train all the shifts of meaning, the overtones and the ambiguities, between *gauche* and *adroit* and *dexterous*, between *sinister* and the sense of right. When a man counts *one, two, three*, he is not only doing mathematics; he is on the path to the mysticism of numbers in Pythagoras and Vitruvius and Kepler, to the Trinity and the signs of the Zodiac.

I have described imagination as the ability to make images and to move them about inside one's head in new arrangements. This is the faculty that is specifically human, and it is the common root from which science and literature both spring and grow and flourish together. For they do flourish (and languish) together; the great ages of science are the great ages of all the arts, because in them powerful minds have taken fire from one another, breathless and higgledy-piggledy, without asking too nicely whether they ought to tie their imagination to falling balls or a haunted island. Galileo and Shakespeare, who were born in the same year, grew into greatness in the same age; when Galileo was looking through his telescope at the moon, Shakespeare was writing *The Tempest* and all Europe was in ferment, from Johannes Kepler to Peter Paul Rubens, and from the first table of logarithms by John Napier to the Authorized Version of the Bible.

Let me end with a last and spirited example of the common inspiration of literature and science, because it is as much alive today as it was three hundred years ago. What I have in mind is man's ageless fantasy, to fly to the moon. I do not display this to you as a high scientific enterprise; on the contrary, I think we have more important discoveries to make here on earth than wait for us, beckoning, at the horned surface of the moon. Yet I cannot belittle the fascination which that ice-blue journey has had for the imagination of men, long before it drew us to our television screens to watch the tumbling astronauts. Plutarch and

Lucian, Ariosto and Ben Jonson wrote about it, before the days of Jules Verne and H. G. Wells and science fiction. The seventeenth century was heady with new dreams and fables about voyages to the moon. Kepler wrote one full of deep scientific ideas, which (alas) simply got his mother accused of witchcraft. In England, Francis Godwin wrote a wild and splendid work, *The Man in the Moone,* and the astronomer John Wilkins wrote a wild and learned one, *The Discovery of a New World.* They did not draw a line between science and fancy; for example, they all tried to guess just where in the journey the earth's gravity would stop. Only Kepler understood that gravity has no boundary, and put a law to it—which happened to be the wrong law.

All this was a few years before Isaac Newton was born, and it was all in his head that day in 1666 when he sat in his mother's garden, a young man of twenty-three, and thought about the reach of gravity. This was how he came to conceive his brilliant image, that the moon is like a ball which has been thrown so hard that it falls exactly as fast as the horizon, all the way round the earth. The image will do for any satellite, and Newton modestly calculated how long therefore an astronaut would take to fall round the earth once. He made it ninety minutes, and we have all seen now that he was right; but Newton had no way to check that. Instead he went on to calculate how long in that case the distant moon would take to round the earth, if indeed it behaves like a thrown ball that falls in the earth's gravity, and if gravity obeyed a law of inverse squares. He found that the answer would be twenty-eight days.

In that telling figure, the imagination that day chimed with nature, and made a harmony. We shall hear an echo of that harmony on the day when we land on the moon, because it will be not a technical but an imaginative triumph, that reaches back to the beginning of modern science and literature both. All great acts of imagination are like this, in the arts and in science, and convince us because they fill out reality with a deeper sense of rightness. We start with the simplest vocabulary of images, with *left* and *right* and *one, two, three,* and before we know how it happened the words and the numbers have conspired to make a match with nature: we catch in them the pattern of mind and matter as one.

READING

Another aspect of the prewriting process that is helpful as preparation for a writing assignment is close reading for ideas and specific structural and stylistic devices. It is the combination of these two—content and rhetoric—that the essays in this section deal with. For most, the experience of reading for *what* (content and ideas) is being communicated is quite familiar, but the experience of reading for *how* (style and structure) it is communicated may be less familiar. Proceeding from that assumption, the selections that follow explore the *hows* of written expression rather than the *whats*.

One of the most effective methods for this type of study is the outline. An outline is constructed as a visual representation of the developmental pattern or structure of an essay, and it can help to reveal the several rhetorical techniques at work. For example, an outline of the following dedicatory address by John F. Kennedy will demonstrate something of the structure of the address and will suggest many of the rhetorical qualities associated with the Kennedy style.

Poetry and Power

1   This day, devoted to the memory of Robert Frost, offers an opportunity for reflection which is prized by politicians as well as by others and even by poets. For Robert Frost was one of the

granite figures of our time in America. He was supremely two things: an artist and an American. A nation reveals itself not only by the men it produces but also by the men it honors, the men it remembers.

2   In America our heroes have customarily run to men of large accomplishments. But today this college and country honor a man whose contribution was not to our size but to our spirit; not to our political beliefs but to our insight; not to our self-esteem but to our self-comprehension.

3   In honoring Robert Frost we therefore can pay honor to the deepest sources of our national strength. That strength takes many forms, and the most obvious forms are not always the most significant.

4   The men who create power make an indispensable contribution to the nation's greatness, but the men who question power make a contribution just as indispensable, especially when that questioning is disinterested, for they determine whether we use power or power uses us. Our national strength matters; but the spirit which informs and controls our strength matters just as much. This was the special significance of Robert Frost.

5   He brought an unsparing instinct for reality to bear on the platitudes and pieties of society. His sense of the human tragedy fortified him against self-deception and easy consolation.

6   "I have been," he wrote, "one acquainted with the night." And because he knew the midnight as well as the high noon, because he understood the ordeal as well as the triumph of the human spirit, he gave the age strength with which to overcome despair.

7   At bottom he held a deep faith in the spirit of man. And it is hardly an accident that Robert Frost coupled poetry and power, for he saw poetry as the means of saving power from itself.

8   When power leads man toward arrogance, poetry reminds him of his limitations. When power narrows the areas of man's concern, poetry reminds him of the richness and diversity of his existence. When power corrupts, poetry cleanses, for art establishes the basic human truths which must serve as the touchstones of our judgment. The artist, however faithful to his personal vision of reality, becomes the last champion of the individual mind and sensibility against an intrusive society and an officious state. The great artist is thus a solitary figure. He has, as Frost said, "a lover's quarrel with the world." In pursuing his perceptions of reality he must often sail against the currents of his time. This is

not a popular role. If Robert Frost was much honored during his lifetime, it was because a good many preferred to ignore his darker truths. Yet, in retrospect, we see how the artist's fidelity has strengthened the fiber of our national life.

9   If sometimes our great artists have been the most critical of our society, it is because their sensitivity and their concern for justice, which must motivate any true artist, make them aware that our nation falls short of its highest potential.

10   I see little of more importance to the future of our country and our civilization than full recognition of the place of the artist. If art is to nourish the roots of our culture, society must set the artist free to follow his vision wherever it takes him.

11   We must never forget that art is not a form of propaganda; it is a form of truth. And as Mr. MacLeish once remarked of poets, "There is nothing worse for our trade than to be in style."

12   In a free society art is not a weapon, and it does not belong to the sphere of polemics and ideology. Artists are not engineers of the soul. It may be different elsewhere. But in a democratic society the highest duty to the writer, the composer, the artist, is to remain true to himself and to let the chips fall where they may. In serving his vision of the truth, the artist best serves his nation. And the nation which disdains the mission of art invites the fate of Robert Frost's hired man—the fate of having "nothing to look backward to with pride, and nothing to look forward to with hope."

13   I look forward to a great future for America—a future in which our country will match its military strength with our moral strength, its wealth with our wisdom, its power with our purpose.

14   I look forward to an America which will not be afraid of grace and beauty, which will protect the beauty of our natural environment, which will preserve the great old American houses and squares and parks of our national past, and which will build handsome and balanced cities for our future.

15   I look forward to an America which will reward achievement in the arts as we reward achievement in business or statecraft.

16   I look forward to an America which will steadily raise the standards of artistic accomplishment and which will steadily enlarge cultural opportunities for all of our citizens.

17   And I look forward to an America which commands respect throughout the world, not only for its strength but for its civilization as well.

18   And I look forward to a world which will be safe, not only for
democracy and diversity but also for personal distinction.[1]

I. Tribute to Robert Frost
   A. An artist and an American (1)
   B. His contribution (2)
   C. His strengths
      1. A deep source of national strength (3)
      2. An informing and controlling spirit of nation's power (4)
      3. An instinct for reality and a sense of tragedy (5)
      4. An understanding of ordeal (6)
      5. A deep faith in the spirit of man (7)

II. Tribute to Poetry
   A. Its saving qualities (8)
   B. Its critical value (9)

III. Tribute to the Arts
   A. As free expression
      1. Nourishes our culture (10)
      2. A form of truth (11)
      3. A service to the nation (12)
   B. As inspiration
      1. Integration of our best qualities (13)
      2. Pride in our past and beauty (14)
      3. Equal achievement and reward (15)
      4. Enhancement of itself and our citizens (16)
      5. Creator of prestige (17)
      6. Guardian of the democratic aspiration (18)

As the outline shows, the structural movement in the essay is
from specific to general, or from part to whole. This kind of pattern is employed by the author to expand the content; that is, it
obviously gives him an opportunity to talk about more than
Robert Frost, though coherence is never lost since Parts II and
III grow naturally out of the personal tribute.

There are several other questions that will be instructive for

[1]Reprinted by permission of the Atlantic Monthly Company, from the
speech of John F. Kennedy given at Amherst College, Massachusetts, October
26, 1963. © 1964 by The Atlantic Monthly Company, Boston, Massachusetts.

the reader to answer: What is the structural device that ties the last seven paragraphs together? What is the basis for the ordering of paragraphs 3–7? How does the style (sentence structure and word choice) contribute to the structure in the last seven paragraphs? When paragraph 5 is read aloud what effect do the sound patterns have on the meaning and structure? If one can answer questions such as these, he is beginning to understand some of the responsibilities attendant upon clear, effective, and rational written expression.

The following essays approach the problem of reading as it relates to writing in a variety of ways—from the analysis of structure to the reading of poetry. An awareness of structure and a sensitivity to style in the writing of others will go a long way toward the development of those quailties in one's own work.

seeing the skeleton
MORTIMER ADLER

1

Every book has a skeleton hidden between its boards. Your job
is to find it. A book comes to you with flesh on its bare bones
and clothes over its flesh. It is all dressed up. I am not asking
you be impolite or cruel. You do not have to undress it or tear
the flesh off its limbs to get at the firm structure that underlies
the soft. But you must read the book with X-ray eyes, for it is an
essential part of your first apprehension of any book to grasp its
structure.

You know how violently some people are opposed to vivisec-
tion. There are others who feel as strongly against analysis of
any sort. They simply do not like to have things taken apart,
even if the only instrument used in cutting up is the mind. They
somehow feel that something is being destroyed by analysis. This
is particularly true in the case of works of art. If you try to show
them the inner structure, the articulation of the parts, the way
the joints fit together, they react as if you had murdered the poem
or the piece of music.

That is why I have used the metaphor of the X ray. No harm
is done to the living organism by having its skeleton lighted up.
The patient does not even feel as if his privacy had been in-

Reprinted with permission of Simon & Schuster, Inc., from *How To Read
a Book*, by Mortimer Adler. © 1940, 1966 by Mortimer J. Adler.

fringed upon. Yet the doctor has discovered the disposition of the parts. He has a visible map of the total layout. He has an architect's ground plan. No one doubts the usefulness of such knowledge to help further operations on the living organism.

Well, in the same way, you can penetrate beneath the moving surface of a book to its rigid skeleton. You can see the way the parts are articulated, how they hang together, and the thread that ties them into a whole. You can do this without impairing in the least the vitality of the book you are reading. You need not fear that Humpty-Dumpty will be all in pieces, never to come together again. The whole can remain in animation while you proceed to find out what makes the wheels go round.

I had one experience as a student which taught me this lesson. Like other boys of the same age, I thought I could write lyric poetry. I may have even thought I was a poet. Perhaps that is why I reacted so strongly against a teacher of English literature who insisted that we be able to state the unity of every poem in a single sentence and then give a prosaic catalogue of its contents by an orderly enumeration of all its subordinate parts.

To do this with Shelley's *Adonais* or with an ode by Keats seemed to me nothing short of rape and mayhem. When you got finished with such cold-blooded butchery, all the "poetry" would be gone. But I did the work I was asked to do and, after a year of analysis, I found otherwise. A poem was not destroyed by such tactics in reading. On the contrary, the greater insight which resulted seemed to make the poem more like a vital organism. Instead of its being an ineffable blur, it moved before one with the grace and proportion of a living thing.

That was my first lesson in reading. From it I learned two rules, which are the second and third rules for the first reading of any book. I say "any book." These rules apply to science as well as poetry, and to any sort of expository work. Their application will be somewhat different, of course, according to the kind of book they are used on. The unity of a novel is not the same as the unity of a treatise on politics; nor are the parts of the same sort, or ordered in the same way. But every book which is worth reading at all has a unity and an organization of parts. A book which did not would be a mess. It would be relatively unreadable, as bad books actually are.

2

I am going to state these two rules as simply as possible. Then I shall explain them and illustrate them. The first rule is: *Classify the book according to kind and subject matter.*

The second rule—I say "second" because I want to keep the numbering of the four rules which comprise the first way of reading—can be expressed as follows: *State the unity of the whole book in a single sentence, or at most in several sentences (a short paragraph).*

This means that you must be able to say what the whole book is about as briefly as possible. To say what the whole book is about is not the same as saying what kind of book it is. The word "about" may be misleading here. In one sense, a book is *about* a certain type of subject matter, which it treats in a certain way. If you know this, you know what *kind* of book it is. But there is another and perhaps more colloquial sense of "about." We ask a person what he is about, what he is up to. So we can wonder what an author is trying to do. To find out what a book is *about* in this sense is to discover its *theme* or main *point.*

Everyone, I think, will admit that a book is a work of art. Furthermore, they will agree that in proportion as it is good, as a book and as a work of art, it has a more perfect and pervasive unity. They know this to be true of music and paintings, novels and plays. It is no less true of books which convey knowledge. But it is not enough to acknowledge this fact vaguely. You must apprehend the unity with definiteness. There is only one way that I know of being sure you have succeeded. You must be able to tell yourself or anybody else what the unity is and in a few words. Do not be satisfied with "feeling the unity" which you cannot express. The student who says, "I know what it is, but I just can't say it," fools no one, not even himself.

The third rule can be expressed as follows: *Set forth the major parts of the book, and show how these are organized into a whole, by being ordered to one another and to the unity of the whole.*

The reason for this rule should be obvious. If a work of art were absolutely simple, it would, of course, have no parts. But that is not the case. None of the sensible, physical things man knows is simple in this absolute way, nor is any human production. They are all complex unities. You have not grasped a complex unity if all you know about it is how it is one. You must also know how it is many, not a many which consists of a lot of separate things, but an organized many. If the parts were not organically related, the whole which they composed would not be one. Strictly speaking, there would be no whole at all but merely a collection.

You know the difference between a heap of bricks, on the one hand, and the single house they can constitute, on the other. You know the difference between one house and a collection of houses. A book is like a single house. It is a mansion of many rooms on different levels, of different sizes and shapes, with different outlooks, rooms with different functions to perform. These rooms are independent, in part. Each has its own structure and interior decoration. But they are not absolutely independent and separate. They are connected by doors and arches, by corridors and stairways. Because they are connected, the partial function which each performs contributes its share to the usefulness of the whole house. Otherwise the house would not be genuinely livable.

The architectural analogy is almost perfect. A good book, like a good house, is an orderly arrangement of parts. Each major part has a certain amount of independence. As we shall see, it may have an interior structure of its own. But it must also be connected with the other parts—that is, related to them functionally—for otherwise it could not contribute its share to the intelligibility of the whole.

As houses are more or less livable, so books are more or less readable. The most readable book is an architectural achievement on the part of the author. The best books are those that have the most intelligible structure and, I might add, the most apparent. Though they are usually more complex than poorer books, their greater complexity is somehow also a great simplicity, because their parts are better organized, more unified.

That is one of the reasons why the great books are most readable. Lesser works are really more bothersome to read. Yet to read them well—that is, as well as they can be read—you must try to find some plan in them. They would have been better if the author had himself seen the plan a little more clearly. But if they hang together at all, if they are a complex unity to any degree, there must be a plan and you must find it.

3

Let me return now to the second rule which requires you to state the unity. A few illustrations of this rule in operation may guide you in putting it into practice. I begin with a famous case. Many of you probably read Homer's *Odyssey* in school. Certainly most of you know the story of Ulysses, the man who took ten years to return from the siege of Troy only to find his faithful wife Penelope herself besieged by suitors. It is an elaborate story as Homer tells it, full of exciting adventures on land and sea, replete with episodes of all sorts and many complications of plot. Being a good story, it has a single unity of action, a main thread of plot which ties everything together.

Aristotle, in his *Poetics,* insists that this is the mark of every good story, novel, or play. To support his point, he shows you how the unity of the *Odyssey* can be summarized in a few sentences.

> A certain man is absent from home for many years; he is jealously watched by Neptune, and left desolate. Meanwhile his home is in a wretched plight; suitors are wasting his substance and plotting against his son. At length, tempest-tost, he himself arrives; he makes certain persons acquainted with him; he attacks the suitors with his own hand, and is himself preserved while he destroys them.

"This," says Aristotle, "is the essence of the plot; the rest is episode."

After you know the plot in this way, and through it the unity of the whole narrative, you can put the parts into their proper places. You might find it a good exercise to try this with some novels you have read. Try it on some great ones, such as *Tom*

Jones or *Crime and Punishment* or the modern *Ulysses*. Once when Mr. Clifton Fadiman was visiting Chicago, Mr. Hutchins and I asked him to lead our class in the discussion of Fielding's *Tom Jones*. He reduced the plot to the familiar formula: boy meets girl, boy wants girl, boy gets girl. This is the plot of every romance. The class learned what it means to say that there are only a small number of plots in the world. The difference between good and bad fiction having the same essential plot lies in what the author does with it, how he dresses up the bare bones.

. . .

Sometimes an author obligingly tells you on the title page what the unity is. In the eighteenth century, writers had the habit of composing elaborate titles which told the reader what the whole book was about. Here is a title by Jeremy Collier, an English divine who attacked the obscenity of the Restoration drama much more learnedly than the Legion of Decency has recently attacked the movies: *A Short View of the Immorality and Profaneness of the English Stage, together with the Sense of Antiquity upon this Argument.* You know from this that Collier recites many flagrant instances of the abuse of public morals and that he is going to support his protest by quoting texts from those ancients who argued, as Plato did, that the stage corrupts youth, or, as the early Church fathers did, that plays are seductions of the flesh and the devil.

Sometimes the author tells you the unity of his plan in his preface. In this respect, expository books differ radically from fiction. A scientific or philosophical writer has no reason to keep you in suspense. In fact, the less suspense such an author keeps you in, the more likely you are to sustain the effort of reading him through. Like a newspaper story, an expository book may summarize itself in its first paragraph.

Do not be too proud to accept the author's help if he proffers it, but do not rely too completely on what he says in the preface. The best-laid plans of authors, like those of other mice and men, gang aft agley. Be somewhat guided by the prospectus the author gives you, but always remember that the obligation of finding the unity belongs to the reader, as much as having one belongs to the writer. You can discharge that obligation honestly only by reading the whole book.

The opening paragraph of Herodotus' history of the war between the Greeks and the Persians provides an excellent summary of the whole. It runs:

> These are the researches of Herodotus of Halicarnassus, in order that the actions of men may not be effaced by time, nor the great and wondrous deeds displayed by Greeks and barbarians be deprived of renown; and for the rest, for what cause they waged war upon one another.

That is a good beginning for you as a reader. It tells you succinctly what the whole book is about.

But you had better not stop there. After you have read the nine parts through, you will probably find it necessary to elaborate on that statement to do justice to the whole. You may want to mention the Persian kings—Cyrus, Darius, and Xerxes—the Greek heroes of Salamis and Thermopylae, and the major events —the crossing of the Hellespont and the decisive battles of the war.

All the rest of the fascinating details, with which Herodotus richly prepares you for his climax, can be left out of the plot. Note, here, that the unity of a history is a single thread of plot, very much as in fiction. That is part of what I meant in the last chapter by saying that history is an amalgam of science and poetry. So far as unity is concerned, this rule of reading elicits the same kind of answer in history and fiction. But there are other rules of reading which require the same kind of analysis in history as in science and philosophy.

. . .

4

Now we can turn to the other structural rule, the rule which requires us to set forth the major parts of the book in their order and relation. This third rule is closely related to the second which we have just discussed. You may have noticed already how a well-stated unity indicates the major parts that compose the whole. You cannot apprehend a whole without somehow seeing its parts. But it is also true that unless you grasp the organization of its parts, you cannot know the whole comprehensively.

You may wonder, therefore, why I have made two rules here instead of one. It is primarily a matter of convenience. It is easier to grasp a complex and unified structure in two steps rather than in one. The second rule directs your attention toward the unity, and the third toward the complexity, of a book. There is another reason for the separation. The major parts of a book may be seen at the moment when you grasp its unity. But these parts are usually themselves complex and have an interior structure you must see. Hence the third rule involves more than just an enumeration of the parts. It means treating the parts as if they were subordinate wholes, each with a unity and a complexity of its own.

I can write out the formula for operating according to this third rule. Because it is a formula, it may guide you in a general way. According to the second rule, you will remember, we had to say: the whole book is about so and so and such and such. That done, we can proceed as follows: (1) the author accomplished this plan in five major parts, of which the first part is about so and so, the second part is about such and such, the third part is about this, the fourth part about that, and the fifth about still another thing. (2) The first of these major parts is divided into three sections, of which the first considers X, the second considers Y, and the third considers Z. Each of the other major parts is then similarly divided. (3) In the first section of the first part, the author makes four points, of which the first is A, the second B, the third C, and the fourth D. Each of the other sections is then similarly analyzed, and this is done for each of the sections of each of the other major parts.

Terrifying? I can see why it might be. All this to do, you say, and on what is only the first reading of a book. It would take a lifetime to read a book that way. If you feel this way, I can also see that all my warnings have done no good. When put down this way in a cold and exacting formula, the rule looks as if it required an impossible amount of work from you. But you have forgotten that the good reader does this sort of thing habitually, and hence easily and naturally. He may not write it all out. He may not even at the time of reading have made it all verbally explicit. But if he were called upon to give an account of the structure of a book, he would do something that approximated the formula I have suggested.

The word "approximation" should relieve your anxiety. A good rule always describes the ideal performance. But a man can be skilled in an art without being the ideal artist. He can be a good practitioner if he merely approximates the rule. I have stated the rule here for the ideal case. I would be satisfied, and so should you be with yourself, if you made a very rough approximation to what is required. Even when you become more skilled, you will not wish to read every book with the same degree of effort. You will not find it profitable to expend all your skill on some books.

I have tried to make a close approximation to the requirements of this rule in the case of relatively few books. In other instances, which means for the most part, I am satisfied if I have a fairly rough notion of the book's structure. You will find, as I have, that the degree of approximation you wish to make varies with the character of the book and your purpose in reading it. Regardless of this variability, the rule remains the same. You must know how to follow it, whether you follow it closely and strictly or only in a rough fashion.

The forbidding aspect of the formula for setting forth the order and relation of the parts may be somewhat lessened by a few illustrations of the rule in operation. Unfortunately, it is more difficult to illustrate this rule than the other one about stating the unity. A unity, after all, can be stated in a sentence or two, at most a short paragraph. But in the case of any large and complex book, a careful and adequate recital of the parts, and their parts, and *their* parts down to the least structural units, would take a great many pages to write out.

Some of the greatest medieval commentaries on the works of Aristotle are longer than the originals. They include, of course, more than a structural analysis, for they undertake to interpret the author sentence by sentence. The same is true of certain modern commentaries, such as the great ones on Kant's *The Critique of Pure Reason*. I suggest that you look into a commentary of this sort if you want to see this rule followed to perfection. Aquinas, for instance, begins each section of his commentary with a beautiful outline of the points that Aristotle has made in that part of his work; and he always says explictly how that part fits into the structure of the whole, especially in relation to the parts that come before and after.

On second thought, perhaps you had better not look at masterly commentaries. A beginner in reading might be depressed by their perfection. He might feel as the beginner in climbing feels at the bottom of the Jungfrau. A poor and slight sample of analysis by me might be more encouraging, though certainly less uplifting. It is all right to hitch your wagon to a star, but you had better be sure it is well lubricated before you take the reins.

5

. . . I may be able to give you a few . . . examples of applying this rule if I do not try to carry the process out in all its details. Take the Constitution of the United States. That is an interesting, practical document, and a very well-organized piece of writing, indeed. You should have no difficulty in finding its major parts. They are pretty clearly indicated, though you have to do some analysis to make the main divisions. I suggest the following:

FIRST: The preamble, setting forth the purpose of the Constitution;

SECOND: The first article, dealing with the legislative department of the government;

THIRD: The second article, dealing with the executive department of the government;

FOURTH: The third article, dealing with the judicial department of the government;

FIFTH: The fourth article, dealing with the relationship between state and Federal governments;

SIXTH: The fifth, sixth, and seventh articles, dealing with the amendment of the Constitution, its status as the supreme law of the land, and provisions for its ratification;

SEVENTH: The first ten amendments, constituting the Bill of Rights;

EIGHTH: The remaining amendments up to the present day.

This is only one way of doing the job. There are many others. The first three articles could be grouped together in one division, for instance; or instead of two divisions with respect to the amendments, more divisions could be introduced, grouping the amendments according to the problems they dealt with. I suggest that you try your hand at making your own division of the Constitution into its main parts. Go further than I did, and try to state the parts of the parts as well. You may have read the Constitution many times before this, but if you exercise this rule on it for another reading, you will find a lot there you never saw before.

I am going to attempt one more example, with great brevity. I have already stated the unity of Aristotle's *Ethics*. Now let me give you a first approximation of its structure. The whole is divided into the following main parts: a first, treating of happiness as the end of life, and discussing it in relation to all other practicable goods; a second, treating of the nature of voluntary action, and its relation to the formation of virtuous and vicious habits; a third, discussing the various virtues and vices, both moral and intellectual; a fourth, dealing with moral states which are neither virtuous nor vicious; a fifth, treating of friendship, and a sixth and last, discussing pleasure, and completing the account of human happiness begun in the first.

These divisions obviously do not correspond to the ten books of the *Ethics*. Thus, the first part is accomplished in the first book; the second part runs through book two and the first half of book three; the third part extends from the rest of book three to the end of the sixth book; the discussion of pleasure occurs at the end of book seven and again at the beginning of book ten.

I mention all this to show you that you need not follow the apparent structure of a book as indicated by its chapter divisions. It may, of course, be better than the blueprint you develop, but it may also be worse; in any case, the point is to make your own blueprint. The author made his in order to write a good book. You must make yours in order to read it well. If he were a perfect writer and you a perfect reader, it would naturally follow that the two would be the same. In proportion as either of you or both fall away from perfection, all sorts of discrepancies will inevitably result.

I do not mean that you should totally ignore chapter headings and sectional divisions made by the author. They are intended to help you, just as titles and prefaces are. But you must use them as guides for your own activity, and not rely on them passively. There are few authors who execute their plan perfectly, but there is often more plan in a great book than meets the eye at first. The surface can be deceiving. You must look beneath to discover the real structure.

6

In general, these two rules of reading which we have been discussing look as if they were rules of writing also. Of course, they are. Writing and reading are reciprocal, as are teaching and being taught. If authors or teachers did not organize their communications, if they failed to unify them and order their parts, there would be no point in directing readers or listeners to search for the unity and uncover the structure of the whole.

Though there are reciprocal rules in the two cases, they are not followed in the same way. The reader tries to *uncover* the skeleton the book conceals. The author starts with it and tries to *cover it up*. His aim is to conceal the skeleton artistically or, in other words, to put flesh on the bare bones. If he is a good writer, he does not bury a puny skeleton under a mass of fat. The joints should not show through where the flesh is thin, but if flabbiness is avoided, the joints will be detectable and the motion of the parts will reveal the articulation.

I made a mistake several years ago which was instructive on this point. I wrote a book in outline form. I was so obsessed with the importance of structure that I confused the arts of writing and reading. I outlined the structure of a book, and published it. Naturally, it was repulsive to most self-respecting readers who thought that they could do their job, if I did mine. I learned from their reactions that I had given them a reading of a book I had not written. Writers should write books and leave commentaries to readers.

Let me summarize all this by reminding you of the old-fashioned maxim that a piece of writing should have unity, clarity, and coherence. That is a basic maxim of good writing. The two rules we have been discussing in this chapter respond to writing which follows that maxim. If the writing has unity, we must find it. If the writing has clarity and coherence, we must appreciate it by finding the distinction and the order of the parts. What is clear is so by the distinctness of its outlines. What is coherent hangs together in an orderly disposition of parts.

These two rules, I might add, can be used in reading any substantial part of an expository book, as well as the whole. If the part chosen is itself a relatively independent, complex unity, its unity and complexity must be discerned for it to be well read. Here there is a significant difference between books conveying knowledge and poetical works, plays, and novels. The parts of the former can be much more autonomous than the parts of the latter. The student who is supposed to have read a novel and who says he has "read enough to get the idea" does not know what he is talking about. If the novel is any good at all, the idea is in the whole, and cannot be found short of reading the whole. But you can get *the* idea of Aristotle's *Ethics* or Darwin's *The Origin of Species* by reading some parts of it carefully.

7

So long ago that you may have forgotten it, I mentioned a fourth rule to complete the first ways of reading a book. It can be stated briefly. It needs little explanation and no illustration. It really repeats in another form what you have already done if you have applied the second and third rules. But it is a useful repetition because it throws the whole and its parts into another light.

This fourth rule requires you to *find out what the author's problems were*. This rule is most pertinent, of course, to the great books. If you remember that they are original communications, you will realize that the man who wrote them started out with problems and ended by writing what the solutions were. A problem is a question. The book ostensibly contains one or more answers to it.

The writer may or may not tell you what the questions were as well as give you the answers which are the fruits of his work. Whether he does or does not, and especially if he does not, it is your task as a reader to formulate the problem as precisely as you can. You should be able to state the main problem or problems which the book tries to answer, and you should be able to state the subordinate problems if the main questions are complex and have many parts. You should not only have a fairly adequate grasp of all the questions involved, but you should be able to put the questions in an intelligible order. Which are primary and which secondary? Which questions must be answered first, if others are to be answered later?

You see how this fourth rule duplicates, in a sense, work you have already done in stating the unity and finding its parts. It may, however, actually help you to do that work. In other words, following the fourth rule is a useful procedure in conjunction with obeying the other two.

If you know the kinds of questions *anyone can ask about anything*, you will become adept in detecting an author's problems. They can be briefly formulated. Does something exist? What kind of thing is it? What caused it to exist, or under what conditions can it exist, or why does it exist? What purpose does it serve? What are the consequences of its existence? What are its characteristic properties, its typical traits? What are its relations to other things of a similar sort, or of a different sort? How does it behave? *The foregoing are all theoretical questions. The following are practical.* What ends should be sought? What means should be chosen to a given end? What things must one do to gain a certain objective, and in what order? Under these conditions, what is the right thing to do, or the better rather than the worse? Under what conditions would it be better to do this rather than that?

This list of questions is far from being exhaustive or analytically refined, but it does represent the types of most frequently asked questions in the pursuit of theoretic or practical knowledge. It may help you to discover the problems a book has tried to solve.

When you have followed the four rules . . . , you can put down the book you have in hand for a moment. You can sigh and say: "Here endeth the first reading."

reading for analysis of reasoning
ALEXANDER SCHARBACH

A newspaper banner over a column bearing a Washington Associated Press dateline reads: "Critic Claims Professors Lazy." The article is a report of a meeting of the American Council on Education and begins: "College professors are lazy, tradition-bound, inefficient, conceited and devoted to their own comfort, a former colleague says."

In news style, this opening is the conclusion of the argument as the AP reporter analyzed the speech. The speaker was a vice president of the Ford Foundation's fund for the advancement of education, and his audience was one thousand college professors and administrators at their Washington meeting. He complained that after the foundation spent 60 million dollars on attempts at improving schools and colleges and saw some success in experiments, the institutions returned to traditonal teaching procedures. Particularly, they refused to teach by television, and they still preferred, as surveys showed, to continue teaching small classes by the lecture method. He was highly displeased that out of thirty teaching procedures included in the survey questionnaire, teaching by television rated no higher than eighteenth.

Readers of the AP summary of the probably long speech would be left wondering what portions had been left omitted and what their bearing would have been on the part reported. They would

Reprinted with permission of McGraw-Hill Book Company, from *Critical Reading and Writing*, by Alexander Scharbach. © 1965 by McGraw-Hill, Inc.

have to remember that newspaper reports of learned society meetings are generally colored by the reporter's eagerness to find a dramatic story that might make headlines, as did this one.

The conclusion opening the report is inferred from two basic syllogisms:

1. Whoever underwrites TV experiments can expect college professors to adopt new methods.
2. The foundation spent 60 million dollars on such experiments!
3. The foundation can expect the professors to adopt new methods.

1. All those not living up to foundation expectations are lazy, tradition-bound, etc.
2. College professors did not live up to foundation expectations.
3. College professors are lazy, tradition-bound, etc.

Both syllogisms reveal assumed premises in their first statement. It would appear to an uninformed reader that perhaps the foundation took too much for granted when it gave the huge sums for the experiments. What solid evidence of possible success did it have to justify expending such amounts? How successful, really, were *the many cases* deemed such by the speaker, and would the new methods bring savings? Must teachers who do not feel convinced by the new methods necessarily be *lazy, tradition-bound,* etc.? Perhaps faulty communication may be the cause of this professorial intransigence. We are not told whether the questionnaire was given to only participating institutions or to others as well.

A proposition that unwisely includes all of a class or kind is called a *hasty generalization.* This fallacy in reasoning appears in the newspaper headline and opening lead: "College professors are lazy." It does not say *some* or *a number,* or even *many.* On the contrary, it implies that *all* are such. (Incidentally, the report lumps all levels of college and university teaching staff into one rank—*professors.* Now, everyone knows that the low men on the totem pole—the instructors and the assistant professors—who are engaged in teaching composition are not *lazy.* Look at the mountains of papers they have to correct!)

.   .   .

RECOGNIZING TYPES OF ARGUMENTS

Syllogistic analysis can spotlight the skeletal logic of any lecture or reading assignment developing a proposition. It can reveal flaws and strengths in inferences and conclusions. But a convincing argument needs the shaping features of rhetoric as much as it does those of logic. These rhetorical qualities are best seen in the basic forms or outlines that tradition considers effective for convincing speech and writing.

To begin with, remember that argumentation is one of the four kinds of discourse—exposition, description, and narration being the other three, and each having techniques of its own. Its purpose to convince and persuade implies that there will be those who will disagree. More than likely, they will not disagree with everything, only with certain points. These chief points of difference on which the argument stands or falls are called *the issues*. Issues raise the questions that have to be answered, and every type of argument has certain standard inquiries to determine its chief issues. Skilled debaters know them by heart and become expert in applying them.

Before listing any types and their formula issues, let's see what happens in one typical argument. In this passage, what is James Boswell asking himself?

> I was deeply offended with the behaviour of this nobleman. I had resolved to give up all regard for him; and now, by our coming to an explanation, I am perfectly convinced that he was not to blame. I hope this acknowledgment is not owing to mere goodness and easiness of temper. For his facts and arguments, which are all just, are very strong in his favour. I think my candid soul is to be admired for yielding my resentful feelings to truth. This even makes me very happy. I shall now enjoy his elegant company and conversations as fully and freely as formerly. We shall be intimate companions.

Paraphrasing, we can say he had been angered by a nobleman and was ready to break off all dealings with him. After hearing an explanation based on facts and reasoning, however, young

Boswell gladly changes his plans and will become the other's close friend. In brief, this is a *change of policy* argument and illustrates the various issues to be found in that type. These are the general issue questions:

1. Is the old policy just and beneficial?
2. Can its defects be remedied?
3. Is the new policy just and beneficial?
4. Will it work under the conditions proposed?

James Boswell ran through these classic questions, it would seem, to prove to himself and the future readers of his *Journal* that his earlier plan to be hostile to the nobleman was neither just nor beneficial. He told himself that it was not just his good nature and desire to be at peace with a possible benefactor which made him change his mind. No, the nobleman had good reason and facts on his side. So Boswell can congratulate himself on his own open mind and his good heart and look forward to enjoying a delightful, beneficial friendship. . . .

Change of policy arguments naturally abound in the many volumes of the *Congressional Record*. Also, thanks to the custom of *inserting remarks,* an occasional bizarre argument shows up among the serious debates over proposals to eliminate luxury taxes on furs, to build new power dams, to decrease foreign aid, and to make other such weighty changes in policy. One unusual argument comes with the insertion in 1950 of an article written by a physical culturist who proposed a new policy: The American people should stop eating and wearing anything derived from *down deep in the earth*. His issues and their answers can be stated thus:

1. Is the old (or present) policy of what people eat and wear just and beneficial? No. Everybody knows what harmful effects mineral oils, chemicals, and gases can have on the human body.
2. Can the old policy be retained and remedied? Not at all. It has to be done away with. All synthetics are harmful.
3. Is the new policy of diet change just and beneficial? Absolutely! "I believe that since we live on top of the earth, foods, etc. taken from the top of the earth, or near the top, are best for the human body."

4. Will it work? Of course. There are cotton, wool, and linen enough to clothe everybody. Enough food also.

Asking such basic questions quickly reveals the essential ludicrousness of such an argument, but the same questions can be applied to arguments proposing changes in student body rules, in personal life, and in government at all levels.

Argument of analogy is most persuasive, and perhaps sells products and convinces unquestioning minds more easily than do the other forms of argument. *Analogy* can be defined as the likeness between two things consisting of similarity not of the things themselves but of some features. In logic, analogy is a form of inferring that if two or more things agree in some respects, they probably also agree in others.

Analogy works in all manner of situations. After World War II ended, many cautious people looked at shipyards and industries that had been geared to the war effort and began thinking in terms of comparison thus: "After World War I there was a bad depression and much unemployment because there was no more need of war equipment. So now we had better prepare for another depression." Those who acted in such a fearful fashion lost wonderful opportunities to invest in firms that since the war have climbed to record heights of business. These skeptics failed to ask the issue question: *Are the points of similarity stronger than the points of difference?* Or if they asked the question, they were unable to answer it correctly. At the time, it was an inquiry that many respected economists also found it difficult to answer.

Some people allow even a single common term to confuse them into viewing totally different situations as being analogous, as in the following letter to an editor:

> Really, there is nothing new under the sun. We have the Crusade of the Students Non-Violent Co-ordinating Committee today. We had the Children's Crusade to the Holy Land in 1212. Will they be equally futile?

No possible analogies could be made between two such dissimilar situations; only *crusade* relates them, and the referents are not at all identical in the two instances.

Argument of cause brings in the profound matter of causation: Can *A* cause *B* to come into existence? If *A* is always seen as appearing prior to *B* in a phenomenon, does *A* cause *B*? These are some of the puzzles that bother unthinking persons not at all; they take a cause-effect world for granted, as they do their language. For them, clouds in the sky *cause* rain; warm air *causes* milk to sour; strikes *cause* higher prices. Even the somewhat scholarly persons who write learnedly of baffling subjects can be confused about *cause*. Dr. Immanuel Velikovsky's *Worlds in Collision* is a book providing excellent illustration of the argument of cause.

Velikovsky was evidently trying to find the natural cause or explanation for two stupendous events recorded in the Old Testament: the dividing of the waters of the Red Sea, enabling Moses to lead the Israelites dry-shod across it, and Joshua's feat of commanding the sun to stand still so that he could finish his great battle for the Promised Land. Through a complex fusion of inductive and deductive thinking and feeling, Velikovsky finally arrived at his cause. Despite all refutation, he still holds that a comet split off from the planet Jupiter and, on two different occasions, passed close to Earth, was drawn into the orbit of Mars, and finally, after producing many smaller comets, ended up as the planet Venus. On the first pass near Earth, it providentially made possible the dividing of waters, and on the second the halting of the sun. The comet likewise accounts for the storm on Mt. Sinai when Moses was given the Commandments and for the manna which kept the Israelites alive in the desert.

His *argument of cause* can be and has extensively been questioned on these issue points:

1. Is the assumed cause the only possible one?
2. Is not the cause perhaps only a factor in the conditions?
3. Could the cause produce all of the phenomena observed?

Scholars have given Dr. Velikovsky's comet theory severe criticism on the grounds of the inadequacy of the evidence he offers in geology and astronomy as well as the fallacies of his reasoning upon that evidence. These issue questions indicate the care readers must take in considering arguments.

The *argument of fact* also has its basic issues. Paperback thrillers and television courtroom dramas have popularized the standard inquiries: "What was the condition of the body, Doctor?" "Mr. Crosseyes, where were you standing at the time? Are you sure you saw it all?" In every case, the questions concern the facts of evidence and the competence of the witnesses:

1. Are the facts in evidence relevant and unquestionable?
2. Are the characters of the witnesses reliable?
3. Are the witnesses competent to testify on the subject in question?

The same issues apply to attempts at proving that Homer's Troy has been located, that man's ancestors were carnivorous, or that someone other than Shakespeare wrote "Shakespeare's" plays. They apply as well to interminable efforts to establish before law whether an aluminum plant in the vicinity is directly responsible for the death of a dairy farmer's cows and the ruination of pasture grass. The issues relate also to questions of fact about value judgments such as this one: Is it reprehensible for a student newspaper to publish the statement: "Grades are your means of getting into graduate school; your means of keeping your parents happy; your means of avoiding the Army. . . . [But] Do not give the professor reason to suppose that your interest is in the grade. You must always act like an interested intellectual, no matter what your motive"?

To avoid undue controversy over examples, let's examine how argument-of-fact issues can be applied to a magazine article dealing with this question of fact: "Does the violence of television shows harmfully affect children viewers?" These are the conclusions reached:

A child who watches violence on a screen is not necessarily going to attack the first person he sees. But if he is provoked enough on some future occasion, he may very well copy aggressive patterns of behavior that he has learned from a pictorial medium like television. This is clearly illustrated by an episode in which a boy was seriously wounded during the reenactment, with a friend, of a switchblade knife fight seen in a television rerun of the movie *Rebel Without a Cause*. The impact of the scene upon the boys did not become apparent until the day after the program, when one of them adopted the James Dean role and challenged his friend to a fight. Only after the fight had begun did the *Rebel*-style knife play emerge. . . .

We now see clearly that violence on a television or movie screen affects viewers by:

1. Reducing their inhibitions against violent, aggressive behavior.
2. Teaching them forms of aggression—that is, giving them information about how to attack someone else when the occasion arises.

And, third, let us keep in mind that the ethical ending, in which the villain is punished, may keep viewers from reproducing villainy right away, but does not make them forget how to do it. The ethical ending is just a suppressor of violence; it does not erase.

Since the amount of time that children are exposed to television makes it one of the most important influences in their lives, these laboratory findings do not present a pretty picture—unless our society is interested in increasing the aggressive tendencies of a growing generation.

Now the issue questions: Are the facts relevant and unquestionable? Are the witnesses reliable and competent?

The author of this report is a prominent university psychologist; he carried out a series of experiments with ninety-six boys and girls, most of them four-year-olds, from middle-class homes in the Palo Alto, California, area. In this *Look* article he explains in some detail the experiments wherein children were exposed to patterns of violence "shown by adult models in three different situations: in real life, on film, and as cartoon characters on film." Since the conclusions were arrived at through experiments, other investigators can repeat the tests and check the findings reported. It is evident that the author-experimenter anticipated just such questions. How well his conclusions have held up may possibly be learned by consulting *The Psychological Index*.

As has been suggested, value judgments become the ones most difficult to establish as facts, such as, for example, this judgment by Montaigne:

> Experience has taught us to rank the virtue of housekeeping above all others in married women. I put my wife to it, as her own concern, leaving her during my absence the entire government of my affairs. It is the most useful and honorable occupation for the mother of a family. Nevertheless, though I have seen many an avaricious woman, I have seldom known a good manager. It

is the supreme quality a man should seek in a wife—the only dowry that can ruin or preserve our houses.

Montaigne's is an *argument of values*. Before trying to discuss issues for it, let us consider an even more extreme statement of values, or interpretations, by Oscar Wilde:

> It is the imaginative quality of Christ's own nature that makes him this palpitating centre of romance. The strange figures of poetic drama and ballad are made by the imagination of others, but out of his own imagination entirely did Jesus of Nazareth create himself. The cry of Isaiah had really no more to do with his coming than the song of the nightingale has to do with the rising of the moon—no more, perhaps no less. He was the denial as well as the affirmation of prophecy. For every expectation that he fulfilled there was another that he destroyed. "In all beauty," says Bacon, "there is some strangeness of proportion," and of those who are born of the spirit—of those, that is to say, who like himself are dynamic forces—Christ says that they are like the wind that "bloweth where it listeth, and no man can tell whence it cometh and whither it goeth." That is why he is so fascinating to artists. He has all the colour elements of life: mystery, strangeness, pathos, suggestion, ecstasy, love. He appeals to the temper of wonder and creates that mood in which alone he can be understood.

An *argument of values* almost always involves personal beliefs, both those of the writer and of the reader. They relate to such private matters as religion, philosophy, art, and literature. Because they are intangible, they may often be difficult to appraise fairly. Unlike sciences such as astronomy and geology, wherein experts can agree on many basic facts because they are establishable in laboratories, the liberal arts subjects seldom have experts who are at all universally accepted as infallible. Even the language of the arts of human values differs from that of science, which is mainly mathematical symbols, permitting no errant connotations.

But in a democratic society where citizen often lives elbow-to-elbow with citizen, it is difficult to dismiss all subjective values as merely peculiarities of taste. For as the Constitution founders long ago realized, we remember, men are easily aroused in their passions, and violence may quickly flare. Still, we stand on the rights guaranteed us of freedom of speech and belief. At the same time we are equally bound to respect those rights in others.

What, then, as a critical reader, should one demand of persuasive statements of values? What does he owe himself, the author, and his fellowman? Perhaps a few general questions of issues may provide some answers. (It is better yet if you can provide your own criteria for judgment.)

1. What exactly are the beliefs herein advanced? . . .
2. Do the views offered propose physical or mental harm to anyone?
3. Do they make daily life more meaningful to the author? More agreeable to others?

These are broad measurements written with the realization that our American civilization has cherished such individualists as Thomas Jefferson, Benjamin Franklin, Henry David Thoreau, Abraham Lincoln, Walt Whitman, and Robert Frost.

To ignore values, stated or implied, in what we read is to miss basic meanings. We must learn to be as quick to detect shoddy half-truths and unacceptable doctrines as we are to note the fallacies in reasoning. Unfortunately, however, as one college entrance examiner was shocked to discover, too many entering college students seem unable, or are unwilling, to detect the unacceptable:

> The students who wrote them [the comments on the test paragraph] know how to put sentences together; they come close to knowing how to read. What they don't know is how to evaluate what they read, how to see it in terms of who they are and the other things they know, how to test on their pulses the real assumptions beneath the ostensible ones. Most of the students, I suppose, would have been ready to condemn totalitarianism if they had seen it. The problem is to get them to recognize it *when* they see it.

It could not be said better: critical readers *test on their pulses the real assumptions beneath the ostensible ones.* Logic can show you how to find the assumptions, but your family and you, with perhaps some outside help, must provide *the testing pulse.*

. . . .

THE MOCKING LANGUAGE OF FALLACIES

. . . The smokescreens, mousetraps, false appeals, and misleading use of the devices of propaganda somewhat overlap with the errors—deliberate or otherwise—made by many writers and speakers in logic. These errors in reasoning are called *fallacies;* we have already noted the examples of *hasty generalizations* and *false assumptions*, but there are others.

False analogy misleads and beguiles by painting a picture wholly lacking in truth but seeming to be what it claims. *Analogy*, we have said, is "a form of inference in which it is reasoned that if two (or more) things agree with one another in one or more respects, they will (probably) agree in yet other respects." A *false* analogy, therefore, will be one wherein the points of resemblance between two things may seem striking enough to warrant identifying the two as wholly alike, but further examination will show that the points of difference are stronger than the points of similarity. For example, an opponent of Federal aid to state education may contend: "Giving Federal funds to the states for their schools won't work out well for anybody. It will be the case of a father's putting himself into the embarrassing position of handing out money to his children, and then not being able to stop them from wasting or misusing it." The homely comparison may win a delighted chuckle from an audience identifying itself with the nonplussed parent, but the Federal government looks quite awkward in the role of "Dad." Orators fall into analogies as naturally as rain into puddles. "The battle of Waterloo was won on the playing fields of Eton" is a famous progenitor of the many faulty comparisons of sports to the "game of life," which generally confuse one about sports and life.

A writer or speaker *ignoring the issue* may suddenly grow long-winded when challenged on a touchy point. If unable to answer, he may turn nasty and abusive, resorting to name-calling. In other eras he might have evaded the issue by challenging the questioner to a duel—as if being able to slice up an opponent proved a point of logic. The skilled issue dodger has a whole bag of tricks. He may cite undisputable facts, one after the other, but the facts may not be *evidence* relevant to the issue. In arguing that automation really is no monster but a servant, he might give examples and figures of the many new jobs and industries that automation has produced, but he would neglect the charge that it has also brought increased unemployment. Or he might resort to *ad hoc* defense of automation by limiting his explanation to the description of one particular plant or industry which had achieved a remarkable record of employment expansion, ignoring the fact that a neighboring city might consequently have been adversely affected.

Ignoring the issue may take many different forms, but it becomes a particularly bitter charge in a situation wherein what one person feels are his "convictions" others call his "prejudices." Recently *The New York Times* editorially took a congressman to task for ignoring the issues of the merits of a book and attacking instead everyone connected with it:

How Not to Read a Book

Behind the immunity of the Congressional Record, Representative James B. Utt, a rightwing California Republican, has made a McCarthyite attack on the Columbia Broadcasting System, the American Booksellers Association, The New York Herald Tribune, Simon & Schuster and Jessica Mitford, author of the current best seller, "The American Way of Death." Mr. Utt indicts the network, the newspaper and the booksellers because in one way or another they are helping to publicize Miss Mitford's book.

The fact that her discussion of the flamboyance and high cost of funerals has evoked high praise from Catholic, Protestant and Jewish clergymen, as well as from reviewers and other commentators in all parts of the country, is of no concern to Mr. Utt. What makes the book intolerable to him is that Miss Mitford a dozen years ago was accused of membership in subversive organizations and that someone once identified her husband as a Communist.

The Congressman's general approach to all such matters is perhaps best indicated by some of his past estimates of other individuals and organizations. He has called President Kennedy "a pathological liar" and United Nations Under Secretary Ralph J. Bunche "a Communist sympathizer," and he has urged that the United States quit the U.N. because the world body is "a tool of Communism." On that basis his credentials as a book and television critic can safely be dismissed as nil; his credentials as a legislator cannot be examined with equal safety without the immunity the Congressional Record provides.

This editorial, in making its point, also exemplifies several different forms of verbal weaponry. What are they?

Avoiding the issue is sometimes confused with *begging the question*—assuming that the question raised has been proved. When two famous scholars go after one another—one claiming *certainty* and *facts* of literary history and the other in favor of literary criticism, or the study of literature as an art—they will be most conscientious to avoid being accused of *begging the question,* as is F. R. Leavis herein:

> Any history that deals in influences is committed to criticism— as Mr. Bateson, in his own way, is committed. This general proposition will surprise Mr. Bateson—or rather, he will feel, and perhaps rightly, that it justified his ascribing to me the more general proposition. It brings me, at any rate, to my essential point against him: the radical distinction he invokes, the distinction that he reduces to the difference between fact and opinion, seems to me extraordinarily uncritical (I hope he won't think this begging the question). What is this "fact" of "the dependence of Dryden's poetry on Waller's"? I should like to see by what "sober evidence-weighing" Mr. Bateson would set out to establish it. The only evidence he specifies is "that provided by parallel passages" —by which, indeed, Dryden can be proved to have read Waller just as he can be proved to have read Cowley and Milton.

The loaded question may not be a fallacy, but it leads to responses compounding the errors of any flaw in reasoning. Archetype of all such threatening inquiries is the one we referred to in the discussion of political devices used in mass persuasion: "Answer yes or no—Are you still beating your wife?" It has its multitude of variants: "Mr. Mayor, are you going to announce your candidacy for governor soon?" "Are you going to be a renegade all your life?" Anyone seeking to embarrass his opponent may fire a "challenge" at him in the form of a complex question, which, if answered directly, can only offend one group or another of supporters, as this one: "Senator, in all your speeches and articles on this topic of *featherbedding* and the unions, you keep telling the union leaders the same thing—

'Take a good realistic look at the tremendous technological advances being made in your plants and factories.' Now tell us the truth, Senator. Don't you still really think that the fight of any union to keep its members employed on unnecessary jobs is *featherbedding?*" That this question is a booby trap is clear. But then, the wily senator may turn about and ignore the issue by looking properly indignant and counter attacking with the cry, "Let's look at the record and see what the real facts are!"

When the reader is offered only two alternatives, two choices of action or decision, and both are highly displeasing to him, he is said to be *on the horns of the dilemma*. It is often most difficult to find a third alternative which may deliver one from both of the *horns*. In *The Decline of the West*, Oswald Spengler posed a famous dilemma that helped eventually to drive the German people onto the horn of Nazism. When he wrote that every event was "the prelude of a future . . . with which the history of West-European mankind will be definitely *closed*," he proceeded to set before them two almost equally unbearable choices:

> He who does not understand that this outcome is obligatory and insusceptible of modification, that our choice is between will *this* and willing nothing at all, between cleaving to *this* destiny or despairing of the future and of life itself; he who cannot feel that there is grandeur also in the realizations of powerful intelligences, in the energy and discipline of metal-hard natures, in battles fought with the coldest and most abstract means; he who is obsessed with the idealism of a provincial and would pursue the ways of life of past ages—must forgo all desire to comprehend history, to live through history or to make history.

Does it seem possible that a nation of readers would accept such meager choices? It is strange that a country that had produced great philosophers could not come up with more suitable alternatives than the ones of despair and callous destruction offered them by Spengler and then by Adolph Hitler. Had readers ceased to be critical and become wholly permissive?

Making an unhappy choice usually leads to *rationalization*. One who rationalizes finds "good" reasons to justify making errors in judgment and action. It may take on the form of *sour grapes* thinking found expressed in the attitude: "Aw, who wanted it anyway?" If not given what he considers his due, he sulks and blames everyone but himself without giving up any of his sense of superiority. Dostoyevsky has made a powerful novel of the rationalizations of an "underground" character. Here is the tormented man at a bachelor dinner party which he knew he should never have insisted on being invited to:

> They forgot about me, and I sat there crushed and humiliated.
> "Good God, what kind of company are they for me!" I thought. "What a stupid light I've shown myself in! And I've let Ferfichkin get away with too much. These lumps think they're doing me a great honor, allowing me to sit down to dinner with them, whereas it's I who condescend to dine with them! So I've grown thin and my clothes are shabby? Ah, the damned trousers! Zverkov probably noticed the yellow stain on the knee right away. Ah, why bother! I ought to get up right away, take my hat, and leave without saying a word. And tomorrow, I could challenge any of them to a duel. The miserable pigs! I don't have to stick it out to get my seven rubles' worth of food. They might think, though, —damn it all! To hell with the seven rubles! I'm leaving right now!"
> It goes without saying that I didn't leave.

Perhaps the most vicious kind of self-justification through self-deception appears in the language of the "poison pen" writer or speaker. He demands that the silence of the one accused or slandered be interpreted as proof of guilt. His repeated theme is: "If he's not what I say he is, why doesn't he defend himself? What's keeping him from talking up, the way an honest man would do? He doesn't dare. That's why. If what I say isn't gospel fact, he can take me to court, can't he? But no, he keeps still, hoping you'll forget all about this business until after the election." In such a case, whatever denials are issued by the aggrieved party go unheard by the accuser. Unless constrained by court order, he continues making the same charges to different audiences even long after the claims have been proved false.

Post hoc ergo propter hoc—literally, "after this, therefore on account of this"—is the common error of attributing a cause-effect relationship where there is only one of time. If a family go on a long vacation without notifying their newspaper boy to discontinue delivery of the daily newspaper, they can expect to find a stack of yellowing papers behind the screen door or littering the yard. Here there is a causal relation between events. A sudden fall in barometric pressure will warn of a change in the weather, but the barometer reading itself is not the cause of that change. During the seventy-two-year reign of Louis XIV, many "glories and disasters" came to France, but they were not caused merely by the fact that Louis occupied the throne. He does not deserve either the credit or the blame for many of them, any more than President Herbert Hoover was the cause of the Great Depression which began during his term of office. What comes first may not be at all the cause of what follows subsequently.

reading for ideas
KEN MACORIE

When you want to get everything possible out of a piece of writing, you will have to read closely. The close reader does not passively soak up what someone has written. He is active. He analyzes. He reacts. He takes an attitude. He *thinks*. He is always saying to himself, "Is this fellow making sense? Is his point worth making? Do his examples suggest that he is right?" Suppose you pick up your evening newspaper and glance at a sports column which says:

> Appearance of meteoric Dave Sime on our track and field scene, especially in an Olympic year, amounts to almost a miracle.
>
> Where else in the world, please, could they come up with a kid from the blue who could tear up the record book and toss it to the winds as this University of North Carolina sophomore has done, is doing and apparently will continue to do. . . .
>
> The 19-year-old speedster who wants to be a ball player now has surpassed all standards in the 220-yard dash and the 220-yard low hurdles. He has equalled the world record in the 100-yard dash. What about the broad jump? With his kind of speed he must be able to fly!
>
> He calls up his mother after breaking the 220-yard mark and casually says, "Mom—I did it—I set a world record," as casually

Reprinted with permission of Harcourt, Brace & World, Inc., from *The Perceptive Writer, Reader and Speaker,* by Ken Macorie. © 1959 by Harcourt, Brace & World, Inc.

as he would report to her that he had drawn an "A" in the math final.

He still has his eye on that baseball diamond, and as soon as he has helped Uncle Sam in the Olympics, he is going back to it and to heck with this track business!

No place but in the U.S. could that happen!

When you see the question, "Where else in the world, please, could they come up with a kid from the blue . . ." you should think back to your own knowledge and experience to test the statement. You might conclude that any country in the world might produce a Dave Sime. You may have known several persons who suddenly proved to be good trackmen in college.

When you read that Dave Sime "calls up his mother after breaking the 220-yard mark and casually says, 'Mom—I did it— I set a world record,' as casually as he would report to her that he had drawn an 'A' in the math final," you should question the writer's description. In the first place, the statement "Mom—I did it—I set a world record," does not sound casual, but excited. In the second place, a boy probably doesn't tell his mother casually that he got an "A" in a math final. In the third place, you may not see why Dave Sime should be given special credit for making a normal statement about winning to his mother.

You might next ask what the writer is trying to prove with his praise for Dave Sime. What is his point? Is it that the United States provides greater opportunity for its athletes than any other country? If so, one example of an athlete who has broken several world records does not seem to prove that point. And furthermore, the argument that the United States encourages athletics more than the Soviet Union or any other country is the kind for which proof is hard to gather. One country may spend more money; the other may allow more free competition, and so forth. After such an active reading of the passage, you probably conclude that the writer has made no significant points at all. The only valuable message in his column is the simple fact that Dave Sime was little known before he broke several world records in track.

This example from a sports editor's column may seem elementary to you. You may feel that you could spot the holes in its argument immediately by yourself. I have used it for two reasons: (1) to remind you that unless you get into the habit of reading closely, you will accept sloppy thinking in your every-day reading without knowing that you are doing it, and (2) to give you a relatively simple piece of writing to study before you tackle more difficult passages later in the chapter by such men as Albert Einstein, John Dewey, and Robert Redfield.

Like thinking, the process of reading involves a number of actions. For example, the expert reader usually

> searches for the author's controlling idea and main points,
> anticipates what he will find,
> tests the validity of what the author says,
> relates ideas to experience and knowledge.

SEARCH FOR A CONTROLLING IDEA AND MAIN POINTS

You can understand the main points and even the examples of an author and still miss his controlling idea. Many students understand and sometimes even enjoy every paragraph in a chapter; but when their teacher asks them what the author was driving at, they are. at a loss for words. You may have suffered this embarrassment yourself. Perhaps in this situation you wanted to say, "I know what he was driving at, but I just can't put it into words." But putting an idea into words is part of knowing it.

Often a writer states only one idea in a piece of writing; then your job of finding it is easy. But even if he asserts that idea six or seven times, as in the following article, you need to force yourself to state it or you may come away with only a vague notion of what it is.

> One of my more intellectual friends brought up a point the other day that stimulates some serious thinking. *He asked why the spirit of a college or university must always be connected with its sports program.*
>
> Citing a definite lack of pride in intellectual conquests, he added that he would like to put on a pair of Bermudas, stand in the middle of the campus, and lead a few yells for the philosophy department.

He's right too. All over the United States, with the possible exception of a few schools which are solely academic, *the value and standing of an institution is based on its "spirit" and its football team.*

Here at Long Beach State we have heard so much about the lack of spirit on the part of the students that it is beginning to leave a bad taste in the mouth. *Why should a person have to sit in the bleachers and yell his lungs out to prove that he is loyal to his college?*

I am not advocating the overthrow of football or of the time-honored "spirit." This type of loyalty is just as vital to the school as intellectual spirit. It is especially important to a certain type of student. *I do feel, however, that we should realize that Long Beach State has many students to whom this rah-rah bit is not essential.*

We shouldn't worry too much if our crowds at football games are not the biggest or our yells the loudest. *Perhaps we already possess in mature intellect what we are seemingly missing in the boola-boola department.*

JERRY RUSSOM,
in *The Long Beach State College Forty-Niner,*
as reprinted in *The Ohio State Lantern,* January 9, 1957

All the statements in the above passage drive toward a single idea; yet if you were asked to state that idea, you might find yourself groping for words, and finally saying, "He doesn't seem to like football." This may be true, but it is a totally inadequate statement of the writer's point. You must force yourself as a reader to fix on one statement as the controlling idea. Which of the ideas printed in italics above do you think is the best statement of the writer's controlling idea? Can you sum up this idea better in your own words?

Look for Signal Words

How do you spot a main point? Fundamentally, you find it by understanding the whole passage you read and using your powers of evaluation to decide which points are major and which minor. You cannot always be certain that the author would agree with your decision. However, you can usually be fairly certain; for the author ordinarily provides you with signal words that show he is making what he considers an important point. Try to spot the main points in the following article:

> What goes on in the minds of my class is a mystery. They are a good class; that is, they are attentive. They are always respectful; they smile, at least tepidly, at my occasional story or witticism. But do these attitudes, I wonder, reflect the inner man or woman? How much of their real selves are in my Psychology class?
>
> Let me illustrate. I have in mind a girl student. She never hands in an exercise late. She masters the readings I assign. But she sits in every class sober as an owl, never giving the slightest twitch of the face at any of my humorous sallies. This young Minerva I saw one night at a basketball game. Or was she the same? I could hardly believe it. For her eyes were aglow with enthusiasm; her cheeks were flushed with excitement; her hands, ordinarily quiet, were a whirlwind of waving, clapping, and fist-clenching. Next day in class she was as quiet and placid as always.
>
> This taught me something or rather enforced what I had thought of before. It is this, that we know little about what our students are thinking, and that is what we teachers need *most* to know. We need to know whether they want our instruction and if not, why not. We need to know whether first in their thoughts is the sentence we are analyzing, or the idea we are examining. If it is not, we are spitting against the wind.
>
> We need to know our students as persons—whether their home-life is happy, their love-affairs smooth, their economic status secure, their inner life calm and easy. But most of these are locked secrets, known not even to professional counselors. And there is another side, too—one not so dismal. Last night may have been a rainbow-colored date, a hilarious stag-party, or an unforgettable gab-fest. These things take the main track of the student's mind, while the instructor, explaining the difference between the participle and the gerund, wastes his sweetness on the desert air.
>
> These are the subconscious speculations I indulge in some mornings as I stand, pulpit-enthroned, before my class. And I wish I could know what goes on behind those 81 locked doors.
>
> PROFESSOR DAVID W. SMITH,
> in the column "Faculty Says,"
> University of Arizona *Wildcat*, February 27, 1957

The first sentence in the above article involves a question— "What goes on in the minds of my class?" Often the leading question of an article will signal its main points or controlling idea, which may simply be an answer to that question. Do you think the answer to this question is the author's controlling idea, or just one of his main points?

The writer of the above column on college students has helped the reader by including, in addition to the leading question, the phrase "we need to know," which acts as another signal of the main points. Writers employ a great number of words or phrases which act as earmarks, such as *fundamentally, in the last analysis, most important, chief, without doubt, when in fact, and so, in conclusion, the point is, the real issue,* and so forth. Often a writer takes a whole sentence to tell you that he is about to state his central idea or a main point. For example, he may say: "Meanwhile, one very simple and practical principle emerges," or "One fact now stands out."

In the above column on college students, the italicized word *most* in the third paragraph is a signal to an expert reader that the writer must be making one of his main points there. The point might be written:

1. Most of all, we teachers need to know what our students *are thinking.*

The author makes other points as well:

2. We need to know whether they want our instruction and if not, why not.
3. We need to know whether first in their thoughts is the sentence we are analyzing, or the idea we are examining.
4. We need to know our students as persons.

Differentiate Between Controlling Idea and Main Points

Above you see four points made by the author. Is one point so much more important than the others that it might be called the central, controlling idea? If you had to eliminate one point as being less important, which one would it be?

The first point seems to include the others and therefore might be chosen as the controlling idea. The third point seems very detailed in contrast to the others and thus might be eliminated if the reader wanted to confine himself to one controlling idea and two main points.

Know Where to Look for Key Sentences

You have probably heard teachers emphasizing the need for writers to use "topic" sentences and for readers to discover them. The term "topic sentence" may be somewhat misleading, suggesting not a sentence which makes the point of a paragraph, but one which states the topic or subject, a relatively obvious matter. I shall call the sentences which carry the point of a paragraph *key sentences*. They are the ones that count. Frequently an author puts them first in his paragraph. As a good reader, you will commonly look for them there first. For example:

> *In this absorption in work, many people believe, lies the seat of the executive neurosis.* From Dodsworth on, the figure of the businessman self-alienated from the wider life has been held up to Americans as a somewhat tragic figure. Why, when the purpose of our vast productive apparatus is the release of man from toil, do the people in charge of it so willfully deny themselves the fruits of it? Even the executive, as he curses the demon within him, tends to feel a little guilty about it.
>
> WILLIAM H. WHYTE,
> *The Organization Man*,
> New York, Simon & Schuster, 1956

If you do not find that the key sentence is the first one in the paragraph, look at the last sentence, the next most likely position for it. For example:

> All this is not to say by any means that man is, biologically speaking, a jack-of-all-trades and master of none. Because of his thickened and heavily wrinkled brain cortex, there is one particular thing he does better, much better, than any other creature, and in this respect he is a specialist in the usual sense of the term. *He can create and use symbols so elaborately and with such effects as to make it impractical and misleading to classify man as an animal at all for many purposes.*
>
> WENDELL JOHNSON,
> *Your Most Enchanted Listener*,
> Harper & Brothers, New York, 1956

Occasionally the key sentence may occur in the middle of a paragraph:

> Twelve years after World War I the world was sinking into its worst depression; Italy had already been conquered by fascism, and Hitler's Nazis were marshaling forces for the final push to power—and war. *Today Europe is a picture of prosperity*, the coffee houses are full, the people well-dressed by previous standards, and there is no sign of any Austrian painter with a Charlie Chaplin moustache. Even in Germany there is not a single vocal force that can be called "fascist."
>
> SIDNEY LENS, "The Revival of Europe,"
> *The Progressive*, Vol. 21, August, 1957

If you read an essay or article whose central idea eludes you, you might stop and inspect quickly the first sentences of each paragraph. Often they will give you the pattern of development the writer is using and suggest where you are apt to find the controlling idea.

Consider Headings and Subheadings

The type of writing you read in college often is marked off by headings and subheadings which help you find main points. Some students believe that if they remember the headings, they need not read the paragraphs below them. Headings are useful for the skimmer and for the person trying to locate main points and the controlling idea, especially for purposes of review, but they normally will not give you the body of the argument or explanation you are reading. For example, the following headings from a magazine article are helpful, but if you were to repeat them without understanding the basis on which the writer stated them, you would know very little.

The American Press Is the Best in the World Today
The American Press on the Whole Is Improving
Censorship by Publishers Is Worse Than That by Advertisers
Newspapers Are Edited by Business Men
Monopoly Is a Grave Danger in the Press
There Is a Dangerous Tendency Toward Standardized and Syndicated Material
The Middle Class Is Overrepresented in the Press

Journalists and Papers Get Old, Fat, and Timid
In Technology There Is Hope
We Get About What We Deserve

BRUCE BLIVEN, "Balance Sheet of American Journalism,"
The New Republic, Vol. 104, March 10, 1941

These statements in themselves suggest the author's general attitude toward the press, but they do not present his reasoning or his evidence. As soon as someone asks you why the author thinks the American press is the best in the world or what difference it makes if papers are edited by businessmen, you might be lost. Some headings such as "In Technology There Is Hope," tell almost nothing by themselves. What kind of technology? Hope for what? Actually, the author was speaking of typesetting machines controlled by tapes like teletypes, self-justifying typewriters, telephotos, and radio printers.

A heading may act as a signal of a main point. If you have read the complete piece of writing carefully, remembering a few headings may be valuable as a trigger which sets off recall of the author's ideas.

ANTICIPATE WHAT WILL BE SAID

We know from studies in perception that persons frequently do not see what is before them because they do not expect it. Anticipating as a listener or reader may be dangerous or helpful. If a man anticipates in the wrong way, he will be so sure of what he will read or hear before he comes to it that he will perceive the ideas in his mind, rather than those in the mind of the person communicating to him. If he anticipates wisely, attempting to predict tentatively what he will hear or read, he will come to it with a frame of reference that will help him understand and remember. Suppose you go to a football game at which you expect the team with an exceptional record to "slaughter" the other team. The underdog wins, 12-0. You will not forget that game quickly because it broke an anticipated pattern. But if you had been a stranger in town, you might have watched the game with little feeling and never remembered a thing about it.

The good reader anticipates the point he expects to encounter.

If he is wrong in his guess, he discards his anticipation immediately. But even then, as a result of his anticipation, he will spot the right point faster and remember it longer. He can compare what the author actually says to what he expected him to say. This will help him fix the new idea in his mind.

Avoid Reader's Trance

The most dangerous habit a reader can develop is to read without thinking. Lulled by apparently obvious statements and dull examples, you have probably caught yourself reading this way—thinking of something else while your eyes pass over the lines. You can prevent such trances if you try to think ahead to what point the author is working toward. Try this with the following passage.

The Limits of Disloyalty

Nominally the same Bill of Rights which protects free speech in peacetime also protects free speech in time of war. This was decided as far as civilians are concerned in the famous case *Ex parte Milligan* in 1866. But since the limits of permissible free speech have been defined in terms of danger, and since the danger in time of war is infinitely greater than in time of peace, we actually have a double standard. Citizens do not have the same right to read in wartime as in peacetime. "Words," as Judge Learned Hand has said, "are not only the keys of persuasion, but the triggers of action." The same words which serve as keys of persuasion in peacetime are likely to serve as triggers of action in a national emergency.

The writer followed this paragraph with three examples of suppression of freedom during wartime: the jailing of socialist Eugene V. Debs for attacking "capitalist" wars during World War I; a New York State law requiring that public-school textbooks used during a war not contain material favorable to the enemy; the use of two thousand censors of foreign mail in Washington during World War II. You might now properly ask whether the writer had a point worth making. Everyone knows that censorship is more frequent in wartime than in peacetime.

When you come upon a paragraph like this, which seems to make no worthwhile point, you should anticipate that an important point is coming. The author may never present it. In that case, you may conclude he is a dud and a bore. But if he does present it, you will be ready for it and you will have found some significance in the material which preceded it. The author of the above passage was leading up to a significant point, as a later paragraph shows:

> Few citizens question the right or wisdom of the government in imposing such limitations on the distribution of the written word. They are quite willing to subordinate their personal aspirations for unrestricted freedom to the national need. What disturbs them at the present moment is that the distinctions between wartime and peacetime have broken down, and that military men may take advantage of a blurred frontier to restrict the literature of minority criticism. Admiral Arthur Radford, chairman of the Joint Chiefs of Staff, estimated in 1954 that "the period of tension" between the Communist world and the west might last one hundred years. If wartime rules of control should gradually win acceptance during that century because of national necessity, what would happen to the minimum demand of Justice Holmes, expressed in the Abrams case in 1919, that even in wartime "Congress certainly cannot forbid all effort to change the mind of the country"?
>
> PAUL BLANSHARD, *The Right to Read,*
> Beacon Press, Boston, 1955

Now it becomes plain that in discussing the stronger controls on expression which are exercised in wartime, the author was leading up to the warning that during peacetime military leaders might continue wartime limitations on freedom of expression for the reason that peace is now only a "cold war." That is his main point in this part of his book, and one worth making.

Note the Drift of Examples

Sometimes even the expert reader is not quite certain what the author is trying to say. When the point of a passage eludes him, he studies the examples. If, for instance, one shows that a boy raised in the slums experienced love, affection, and happiness in his home life, and another shows that a boy was led into crime because his only playground was a pool hall where he met petty criminals, the author is obviously not trying to prove that slum environments always breed criminals. The expert reader, noting these examples, will look for a point other than this conventional one. Normally the examples of a writer plainly "drift" in the direction of his point.

In the following passage from *The Evolution of Physics* by Albert Einstein and Leopold Infeld, see whether you can infer the main point toward which the examples drift.

> The output of a coal mine can change in a continuous way. The amount of coal produced can be decreased or increased by arbitrarily small steps. But the number of miners employed can change only discontinuously. It would be pure nonsense to say: "Since yesterday, the number of employees has increased by 3.783."
>
> Asked about the amount of money in his pocket, a man can give a number containing only two decimals. A sum of money can change only by jumps, in a discontinuous way. In America the smallest permissible change or, as we shall call it, the "elementary quantum" for American money, is one cent. The elementary quantum for English money is one farthing, worth only half the American elementary quantum. Here we have an example of two elementary quanta whose mutual values can be compared. The ratio of their values has a definite sense since one of them is worth twice as much as the other.
>
> We can say: some quantities can change continuously and others can change only discontinuously, by steps which cannot be further decreased. The indivisible steps are called the *elementary quanta* of the particular quantity to which they refer.
>
> We can weigh large quantities of sand and regard its mass as continuous even though its granular structure is evident. But if the sand were to become very precious and the scales used very sensitive, we should have to consider the fact that the mass always changes by a multiple number of one grain. The mass of this one grain would be our elementary quantum.
>
> New York, Simon & Schuster, 1938

In this passage, Einstein and Infeld have not stated their main point. With three examples, coal mine, money, and sand, they have established what they mean by *continuous, discontinuous,* and *quantum.* But as a good reader, you should gain more than the meaning of these three terms from the passage. You should anticipate that the examples are building toward a general point and try to guess what that point is. In the next sentence after those quoted above, Einstein and Infeld state their point more explicitly. Stop reading and go back to the passage. Can you guess what point they are about to state?

What they say in their next sentence is: "From this example we see how the discontinuous character of a quantity, so far regarded as continuous, can be detected by increasing the precision of our measurements." In other words, they are saying that we must assume that some physical quantities which have been regarded in the past as continuous actually will prove discontinuous when broken down. They will be found to be composed of elementary quanta, like the grain of sand.

You should value specific examples, for they often make clear the meanings of difficult terms or ideas. As you read examples, try to determine what general point they illustrate. In the paragraphs by Einstein and Infeld, you should not have missed the central idea even if it was never stated explicitly. In your reading, look to examples; they may lead you to a main point.

Consider the Author and the Publication

Looking for clues to meaning is part of anticipation in reading. A good reader uses every clue available. For example, if he is asked to read a hard-to-understand writer like John Dewey, the American philosopher, he attempts to find out something about Dewey before he begins reading. We all do this sort of thing in everyday life. When we know we must talk to someone, perhaps a prospective employer, we naturally ask others who know him what kind of person he is in an effort to prepare ourselves so that we will not go into the interview "cold." In the same way, try not to go into your reading "cold." In many of the college texts you use, short statements are made about the author of a chapter or an essay. Preceding a selection from John Dewey, you might find a description such as this:

JOHN DEWEY, 1859–1952. Columbia University philosopher who espoused the doctrine of "learning by doing." A founder of *pragmatism*, he believed that theories should be tested in practice in the real world and that one's acts, if intelligent, should be traceable to sound theory. Dewey has been admired in foreign countries as America's foremost philosopher and at home attacked as the founder of "progressive education," in which—say his critics—children are allowed to do whatever they want to do without discipline. He has been taken to task for writing "educational jargon," sentences full of abstract words and needless repetition.

After noting this description, expect to find difficulty with Dewey. Do not be dismayed by the language in this passage from his introduction to *Reconstruction in Philosophy,* for example:

> Science is a pursuit, not a coming into possession of the immutable; new theories as points of view are more prized than discoveries that quantitatively increase the store on hand. . . . the great innovators in science "are the first to fear and doubt their discoveries."

Your first step may be to look up *immutable* if you don't know its meaning. Read the whole passage again. Perhaps you still don't understand it. Break it down into sentences and phrases to see whether you can find some idea that makes sense to you. Try to find echoes of ideas given in the description of Dewey earlier.

Dewey's last idea, that discoverers of new ideas in science fear and doubt their discoveries, looks like the easiest one to comprehend. Coupled with the idea that scientific theories are not immutable, it suggests that Dewey is saying that great scientists devise new theories but drop them as soon as they turn up evidence contradicting them. This is much the same idea as the one in the statement "theories should be tested in practice in the real world," which appears in the description of John Dewey presented above. Once you have understood this much, you can probably go on to puzzle out the meaning of what appears to be the main point: "new theories as points of view are more prized than discoveries that quantitatively increase the store on hand." Can you explain the meaning of that statement?

The expert reader or listener sees that familiar persons, magazines, newspapers, or television programs have certain patterns of thought. He examines their past patterns in order to improve his predictions or anticipations of what he will find in them in

the future. He expects the "lines" of thought in political magazines like *Time* and *The New Republic* to differ. He expects
different philosophies behind the reports of two news commentators. He expects a different treatment of sex and crime news
in *The New York Times* from that in a tabloid newspaper like
the New York *Daily News*.

Anticipating patterns of communication is helpful, but not
easy. It takes work, for only the person who reads widely and
with mind awake can make himself aware of the multitude of
communication patterns or techniques in use today. He must
have some idea of the nature of these patterns before he can
anticipate and detect them.

Be Prepared for Irony

Frequently the best thinkers state their points obliquely, without coming right out and saying, "My point is . . ." They may do
this because they want to get the reader's attention by shock or
surprise. They have style: they do not state their ideas flatly and
dully. They expect the reader to enjoy the way they say things
as well as to learn from what they say.

A special instance of obliqueness is *irony* . . . in which a writer
says the opposite of what he means. If you are not prepared for
it when it comes, you will not only miss the point but will take
the author's meaning to be just the opposite of what he really
meant. Here is an example from *Gulliver's Travels* by a master
of irony, Jonathan Swift. He is letting his hero explain to a person in the land of the Houyhnhnms why eighteenth-century
Englishmen make war.

> It is a very justifiable cause of a war to invade a country after
> the people have been wasted by famine, destroyed by pestilence,
> or embroiled by factions among themselves. It is justifiable to
> enter into war against our nearest ally, when one of his towns lies
> convenient for us, or a territory of land, that would render our
> dominions round and complete. If a prince sends forces into a
> nation where the people are poor and ignorant, he may lawfully
> put half of them to death, and make slaves of the rest, in order to
> civilize and reduce them from their barbarous way of living.

What is Swift's point? His list of justifiable reasons for making war are examples, not a main point. Nevertheless, taken together, they imply a central idea. An expert reader would enjoy the ironical humor of Swift's examples, but not get lost in them. He would grasp that in these sentences Swift is condemning the colonial exploitation that all powerful nations of the world have carried out at some time in their history.

Another form of irony is *paradox*, in which a statement is made which on the surface seems nonsensically contradictory but which, upon closer examination, makes good sense. For example: "A strong man knows his weaknesses." If you enjoy this kind of style, try the writing of Gilbert Chesterton, Samuel Butler, or Bernard Shaw. An example of paradox occurs in an article in *The University of Chicago Magazine* (October, 1951) by Robert Redfield, a distinguished professor of anthropology. Professor Redfield began his essay by saying that the University had been investigated a number of times for alleged subversive activities and had gained a reputation for radical thought. He went on to say:

> I put forward the view that this reputation for dangerous radicalism is an evidence that the University is doing its duty. It shows that the University is engaged in defending the very liberties which its detractors believe it to be endangering. I would go so far as to say that if the University were not from time to time accused of dangerous thoughts its professors could not then be doing their duty to think. It is good that university people make some other people a little uneasy because that uneasiness is a sign of their activity in the public service.

This statement is unusual, to say the least. But Professor Redfield meant what he said: that dangerous radicalism is necessary for progress. By "radicalism" he meant innovations and experiments—changes from customary ways of doing things. In this way he emphasized his point that persons cannot blithely condemn all new ideas as "subversive" without putting a damper on creative thinking. He believes that drawing a neat line between which radical thoughts will be helpful and which harmful is difficult.

.   .   .

RELATE IDEAS TO EXPERIENCE AND KNOWLEDGE

You can read through a difficult philosophical essay without learning a thing if you do not slow down to understand its abstract language. Apply your own examples to "sound out" the general statements and you will find the essay gaining meaning for you. Let us return to the passage from Mill's *On Liberty,* quoted above:

> The fatal tendency of mankind to leave off thinking about a thing when it is no longer doubtful is the cause of half their errors.

Reading this statement, you should ask yourself, "What kind of thing do men quit thinking about when it is no longer doubtful? One example might be the idea that matter is solid and permanent, which man knew was not doubtful when he hit his hand against hard matter. It took a doubter to discover that matter is atomic and shifting in nature.

In this essay, John Stuart Mill also said:

> He who knows only his own side of the case, knows little of that. His reasons may be good, and no one may have been able to refute them. But if he is equally unable to refute the reasons on the opposite side; if he does not so much as know what they are, he has no ground for preferring either opinion. . . .

Do you believe Mill is right? Have you known persons, maybe even yourself, who didn't know their side of a question well because they didn't know their opponent's side? If you can't give a specific example of someone like this, perhaps you really don't know what Mill means.

When an expert reader has trouble understanding an abstract passage, he may look for those sentences which have meaning for him and hurry over those which do not. Then, with enlarged understanding, he goes back to the sentences which puzzled him. He moves quickly from one point of understanding to another. In *On Liberty,* Mill went on to say:

This is not the way to do justice to the arguments, or bring them into real contact with his own mind. He must be able to hear them from persons who actually believe them; who defend them in earnest, and do their very utmost for them. *He must know them in their most plausible and persuasive form; he must feel the whole force of the difficulty which the true view of the subject has to encounter and dispose of, else he will never really possess himself of the portion of truth which meets and removes that difficulty.* Ninety-nine in a hundred of what are called educated men are in this condition, even of those who can argue fluently for their opinions. Their conclusion may be true, but it might be false for anything they know: they have never thrown themselves into the mental position of those who think differently from them, and considered what such persons may have to say; and consequently they do not, in any proper sense of the word, know the doctrine which they themselves profess.

The most difficult passage to understand seems to be the one in italics. If you do not understand it, read the sentences before and after it and see whether you can then get its point.

In reading a selection like this by Mill, remember that you do not really understand it unless you can see what its ideas would mean if put into practice today. For example, if we were arguing about Communism, what would we have to do to follow Mill's ideas? We would not simply have to hear an expert on Communism; we would have to hear a Communist himself argue as strongly as he could for his beliefs. The implication for us of Mill's idea is that until a democratic capitalist has heard a Communist argue his side, he doesn't know his own case for capitalism. This application of Mill's idea may disturb you, but it brings home the significance of his statement. You now have a chance to say whether you agree with him or not, because you really understand him. Testing his ideas in this way lets you examine them thoroughly.

The reflective reader of general ideas or principles always asks what the consequences would be if these principles were followed in the practical world. Such a reader is on the lookout for any happenings which test Mill's idea in everyday life. Look, for instance, at this headline which appeared in *The New York Times* on March 19, 1957 over a story about a student meeting.

COLUMBIA SESSION CRITICAL OF GATES
Student Meeting Is Orderly as
Editor of Daily Worker Takes Part in Panel

Upon close investigation, the alert reader would have discovered that John Gates, a Communist who had served time in prison for conspiring to teach and advocate the forcible overthrow of the government, participated in a well-attended forum held by a student organization on the Columbia University campus. Two other speakers at the forum appeared to oppose Mr. Gates. They were Norman Thomas, socialist, and Bertram D. Wolfe, author of several anti-Communist books. The reader who was keeping his eyes open for material about Mr. Gates after that meeting might have noticed that the March, 1958, issue of *Progressive* magazine carried a statement by John Gates telling why he later resigned from the Communist Party. In his statement, "The Failure of Communism in America," he wrote:

> It never occurred to me that *this movement*, based on a theory of change as Marxism is supposed to be, *might find itself left behind by the changes in American life itself*. This thought has come late. It hit me hardest one afternoon, just a year ago, when 1,200 students on the Columbia University campus came to hear me speak.
>
> "Mr. Gates," one young man shouted in the question period, "you say the Communist Party did big things for America. What were they?"
>
> I started to answer, as so many Communist speakers do, beginning with the long, bitter fight for social insurance, the payments to the aged and the unemployed on which so many depend today. Who does not remember how splendidly the Communists fought for that?
>
> A wave of laughter flooded McMillan Theater, swept through every corner of the hall. My face flushed, as though something had hit me.
>
> I rode the subways home that night in grim bewilderment: I can still hear that laughter.

These accounts show that certain students at Columbia University were, as Mill advised, listening to the other side, not to a lecturer speaking on Communism, but to a man who believed in Communism, who defended it "in earnest" and did his "very utmost" for it. What he said perhaps surprised them. They asked him embarrassing questions and laughed at some of his answers. But they did listen. The experience of exchanging responses with persons believing in the other side apparently had an effect on Mr. Gates as well.

You should apply to everyday life the general ideas you read or listen to not only to remember them better, but to extend your experience vicariously. True, experience is a good teacher, but reading and experience together are a better teacher.

. . .

Understand Allusions

One of the reasons your college reading is difficult is that authors are constantly presupposing that you have a wide reading background and will understand the allusions, or references, they make to books, ideas, and persons. When they speak of a man as an Othello or an Iago, they expect you to know Shakespeare's characters, Othello, the noble-hearted warrior, jealous and gullible; Iago, the poisonous, diabolically clever master of deceit. If you are reading English literary criticism, authors are apt to refer to someone as a "motiveless malignity," a term applied by a literary critic to Iago. They will expect you to know and understand that reference.

The question of whether writers and speakers should or should not presuppose this kind of knowledge in their audience is somewhat pointless. They do presuppose it, and you will be lost if you do not catch at least some of their allusions. In subjects you know well, whether physics or baseball, you would not want to converse long with persons whose lack of knowledge required you to identify Einstein, von Braun, Oppenheimer, and Teller, or to explain the dominance of the Yankees or the position of Babe Ruth in history. Communication is a sharing of responses and often is possible only on the basis of commonly held knowledge and experience. Allusions are necessary for this sharing. You should be aware of their importance and be alert to look up or inquire about those whose meanings are reasonably accessible to you.

In the long run, the best way to prevent allusive writing from frustrating and confusing you is to widen your reading experience. Many times we do not know what we have missed when an allusion goes by us unnoticed. And yet, to be reminded of something you know and like is one of the joys of life. Writers know this. They use allusions not only to save time and words, but to give you the pleasure that comes from seeing similarities or hearing echoes of ideas. The more you have read, the more you will enjoy this kind of overlapping of idea and word. For example, Andrew Marvell in the seventeenth century wrote a great and beautiful poem called "To His Coy Mistress," in which appeared these lines:

> The grave's a fine and private place,
> But none, I think, do there embrace.

If you knew these lines, as many people do, you would appreciate more the title of a novel about two Southern families written by Ann Hebson in 1958: *A Fine and Private Place.* If you read the book, you will further enjoy thinking of why the author chose this phrase.

Writers frequently make allusion to another piece of writing by echoing or repeating part of it in their titles. Ernest Hemingway called his novel about the Spanish civil war *For Whom the Bell Tolls,* in reference to the meditation by John Donne which is quoted in this book. Humor is often achieved by a play on words, which alludes to a well-known phrase. Wordsworth wrote a lovely poem entitled "Lines Composed a Few Miles above Tintern Abbey." Maurice Crane, a writer discussing popular songs, called an article, "Lines Composed Quite a Few Miles from Tin Pan Alley." The humor of his title would be lost on anyone who was not reminded of Wordsworth's poem. Only through reading widely and being curious enough to ask and inquire about allusions can you insure that they will perform their function for you.

This chapter has presented a number of techniques for close reading. You will probably never employ all of them in studying any one piece of writing; but you can develop each of them during your college years and have them ready to apply when needed. Look at these techniques of reading once again and ask yourself which ones you think you need to work on most:

Search for a controlling idea and main points
    Look for signal words
    Differentiate between controlling idea and main points
    Know where to look for key sentences
    Consider headings and subheadings
Anticipate what will be said
    Avoid reader's trance
    Note the drift of examples
    Consider the author and the publication
    Be prepared for irony
Relate ideas to experience and knowledge
    Understand allusions

how should one read a book?

VIRGINIA WOOLF

In the first place, I want to emphasize the note of interrogation at the end of my title. Even if I could answer the question for myself, the answer would apply only to me and not to you. The only advice, indeed, that one person can give another about reading is to take no advice, to follow your own instincts, to use your own reason, to come to your own conclusions. If this is agreed between us, then I feel at liberty to put forward a few ideas and suggestions because you will not allow them to fetter that independence which is the most important quality that a reader can possess. After all, what laws can be laid down about books? The battle of Waterloo was certainly fought on a certain day; but is *Hamlet* a better play than *Lear*? Nobody can say. Each must decide that question for himself. To admit authorities, however heavily furred and gowned, into our libraries and let them tell us how to read, what to read, what value to place upon what we read, is to destroy the spirit of freedom which is the breath of those sanctuaries. Everywhere else we may be bound by laws and conventions—there we have none.

But to enjoy freedom, if the platitude is pardonable, we have of course to control ourselves. We must not squander our powers,

Reprinted with permission of Harcourt, Brace & World, Inc., Quentin Bell and Angelica Garnett, and The Hogarth Press, from *The Second Common Reader*, by Virginia Woolf. Copyright 1932 by Harcourt, Brace & World., Inc.; renewed 1960 by Leonard Woolf.

helplessly and ignorantly, squirting half the house in order to water a single rose-bush; we must train them, exactly and powerfully, here on the very spot. This, it may be, is one of the first difficulties that faces us in a library. What is "the very spot"? There may well seem to be nothing but a conglomeration and huddle of confusion. Poems and novels, histories and memoirs, dictionaries and blue-books; books written in all languages by men and women of all tempers, races, and ages jostle each other on the shelf. And outside the donkey brays, the women gossip at the pump, the colts gallop across the fields. Where are we to begin? How are we to bring order into this multitudinous chaos and so get the deepest and widest pleasure from what we read?

It is simple enough to say that since books have classes—fiction, biography, poetry—we should separate them and take from each what it is right that each should give us. Yet few people ask from books what books can give us. Most commonly we come to books with blurred and divided minds, asking of fiction that it shall be true, of poetry that it shall be false, of biography that it shall be flattering, of history that it shall enforce our own prejudices. If we could banish all such preconceptions when we read, that would be an admirable beginning. Do not dictate to your author; try to become him. Be his fellow-worker and accomplice. If you hang back, and reserve and criticize at first, you are preventing yourself from getting the fullest possible value from what you read. But if you open your mind as widely as possible, then signs and hints of almost imperceptible fineness, from the twist and turn of the first sentences, will bring you into the presence of a human being unlike any other. Steep yourself in this, acquaint yourself with this, and soon you will find that your author is giving you, or attempting to give you, something far more definite. The thirty-two chapters of a novel—if we consider how to read a novel first—are an attempt to make something as formed and controlled as a building: but words are more impalpable than bricks; reading is a longer and more complicated process than seeing. Perhaps the quickest way to understand the elements of what a novelist is doing is not to read, but to write; to make your own experiment with the dangers and difficulties of words. Recall, then, some event that has left a distinct impression on you—how at the corner of the street, perhaps, you passed two people talking. A tree shook; an electric light danced; the tone of the talk was comic, but also tragic; a whole vision, an entire conception, seemed contained in that moment.

But when you attempt to reconstruct it in words, you will find that it breaks into a thousand conflicting impressions. Some must be subdued; others emphasized; in the process you will lose, probably, all grasp upon the emotion itself. Then turn from your blurred and littered pages to the opening pages of some great novelist—Defoe, Jane Austen, Hardy. Now you will be better able to appreciate their mastery. It is not merely that we are in the presence of a different person—Defoe, Jane Austen, or Thomas Hardy—but that we are living in a different world. Here, in *Robinson Crusoe,* we are trudging a plain high road; one thing happens after another; the fact and the order of the fact is enough. But if the open air and adventure mean everything to Defoe they mean nothing to Jane Austen. Hers is the drawing-room, and people talking, and by the many mirrors of their talk revealing their characters. And if, when we have accustomed ourselves to the drawing-room and its reflections, we turn to Hardy, we are once more spun round. The moors are round us and the stars are above our heads. The other side of the mind is now exposed—the dark side that comes uppermost in solitude, not the light side that shows in company. Our relations are not towards people, but towards Nature and destiny. Yet different as these worlds are, each is consistent with itself. The maker of each is careful to observe the laws of his own perspective, and however great a strain they may put upon us they will never confuse us, as lesser writers so frequently do, by introducing two different kinds of reality into the same book. Thus to go from one great novelist to another—from Jane Austen to Hardy, from Peacock to Trollope, from Scott to Meredith—is to be wrenched and uprooted; to be thrown this way and then that. To read a novel is a difficult and complex art. You must be capable not only of great fineness of perception, but of great boldness of imagination if you are going to make use of all that the novelist—the great artist—gives you.

But a glance at the heterogeneous company on the shelf will show you that writers are very seldom "great artists"; far more often a book makes no claim to be a work of art at all. These biographies and autobiographies, for example, lives of great men, of men long dead and forgotten, that stand cheek by jowl with the novels and poems, are we to refuse to read them because they are not "art"? Or shall we read them, but read them in a different way, with a different aim? Shall we read them in the first place to satisfy that curiosity which possesses us sometimes when in the evening we linger in front of a house where the lights are lit and the blinds not yet drawn, and each floor of the house shows us a different section of human life in being? Then we are consumed with curiosity about the lives of these people—the servants gossiping, the gentlemen dining, the girl dressing for a party, the old woman at the window with her knitting. Who are they, what are they, what are their names, their occupations, their thoughts, and adventures?

Biographies and memoirs answer such questions, light up innumerable such houses; they show us people going about their daily affairs, toiling, failing, succeeding, eating, hating, loving, until they die. And sometimes as we watch, the house fades and the iron railings vanish and we are out at sea; we are hunting, sailing, fighting; we are among savages and soldiers; we are taking part in great campaigns. Or if we like to stay here in England, in London, still the scene changes; the street narrows; the house becomes small, cramped, diamond-paned, and malodorous. We see a poet, Donne, driven from such a house because the walls were so thin that when the children cried their voices cut through them. We can follow him, through the paths that lie in the pages of books, to Twickenham; to Lady Bedford's Park, a famous meeting-ground for nobles and poets; and then turn our steps to Wilton, the great house under the downs, and hear Sidney read the *Arcadia* to his sister; and ramble among the very marshes and see the very herons that figure in that famous romance; and then again travel north with that other Lady Pembroke, Anne Clifford, to her wild moors, or plunge into the city and control our merriment at the sight of Gabriel Harvey in his black velvet suit arguing about poetry with Spenser. Nothing is more fascinating than to grope and stumble in the alternate darkness and splendour of Elizabethan London. But there is no staying there. The Temples and the Swifts, the Harleys and the St. Johns beckon us on; hour upon hour can be spent disentangling their quarrels and deciphering their characters; and when we tire of them we can stroll on, past a lady in black wearing diamonds, to Samuel Johnson and Goldsmith and Garrick; or cross the channel, if we like, and meet Voltaire and Diderot, Madame du Deffand; and so back to England and Twickenham—how certain places repeat themselves and certain names!—where Lady Bedford had her Park once and Pope lived later, to Walpole's home at Strawberry Hill. But Walpole introduces us to such a swarm of new acquaintances, there are so many houses to visit and bells to ring that we may well hesitate for a moment, on the Miss Berrys' doorstep, for example, when behold, up comes Thackeray; he is the friend of the woman whom Walpole loved; so that merely by going from friend to friend, from garden to garden, from house to house, we have passed from one end of English literature to another and wake to find ourselves here again in the present, if we can so differentiate this moment from all that have gone before. This, then, is one of the ways in which we can read these lives and letters; we can make them light up the many windows of the past; we can watch the famous dead in their familiar habits and fancy sometimes that we are very close and can surprise their secrets, and sometimes we may pull out a play or a poem that they have written and see whether it reads differently in the presence of the author. But this again rouses other questions. How far, we must ask ourselves, is a book influenced by its writer's life—how far is it safe to let the man interpret the writer? How far shall we resist or give way to the sympathies and antipathies that the man himself rouses in us—so sensitive are words, so receptive of the character of the author? These are questions that press upon us when we read lives and letters, and we must answer them for ourselves, for nothing can be more fatal than to be guided by the preferences of others in a matter so personal.

But also we can read such books with another aim, not to throw light on literature, not to become familiar with famous people, but to refresh and exercise our own creative powers. Is there not an open window on the right hand of the bookcase? How delightful to stop reading and look out! How stimulating the scene is, in its unconsciousness, its irrelevance, its perpetual movement—the colts galloping round the field, the woman filling her pail at the well, the donkey throwing back his head and emitting his long, acrid moan. The greater part of any library is nothing but the record of such fleeting moments in the lives of men, women, and donkeys. Every literature, as it grows old, has its rubbish-heap, its record of vanished moments and forgotten lives told in faltering and feeble accents that have perished. But if you give yourself up to the delight of rubbish-reading you will be surprised, indeed you will be overcome, by the relics of human life that have been cast out to moulder. It may be one letter— but what a vision it gives! It may be a few sentences—but what vistas they suggest! Sometimes a whole story will come together with such beautiful humour and pathos and completeness that it seems as if a great novelist had been at work, yet it is only an old actor, Tate Wilkinson, remembering the strange story of Captain Jones; it is only a young subaltern serving under Arthur Wellesley and falling in love with a pretty girl at Lisbon; it is only Maria Allen letting fall her sewing in the empty drawing-room and sighing how she wishes she had taken Dr. Burney's good advice and had never eloped with her Rishy. None of this has any value; it is negligible in the extreme; yet how absorbing it is now and again to go through the rubbish-heaps and find rings and scissors and broken noses buried in the huge past and try to piece them together while the colt gallops round the field, the woman fills her pail at the well, and the donkey brays.

But we tire of rubbish-reading in the long run. We tire of searching for what is needed to complete the half-truth which is all that the Wilkinsons, the Bunburys, and the Maria Allens are able to offer us. They had not the artist's power of mastering and eliminating; they could not tell the whole truth even about their own lives; they have disfigured the story that might have been so shapely. Facts are all that they can offer us, and facts are a very inferior form of fiction. Thus the desire grows upon us to have done with half-statements and approximations; to cease from searching out the minute shades of human character, to enjoy the greater abstractness, the purer truth of fiction. Thus we create the mood, intense and generalised, unaware of detail, but stressed by some regular, recurrent beat, whose natural expression is poetry; and this is the time to read poetry when we are almost able to write it.

> Western wind, when wilt thou blow?
> The small rain down can rain.
> Christ, if my love were in my arms,
> And I in my bed again!

The impact of poetry is so hard and direct that for the moment there is no other sensation except that of the poem itself. What profound depths we visit then—how sudden and complete is our immersion! There is nothing here to catch hold of; nothing to stay us in our flight. The illusion of fiction is gradual; its effects are prepared; but who when they read these four lines stops to ask who wrote them, or conjures up the thought of Donne's house or Sidney's secretary; or enmeshes them in the intricacy of the past and the succession of generations? The poet is always our contemporary. Our being for the moment is centred and constricted, as in any violent shock of personal emotion. Afterwards, it is true, the sensation begins to spread in wider rings through our minds; remoter senses are reached; these begin to sound and to comment and we are aware of echoes and reflections. The intensity of poetry covers an immense range of emotion. We have only to compare the force and directness of

> I shall fall like a tree, and find my grave,
> Only remembering that I grieve,

with the wavering modulation of

> Minutes are numbered by the fall of sands,
> As by an hour glass; the span of time
> Doth waste us to our graves, and we look on it;
> An age of pleasure, revelled out, comes home
> At last, and ends in sorrow; but the life,
> Weary of riot, numbers every sand,
> Wailing in sighs, until the last drop down,
> So to conclude calamity in rest,

or place the meditative calm of

> whether we be young or old,
> Our destiny, our being's heart and home,

Is with infinitude, and only there;
With hope it is, hope that can never die,
Effort, and expectation, and desire,
And something evermore about to be,

beside the complete and inexhaustible loveliness of

The moving Moon went up the sky,
And no where did abide:
Softly she was going up,
And a star or two beside—

or the splendid fantasy of

And the woodland haunter
Shall not cease to saunter
    When, far down some glade,
Of the great world's burning,
One soft flame upturning
Seems, to his discerning,
    Crocus in the shade.

to bethink us of the varied art of the poet; his power to make us
at once actors and spectators; his power to run his hand into
character as if it were a glove, and be Falstaff or Lear; his power
to condense, to widen, to state, once and for ever.

"We have only to compare"—with those words the cat is out
of the bag, and the true complexity of reading is admitted. The
first process, to receive impressions with the utmost understanding, is only half the process of reading; it must be completed, if
we are to get the whole pleasure from a book, by another. We
must pass judgment upon these multitudinous impressions; we
must make of these fleeting shapes one that is hard and lasting.
But not directly. Wait for the dust of reading to settle; for the
conflict and the questioning to die down; walk, talk, pull the
dead petals from a rose, or fall asleep. Then suddenly without
our willing it, for it is thus that Nature undertakes these transi-
tions, the book will return, but differently. It will float to the
top of the mind as a whole. And the book as a whole is different
from the book received currently in separate phrases. Details now
fit themselves into their places. We see the shape from start to
finish; it is a barn, a pig-sty, or a cathedral. Now then we can
compare book with book as we compare building with building.

But this act of comparison means that our attitude has changed; we are no longer the friends of the writer, but his judges; and just as we cannot be too sympathetic as friends, so as judges we cannot be too severe. Are they not criminals, books that have wasted our time and sympathy; are they not the most insidious enemies of society, corrupters, defilers, the writers of false books, faked books, books that fill the air with decay and disease? Let us then be severe in our judgments; let us compare each book with the greatest of its kind. There they hang in the mind the shapes of the books we have read solidified by the judgments we have passed on them—*Robinson Crusoe, Emma, The Return of the Native.* Compare the novels with these—even the latest and least of novels has a right to be judged with the best. And so with poetry—when the intoxication of rhythm has died down and the splendour of words has faded a visionary shape will return to us and this must be compared with *Lear,* with *Phèdre,* with *The Prelude;* or if not with these, with whatever is the best or seems to us to be the best in its own kind. And we may be sure that the newness of new poetry and fiction is its most superficial quality and that we have only to alter slightly, not to recast, the standards by which we have judged the old.

It would be foolish, then, to pretend that the second part of reading, to judge, to compare, is as simple as the first—to open the mind wide to the fast flocking of innumerable impressions. To continue reading without the book before you, to hold one shadow-shape against another, to have read widely enough and with enough understanding to make such comparisons alive and illuminating—that is difficult; it is still more difficult to press further and to say, "Not only is the book of this sort, but it is of this value; here it fails; here it succeeds; this is bad; that is good". To carry out this part of a reader's duty needs such imagination, insight, and learning that it is hard to conceive any one mind sufficiently endowed; impossible for the most self-confident to find more than the seeds of such powers in himself. Would it not be wiser, then, to remit this part of reading and to allow the critics, the gowned and furred authorities of the library, to decide the question of the book's absolute value for us? Yet how impossible! We may stress the value of sympathy; we may try to sink our own identity as we read. But we know that we cannot sympathise wholly or immerse ourselves wholly; there is always a demon in us who whispers, "I hate, I love", and we cannot silence him. Indeed, it is precisely because we hate and we love that our relation with the poets and novelists is so intimate that we find the presence of another person intolerable. And even if the results are abhorrent and our judgments are wrong, still our taste, the nerve of sensation that sends shocks through us, is our chief illuminant; we learn through feeling; we cannot suppress our own idiosyncrasy without impoverishing it. But as time goes on perhaps we can train our taste; perhaps we can make it submit to some control. When it has fed greedily and lavishly upon books of all sorts—poetry, fiction, history, biography—and has stopped reading and looked for long spaces upon the variety, the incongruity of the living world, we shall find that it is changing a little; it is not so greedy, it is more reflective. It will begin to bring us not merely judgments on particular books, but it will tell us that there is a quality common to certain books. Listen, it will say, what shall we call *this*? And it will read us perhaps *Lear* and then perhaps the *Agamemnon* in order to bring out that common quality. Thus, with our taste to guide us, we shall venture beyond the particular book in search of qualities that group books together; we shall give them names and thus frame a rule that brings order into our perceptions. We shall gain a further and a rarer pleasure from that discrimination. But as a rule only lives when it is perpetually broken by contact with the books themselves—nothing is easier and more stultifying than to make rules which exist out of touch with facts, in a vacuum— now at last, in order to steady ourselves in this difficult attempt, it may be well to turn to the very rare writers who are able to enlighten us upon literature as an art. Coleridge and Dryden and Johnson, in their considered criticism, the poets and novelists themselves in their unconsidered sayings, are often surprisingly relevant; they light up and solidify the vague ideas that have been tumbling in the misty depths of our minds. But they are only able to help us if we come to them laden with questions and suggestions won honestly in the course of our own reading. They can do nothing for us if we herd ourselves under their authority and lie down like sheep in the shade of a hedge. We can only understand their ruling when it comes in conflict with our own and vanquishes it.

If this is so, if to read a book as it should be read calls for the

rarest qualities of imagination, insight, and judgment, you may
perhaps conclude that literature is a very complex art and that
it is unlikely that we shall be able, even after a lifetime of reading, to make any valuable contribution to its criticism. We must
remain readers; we shall not put on the further glory that belongs to those rare beings who are also critics. But still we have
our responsibilities as readers and even our importance. The
standards we raise and the judgments we pass steal into the air
and become part of the atmosphere which writers breathe as they
work. An influence is created which tells upon them even if it
never finds its way into print. And that influence, if it were well
instructed, vigorous and individual and sincere, might be of
great value now when criticism is necessarily in abeyance; when
books pass in review like the procession of animals in a shooting
gallery, and the critic has only one second in which to load and
aim and shoot and may well be pardoned if he mistakes rabbits
for tigers, eagles for barndoor fowls, or misses altogether and
wastes his shot upon some peaceful cow grazing in a further field.
If behind the erratic gunfire of the press the author felt that
there was another kind of criticism, the opinion of people reading
for the love of reading, slowly and unprofessionally, and judging
with great sympathy and yet with great severity, might this not
improve the quality of his work? And if by our means books
were to become stronger, richer, and more varied, that would be
an end worth reaching.

Yet who reads to bring about an end however desirable? Are
there not some pursuits that we practise because they are good
in themselves, and some pleasures that are final? And is not this
among them? I have sometimes dreamt, at least, that when the
Day of Judgment dawns and the great conquerors and lawyers
and statesmen come to receive their rewards—their crowns, their
laurels, their names carved indelibly upon imperishable marble—
the Almighty will turn to Peter and will say, not without a
certain envy when He sees us coming with our books under our
arms, "Look, these need no reward. We have nothing to give
them here. They have loved reading."

poetry: a note on reading

HARRY SHAW

The reading of poems is rarely stressed in freshman classes, but poetry does offer certain advantages in learning to read well. Because good poets use language with unusual precision, making words serve their purposes exactly, careful reading of poetry helps you to see how language works. Such reading is not only useful as vocabulary study; it is also an excellent means of discovering how the meaning and effect of words are controlled by the contexts in which they appear. Good poets, moreover, use language with economy and compression for immediate and intense effects. Understanding poetry, where "each word must carry twenty other words upon its back," requires effort which will be repaid by an increase in reading skill.

Certain resources of language have a special importance in poetry. For instance, you should conceive of the rhythm of a poem as a means of communication, reinforcing and combining with the meaning of words, often suggesting or representing the attitude of a poem. But most of all, poetry calls for active contribution from you; the poet makes use of what you know and what you have felt. Good poetry blends sense and sound in ways which evoke images and extend your imagination, memory, and experience beyond the physical limits of your own life.

Reprinted with permission of Harper & Row, Publishers, Inc., from *A Complete Course in Freshman English,* by Harry Shaw. © 1940, 1945, 1949, 1951, 1955 by Harper & Row, Publishers, Inc. © 1959, 1967 by Harry Shaw.

In this textbook, which deals with clear thinking and writing, examples of poetry are provided for further study of methods of communication. The editor hopes that these selections, by standards of clear expression and readability, will stimulate your reflection and curiosity and perhaps encourage the beginnings of an understanding of, and respect for, the power of expression latent in meter, rhyme, and other poetic devices.

A poem is to a piece of prose as an abstract painting is to a realistic portrait. From the same material the poet or artist intensifies by selecting parts or fragments of the idea or image, which he heightens (colors) by sound or pigments and rearranges in order to suggest a more sensitive, frequently more *accurate,* expression of the whole subject. Poetry is the quintessence of written feeling. The poet, departing from strict syntax and the literal sense of every word, discovers new powers of expression and often enriches our language with new words for concepts which we could not express or did not realize before.

Now let's get to some particulars. Six summary statements about poetry may be helpful:

1. Poetry is a language phenomenon—a way of saying things. Whether to teach, preach, or simply thrill, to paint, inform, or spellbind, this is not the language of over-the-counter existence, although many of the words are the same. A new blend of sound and sense is here, rich in connotation, imagery, impression, music, and offering new problems in semantics.

2. Poetry runs a wide gamut of subject matter and experience, familiar and unfamiliar. One age may sing of sea battle, another of a lady's eyes. Or in the same age one man may ponder the skylark while another weaves nightmarish dream-fantasies. The modern poet may use conventional topics, new topics, or apparently no topics at all, remaining content with patterns of sound and rhythm. In any period the gamut may be marked at one end by folk song and at the other by metaphysics.

3. Poetry has organization, purpose, style. Ideas and presentation vary from period to period.

4. Poetry, like music and other arts, has an evocative factor which varies with the experience and personality of the audience. A passage may jog your memory suddenly and help you re-enjoy a lost moment. It may startle you into action or a new

belief. Poetry may help you escape reality for a moment's peace. It may offer you new illusions to replace the old. But it will not sledge-hammer a skeptic into belief. You must meet the poet half-way, then suspend disbelief for a time, "play along" sportingly. This is not to say that you should prostrate yourself as an igno-ramus before genius. If, after reading and thinking, you honestly feel that your original poor impression of a poet, a poem, or poetry itself remains, maintain it stoutly; you will at least know by then why you feel the way you do—that knowledge itself is a step ahead.

5. Poetry comes in various shapes and forms, types and sub-types. Although matter is generally more important than form, the two are inextricably linked, and it is obvious that you should pick up at least a little information on ballads, odes, sonnets, and so on. Certain terms which you will need in studying poetry are briefly defined at the end of this introductory note. Do not memorize these rudimentary definitions, but do refer to them as your need or your instructor suggests.

6. Poetry has pronounced rhythms, generally resolvable into metrical patterns. It often has rhyme, and rhyme comes in varied patterns also. It often is musical. It relies heavily on figurative language and allusion. Quick study, as needed, of terms in the following glossary will provide what help you need in dealing with such matters, but perhaps a further word on rhyme and meter will be useful.

When two words rhyme (see definition of *rhyme* in the glossary), each is noted in what is called a *rhyme scheme* by use of the same letter of the alphabet. For example, if the first and third lines of a stanza rhyme, and the second and fourth do like-wise, the scheme is referred to as *abab*. But be certain not to confuse true rhyme and *assonance* (see the glossary).

The term *meter* in English poetry refers to the pattern of stressed and unstressed syllables in a line, or verse, of a poem. The number of syllables in a line may be fixed and the number of stresses may vary, or the stresses may be fixed and the number of unstressed syllables may change. The number of stresses and syllables is fixed and definite in the most frequent forms of meter in English verse, although actually this basic pattern occasionally varies so as to avoid sounding like a metronome. In some modern poetry, regular meter is largely forsaken, and *cadences* (see the glossary) are employed to approximate the flow of speech. These are the meters most commonly used in English poetry: *iambic, trochaic, anapestic, dactylic,* and *spondaic.* Each is defined and illustrated in the glossary. Every such metrical unit, or group of syllables, is called a *foot;* the number of feet in a line of poetry determines its name as, for example, a verse of three feet is called *trimeter* and one of five feet is called *pentameter.*

With this information at hand in addition to that which is supplied in the glossary, what can you make of this part of Byron's "The Destruction of Sennacherib"?

> The Assyrian came down like a wolf on the fold,
> And his cohorts were gleaming in purple and gold;
> And the sheen of their spears was like stars on the sea,
> Where the blue wave rolls nightly on deep Galilee.

It is impossible to read this material without hearing its music and without realizing that it uses several figures of speech. Technically, the four lines, or verses, constitute a kind of stanza called a *quatrain;* the rhyme scheme is *aabb;* the meter is *anapestic tetrameter:*

And the sheen/ of their spears/ was like stars/ on the sea

As has been mentioned, not every line of poetry is so definitely accented as this one, but your ear, properly attuned, and your mind, filled with basic knowledge about meter, should enable you to read other poetry with understanding allowance for subtly altered rhythmic effects.

Reading poetry requires the same skills and perceptions as reading prose. But since poetry may not be so familiar a form to you, these questions should suggest useful approaches:

1. Study the vocabulary of the poem. What passages are obscure? What key allusions must you check in a reference book? What ordinary words are employed in apparently unusual meanings? What other words must you look up and add to your reading vocabulary? Your writing vocabulary?

2. Who is speaking in the poem? To whom? What is the occasion? (A poem is often dramatic. Do not assume that "I" is the poet speaking in his own person.)

3. What is the attitude in the poem? (Answering this question

is not primarily a matter of describing how the poet felt; it is a matter of describing the attitude that arises for you.)

4. What part of the effect of the poem is accounted for by its rhythm? Does the rhythm represent or suggest any sort of movement? Is the effect of the rhythm consistent with, and does it reinforce, the emotion of the poem?

5. What words or expressions in the poem are so used that, beyond any function they may have in making a statement, they evoke in you images and feelings?

6. Does the poem have a theme which may be stated outside the terms of the poem itself? Is there a line or a short passage which states the theme? Is the theme implicit—suggested instead of being directly stated and left, therefore, for you to formulate?

Without answering these six questions in so many words, a discussion of some points raised by a reading of Robert Herrick's brief "Delight in Disorder"[1] is given in the next paragraphs. This comment may seem too elaborate or too fanciful to you. Very well, then. Write your own commentary on this or some other poem. But remember: if you strive to meet a good poet halfway, your life will be richer for the effort.

The central thought of this poem is that a somewhat negligent dress in women is more exciting than meticulous good grooming. This is hardly a monumental thought. Yet the poem is memorable and affords pleasure by the way in which Herrick conveys the excitement of disorder in dress. After 12 lines in which the poet brings alive the gay bewitchingness of disorder he uses nine words to contrast the dullness and insipidity of superb grooming.

The animation of this poem is achieved in considerable part by the poet's diction. Do you ordinarily think of "disorder" as *sweet?* Of "distraction" as *fine* or of "civility" as *wild?* Herrick continues to transform passive objects into active agents: *erring* lace, *enthrals* the stomacher, *winning* wave, *tempestuous* petti-

---

[1] A sweet disorder in the dress/ Kindles in clothes a wantonness;/ A lawn about the shoulders thrown/ Into a fine distractiòn;/ An erring lace, which here and there/ Enthrals the crimson stomacher;/ A cuff neglectful, and thereby/ Ribbons to flow confusèdly;/ A winning wave (deserving note)/ In the tempestuous petticoat;/ A careless shoe-string, in whose tie/ I see a wild civility:/ Do more bewitch me, than when art/ Is too precise in every part.

coat, *careless* shoe-string, cuff *neglectful*. The various elements of dress *act* riotously, wantonly. A sense of activity permeates the poem; when "sweet disorder" *kindles* wantonness, the thought comes alive with unruliness.

This poem is a tribute to disorder and a contrast between artfulness and naturalness, a creation of a state of feeling that is unusual, to say the least. Even so, the description of clothing follows a definite order. Herrick proceeds to detail items of clothing from head to foot, much as would most men looking at most women. By the time we get to a "careless shoe-string" we are ready to accept the strange, even fantastic, idea of "wild civility." "Sweetness" and "disorder" might go together in an easy concept, but not "wildness" and "civility." What began as subdued whimsy has become a fantastic extravagance. Perhaps that is why the poet, realizing this, descends from Cloud Nine and gets back to ordered movement and language.

All words are born as sounds by which men attempt to convey ideas. This poem is an excellent illustration of how a good poet uses to the fullest, even exaggerates, the emotional content of words inherent in their sound. The way in which the sounds of this poem are manipulated and juggled by the poet greatly reinforces the overall idea. The presence of the clothes (line 2) is made apparent by the combined *l, s,* and *th* sounds, which seem to rustle. The pattern of consonants in "kindles in clothes" indicates that the garments are truly active and flaming. Note, too, the alliteration in "winning wave" and the similar sounds in "tem*pest*uous petticoat." The word *tempestuous* actually sounds like rustling clothing. Notice also how in the last line the sharp syllables of *precise* and the punctuated effect of the percussive *p*'s in *precise* and *part* have a contrasting effect on our senses when set immediately following the poem's main body of sensuous sounds.

Even the meter of the poem conveys a sense of unruliness and disorder. The prevailing meter is iambic tetrameter—four feet, each consisting of an unaccented syllable followed by an accented one, eight syllables to the line. But the crucial word *kindles* reverses the accent and thus acquires special emphasis. In another example of unruliness, note that the last word in line 7, *thereby*, forces the reading on. This difference between a unit of verse and a unit of thought is not uncommon in poetry, but here it adds to the lack of order which fills the poem. If you will compare the first and the last lines of the poem by reading each aloud you will be able to feel rhythmically that, although the first line scans as perfectly as the last, it flows with soft consonants, unlike the staccato effect in the progression of quick, hard sounds composing the final measures of the poem.

More could be said of the technique and content of this little poem, but perhaps for your enjoyment too much has already been written. Yet the poem would not really be enjoyable unless it did employ exaggerated terms in a fanciful manner. The tone is playful and humorous, but this tone would not be so apparent had not the shaping hand of an accomplished poet used many devices of diction, meter, and even rhyme to convey his meaning.

GLOSSARY

ANAPEST A metrical foot of two short syllables followed by one long *(to the end* or *to the end).*

ASSONANCE Similarity in sound between vowels; differs from rhyme in that final consonants involved are not the same *(wine-lime).* (See *Rhyme.*)

BALLAD Originally a song, then a narrative poem with popular and literary traditions, and today (a loose use of the term) a melodramatic or amatory song.

BALLAD STANZA Commonly a four-line stanza with second and fourth lines rhyming and the meter running tetrameter, trimeter, tetrameter, trimeter in order. Many variations exist, however.

BLANK VERSE Unrhymed iambic pentameter used in dignified and lofty passages of epic poetry, drama, etc.

CADENCE Recognizable beat and rhythmic flow of phrase without formal stress pattern, in verse or prose.

CONCEIT Term applied to a strained or involved comparison or idea.

COUPLET A pair of successive lines of verse, especially such as rhyme together and are of identical length.

followed by two unaccented ones *(murmuring).*

DACTYL A metrical foot consisting of an accented syllable

DIMETER A line of poetry made up of two feet.

DRAMATIC MONOLOGUE A poem in which one character speaks to one or more mute listeners and incidentally reveals his own psychological make-up.

ELEGY A formal poem of mourning or brooding on the subject of death.

EPIC A poetic type marked by its length, seriousness, noble characters, central hero, etc.

EPITAPH A subtype, a short poem suitable for a gravestone or valedictory. Sometimes synonymous with an epigram on death. Sometimes wryly humorous like Gay's, written for himself:

> Life is a jest, and all things show it;
> I thought so once, but now I know it.

FOOT The basic rhythmic unit in a recognizable metric pattern. In English the commonest feet are iambic, trochaic, anapestic, and dactylic (which see).

FREE VERSE Verse which has no regular metrical pattern, but which does have cadence, often set up irregularly as to length of line to "look like" poetry; employs imagery and figures of conventional verse and definitely has some organization or over-all unity of effect. Not to be confused with *blank verse*. Often referred to as *vers libre*.

HEPTAMETER A line of poetry having seven feet.

HEROIC COUPLET A pair of rhyming lines in iambic pentameter; may be a "closed" couplet with a unit organization of its own, or one unit with other continuous "open" couplets, with run-on lines.

HEXAMETER A line of poetry having six feet.

IAMBIC Common type of foot with an unaccented syllable followed by an accented one *(ŏmīt)*.

LIGHT VERSE Term (not to be confused with *blank verse* or *free verse*) applied to those forms (limericks, triolets, certain songs) which are light in touch but which require deftness and dexterity nevertheless.

LYRIC Originally a poem to be sung to lyre accompaniment, hence melodic; today, however, generally a short poem with strong emotional basis and marked individual personality evident.

METAPHYSICAL POETRY Loosely, poetry dealing with reasoning

processes and philosophical complexities; in the seventeenth century, it was marked by intellectual pyrotechnics, conceits, subtleties, unusual comparisons.

METER A term used as a combining form to designate the number of feet to a line (pentameter equals five-foot line, etc.). Not in combination, the word refers to any formal arrangement of rhythm.

MONOMETER Literally, a line of poetry having only one foot, obviously seldom found.

OCTAMETER A line of poetry having eight feet.

ODE A subtype of lyric poetry with serious tone, addressed in praise to a person, object, or idea.

PASTORAL A term, adjective or noun, applied to poetry or music or romance dealing with shepherds, flocks, fields, farms, etc. Classically it is an artificial form with lofty language, set themes, and conventional names.

PENTAMETER A line of poetry having five feet.

PETRARCHAN (ITALIAN) SONNET A 14-line love poem, originally introduced to England by Wyatt and Surrey. The first eight lines (octave) rhyme *abba, abba;* the last six (sestet) may take one of several patterns or be irregular, though strictly the last two lines should not rhyme.

PROSODY The study of metrical structure.

QUATRAIN A four-line stanza or a unit group of four lines in a long composition.

REFRAIN The repeated portion of a poem, ballad, song—used for choral effect, audience participation, etc.

RHYME Repetition of sounds at the end of poetic lines (or at the middle and end of a line—"internal" rhyme). Stressed vowels and following consonants should be identical *(wine-mine).* (See *Assonance.*)

SCANSION The act of dividing a line of poetry into feet, placing accent marks, deciding meter, and perhaps reading aloud. The commonest lines in English are tetrameter, pentameter, and hexameter; the four familiar patterns are iambic, trochaic, anapestic, and dactylic.

SESTET The last six lines of a Petrarchan or Italian sonnet (which see).

SHAKESPEAREAN (ENGLISH) SONNET A form taking its name from

the poet who handled it best, although Surrey introduced it. The 14 lines are divided into three quatrains and a couplet with an inflexible rhyme scheme: *abab, cdcd, efef, gg.*

SONNET   A subtype of poetry identified as 14 lines in iambic pentameter with several possible rhyme schemes (see *Petrarchan, Spenserian,* and *Shakespearean sonnet*). In its long history it has been amatory, autobiographical, philosophical, topical.

SPENSERIAN SONNET   A sonnet form with the following rhyme scheme: *abab, bcbc, cdcd, ee.* Superficially, it resembles the Shakespearean, but uses fewer rhymes, achieves coherence by the linking repetitions.

SPONDEE   A foot consisting of two accented syllables, used to prevent monotony in conjunction with commoner set patterns (*dáybréak*).

STANZA   The equivalent in a poem to the paragraph in prose; a unit of verse marked by distinct rhyme, meter, or subject pattern. It is recognized by spacing or indentation.

TETRAMETER   A line of poetry having four feet.

TRIMETER   A line of poetry having three feet.

TROCHEE   A metrical foot consisting of an accented syllable followed by an unaccented one (*tríp ĭt*).

VERSE   Technically, a single line of poetry; also a synonym for poetry; in modern songs, another name for stanza.

WRITING
patterns of thought

DEFINITION

Perhaps the first step in exposition—that is, in writing for the purpose of explaining—is definition. Definition is an analytic method for seeking an answer to the question, What is it? The word itself derives from the Latin *de* and *finire* meaning to set a limit; thus, when we set out to define a word or an idea we attempt to establish boundaries for it, boundaries related in some way to the common usage of the term or to the reality that it represents. Since it is next to impossible to work effectively with either words or ideas unless we understand them as fully as we are able (Mrs. Malaprop, among others, taught us that), definition is fundamental to the communication process.

How can we go about achieving this understanding through definition? There are a number of means, of course, but three are basic and all three proceed by striving to clarify the unknown in terms of the known. The first, most obvious, and commonest method of defining is by synonym, which ordinarily implies an appeal to the dictionary. Thus an unfamiliar word like *exegesis* might be explained by the better known and better understood *interpretation*. By means of the dictionary, definition by synonym has the virtue of ready availability; but it also has certain marked disadvantages. For one thing, no two words are ever precisely synonymous, as even a cursory look at a thesaurus will demonstrate (or consider our example: It is unlikely one would ever be asked, What is your exegesis of that politician's speech?). For another, the typical dictionary—or synonymous— definition *does* set up boundaries; but they are the boundaries of conventional usage, notoriously shifting, unstable boundaries. The point is that synonyms can be of considerable help in clarifying meaning, but one must be wary of relying upon them exclusively.

A much more exact means of definition is through classification. In this method the term to be defined is placed in a class or category, usually called the *genus*, based on likenesses or commonality of traits. Next, the special characteristics of the term are enumerated and specified for the purpose of distinguishing it from other members of the same class. These characteristics are called the *species* or, sometimes, the *differentiae*. Using classification one might define a catamaran as a small boat (class or genus) consisting of a narrow log raft or float, often with two parallel hulls, propelled by sails or paddles (species or differentiae). It goes without saying that for classification to be effective at least one species term must be expressed and the more cited the clearer the definition is likely to be. To define a catamaran as a small boat, for example, would be to define the name associated with a type of seagoing vessel but would hardly clarify the real object designated by that name. The particular virtue of classification as an approach to definition lies in the fact that it attempts to set limits to the reality which a word represents, and so the genus-species test can be applied to any definition that purports to be formal and logical.

A third definition, one that we tend to use almost unconsciously, is definition by example. One may not know the strictly literary meaning of *epic;* but if he is told that the *Iliad, Beowulf,* and *Paradise Lost* are epics he will hopefully have some rudimentary understanding of the term. (You might notice that we are using here the very method we seek to define; that is, the second sentence in this paragraph is used as an example to clarify the concept of definition by example.) On the other hand, if we were to describe an epic as having the formal characteristics of a beginning in medias res and an invocation to the muse, it is quite unlikely we would be of substantial help to a good many people unfamiliar with the term. For definition by example to be of any use, the reader must be aware of and understand some of the specific members of a class even though he may not know the meaning of the general class term. This is to say the obvious; if we have no notion of what the *Iliad* is, then definition by example will help us not at all in understanding the word *epic*. Another distinct weakness of this method is that our examples may share several characteristics (the *Iliad, Beowulf,* and *Paradise Lost* are all poems and all narratives; but there are many poems and more narratives that are not epics), and so the reader may be uncertain as to which characteristic is the appropriate one. Consequently, definition by example works best in conjunction with one or more of the other methods rather than alone.

A good standard dictionary will employ any or all of these methods, but as suggested, it is unwise to rely too heavily upon the dictionary as the sole source for definition. Innumerable essays and speeches begin—rather tediously—something like this: "Webster defines [let our word here be *fascism*] as. . . ." The writer or speaker who commences in this fashion is doubtless blissfully unaware of the fact that lexicographers are concerned with the origin of words, their historical progress, and their present conventional usage but *not* with the realities, whether abstract or concrete, which lie behind those words. Given the temper of the times and the latitude of certain perfectly acceptable dictionary definitions, it would be possible to call a tyrannical parent, a police officer, or a school administrator a fascist; but such usage would scarcely serve as the basis for a definition of the political system of fascism and of those who hold its tenets.

There are other pitfalls in definition which the careful writer should learn to avoid and the reader to distinguish. A common flaw is the *circular definition,* one in which the term being defined or some form of it appears in the definition itself. To define *democracy* as "that sort of state in which all people are treated democratically" is to be not only useless but frustrating as well.

Another sort of error is that occasioned by *overrestriction* in definition. Overrestriction occurs when the definition given for a term is too narrow to encompass everything that the term might denote. To define a *student* as "someone who gains his education at an accredited school" is partly correct, but it over-restricts the possibilities for the word *student*. What of the many persons who attend unaccredited institutions? What of the self-educated? Our definition is satisfactory as far as it takes us, but obviously that is not far enough.

Overinclusion is the opposite face of overrestriction. In errors of this kind the definition given is too sweeping, including possibilities not denoted by the word to be defined. If we define a *student* as "an individual associated with the field of learning" we are, once again, accurate to a degree. However, our definition is faulty because it includes too many people not denoted by the word *student,* as custodians, book salesmen, or certain admin-istrators, to name but a few.

These pitfalls are certainly not the only ones attendant upon close definition; but they are among the most common and, both as writer and reader, one would do well to be constantly on the alert for them. Unfortunately, they will rarely be as obvious as in our rather simplistic examples. It is essential to realize that entire essays in exposition are built around the process of definition; and an essayist, unlike a lexicographer, is frequently subjective and discursive in his approach. And if he is skillful enough and articulate enough, his definition may be extremely convincing though not necessarily accurate. This is not to suggest that the essayist who sets out to define a word or, more likely, an idea is somehow bound to be guilty of deliberately misleading his audience. But the fact that definitions vary so slightly from one dictionary to the next whereas two essayists "defining" the same subject may arrive at totally contradictory conclusions indicates that essays in definition can be, equally, exercises in persuasion as much as in exposition; and the reader should be forewarned to follow the writer's steps in defining with no little care.

Definition is the basis for each of the five selections that follow, varied as they are in subject matter and in form. In each, the writer attempts to pin down some idea or abstract notion to a recognizable, comprehensible reality. In each, the definition itself is extended and the context may bear heavily on the writer's logic and purpose. It will be instructive for the student to examine carefully the processes of definition in these selections, to determine the predominant method or combination of methods at work, to search for flaws and weaknesses, and finally, to judge the success or failure of each.

democracy

CARL BECKER

1 Democracy, like liberty or science or progress, is a word with which we are all so familiar that we rarely take the trouble to ask what we mean by it. It is a term, as the devotees of semantics say, which has no "referent"—there is no precise or palpable thing or object which we all think of when the word is pronounced. On the contrary, it is a word which connotes different things to different people, a kind of conceptual Gladstone bag which, with a little manipulation, can be made to accommodate almost any collection of social facts we may wish to carry about in it. In it we can as easily pack a dictatorship as any other form of government. We have only to stretch the concept to include any form of government supported by a majority of the people, for whatever reasons and by whatever means of expressing assent, and before we know it the empire of Napoleon, the Soviet regime of Stalin, and the Fascist systems of Mussolini and Hitler are all safely in the bag. But if this is what we mean by democracy, then virtually all forms of government are democratic, since virtually all governments, except in times of revolution, rest upon the explicit or implicit consent of the people. In order to discuss democracy intelligently it will be necessary, therefore, to define it, to attach to the word a sufficiently precise meaning to avoid the confusion which is not infrequently the chief result of such discussions.

Reprinted with permission of Yale University Press, from *Modern Democracy*, by Carl L. Becker.

2   All human institutions, we are told, have their ideal forms laid away in heaven, and we do not need to be told that the actual institutions conform but indifferently to these ideal counterparts. It would be possible then to define democracy either in terms of the ideal or in terms of the real form—to define it as government of the people, by the people, for the people; or to define it as government of the people, by the politicians, for whatever pressure groups can get their interests taken care of. But as a historian I am naturally disposed to be satisfied with the meaning which, in the history of politics, men have commonly attributed to the word—a meaning, needless to say, which derives partly from the experience and partly from the aspirations of mankind. So regarded, the term democracy refers primarily to a form of government, and it has always meant government by the many as opposed to government by the one—government by the people as opposed to government by a tyrant, a dictator, or an absolute monarch. This is the most general meaning of the word as men have commonly understood it.

3   In this antithesis there are, however, certain implications, always tacitly understood, which gives a more precise meaning to the term. Peisistratus, for example, was supported by a majority of the people, but his government was never regarded as a democracy for all that. Caesar's power derived from a popular mandate, conveyed through established republican forms, but that did not make his government any the less a dictatorship. Napoleon called his government a democratic empire, but no one, least of all Napoleon himself, doubted that he had destroyed the last vestiges of the democratic republic. Since the Greeks first used the term, the essential test of democratic government has always been this: the source of political authority must be and remain in the people and not in the ruler. A democratic government has always meant one in which the citizens, or a sufficient number of them to represent more or less effectively the common will, freely act from time to time, and according to established forms, to appoint or recall the magistrates and to enact or revoke the laws by which the community is governed. This I take to be the meaning which history has impressed upon the term democracy as a form of government.

liberals and conservatives

LAURENCE SEARS

1   It is one of the significant facts of our time that there is a growing concern with the meaning of political conservatism, and a
dissatisfaction with the way that the term is popularly used. To a
large degree both "liberal" and "conservative" are today little
more than honorific terms used to give a comfortable glow of satisfaction, or else epithets designed to destroy the influence of
those with whom we disagree. But even though the concepts are
blurred, nonetheless one assumption is held in common, that
either one *or* the other is the true belief, and that, although we
may tolerate the opposite and mistaken view, *we* hold the truth
and must be ready to do battle for it. It is the right versus the
wrong. But there is another position which holds: (1) that it is
one of the urgent tasks of our time to get these terms sharply
defined; and (2) that when we do so, we will find that each position holds both a profound and a partial truth. That view needs
reexamination today.

2   One of the difficulties that lies in the path of clear definition
arises from the fact that we have largely forgotten our own political tradition. The picture often drawn of the conservative
does not correspond with the features of men like Burke in
England or James Madison or John Adams in this country. This
is not surprising in the light of the fact that there have been so

Reprinted with permission of the publisher, from *The Antioch Review*,
Volume 13, Number 3.

few clear-headed and consistent conservatives in this country in the last century that we have forgotten what they look like, grown contemptuous of their contribution, and identified them with the reactionary (as fatal a blunder as to identify the liberal with the radical). We are continually faced with this danger of identifying the conservative with men of our own time who are striving to get back to the good old days, who are worshiping at the shrine of the economic gods of the things as they were, and who would formulate a program entirely around such policies as the reduction of taxes, the removal of economic controls, and the cessation of any attempt to break up monopolies. But this is a travesty of our tradition and confirms Reinhold Niebuhr's contention that contemporary American conservatism is little more than a decayed form of nineteenth-century liberalism. It is time that we rescued this word "conservative," and gave to it something of the meaning and dignity that it once had.

3   By way of comparison and contrast, it might be well to look briefly at the tradition of liberalism, of which Jefferson is the outstanding example among the founding fathers. All political philosophies rest back ultimately upon an assumption about human nature. Madison recognized this when he wrote: "What is government itself, but the greatest of all reflections on human nature?" Jefferson was perfectly explicit at this point—he believed profoundly in the potential rationality of man. Hence the appeal to reason by facts was his answer to all political problems. "Enlighten the people generally, and tyranny and oppressions of body and mind will vanish like evil spirits at the dawn of day." Here is the faith of the liberal; men can be appealed to through their intelligence, and in the light of what is wise, they can in the long run be trusted to act not solely in terms of their narrow self-interest, but on behalf of that which is good for all.

4   It is worth noting that it is because of this belief in the reasonableness of man that liberals have to a large extent rejected the necessity of force. L. T. Hobhouse saw this when he declared that it was of the essence of liberalism to oppose the use of force since it was the basis of tyranny.

5   A second characteristic of Jefferson was his deep concern with the rights of man. It was not an accident that it was he who wrote

the Declaration of Independence with its insistence upon the fact
that all men are endowed by their creator with the inalienable
rights of life and liberty and the pursuit of happiness. As time
went on he stressed freedom of speech as the central right in any
democracy. Here again was his faith that men could be trusted
with such freedom and that the state would be the stronger for
it. "If there be any among us who would wish to dissolve this
union or to change its republican form, let them stand undis-
turbed as monuments of the safety with which error of opinion
may be tolerated where reason is left free to combat it." Finally,
there was a commitment on Jefferson's part to the belief that old
ways were never good enough. He sometimes loosely phrased this
attitude so as to make it seem that he was advocating revolution,
when in effect he was stressing the necessity of continually altering the political and social patterns in such a way as to meet the
demands of a new day. Like all liberals, he seemed continually to
be saying: "Hurry; the hour is very late and our work has just
begun."

6   When one turns to the tradition of political conservatism, one
inevitably examines the philosophy of John Adams and James
Madison, and the first discovery is that, contrary to contemporary
notions, theirs is not the position of reactionaries seeking merely
to cling to their privilege, property, and power. These men are
concerned with the achievement of positive values.

7   As regards their view of human nature, one finds a startling
contrast with that of Jefferson. John Adams gives a classic statement:

> It is weakness rather than wickedness which renders men unfit
> to be trusted with unlimited power. The passions are all unlim-
> ited; nature has left them so; if they could be bounded, they
> would be extinct. . . . The love of gold grows faster than the heap
> of acquisition; the love of praise increases by every gratification,
> till it stings like an adder, and bites like a serpent; till the man
> is miserable every moment when he does not snuff the incense.
> Ambition strengthens at every advance, and at last takes posses-
> sion of the whole soul so absolutely that a man sees nothing in
> the world of importance to others or himself but in his object.

Nor is this lack of faith in the rationality of men confined to
those who are uneducated. The élite are mistrusted as much as

the masses. Education is no answer to irrationality and greed. John Adams was suspicious of both groups alike—

> The more knowledge is diffused, the more the passions are extended, and the more furious they grow. . . . The increase and dissemination of knowledge, instead of rendering unnecessary the checks of emulation and the balances of rivalry in the orders of society and constitution of government, augment the necessity of both. . . . Bad men increase in knowledge as fast as good men; and science, arts, taste, sense, and letters are employed for the purposes of injustice and tyranny as well as those of law and liberty; for corruption as well as virtue.

8 Because of his lack of faith in the possibility of a rational appeal to the disinterested behavior of men, his primary concern was with the fact of power. Here is the core of the conservative philosophy, as true in England and on the Continent as it has been in this country. Though it is possible to define power in terms either of coercion or of persuasion, the distinction remains. It is a matter of emphasis. Both sides would agree that the ideal situation is where power is delegated under maximum conditions of persuasion and with a minimum of pressure and force. But the liberal believes that his ends can be largely achieved through persuasion, while the conservative believes that persuasion is inadequate and coercion is inevitable. The play of contending groups seeking power for the achievement of their ends has always been the dominant concern of men like Adams, and they sought to understand not only its source but also its effect. Adams would whole-heartedly have agreed with Lord Acton in his insistence that power always corrupts and absolute power corrupts absolutely. Because of his conviction that this was the effect of power, he was concerned to find the means of distributing and balancing it so that no group or man should hold an inordinate amount. Since we cannot depend upon rational and disinterested behavior, the balance of power is the only answer to the selfishness of men. As John Randolph phrased it, "You may cover whole skins of parchment with limitations, but power alone can limit power."

9 It was James Madison, the man who had more influence in the drafting of our Constitution than anyone else, who formulated the patterns which have become an integral part of our political

life, even though we are scarcely conscious of the philosophy which lies behind them. He started with a recognition of the existence of factions within society which he believed were based upon economic interests. The most common and durable source of factions has always been the various and unequal distribution of property. "Those who hold and those who are without property have ever formed distinct interests in society." It is startling to realize that at this point he was not far from the position of Marx as to the economic basis of politics; in his conviction that men are motivated primarily by their economic interests. But from then on he broke drastically with the Marxian philosophy. Whereas Marx believed that the history of the world lay in the struggle between classes, where one class must inevitably destroy the other, Madison did not believe that it was possible to give to all men the same economic interests, no matter what the economic structure might be, and insisted that any such attempt to remove factions would inevitably destroy liberty. And liberty was always his supreme value. Since, therefore, you cannot remove the causes, you must control the effects, and that can only be done in one of two ways.

10   In the first place, by a check upon the people's direct control over their government. It was because of this that he sought so strenuously for the system of checks and balances which lies at the heart of our Constitution. In the second place, he believed in extending the sphere of interests, of expanding the number of factions and thereby taking in a greater variety of interests, thus giving an effective voice to all.

11   In summarizing this conservative philosophy in order to see more clearly its relevance in our own time, it is redundant to do more than mention the lack of faith in man, which was at its heart. There was little faith in men, either the common people or the aristocracy. Most men are seen as selfish when their interests are involved and many are potentially corrupt. One is reminded of the closing lines of the ballad "Frankie and Johnnie":

> This story has no moral
> This story has no end
> This story only goes to show
> That there ain't no good in men.

Viereck, to whom we are indebted for reminding us of the conservative tradition, has emphasized this fact of human frailty; of the extent to which men are prone to sin and selfishness, and has recognized that this was the foundation of the conservative position.

12   In the second place, because of this mistrust, the conservative has been determined to distribute and balance power. John Adams said, ". . . every project has been found to be no better than committing the lamb to the custody of the wolf, except the one which is called the balance of power. . . ." Power naturally grows because human passions are insatiable, but that power alone can grow which is unchecked, which has no equal power to control it.

13   Contemporary psychology has made an interesting contribution to this analysis of the meaning of power and its relation to democracy. James Marshall has written recently a brilliant article[1] exploring the meaning of power for a theory of democracy. He starts with an insistence that one cannot understand democracy without reducing it to the various elements of power. He goes on to point out that to "exercise power of any nature over people is to that extent to deny or relieve them of responsibility and that such denial limits their personalities, their opportunities for growth, and is the source of immaturity." Hence for him "the measure of a people's democracy is the extent of its freedom from dependence," for dependence has as its corollaries submissiveness and apathy, which are the denial of the whole spirit of democracy. "Freedom from dependence is requisite to maturity." His test of political democracy, therefore, is the freedom from dependence of its people, and its necessary condition is the diffusion of power.

14   In the third place, this conservative philosophy means an acceptance in bluntest terms of pressure politics. In fact, the question is raised as to what other politics there are. The definition of politics as the art of who gets what, when and how is widely accepted. Again it is worth reminding ourselves that the differences between the conservative and the liberal are matters

[1]*Democracy in a World of Tension:* A Symposium prepared by UNESCO, pp. 214–227.

of emphasis; each recognizes the need for persuasion as well as the facing of power by power. Perhaps an illustration will make clearer the distinction. We have in this country many hundreds of thousands of migrant workers who are, politically speaking, the forgotten men. As we face this obvious injustice, the liberal would seem more likely to depend upon an appeal to those who do have political power to share it with those without, trusting to the reason and decency of men to see how grossly unfair this situation is. I suspect that the genuine conservative would spend little time in such an appeal—rather he would try to see the migrants organized so that they could make an effective demand upon the body politic.

15   Such a philosophy implies that the basic economic conflicts of society must always remain. Any political kingdom of heaven where the lions and the lambs lie down together is not likely to transpire, and the philosophy of the Marxian that it is possible to remove these tensions by the destruction of one class is seen to be obvious nonsense, if, of course, one places any value whatever on liberty. This is a hard fact to face. We would like to get rid of the tensions of society. In some cases we will, but essentially any vital society is one which will contain multiple tensions, differences, and interests. As Tannenbaum has put it,[2] "Conflict, strife, divergence, difference of interest and opinion over many things for many reasons, and in varying degrees of intensity, are the conditions of social peace. The conflicting processes of democracy are consistent with and essentially a part of the stresses and strains of life itself." The emphasis lies upon the democratic *process* rather than upon any specific goals. Once again we must remind ourselves that the conservative is not uninterested in justice or in equality, but rather that every achievement is but one step in an endless process which is itself the condition of growth, vitality, and hope.

16   A fourth characteristic of the conservative faith is its emphasis upon expediency rather than upon ultimate rights or principles. An illustration might be drawn from the career of Woodrow Wilson. When he faced the close of World War I, he formulated

2"Balance of Power in Society," in *Political Science Quarterly*, December, 1947.

his famous Fourteen Points, among which was the self-determination of small nations. This was an appealing principle but many came to question whether it did not do more harm than good. The conservative would have been suspicious of any such principle and would certainly have been more likely to seek for adjustments which were at least possible, even though something less than ideal. There is less of a glorious vision held out by the conservative than by the liberal, but there is a sturdy insistence that starting with where we are we may achieve something better even though it falls far short of the dreams of men. There is the belief that although we may never achieve the day when all men may have life and liberty and be free to seek their happiness, yet we will make progress toward this achievement.

17 No specific economic system is necessarily assumed but there is a general approach to our economic problems. The liberal tends to look for that system which will give a maximum of equality and justice based upon deliberate adjustments of means to ends. The conservative tends to trust much more the invisible hand operating through the play of economic forces upon each other than he does to any conscious planning or centralized control. Once again it is the process rather than the results which are important. Galbraith, in *American Capitalism*, has approached the economic problem in such a spirit. He starts with a concern about the extent of governmental power and defends, as an alternative, a system where private economic power is held in check by the countervailing power of those who are subject to it. Politically, this means that the primary rule of the state is to give assistance in the development of such balances of power. Controls, in other words, would be largely automatic, the result of the balancing of forces rather than the deliberate and conscious control by those in power.

18 Finally, it needs to be said that the conservative, although he tends to move more slowly, is not committed to the preservation of a *status quo*. He is not, as was said before, a reactionary, and the distinction needs to be kept clear. He too would move ahead, though more slowly. The great English conservative, Burke, characterized the role of the statesman as "the disposition to preserve and the ability to improve," and any genuine conservative would agree.

19   The contribution of, and commitment to, democracy on the
part of the liberal is widely recognized, but we must understand
clearly what the liberal means. Henry L. Stimson, himself one of
the few consistent conservatives we have had in America in modern times, defined the liberal position acutely, even though he
disagreed with it. Speaking of the dominant philosophy of the
early years of the twentieth century, he said:

> The theoretically easy and emotionally satisfactory solution to
> the failures of democracy lay in "more democracy." If govern-
> ment was inefficient or subservient to powerful private interests,
> turn it back to the people. This solution, which was in direct
> line with the traditions of Jeffersonian democracy, found its ex-
> pression in the movement for the direct election of senators and
> the direct primary and more exuberantly in the campaigns for
> the initiative, the referendum, and the recall. . . . The people
> had lost control of their government because its complexities pro-
> vided a smoke screen for the manipulation of bosses and private
> interests; then let the people themselves take charge.[3]

Give information to the people, put into their hands direct control of their government, and ultimately our problems will be
solved. The liberal would define democracy in other words, as
that system of government where freely elected representatives
are directly responsible to an informed and participating citizenry.

20   The conservative definition is different, though only in emphasis. Since the primary function of government lies in the
maintenance of balance between influences, democracy will mean
the distribution and therefore the minimization of power. It is
not the mere tossing of direct and unlimited power into the
hands of individual citizens, but a balance between competing
groups which is the condition of political health, and compromise between varying interests becomes the condition of liberty.
In fact a conservative might very well define democracy as that
system of government where no one gets all he wants.

[3] *On Active Service in Peace and War*, by Henry L. Stimson and McGeorge
Bundy, Harper and Brothers.

21   But if there are differences of definition, there is certainly as great a commitment to democracy on the part of the conservative as there is with the liberal. However, here again the reason differs. It is less his faith in the goodness of human nature than it is his conviction of the depravity of man which lies behind his devotion to democracy. Niebuhr has said that "Man's capacity for justice makes democracy possible but man's inclination to injustice makes democracy necessary." Thus, by profoundly different roads the liberal and the conservative come to the democratic conclusion that sovereignty must be vested in all the people. In this conviction that we the people hold the ultimate authority, the two philosophies unite.

22   It is not difficult to see the strength of the liberal position. Throughout the entire tradition there has been a deep concern with human rights, with justice and equality, with a recognition of the need for change. Old ways have never been good enough. What is difficult for the liberal is to recognize that there have been weaknesses associated with his faith, that all too often people operating as groups cannot be depended upon to be disinterested, that only under specific conditions are they rational in their decisions. And most of all, the liberal has tended to forget that politics is always power politics and to ignore not merely the source of power but its effect. There were not many liberals who thought Hitler could be met with reason, but there have been many who thought that Stalin could be dealt with on a basis of reasonable compromise. They would have been wiser to have listened more carefully to the warning of Lord Acton.

23   To a liberal, the weaknesses within the conservative's position seem equally obvious. Conservatives forget that man can, under certain conditions, act rationally. There is the tendency for them to be contemptuous of what they call "the masses"; to ignore the fact that there is more than coercive power involved in politics, that men have been and will be moved by the power of ideas and ideals. In their concern with the immediate, they have tended to forget that without a vision the people perish, and all too often they have been complacent in the face of the denial of the rights of man, and smugly timid in the presence of injustice. To be sure, John Morley spoke as a liberal with little respect for the Tory

position, but there was truth in his criticism of the Conservative—

> . . . with his inexhaustible patience of abuses that only torment
> others; his apologetic words for beliefs that may not be so pre-
> cisely true as one might wish, and institutions that are not alto-
> gether so useful as some might think possible; his cordiality
> towards progress and improvement in a general way, and his
> coldness or antipathy to each progressive proposal in particular;
> his pygmy hope that life will one day become somewhat better,
> punily shivering by the side of his gigantic conviction that it
> might well be infinitely worse.[4]

24   So much for the weakness of the conservative position, but its
strength should be equally clear. Based on a recognition of the
fact that men do not often act as wisely as the situations demand—that always groups are in conflict as they strive to further
separate interests, they know that any effective democracy will be
based upon an adequate dividing and balancing of strength. Such
a philosophy must recognize the obvious fact that, as John Adams
said, "power follows property" and that therefore if power is to
be distributed, property must be more equitably held. Such an
honest and consistent conservatism would be far more than a
façade behind which are to be protected the property, privilege
and power of a minority.

25   To one who thinks of himself as a liberal, the value of such a
political philosophy committed to the preservation and extension
of democracy and consistently and honestly devoted to the balancing of pressures through effective organization of all interest
groups would seem to be obvious. It would certainly be a profoundly constructive force in American political history.

26   The reaction from the liberalism of recent years is obvious. In
part it is due to the loss of confidence in human nature that has
accompanied the spectacle of the past decade. In part it is a recognition of the fact that persuasion has seemed relatively impotent during these years, and that power could only be challenged
by power. Whatever the reasons, the swing of the pendulum is
carrying us away from the liberal faith. The danger is that this
may not bring us a genuine conservative movement. Instead we

[4]Quoted by Randall in *The Making of the Modern Mind*, Chapter 7.

may not only destroy the profound contributions of the liberal; we may mistake a decadent reactionism for a constructive conservatism. The radical and the reactionary should have little place in our society, but the liberal *and* the conservative we desperately need.

the negro: an essay on definition
DONALD B. GIBSON

1   When Robert Penn Warren interviews James Baldwin in *Who Speaks for the Negro?* Warren asks a question about the responsibility of the Negro. Baldwin replies initially that he isn't sure what a Negro is. Warren characterizes Baldwin's response as a "tendency to undercut a specific issue and plunge into the shadowy depth." Baldwin's reply, as Warren saw it, could quickly become an academic or even metaphysical problem and therefore of limited relevance to his book. At the same time, however, Warren, as he admits, was wrong. Too few, black and white, liberal and conservative, have asked the question—what is a Negro?—from any perspective whatever; and those who have asked it have not usually questioned the assumption underlying the question itself, the assumption that there exists in reality (rather than metaphorically) a concrete entity described by the term "Negro."

2   Now, I do not wish to argue that there is no such thing as a Negro. Rather, I wish to argue that the assumption of the existence of a clearly definable "Negro" group, as necessary and useful as it may be to the sociologist, has traditionally been and remains one of the major hindrances to understanding of and communication about the problem of race. It is a mistake to assume that there exists a group of people called "Negro" who possess those characteristics of a cultural nature which all other non-native minority groups have had. The implications of this proposition

Reprinted with permission of *The Yale Review*. Copyright Yale University.

explain a great deal about the people called "Negro" in America and point to the unrealized complexity of the racial problem.

3   The present cultural circumstances of the Negro have their roots in the very beginning of his unsought association with America. From the start the groups of Africans transported to America were treated in such a way as to discourage either the continuation of old cultural habits or the establishment of new ones strong enough to replace the old. Though practically all slaves were from West Africa, they came from different areas and tribal groups, spoke different languages, and observed different customs and mores. Those who spoke a common language, possessed a common religion or body of mythology, and honored a common system of institutions were separated in order better to assure compliance in the new environment. Those cultural elements responsible for the internal cohesion of any ethnic group were consciously eliminated by slave traders and slave masters.

4   In point of culture it is clear that the African group differed from all other non-native groups whose native cultures have been more continuous in the American environment. Even if we take into account elements of the African cultural past which have been retained, the fact remains that there does not exist a discrete Negro culture separable in any meaningful degree from the larger American culture. Among Negroes there does not exist, nor has there ever existed, a common language, religion, or mythology, nor a common habit of social interaction. This is to say that though the black man has been enough a part of the American environment to absorb the basic elements of the dominant culture, he has not been separate enough to develop a discrete culture.

5   The fact of the cultural situation of the Negro has many practical ramifications. For example, confusion and lack of communication occurs when people try to think or talk about race and at the same time assume that a Negro-American stands in the same relation to an ethnic group as does an Irish-American or Italian-American individual. Clearly he doesn't.

6   Lacking his own institutions, lacking those basic elements of a culture which allow other groups a firm sense of group identity, the Negro forms a far more diverse element of the population than any other group. Negroes are Negroes primarily because of

the definitions applied by the society; therefore, any cohesiveness which the group has or can have is the result of defense against the white aggressor. Other ethnic groups possessing a common language, religion, or mythology, and common habits of social interaction feel an inner cohesiveness stemming from an internalized system of values. Negroes, on the other hand, only feel a defensive, externally motivated sense of group identity.

7   This explains why Negroes have not been able to emulate the Jewish population, for example, who traditionally have united in order to defend themselves against a hostile majority. Certainly the Jewish people throughout history have had to unite defensively against aggression, but the difference is that the Jews over the centuries developed strong internal links, especially of a religious character, which served to give the group cohesiveness beyond the necessities imposed by external conditions.

8   Jews were never separated from their past in the way Negroes were. The history of the Negro was cut off when he was loaded on ships and brought to America and his past was erased from his memory. At best the Negro can salvage a knowledge of his recent past in America; Jews have records of a past extending far back into antiquity, a past which has been kept alive and an integral part of the Jewish cultural heritage. There is no mode of religious thought and experience among Negroes comparable to Judaism, no mythology comparable to the mythologies which exist in any discrete culture.

9   And finally, language was an important factor which allowed greater cohesion among Jews in America. Though Yiddish was technically not a language, for all practical purposes it was, because in the American environment it differed significantly from the language of the majority. Of course there was never a time when all American Jews spoke Yiddish, yet it was a greater source of internal cohesiveness than Negro dialect, which was never far removed from Southern dialect and from the American language of the majority.

10   The fact that the Negro group is not culturally monolithic also bears on the relation between the middle-class and lower-class Negroes. Recent attention has been focused on the tendency of the Negro middle class to desert the lower classes once middle-class status has been gained, a phenomenon long ago recognized by Negroes themselves. The Negro middle class has been taken to

task for not recognizing its responsibility to the less fortunate Negro. Traditionally, even civil rights groups have been concerned with enlisting middle-class Negroes into their ranks while neglecting and even disparaging alliances with the lower classes. The reasons for the existence of this relationship become obvious when the matter is viewed from the perspective outlined here.

11   In actuality, the attitude of the middle-class Negro does not differ greatly from the attitude of the majority of the middle class toward the lower class. Those who would expect him to act otherwise are simply not aware that the cultural ties which would allow him to reach back and help those he left behind do not exist. He has no cultural basis for feeling united to the lower class. Indeed, the only basis for his feeling identification with the lower class is that stemming from the mutual need for defense against a threatening white society.

12   For this reason, the militant civil rights groups attempt to appeal to the middle-class Negro by reminding him of the forces arrayed against him and of the resulting need for mutual defense. If there were internal cohesiveness within the group, there would be a basis for appeal in terms other than defensive ones. As things presently are, the Negro middle class will continue to be a group unto itself as long as the need for defense grows no greater. It is therefore meaningless to berate the Negro middle class for failure to exercise a responsibility which it has no cultural basis for recognizing.

13   Given the diverse character of the Negro group, it is no wonder that for years Negroes have bemoaned the lack of unity within, even among those in the same or similar economic circumstances. Today, despite the greater appearance of unity than ever before, the cultural makeup of the group legislates against the type of unified thought and action which could take adequate steps toward alleviating the plight of the group in any but the most long-range terms. Unity to the degree achieved by the National Association for the Advancement of Colored People and the Student Nonviolent Coordinating Committee is at best difficult to achieve. Powerful and effective as these groups are, they involve a very small percentage of the Negro population.

14   To be convinced of the diversity of thought and feeling among the Negro group, one need only assess attitudes among Negroes toward the notion of black power. First of all, there is no more

agreement about its meaning among Negroes than there seems to be among whites. And further, there is as much fear, among Negroes, of the term and of its possible implications as there apparently is among the majority of the population. This is evidenced by the large numbers of Negroes of all classes who have publicly repudiated the concept. If the Negro group were monolithic, as it is assumed to be by the majority, and if Negroes interpreted black power as most whites seem to feel it should be interpreted, there might be more justifiable cause for fear of violence than there presently is. The only ground for fear lies in the strength of the white backlash and the withdrawal of sympathy for the Negro's cause by white "liberals." If these actions force Negroes to assume a more defensive posture—thereby uniting the group—then there could be cause for offensive action beyond throwing Coke bottles through the windows of shoeshine parlors.

15   The cultural situation of the Negro has resulted in severe problems of social identity. Though many in the society feel problems of identity, the problem of the Negro is more acute, for his difficulty with identity exists on a more basic plane. There are ways which the most disenchanted white, by virtue of his color alone, can identify with the majority culture which are not available to Negroes.

16   However, larger and larger numbers of Negroes are trying in various ways to solve the problem of social identity by relating to ideals and values different from those embodied in the rejecting culture. The attempt, which is also an effort on the part of many to bring about internal cohesion within the group, has taken many forms. The most full-scale attempt exists among the Black Muslims, who have managed to create internal cohesion within their group primarily by means of religion. The group has its own mythology and instills new habits of life and thought, of custom and manners into its converts. Such a movement could never have existed had there been a culture in the sense that I have defined it with which Negroes could identify.

17   The white majority has only itself to blame for the existence of such a group. It came about entirely as a result of a need for defense in a hostile environment and a need for social identity in a society that withholds it.

18   It is of significance that the Muslims have chosen alien cultural symbols as their basis for union, and that these alien ideas of thought and conduct could come to exist in viable form. The reasons that the group looked to the Middle East for its basis of union underscores the point I am making here: symbols indicating the existence of a monolithic Negro culture do not exist presently in the American environment.

19   Others have looked to Africa for the solution of the problem of social and cultural identity. Not too long ago a Negro might insult another by likening him to an African. Now the reverse is frequently true. Many Negroes look proudly toward Africa, studying its history and culture, buying African art objects. Some groups have gone so far as to adopt certain African native dress in an attempt to identify with an old, established culture.

20   Others have taken elements they feel to be characteristic of the Negro group and attempted to create a culture from these. Many feel positively toward blackness of skin and no longer attach the stigma to it which Negroes previously have done in emulating the ideals of the majority. Fewer Negro men use hair straighteners and some Negro women have begun to wear their hair unstraightened. Some Negroes, even educated ones, prefer to use Negro slang and dialect because they feel it is more theirs than standard American English.

21   The study of Negro literature and history is probably wider in scope and greater in depth than ever before within the Negro group. Many who do not usually read are beginning to read books by and about Negroes in the present and in the past. Some school libraries, often at the insistence of Negro parents, have begun to shelve books having to do with Negroes. All this has come about in an attempt to foster a viable culture.

22   The assumption of a monolithic Negro culture and the consequent lack of awareness of the heterogeneity of the group have been responsible for the existence of what I call the "myth of the race leader." Since the nineteenth century, whites have assumed that if they wanted to know anything about Negroes or to communicate with Negroes, they need only contact a "leader." For years during the late nineteenth and well into the twentieth century, Booker T. Washington was considered *the* Negro leader. Anyone who wanted to know what the Negro thought about any-

thing needed only to ask Booker T. He had the ear of presidents and millionaire philanthropists and was considered by the majority of whites as one who spoke for the Negro. Even he felt so, despite the fact that he could hardly have done so given his own personal interests, limitations, and philosophy.

23   Since that time there has grown up a myth of the Negro leader, of a Negro who may not only speak to the country of affairs concerning the Negro, but is at the same time one who wields power and authority over a homogeneous following. Presidents have frequently met with "leaders" (successful middle-class Negroes) for talks about the Negro question in the same way that they might meet with leaders of foreign countries. The myth of the Negro leader is so deeply embedded in the thinking of the majority that any Negro who leads any organization of Negroes will be referred to by the press as a Negro leader.

24   If the Negro population is as diverse as I have said, it stands to reason that there cannot be any person who will unite even a simple majority into one group. Hence the absurdity of the notion that there are Negro leaders who may speak for the Negro in the same sense that leaders of countries, communities, or religious sects may speak for their citizens or congregations. Only one of the people whom the newspapers designate "leader" (Roy Wilkins of the NAACP) leads as many as a half million people— a small percentage of the twenty-two millions who, according to census figures, live in the United States.

25   The myth of the Negro leader was responsible for Mayor Wagner's calling Martin Luther King during the Harlem riot of 1964. The mayor assumed that since King is indeed a leader of Negroes and the problem at hand involved Negroes, the man could aid in the solution of his problem. Had Wagner recognized the cultural diversity existing among Negroes, he would have known that Dr. King's influence and prestige would not necessarily be effective in that particular slum environment at that particular time. He was probably shocked and puzzled by the hostile reception which Harlemites gave Dr. King.

26   The same faulty thinking which prompted Mayor Wagner to call in Dr. King also prompted President Johnson last summer to urge Negroes to stop rioting in the streets. The President might have saved his breath, for the people rioting were not listening to the speech and could not have cared less about his admoni-

tion. But the President was not talking to the microscopically small minority who were throwing rocks and Molotov cocktails. Mr. Johnson was talking to *the* Negro and assuming that *the* Negro is an entity which can be addressed and influenced as such. If he assumed that the "responsible" Negro community was listening and would exert influence on the violent few, then he was simply being naive, for the relationship between the "responsible" and "irresponsible" is more complex than he might think. But Mr. Johnson was being no more naive than those mayors and governors of places where riots have occurred who have immediately appealed to the "responsible Negro community," the "leaders," in order to control rioting.

27   These are some of the implications of the fact that there exists no discrete, monolithic Negro culture. The major problem emerging from this consideration is that the racial problem is far more complex than most know or are willing publicly to admit. Perhaps, however, I underestimate the thinking behind, for example, the poverty program, which could well be based upon some of the observations made here. That is, is it an accident that one effect of the poverty program is to give jobs to Negroes who are middle class in background or orientation? Is it an accident that giving jobs to these people brings them enough into the mainstream so as to reduce their need for defensive cohesiveness and thus assure that Negroes of the middle and lower classes will not form a single bloc? I do not know the answer to this question.

28   What I've said so far should also reveal the relevance of Baldwin's statement that he isn't sure what a Negro is. What indeed is a Negro? Seen from the perspective I suggest here, the question is not merely an academic one; it has extremely practical ramifications. Most people believe they know what "Negro" means, but I do not know, and I speak from inside. As long as most of us assume that "Negro" implies some kind of discrete identity, understanding is impossible. At the same time, the possibility of the majority of people's recognizing the diversity of the Negro group is dim. At best some may be able to realize and accept the limited reality of the general conception of "Negro," and understand the extent to which it is a kind of metaphor, a poetic expression. Until, however, those talking and thinking about the problem recognize the facts, any kind of meaningful progress toward full solution is unlikely.

letter from birmingham jail
MARTIN LUTHER KING, JR.

MY DEAR FELLOW CLERGYMEN:[1]

1   While confined here in the Birmingham jail, I came across your recent statement calling my present activities "unwise and untimely." Seldom do I pause to answer criticism of my work and ideas. If I sought to answer all the criticisms that cross my desk, my secretaries would have little time for anything other than such correspondence in the course of the day, and I would have no time for constructive work. But since I feel that you are men of genuine good will and that your criticisms are sincerely set forth, I want to try to answer your statement in what I hope will be patient and reasonable terms.

[1]This response to a published statement by eight fellow clergymen from Alabama (Bishop C. C. J. Carpenter, Bishop Joseph A. Durick, Rabbi Hilton L. Grafman, Bishop Paul Hardin, Bishop Holan B. Harmon, the Reverend George M. Murray, the Reverend Edward V. Ramage and the Reverend Earl Stallings) was composed under somewhat constricting circumstances. Begun on the margins of the newspaper in which the statement appeared while I was in jail, the letter was continued on scraps of writing paper supplied by a friendly Negro trusty, and concluded on a pad my attorneys were eventually permitted to leave me. Although the text remains in substance unaltered, I have indulged in the author's prerogative of polishing it for publication [King's note].

Reprinted with permission of Harper & Row, Publishers, Inc., "Letter from Birmingham Jail," April 16, 1963, from *Why We Can't Wait,* by Martin Luther King, Jr. © 1963 by Martin Luther King, Jr.

2   I think I should indicate why I am here in Birmingham, since
you have been influenced by the view which argues against "out-
siders coming in." I have the honor of serving as president of the
Southern Christian Leadership Conference, an organization operating in every southern state, with headquarters in Atlanta,
Georgia. We have some eighty-five affiliated organizations across
the South, and one of them is the Alabama Christian Movement
for Human Rights. Frequently we share staff, educational, and
financial resources with our affiliates. Several months ago the
affiliate here in Birmingham asked us to be on call to engage in
a nonviolent direct-action program if such were deemed necessary. We readily consented, and when the hour came we lived up
to our promise. So I, along with several members of my staff, am
here because I was invited here. I am here because I have organizational ties here.

3   But more basically, I am in Birmingham because injustice is
here. Just as the prophets of the eighth century B.C. left their villages and carried their "thus saith the Lord" far beyond the
boundaries of their home towns, and just as the Apostle Paul left
his village of Tarsus and carried the gospel of Jesus Christ to the
far corners of the Greco-Roman world, so am I compelled to
carry the gospel of freedom beyond my own home town. Like
Paul, I must constantly respond to the Macedonian call for aid.

4   Moreover, I am cognizant of the interrelatedness of all communities and states. I cannot sit idly by in Atlanta and not be concerned about what happens in Birmingham. Injustice anywhere
is a threat to justice everywhere. We are caught in an inescapable
network of mutuality, tied in a single garment of destiny. Whatever affects one directly, affects all indirectly. Never again can we
afford to live with the narrow, provincial "outside agitator" idea.
Anyone who lives inside the United States can never be considered an outsider anywhere within its bounds.

5   You deplore the demonstrations taking place in Birmingham.
But your statement, I am sorry to say, fails to express a similar
concern for the conditions that brought about the demonstrations. I am sure that none of you would want to rest content with
the superficial kind of social analysis that deals merely with effects and does not grapple with underlying causes. It is unfortunate that demonstrations are taking place in Birmingham, but

it is even more unfortunate that the city's white power structure left the Negro community with no alternative.

6   In any nonviolent campaign there are four basic steps: collection of the facts to determine whether injustices exist; negotiation; self-purification; and direct action. We have gone through all these steps in Birmingham. There can be no gainsaying the fact that racial injustice engulfs this community. Birmingham is probably the most thoroughly segregated city in the United States. Its ugly record of brutality is widely known. Negroes have experienced grossly unjust treatment in the courts. There have been more unsolved bombings of Negro homes and churches in Birmingham than in any other city in the nation. These are the hard, brutal facts of the case. On the basis of these conditions, Negro leaders sought to negotiate with the city fathers. But the latter consistently refused to engage in good-faith negotiation.

7   Then, last September, came the opportunity to talk with leaders of Birmingham's economic community. In the course of the negotiations, certain promises were made by the merchants— for example, to remove the stores' humiliating racial signs. On the basis of these promises, the Reverend Fred Shuttlesworth and the leaders of the Alabama Christian Movement for Human Rights agreed to a moratorium on all demonstrations. As the weeks and months went by, we realized that we were the victims of a broken promise. A few signs, briefly removed, returned; the others remained.

8   As in so many past experiences, our hopes had been blasted, and the shadow of deep disappointment settled upon us. We had no alternative except to prepare for direct action, whereby we would present our very bodies as a means of laying our case before the conscience of the local and the national community. Mindful of the difficulties involved, we decided to undertake a process of self-purification. We began a series of workshops on nonviolence, and we repeatedly asked ourselves: "Are you able to accept blows without retaliating?" "Are you able to endure the ordeal of jail?" We decided to schedule our direct-action program for the Easter season, realizing that except for Christmas, this is the main shopping period of the year. Knowing that a strong economic-withdrawal program would be the by-product of direct action, we felt that this would be the best time to bring pressure to bear on the merchants for the needed change.

9   Then it occurred to us that Birmingham's mayoral election was coming up in March, and we speedily decided to postpone action until after election day. When we discovered that the Commissioner of Public Safety, Eugene "Bull" Connor, had piled up enough votes to be in the run-off, we decided again to postpone action until the day after the run-off so that the demonstrations could not be used to cloud the issues. Like many others, we waited to see Mr. Connor defeated, and to this end we endured postponement after postponement. Having aided in this community need, we felt that our direct-action program could be delayed no longer.

10   You may well ask, "Why direct action? Why sit-ins, marches, and so forth? Isn't negotiation a better path?" You are quite right in calling for negotiation. Indeed, this is the very purpose of direct action. Nonviolent direct action seeks to create such a crisis and foster such a tension that a community which has constantly refused to negotiate is forced to confront the issue. It seeks so to dramatize the issue that it can no longer be ignored. My citing the creation of tension as part of the work of the nonviolent-resister may sound rather shocking. But I must confess that I am not afraid of the word "tension." I have earnestly opposed violent tension, but there is a type of constructive, nonviolent tension which is necessary for growth. Just as Socrates felt that it was necessary to create a tension in the mind so that individuals could rise from the bondage of myths and half-truths to the unfettered realm of creative analysis and objective appraisal, so must we see the need for nonviolent gadflies to create the kind of tension in society that will help men rise from the dark depths of prejudice and racism to the majestic heights of understanding and brotherhood.

11   The purpose of our direct-action program is to create a situation so crisis-packed that it will inevitably open the door to negotiation. I therefore concur with you in your call for negotiation. Too long has our beloved Southland been bogged down in a tragic effort to live in monologue rather than dialogue.

12   One of the basic points in your statement is that the action that I and my associates have taken in Birmingham is untimely. Some have asked: "Why didn't you give the new city administration time to act?" The only answer that I can give to this query is that the new Birmingham administration must be prodded

about as much as the outgoing one, before it will act. We are sadly mistaken if we feel that the election of Albert Boutwell as mayor will bring the millennium to Birmingham. While Mr. Boutwell is a much more gentle person than Mr. Connor, they are both segregationists, dedicated to maintenance of the status quo. I have hoped that Mr. Boutwell will be reasonable enough to see the futility of massive resistance to desegregation. But he will not see this without pressure from devotees of civil rights. My friends, I must say to you that we have not made a single gain in civil rights without determined legal and nonviolent pressure. Lamentably, it is an historical fact that privileged groups seldom give up their privileges voluntarily. Individuals may see the moral light and voluntarily give up their unjust posture; but, as Reinhold Niebuhr has reminded us, groups tend to be more immoral than individuals.

13   We know through painful experience that freedom is never voluntarily given by the oppressor; it must be demanded by the oppressed. Frankly, I have yet to engage in a direct-action campaign that was "well timed" in the view of those who have not suffered unduly from the disease of segregation. For years now I have heard the word "Wait!" It rings in the ear of every Negro with piercing familiarity. This "Wait" has almost always meant "Never." We must come to see, with one of our distinguished jurists, that "justice too long delayed is justice denied."

14   We have waited for more than 340 years for our constitutional and God-given rights. The nations of Asia and Africa are moving with jetlike speed toward gaining political independence, but we still creep at horse-and-buggy pace toward gaining a cup of coffee at a lunch counter. Perhaps it is easy for those who have never felt the stinging darts of segregation to say, "Wait." But when you have seen vicious mobs lynch your mothers and fathers at will and drown your sisters and brothers at whim; when you have seen hate-filled policemen curse, kick, and even kill your black brothers and sisters; when you see the vast majority of your twenty million Negro brothers smothering in an airtight cage of poverty in the midst of an affluent society; when you suddenly find your tongue twisted and your speech stammering as you seek to explain to your six-year-old daughter why she can't go to the public amusement park that has just been advertised on televi-

sion, and see tears welling up in her eyes when she is told that Funtown is closed to colored children, and see ominous clouds of inferiority beginning to form in her little mental sky, and see her beginning to distort her personality by developing an unconscious bitterness toward white people; when you have to concoct an answer for a five-year-old son who is asking, "Daddy, why do white people treat colored people so mean?"; when you take a cross-country drive and find it necessary to sleep night after night in the uncomfortable corners of your automobile because no motel will accept you; when you are humiliated day in and day out by nagging signs reading "white" and "colored"; when your first name becomes "nigger," your middle name becomes "boy" (however old you are) and your last name becomes "John," and your wife and mother are never given the respected title "Mrs."; when you are harried by day and haunted by night by the fact that you are a Negro, living constantly at tiptoe stance, never quite knowing what to expect next, and are plagued with inner fears and outer resentments; when you are forever fighting a degenerating sense of "nobodiness"—then you will understand why we find it difficult to wait. There comes a time when the cup of endurance runs over, and men are no longer willing to be plunged into the abyss of despair. I hope, sirs, you can understand our legitimate and unavoidable impatience.

15   You express a great deal of anxiety over our willingness to break laws. This is certainly a legitimate concern. Since we so diligently urge people to obey the Supreme Court's decision of 1954 outlawing segregation in the public schools, at first glance it may seem rather paradoxical for us consciously to break laws. One may well ask: "How can you advocate breaking some laws and obeying others?" The answer lies in the fact that there are two types of laws: just and unjust. I would be the first to advocate obeying just laws. One has not only a legal but a moral responsibility to obey just laws. Conversely, one has a moral responsibility to disobey unjust laws. I would agree with St. Augustine that "an unjust law is no law at all."

16   Now, what is the difference between the two? How does one determine whether a law is just or unjust? A just law is a man-made code that squares with the moral law or the law of God. An unjust law is a code that is out of harmony with the moral law.

To put it in the terms of St. Thomas Aquinas: An unjust law is a human law that is not rooted in eternal law and natural law. Any law that uplifts human personality is just. Any law that degrades human personality is unjust. All segregation statutes are unjust because segregation distorts the soul and damages the personality. It gives the segregator a false sense of superiority and the segregated a false sense of inferiority. Segregation, to use the terminology of the Jewish philosopher Martin Buber, substitutes an "I-it" relationship for an "I-thou" relationship and ends up relegating persons to the status of things. Hence segregation is not only politically, economically, and sociologically unsound, it is morally wrong and sinful. Paul Tillich has said that sin is separation. Is not segregation an existential expression of man's tragic separation, his awful estrangement, his terrible sinfulness? Thus it is that I can urge men to obey the 1954 decision of the Supreme Court, for it is morally right; and I can urge them to disobey segregation ordinances, for they are morally wrong.

17   Let us consider a more concrete example of just and unjust laws. An unjust law is a code that a numerical or power majority group compels a minority group to obey but does not make binding on itself. This is *difference* made legal. By the same token, a just law is a code that a majority compels a minority to follow and that it is willing to follow itself. This is *sameness* made legal.

18   Let me give another explanation. A law is unjust if it is inflicted on a minority that, as a result of being denied the right to vote, had no part in enacting or devising the law. Who can say that the legislature of Alabama which set up that state's segregation laws was democratically elected? Throughout Alabama all sorts of devious methods are used to prevent Negroes from becoming registered voters, and there are some counties in which, even though Negroes constitute a majority of the population, not a single Negro is registered. Can any law enacted under such circumstances be considered democratically structured?

19   Sometimes a law is just on its face and unjust in its application. For instance, I have been arrested on a charge of parading without a permit. Now, there is nothing wrong in having an ordinance which requires a permit for a parade. But such an ordinance becomes unjust when it is used to maintain segregation and to deny citizens the First-Amendment privilege of peaceful assembly and protest.

20 I hope you are able to see the distinction I am trying to point out. In no sense do I advocate evading or defying the law, as would the rabid segregationist. That would lead to anarchy. One who breaks an unjust law must do so openly, lovingly, and with a willingness to accept the penalty. I submit that an individual who breaks a law that conscience tells him is unjust, and who willingly accepts the penalty of imprisonment in order to arouse the conscience of the community over its injustice, is in reality expressing the highest respect for law.

21 Of course, there is nothing new about this kind of civil disobedience. It was evidenced sublimely in the refusal of Shadrach, Meshach, and Abednego to obey the laws of Nebuchadnezzar, on the ground that a higher moral law was at stake. It was practiced superbly by the early Christians, who were willing to face hungry lions and the excruciating pain of chopping blocks rather than submit to certain unjust laws of the Roman Empire. To a degree, academic freedom is a reality today because Socrates practiced civil disobedience. In our own nation, the Boston Tea Party represented a massive act of civil disobedience.

22 We should never forget that everything Adolf Hitler did in Germany was "legal" and everything the Hungarian freedom fighters did in Hungary was "illegal." It was "illegal" to aid and comfort a Jew in Hitler's Germany. Even so, I am sure that, had I lived in Germany at the time, I would have aided and comforted my Jewish brothers. If today I lived in a Communist country where certain principles dear to the Christian faith are suppressed, I would openly advocate disobeying that country's anti-religious laws.

23 I must make two honest confessions to you, my Christian and Jewish brothers. First, I must confess that over the past few years I have been gravely disappointed with the white moderate. I have almost reached the regrettable conclusion that the Negro's great stumbling block in his stride toward freedom is not the White Citizen's Councilor or the Ku Klux Klanner, but the white moderate, who is more devoted to "order" than to justice; who prefers a negative peace which is the absence of tension to a positive peace which is the presence of justice; who constantly says, "I agree with you in the goal you seek, but I cannot agree with your methods of direct action"; who paternalistically believes he can set the timetable for another man's freedom; who lives by a

mythical concept of time and who constantly advises the Negro to wait for a "more convenient season." Shallow understanding from people of good will is more frustrating than absolute misunderstanding from people of ill will. Lukewarm acceptance is much more bewildering than outright rejection.

24   I had hoped that the white moderate would understand that law and order exist for the purpose of establishing justice and that when they fail in this purpose they become the dangerously structured dams that block the flow of social progress. I had hoped that the white moderate would understand that the present tension in the South is a necessary phase of the transition from an obnoxious negative peace, in which the Negro passively accepted his unjust plight, to a substantive and positive peace, in which all men will respect the dignity and worth of human personality. Actually, we who engage in nonviolent direct action are not the creators of tension. We merely bring to the surface the hidden tension that is already alive. We bring it out in the open, where it can be seen and dealt with. Like a boil that can never be cured so long as it is covered up but must be opened with all its ugliness to the natural medicines of air and light, injustice must be exposed, with all the tension its exposure creates, to the light of human conscience and the air of national opinion, before it can be cured.

25   In your statement you assert that our actions, even though peaceful, must be condemned because they precipitate violence. But is this a logical assertion? Isn't this like condemning a robbed man because his possession of money precipitated the evil act of robbery? Isn't this like condemning Socrates because his unswerving commitment to truth and his philosophical inquiries precipitated the act by the misguided populace in which they made him drink hemlock? Isn't this like condemning Jesus Christ because his unique God-consciousness and never-ceasing devotion to God's will precipitated the evil act of crucifixion? We must come to see that, as the federal courts have consistently affirmed, it is wrong to urge an individual to cease his efforts to gain his basic constitutional rights because the quest may precipitate violence. Society must protect the robbed and punish the robber.

26   I had also hoped that the white moderate would reject the myth concerning time in relation to the struggle for freedom. I

have just received a letter from a white brother in Texas. He writes: "All Christians know that the colored people will receive equal rights eventually, but it is possible that you are in too great a religious hurry. It has taken Christianity almost two thousand years to accomplish what it has. The teachings of Christ take time to come to earth." Such an attitude stems from a tragic misconception of time, from the strangely irrational notion that there is something in the very flow of time that will inevitably cure all ills. Actually, time itself is neutral; it can be used either destructively or constructively. More and more I feel that the people of ill will have used time much more effectively than have the people of good will. We will have to repent in this generation not merely for the hateful words and actions of the bad people, but for the appalling silence of the good people. Human progress never rolls in on wheels of inevitability; it comes through the tireless efforts of men willing to be co-workers with God, and without this hard work, time itself becomes an ally of the forces of social stagnation. We must use time creatively, in the knowledge that the time is always ripe to do right. Now is the time to make real the promise of democracy and transform our pending national elegy into a creative psalm of brotherhood. Now is the time to lift our national policy from the quicksand of racial injustice to the solid rock of human dignity.

27   You speak of our activity in Birmingham as extreme. At first I was rather disappointed that fellow clergymen would see my non-violent efforts as those of an extremist. I began thinking about the fact that I stand in the middle of two opposing forces in the Negro community. One is a force of complacency, made up in part of Negroes who, as a result of long years of oppression, are so drained of self-respect and a sense of "somebodiness" that they have adjusted to segregation; and in part of a few middle-class Negroes who, because of a degree of academic and economic security and because in some ways they profit by segregation, have become insensitive to the problems of the masses. The other force is one of bitterness and hatred, and it comes perilously close to advocating violence. It is expressed in the various black nationalist groups that are springing up across the nation, the largest and best-known being Elijah Muhammad's Muslim movement. Nourished by the Negro's frustration over the continued exist-

ence of racial discrimination, this movement is made up of
people who have lost faith in America, who have absolutely repudiated Christianity, and who have concluded that the white
man is an incorrigible "devil."

28   I have tried to stand between these two forces, saying that we
need emulate neither the "do-nothingism" of the complacent nor
the hatred and despair of the black nationalist. For there is the
more excellent way of love and nonviolent protest. I am grateful
to God that, through the influence of the Negro church, the way
of nonviolence became an integral part of our struggle.

29   If this philosophy had not emerged, by now many streets of the
South would, I am convinced, be flowing with blood. And I am
further convinced that if our white brothers dismiss as "rabble-
rousers" and "outside agitators" those of us who employ nonviolent direct action, and if they refuse to support our nonviolent
efforts, millions of Negroes will, out of frustration and despair,
seek solace and security in black-nationalist ideologies—a development that would inevitably lead to a frightening racial nightmare.

30   Oppressed people cannot remain oppressed forever. The yearning for freedom eventually manifests itself, and that is what has
happened to the American Negro. Something within has reminded him of his birthright of freedom, and something without
has reminded him that it can be gained. Consciously or unconsciously, he has been caught up by the *Zeitgeist*, and with his
black brothers of Africa and his brown and yellow brothers of
Asia, South America, and the Caribbean, the United States Negro
is moving with a sense of great urgency toward the promised
land of racial justice. If one recognizes this vital urge that has
engulfed the Negro community, one should readily understand
why public demonstrations are taking place. The Negro has many
pent-up resentments and latent frustrations, and he must release
them. So let him march; let him make prayer pilgrimages to the
city hall; let him go on freedom rides—and try to understand
why he must do so. If his repressed emotions are not released in
nonviolent ways, they will seek expression through violence; this
is not a threat but a fact of history. So I have not said to my people, "Get rid of your discontent." Rather, I have tried to say that
this normal and healthy discontent can be channeled into the

creative outlet of nonviolent direct action. And now this approach is being termed extremist.

31   But though I was initially disappointed at being categorized as an extremist, as I continued to think about the matter I gradually gained a measure of satisfaction from the label. Was not Jesus an extremist for love: "Love your enemies, bless them that curse you, do good to them that hate you, and pray for them which despitefully use you, and persecute you." Was not Amos an extremist for justice: "Let justice roll down like waters and righteousness like an ever-flowing stream." Was not Paul an extremist for the Christian gospel: "I bear in my body the marks of the Lord Jesus." Was not Martin Luther an extremist: "Here I stand; I cannot do otherwise, so help me God." And John Bunyan: "I will stay in jail to the end of my days before I make a butchery of my conscience." And Abraham Lincoln: "This nation cannot survive half slave and half free." And Thomas Jefferson: "We hold these truths to be self-evident, that all men are created equal. . . ." So the question is not whether we will be extremists, but what kind of extremists we will be. Will we be extremists for hate or for love? Will we be extremists for the preservation of injustice or for the extension of justice? In that dramatic scene on Calvary's hill three men were crucified. We must never forget that all three were crucified for the same crime —the crime of extremism. Two were extremists for immorality, and thus fell below their environment. The other, Jesus Christ, was an extremist for love, truth, and goodness, and thereby rose above his environment. Perhaps the South, the nation, and the world are in dire need of creative extremists.

32   I had hoped that the white moderate would see this need. Perhaps I was too optimistic; perhaps I expected too much. I suppose I should have realized that few members of the oppressor race can understand the deep groans and passionate yearnings of the oppressed race, and still fewer have the vision to see that injustice must be rooted out by strong, persistent, and determined action. I am thankful, however, that some of our white brothers in the South have grasped the meaning of this social revolution and committed themselves to it. They are still all too few in quantity, but they are big in quality. Some—such as Ralph McGill, Lillian Smith, Harry Golden, James McBride Dabbs, Ann

Braden and Sarah Patton Boyle—have written about our struggle
in eloquent and prophetic terms. Others have marched with us
down nameless streets of the South. They have languished in
filthy, roach-infested jails, suffering the abuse and brutality of
policemen who view them as "dirty nigger-lovers." Unlike so
many of their moderate brothers and sisters, they have recognized
the urgency of the moment and sensed the need for powerful
"action" antidotes to combat the disease of segregation.

33   Let me take note of my other major disappointment. I have
been so greatly disappointed with the white church and its
leadership. Of course, there are some notable exceptions. I am
not unmindful of the fact that each of you has taken some
significant stands on this issue. I commend you, Reverend
Stallings, for your Christian stand on this past Sunday, in welcom-
ing Negroes to your worship service on a nonsegregated basis. I
commend the Catholic leaders of this state for integrating Spring
Hill College several years ago.

34   But despite these notable exceptions, I must honestly reiterate
that I have been disappointed with the church. I do not say this
as one of those negative critics who can always find something
wrong with the church. I say this as a minister of the gospel, who
loves the church; who was nurtured in its bosom; who has been
sustained by its spiritual blessings and who will remain true to
it as long as the cord of life shall lengthen.

35   When I was suddenly catapulted into the leadership of the
bus protest in Montgomery, Alabama, a few years ago, I felt we
would be supported by the white church. I felt that the white
ministers, priests, and rabbis of the South would be among our
strongest allies. Instead, some have been outright opponents,
refusing to understand the freedom movement and misrepresenting its leaders; all too many others have been more cautious
than courageous and have remained silent behind the anesthetiz-
ing security of stained-glass windows.

36   In spite of my shattered dreams, I came to Birmingham with
the hope that the white religious leadership of this community
would see the justice of our cause and, with deep moral concern,
would serve as the channel through which our just grievances
could reach the power structure. I had hoped that each of you
would understand. But again I have been disappointed.

37 I have heard numerous southern religious leaders admonish their worshippers to comply with a desegregation decision because it is the law, but I have longed to hear white ministers declare: "Follow this decree because integration is morally right and because the Negro is your brother." In the midst of blatant injustices inflicted upon the Negro, I have watched white churchmen stand on the sideline and mouth pious irrelevancies and sanctimonious trivialities. In the midst of a mighty struggle to rid our nation of racial and economic injustice, I have heard many ministers say: "Those are social issues, with which the gospel has no real concern." And I have watched many churches commit themselves to a completely otherworldly religion which makes a strange, un-Biblical distinction between body and soul, between the sacred and the secular.

38 I have traveled the length and breadth of Alabama, Mississippi, and all the other southern states. On sweltering summer days and crisp autumn mornings I have looked at the South's beautiful churches with their lofty spires pointing heavenward. I have beheld the impressive outlines of her massive religious-education buildings. Over and over I have found myself asking: "What kind of people worship here? Who is their God? Where were their voices when the lips of Governor Barnett dripped with words of interposition and nullification? Where were they when Governor Wallace gave a clarion call for defiance and hatred? Where were their voices of support when bruised and weary Negro men and women decided to rise from the dark dungeons of complacency to the bright hills of creative protest?"

39 Yes, these questions are still in my mind. In deep disappointment I have wept over the laxity of the church. But be assured that my tears have been tears of love. There can be no deep disappointment where there is not deep love. Yes, I love the church. How could I do otherwise? I am in the rather unique position of being the son, the grandson, and the great-grandson of preachers. Yes, I see the church as the body of Christ. But, oh! How we have blemished and scarred that body through social neglect and through fear of being nonconformists.

40 There was a time when the church was very powerful—in the time when the early Christians rejoiced at being deemed worthy to suffer for what they believed. In those days the church was

not merely a thermometer that recorded the ideas and principles of popular opinion; it was a thermostat that transformed the mores of society. Whenever the early Christians entered a town, the people in power became disturbed and immediately sought to convict the Christians for being "disturbers of the peace" and "outside agitators." But the Christians pressed on, in the conviction that they were "a colony of heaven," called to obey God rather than man. Small in number, they were big in commitment. They were too God-intoxicated to be "astronomically intimidated." By their effort and example they brought an end to such ancient evils as infanticide and gladiatorial contests.

41   Things are different now. So often the contemporary church is a weak, ineffectual voice with an uncertain sound. So often it is an archdefender of the status quo. Far from being disturbed by the presence of the church, the power structure of the average community is consoled by the church's silent—and often even vocal—sanction of things as they are.

42   But the judgment of God is upon the church as never before. If today's church does not recapture the sacrificial spirit of the early church, it will lose its authenticity, forfeit the loyalty of millions, and be dismissed as an irrelevant social club with no meaning for the twentieth century. Every day I meet young people whose disappointment with the church has turned into outright disgust.

43   Perhaps I have once again been too optimistic. Is organized religion too inextricably bound to the status quo to save our nation and the world? Perhaps I must turn my faith to the inner spiritual church, the church within the church, as the true *ekklesia*[2] and the hope of the world. But again I am thankful to God that some noble souls from the ranks of organized religion have broken loose from the paralyzing chains of conformity and joined us as active partners in the struggle for freedom. They have left their secure congregations and walked the streets of Albany, Georgia, with us. They have gone down the highways of the South on tortuous rides for freedom. Yes, they have gone to jail with us. Some have been dismissed from their churches, have lost the support of their bishops and fellow ministers. But they

[2]The Greek New Testament word for the early Christian church.

have acted in the faith that right defeated is stronger than evil triumphant. Their witness has been the spiritual salt that has preserved the true meaning of the gospel in these troubled times. They have carved a tunnel of hope through the dark mountain of disappointment.

44 I hope the church as a whole will meet the challenge of this decisive hour. But even if the church does not come to the aid of justice, I have no despair about the future. I have no fear about the outcome of our struggle in Birmingham, even if our motives are at present misunderstood. We will reach the goal of freedom in Birmingham and all over the nation, because the goal of America is freedom. Abused and scorned though we may be, our destiny is tied up with America's destiny. Before the pilgrims landed at Plymouth, we were here. Before the pen of Jefferson etched the majestic words of the Declaration of Independence across the pages of history, we were here. For more than two centuries our forebears labored in this country without wages; they made cotton king; they built the homes of their masters while suffering gross injustice and shameful humiliation—and yet out of a bottomless vitality they continued to thrive and develop. If the inexpressible cruelties of slavery could not stop us, the opposition we now face will surely fail. We will win our freedom because the sacred heritage of our nation and the eternal will of God are embodied in our echoing demands.

45 Before closing I feel impelled to mention one other point in your statement that has troubled me profoundly. You warmly commended the Birmingham police force for keeping "order" and "preventing violence." I doubt that you would have so warmly commended the police force if you had seen its dogs sinking their teeth into unarmed, nonviolent Negroes. I doubt that you would so quickly commend the policemen if you were to observe their ugly and inhumane treatment of Negroes here in the city jail; if you were to watch them push and curse old Negro women and young Negro girls; if you were to see them slap and kick old Negro men and young boys; if you were to observe them, as they did on two occasions, refuse to give us food because we wanted to sing our grace together. I cannot join you in your praise of the Birmingham police department.

46 It is true that the police have exercised a degree of discipline in

handling the demonstrators. In this sense they have conducted themselves rather "nonviolently" in public. But for what purpose? To preserve the evil system of segregation. Over the past few years I have consistently preached that nonviolence demands that the means we use must be as pure as the ends we seek. I have tried to make clear that it is wrong to use immoral means to attain moral ends. But now I must affirm that it is just as wrong, or perhaps even more so, to use moral means to preserve immoral ends. Perhaps Mr. Connor and his policemen have been rather nonviolent in public, as was Chief Pritchett in Albany, Georgia, but they have used the moral means of nonviolence to maintain the immoral end of racial injustice. As T. S. Eliot has said, "The last temptation is the greatest treason: To do the right deed for the wrong reason."

47   I wish you had commended the Negro sit-inners and demonstrators of Birmingham for their sublime courage, their willingness to suffer, and their amazing discipline in the midst of great provocation. One day the South will recognize its real heroes. They will be the James Merediths, with the noble sense of purpose that enables them to face jeering and hostile mobs, and with the agonizing loneliness that characterizes the life of the pioneer. They will be old, oppressed, battered Negro women, symbolized in a seventy-two-year-old woman in Montgomery, Alabama, who rose up with a sense of dignity and with her people decided not to ride segregated buses, and who responded with ungrammatical profundity to one who inquired about her weariness: "My feets is tired, but my soul is at rest." They will be the young high school and college students, the young ministers of the gospel and a host of their elders, courageously and nonviolently sitting in at lunch counters and willingly going to jail for conscience's sake. One day the South will know that when these disinherited children of God sat down at lunch counters, they were in reality standing up for what is best in the American dream and for the most sacred values in our Judaeo-Christian heritage, thereby bringing our nation back to those great wells of democracy which were dug deep by the founding fathers in their formulation of the Constitution and the Declaration of Independence.

48   Never before have I written so long a letter. I'm afraid it is

much too long to take your precious time. I can assure you that it would have been much shorter if I had been writing from a comfortable desk, but what else can one do when he is alone in a narrow jail cell, other than write long letters, think long thoughts, and pray long prayers?

49   If I have said anything in this letter that overstates the truth and indicates an unreasonable impatience, I beg you to forgive me. If I have said anything that understates the truth and indicates my having a patience that allows me to settle for anything less than brotherhood, I beg God to forgive me.

50   I hope this letter finds you strong in the faith. I also hope that circumstances will soon make it possible for me to meet each of you, not as an integrationist or a civil-rights leader but as a fellow clergyman and a Christian brother. Let us all hope that the dark clouds of racial prejudice will soon pass away and the deep fog of misunderstanding will be lifted from our fear-drenched communities, and in some not too distant tomorrow the radiant stars of love and brotherhood will shine over our great nation with all their scintillating beauty.

Yours for the cause of Peace and Brotherhood.
Martin Luther King, Jr.

spring
GERARD MANLEY HOPKINS

Nothing is so beautiful as spring—
  When weeds, in wheels, shoot long and lovely and lush;
  Thrush's eggs look little low heavens, and thrush
Through the echoing timber does so rinse and wring
The ear, it strikes like lightnings to hear him sing;   5
  The glassy peartree leaves and blooms, they brush
  The descending blue; that blue is all in a rush
With richness; the racing lambs too have fair their fling.

What is all this juice and all this joy?   9
  A strain of the earth's sweet being in the beginning
In Eden garden.—Have, get, before it cloy,
  Before it cloud, Christ, lord, and sour with sinning,
Innocent mind and Mayday in girl and boy,
  Most, O maid's child, thy choice and worthy the winning. 14

Reprinted with permission of Oxford University Press, from *Poems of Gerard Manley Hopkins*, third edition, edited by W. H. Gardner. Copyright 1948 by Oxford University Press.

DISCUSSION AND WRITING MATERIAL

"Democracy"

What function does each of the three paragraphs perform in the definition? What is the difference between the political and historical meanings of the term? Extend Becker's definition of democracy by offering an illustration from a personal experience.

"Liberals and Conservatives"

What are the basic differences between the two philosophies? How do these differences manifest themselves in the political arena today? Present an argument from both a conservative and liberal point of view on a contemporary issue (for example, the legalization of marijuana, censorship, the control of the environment, etc.).

Complete the following outline by putting in the paragraph numbers and subheadings.

Introduction ( )
I.   The liberal tradition ( )
II. The conservative tradition ( )
III. The liberal and conservative contributions to Democracy ( )
IV. Weaknesses and strengths of both positions ( )
     Conclusion ( )

What is the basic method used to extend the definition of the two terms? What function does the material in Part IV of the above outline serve in the essay?

"The Negro: An Essay on Definition"

Explain the structural purposes of paragraphs 7–9. Discuss the basis for the extension of the term. What structural function do paragraphs 16–21 perform? Outline the different facets that have led to the situation where there is no "discrete, monolithic Negro culture."

"Letter from Birmingham Jail"

From your personal experience, how effective do you feel the approach Dr. King suggests in paragraph 6 would be? What is the basis of development in paragraphs 6–11 and 31? Explain the definition process that is used in paragraph 15. Analyze the effectiveness of the sentence structure in paragraph 14. How does the repetition of sounds contribute to the overall effect of the paragraph? How effective is the use of imagery and metaphor in paragraph 14? Discuss the use of metaphor in paragraph 26. How effective is the thermometer–thermostat metaphor in paragraph 40?

"Spring"

Explain how the poet defines Spring in his poem. What is the relationship between the two stanzas? Compare the imagery and sound patterns of the two stanzas. What is the function of the poet's question?

ANALYSIS

Like most rhetorical techniques, analysis is a process we perform unconsciously nearly every day of our lives. For example, each time we budget our paychecks, or plan a work-study schedule, or examine the contents of an editorial, or explain the workings of a piece of machinery, we are almost surely engaging in some form of analysis, however informal. As a technique of expository writing, analysis has as its purpose the *informing* of the reader of the components and composition of a particular subject. Analyzing can be applied to both static and dynamic subject matter, though in the latter case it frequently assumes many of the techniques of narration; consequently, we will confine ourselves here to the former, that is, such static subjects as ideas, structured groups, and objects. Topics of this sort can be analyzed by one of two methods (or in some cases by a combination of both): classification or division.

Almost invariably, classification analysis is applicable when the subject under consideration is plural in number. Airplanes, for instance, may be classified by their use. Thus we can designate some planes as private, others as commercial, and still others as military. Literature can be—and often is—classified generically as poetry, drama, the short story, and the novel. The federal government can be classified by its branches: executive, judicial, and legislative. The point is that classification analysis presumes that the resultant categories will be wholes or totalities in themselves rather than single parts of a larger subject.

Not surprisingly then, analysis by division carries this process several steps further and breaks the single entity down into its constituent parts. By way of illustration we might simply expand on our examples of the preceding paragraph. An airplane may be divided into its wings, engines, fuselage, tail, etc.; similarly, poetry may be divided into such types as epic, dramatic, lyric, and narrative, to name but a few (and of course it can be further divided into metrical lines and words, if desired); and finally, the legislative arm of government can be divided into the two houses of congress and, ultimately, into their individual members. Here again the point is that the results of analysis by division are singular, that is, the individual *parts* of the subject or object being analyzed.

Regardless of the method of analysis employed, there are certain pitfalls to be avoided and certain guidelines to follow. It goes without saying that all analyses should be logically sound and, depending on the extent of information required, all should be thorough. Logic is the sort of self-evident virtue we all pay lip service to, but in rhetorical analysis it is easy enough to slip into some common fallacies. For example, one might base an analysis on two or more principles of classification or division; and in such a case the results could be grossly misleading. If the manager of a plant classified his employees as technical, sales, and administrative personnel and then added the category of employees over forty, it is clear that two distinct principles of classification would be operative at the same time: classification by duty or training and by age. Granted, the manager might very well want to know the ages of his employees and he might want that information broken down by duty or branch; but what he is looking for then is an entirely different sort of classification from our original list, which doubtless would include inadvertent and indeed irrelevant overlapping. Analysis will produce certain kinds of information, but the purpose of that information must be clearly in mind before it is undertaken.

Another related fallacy, not uncommon to analysis, is the failure to create categories of division or classification which are mutually exclusive. An analysis of a military unit into officers, warrant officers, Captain Smith, and enlisted men would obviously be fallacious on these grounds simply because Captain Smith belongs in the first category cited. And the example noted in the preceding paragraph would also serve to illustrate this weakness in analysis (though of course it illustrates the error of analysis by two different principles as well), *if* any employees over forty were found in any of the three branches employed.

Finally, logical analysis requires that the categories at each stage of the analysis be roughly comparable. To extend our military example a bit further, to classify the organization of the army as General Jones, warrant officers, and enlisted men is to violate this principle of analysis, for the three items are clearly not comparable (no matter how swollen General Jones' view of his role may be). In other words, comparability implies a reasonable numerical correspondence. Thus, this breakdown should read officers, warrant officers, and enlisted men.

The problem of thoroughness in analysis is generally a matter of degree, and inevitably this becomes a matter of judgment. Certainly there exist a vast number of stages or levels to which the analysis of virtually any subject can be taken, and it is the responsibility of the writer to determine which levels are appropriate to his audience and to his purpose. And no one can do this for him. For a general study of the committee structure of the United States Senate, a simple classification of those committees and their predominant function might well suffice. But if the writer is addressing himself to a politically more knowledgeable and sophisticated audience, he would be well advised to continue his analysis through subcommittees, individual efforts, and delegated responsibilities—as far, indeed, as he had to go to fully clarify his subject.

In organizing analyses of any kind, the novice writer might feel most at ease if he states initially his subject, the principle of analysis to be used, and the components to be considered. Proceeding in this fashion, he will have at once a built-in structure for his essay, for the several components of the subject will frequently serve as the logical steps in the paper; in effect, such an initial statement acts as an outline for writer and reader alike.

In the following section, analysis in one form or another is the guiding principle of each writer. The examples we have employed in this introduction are, like most such illustrations, absurdly simple, and even a cursory reading of the five selections in the unit will make it painfully clear that a complete analysis is most often a highly complex process, one in which many rhetorical principles are often at work. Nevertheless, for our immediate purposes, it will be profitable to examine these selections on the bases of analysis suggested here and to judge especially the logic, thoroughness, and clarity of each author.

the best-known monument of american prose

GILBERT HIGHET

Fourscore and seven years ago . . .[1]

1 These five words stand at the entrance to the best-known monument of American prose, one of the finest utterances in the

[1] Fourscore and seven years ago our fathers brought forth on this continent
a new nation, conceived in liberty, and dedicated to the proposition that all
men are created equal.

Now we are engaged in a great civil war, testing whether that nation, or
any nation so conceived or so dedicated, can long endure. We are met on a
great battle-field of that war. We have come to dedicate a portion of that
field, as a final resting place for those who here gave their lives that that nation might live. It is altogether fitting and proper that we should do this.

But, in a larger sense, we cannot dedicate—we cannot consecrate, we cannot hallow—this ground. The brave men, living and dead, who struggled
here, have consecrated it, far above our poor power to add or detract. The
world will little note, nor long remember, what we say here, but it can never
forget what they did here. It is for us the living, rather, to be dedicated here
to the unfinished work which they who fought here have thus far so nobly
advanced. It is rather for us to be here dedicated to the great task remaining
before us—that from these honored dead we take increased devotion to that
cause for which they gave the last full measure of devotion—that we here
highly resolve that these dead shall not have died in vain—that this nation,
under God, shall have a new birth of freedom—and that government of the
people, by the people, for the people, shall not perish from the earth.

Reprinted with permission of Oxford University Press, Inc., from *A Clerk
of Oxenford*, by Gilbert Highet. Copyright 1954 by Gilbert Highet.

entire language, and surely one of the greatest speeches in all history. Greatness is like granite: it is molded in fire, and it lasts for many centuries.

2   Fourscore and seven years ago . . . It is strange to think that President Lincoln was looking back to the 4th of July 1776, and that he and his speech are now further removed from us than he himself was from George Washington and the Declaration of Independence. Fourscore and seven years before the Gettysburg Address, a small group of patriots signed the Declaration. Fourscore and seven years after the Gettysburg Address, it was the year 1950 (in November 1950 the Chinese had just entered the war in Korea), and that date is already receding rapidly into our troubled, adventurous, and valiant past.

3   Inadequately prepared and at first scarcely realized in its full importance, the dedication of the graveyard at Gettysburg was one of the supreme moments of American history. The battle itself had been a turning point of the war. On the 4th of July 1863, General Meade repelled Lee's invasion of Pennsylvania. Although he did not follow up his victory, he had broken one of the most formidable aggressive enterprises of the Confederate armies. Losses were heavy on both sides. Thousands of dead were left on the field, and thousands of wounded died in the hot days following the battle. At first, their burial was more or less haphazard; but thoughtful men gradually came to feel that an adequate burying place and memorial were required. These were established by an interstate commission that autumn, and the finest speaker in the North was invited to dedicate them. This was the scholar and statesman Edward Everett of Harvard. He made a good speech—which is still extant: not at all academic, it is full of close strategic analysis and deep historical understanding.

4   Lincoln was not invited to speak, at first. Although people knew him as an effective debater, they were not sure whether he was capable of making a serious speech on such a solemn occasion. But one of the impressive things about Lincoln's career is that he constantly strove to *grow*. He was anxious to appear on that occasion and to say something worthy of it. (Also, it has been suggested, he was anxious to remove the impression that he did not know how to behave properly—an impression which

had been strengthened by a shocking story about his clowning on the battlefield of Antietam the previous year.) Therefore when he was invited he took considerable care with his speech. He drafted rather more than half of it in the White House before leaving, finished it in the hotel at Gettysburg the night before the ceremony (not in the train, as sometimes reported), and wrote out a fair copy next morning.

5   There are many accounts of the day itself, 19 November 1863. There are many descriptions of Lincoln, all showing the same curious blend of grandeur and awkwardness, or lack of dignity, or—it would be best to call it humility. In the procession he rode horseback: a tall lean man in a high plug hat, straddling a short horse, with his feet too near the ground. He arrived before the chief speaker, and had to wait patiently for half an hour or more. His own speech came right at the end of a long and exhausting ceremony, lasted less than three minutes, and made little impression on the audience. In part this was because they were tired, in part because (as eyewitnesses said) he ended almost before they knew he had begun, and in part because he did not speak the Address, but read it, very slowly, in a thin high voice, with a marked Kentucky accent, pronouncing "to" as "toe" and dropping his final R's.

6   Some people of course were alert enough to be impressed. Everett congratulated him at once. But most of the newspapers paid little attention to the speech, and some sneered at it. The *Patriot and Union* of Harrisburg wrote, "We pass over the silly remarks of the President; for the credit of the nation we are willing . . . that they shall no more be repeated or thought of"; and the London *Times* said, "The ceremony was rendered ludicrous by some of the sallies of that poor President Lincoln," calling his remarks "dull and commonplace." The first commendation of the Address came in a single sentence of the Chicago *Tribune,* and the first discriminating and detailed praise of it appeared in the Springfield *Republican,* the Providence *Journal,* and the Philadelphia *Bulletin.* However, three weeks after the ceremony and then again the following spring, the editor of *Harper's Weekly* published a sincere and thorough eulogy of the Address, and soon it was attaining recognition as a masterpiece.

7   At the time, Lincoln could not care much about the reception
of his words. He was exhausted and ill. In the train back to
Washington, he lay down with a wet towel on his head. He had
caught smallpox. At that moment he was incubating it, and he
was stricken down soon after he re-entered the White House.
Fortunately it was a mild attack, and it evoked one of his best
jokes: he told his visitors, "At last I have something I can give
to everybody."

8   He had more than that to give to everybody. He was a unique
person, far greater than most people realize until they read his
life with care. The wisdom of his policy, the sources of his states-
manship—these were things too complex to be discussed in a
brief essay. But we can say something about the Gettysburg
Address as a work of art.

9   A work of art. Yes: for Lincoln was a literary artist, trained
both by others and by himself. The textbooks he used as a boy
were full of difficult exercises and skillful devices in formal
rhetoric, stressing the qualities he practiced in his own speaking:
antithesis, parallelism, and verbal harmony. Then he read and
reread many admirable models of thought and expression: the
King James Bible, the essays of Bacon, the best plays of Shakespeare. His favorites were *Hamlet, Lear, Macbeth, Richard III,*
and *Henry VIII,* which he had read dozens of times. He loved
reading aloud, too, and spent hours reading poetry to his friends.
(He told his partner Herndon that he preferred getting the
sense of any document by reading it aloud.) Therefore his serious
speeches are important parts of the long and noble classical
tradition of oratory which begins in Greece, runs through Rome
to the modern world, and is still capable (if we do not neglect it)
of producing masterpieces.

10   The first proof of this is that the Gettysburg Address is full of
quotations—or rather of adaptations—which give it strength. It
is partly religious, partly (in the highest sense) political: therefore
it is interwoven with memories of the Bible and memories of
American history. The first and the last words are biblical
cadences. Normally Lincoln did not say "fourscore" when he
meant eighty; but on the solemn occasion he recalled the important dates in the Bible—such as the age of Abraham when
his first son was born to him, and he was "fourscore and six

years old" (Gen. 16:16; cf. Exod. 7:7). Similarly he did not say there was a chance that democracy might die out: he recalled the somber phrasing of the Book of Job—where Bildad speaks of the destruction of one who shall vanish without a trace, and says that "his branch shall be cut off; his remembrance shall perish from the earth" (Job 18:16–17; cf. Jer. 10:11, Micah 7:2). Then again, the famous description of our State as "government of the people, by the people, for the people" was adumbrated by Daniel Webster in 1830 (he spoke of "the people's government, made for the people, made by the people, and answerable to the people") and then elaborated in 1854 by the abolitionist Theodore Parker (as "government of all the people, by all the people, for all the people"). There is good reason to think that Lincoln took the important phrase "under God" (which he interpolated at the last moment) from Weems, the biographer of Washington; and we know that it had been used at least once by Washington himself.

11   Analyzing the Address further, we find that it is based on a highly imaginative theme, or groups of themes. The subject is—how can we put it so as not to disfigure it?—the subject is the kinship of life and death, that mysterious linkage which we see sometimes as the physical succession of birth and death in our world, sometimes as the contrast, which is perhaps a unity, between death and immortality. The first sentence is concerned with birth:

> Our *fathers brought forth a new* nation, *conceived* in liberty.

The final phrase but one expresses the hope that

> this nation, under God, shall have a *new birth* of freedom.

And the last phrase of all speaks of continuing life as the triumph over death. Again and again throughout the speech, this mystical contrast and kinship reappear: "those who *gave their lives* that that nation might *live*," "the brave men *living* and *dead*," and so in the central assertion that the dead have already consecrated their own burial place, while "it is for us, the *living*, rather to be dedicated . . . to the great task remaining." The Gettysburg Address is a prose poem; it belongs to the same world as the great elegies, and the adagios of Beethoven.

12 Its structure, however, is that of a skillfully contrived speech. The oratorical pattern is perfectly clear. Lincoln describes the occasion, dedicates the ground, and then draws a larger conclusion by calling on his hearers to dedicate themselves to the preservation of the Union. But within that, we can trace his constant use of at least two important rhetorical devices.

13 The first of these is *antithesis:* opposition, contrast. The speech is full of it. Listen:

> The world will little *note*
>   nor long *remember*   what *we say here*
> but   it can never *forget*   what *they did here*.

And so in nearly every sentence: "brave men, *living* and *dead*"; "to *add* or *detract*." There is antithesis of the Founding Fathers and the men of Lincoln's own time:

> Our *fathers brought forth* a new nation . . .
> now *we* are testing whether that nation . . . can *long endure*.

And there is the more terrible antithesis of those who have already died and those who still live to do their duty. Now, antithesis is the figure of contrast and conflict. Lincoln was speaking in the midst of a great civil war.

14 The other important pattern is different. It is technically called *tricolon*—the division of an idea into three harmonious parts, usually of increasing power. The most famous phrase of the Address is a tricolon:

> government of the people
>   by the people
> and   for the people.

The most solemn sentence is a tricolon:

> we cannot dedicate
> we cannot consecrate
> we cannot hallow   this ground.

And above all, the last sentence (which has sometimes been criticized as too complex) is essentially two parallel phrases, with a tricolon growing out of the second and then producing another tricolon: a trunk, three branches, and a cluster of flowers. Lincoln says that it is for his hearers to be dedicated to the great task remaining before them. Then he goes on:

that from these honored dead

—apparently he means "in such a way that from these honored dead"—

we take increased devotion to that cause . . .

Next, he restates this more briefly:

that we here highly resolve . . .

And now the actual resolution follows, in three parts of growing intensity:

that these dead shall not have died in vain
that this nation, under God, shall have a new birth of freedom
and that

(one more tricolon)

government of the people
　　　　　　by the people
and　　　　　for the people
shall not perish from the earth.

Now, the tricolon is the figure which, through division, emphasizes basic harmony and unity. Lincoln used antithesis because he was speaking to a people at war. He used the tricolon because he was hoping, planning, praying for peace.

15 No one thinks that when he was drafting the Gettysburg Address, Lincoln deliberately looked up these quotations and consciously chose these particular patterns of thought. No, he chose the theme. From its development and from the emotional tone of the entire occasion, all the rest followed, or grew—by that marvelous process of choice and rejection which is essential to artistic creation. It does not spoil such a work of art to analyze it as closely as we have done; it is altogether fitting and proper that we should do this: for it helps us to penetrate more deeply into the rich meaning of the Gettysburg Address, and it allows us the very rare privilege of watching the workings of a great man's mind.

politics and the english language
GEORGE ORWELL

1 Most people who bother with the matter at all would admit that the English language is in a bad way, but it is generally assumed that we cannot by conscious action do anything about it. Our civilization is decadent, and our language—so the argument runs—must inevitably share in the general collapse. It follows that any struggle against the abuse of language is a sentimental archaism, like preferring candles to electric light or hansom cabs to aeroplanes. Underneath this lies the half-conscious belief that language is a natural growth and not an instrument which we shape for our own purposes.

2 Now, it is clear that the decline of a language must ultimately have political and economic causes: it is not due simply to the bad influence of this or that individual writer. But an effect can become a cause, reinforcing the original cause and producing the same effect in an intensified form, and so on indefinitely. A man may take to drink because he feels himself to be a failure, and then fail all the more completely because he drinks. It is rather the same thing that is happening to the English language. It becomes ugly and inaccurate because our thoughts are foolish, but the slovenliness of our language makes it easier for us to have foolish thoughts. The point is that the process is reversible. Modern English, especially written English, is full of bad habits

Reprinted with permission of Harcourt, Brace & World, Inc., from *Shooting an Elephant and Other Essays*, by George Orwell. Copyright 1945, 1946, 1949, 1950 by Sonia Brownell Orwell.

which spread by imitation and which can be avoided if one is willing to take the necessary trouble. If one gets rid of these habits one can think more clearly, and to think clearly is a necessary first step towards political regeneration: so that the fight against bad English is not frivolous and is not the exclusive concern of professional writers. I will come back to this presently, and I hope that by that time the meaning of what I have said here will have become clearer. Meanwhile, here are five specimens of the English language as it is now habitually written.

3   These five passages have not been picked out because they are especially bad—I could have quoted far worse if I had chosen —but because they illustrate various of the mental vices from which we now suffer. They are a little below the average, but are fairly representative samples. I number them so that I can refer back to them when necessary:

(1) I am not, indeed, sure whether it is not true to say that the Milton who once seemed not unlike a seventeenth-century Shelley had not become, out of an experience ever more bitter in each year, more alien [*sic*] to the founder of that Jesuit sect which nothing could induce him to tolerate.

PROFESSOR HAROLD LASKI
(Essay in *Freedom of Expression*)

(2) Above all, we cannot play ducks and drakes with a native battery of idioms which prescribes such egregious collocations of vocables as the Basic *put up with* for *tolerate* or *put at a loss* for *bewilder*.

PROFESSOR LANCELOT HOGBEN (*Interglossa*)

(3) On the one side we have the free personality: by definition it is not neurotic, for it has neither conflict nor dream. Its desires, such as they are, are transparent, for they are just what institutional approval keeps in the forefront of consciousness; another institutional pattern would alter their number and intensity; there is little in them that is natural, irreducible, or culturally dangerous. But *on the other side,* the social bond itself is nothing but the mutual reflection of these self-secure integrities. Recall the definition of love. Is not this the very picture of a small academic? Where is there a place in this hall of mirrors for either personality or fraternity?

Essay on psychology in *Politics* (New York)

(4) All the "best people" from the gentlemen's clubs, and all the frantic fascist captains, united in common hatred of Socialism and bestial horror of the rising tide of the mass revolutionary movement, have turned to acts of provocation, to foul incendiarism, to medieval legends of poisoned wells, to legalize their own destruction of proletarian organizations, and rouse the agitated petty-bourgeoisie to chauvinistic fervor on behalf of the fight against the revolutionary way out of the crisis.

Communist pamphlet

(5) If a new spirit *is* to be infused into this old country, there is one thorny and contentious reform which must be tackled, and that is the humanization and galvanization of the B.B.C. Timidity here will bespeak canker and atrophy of the soul. The heart of Britain may be sound and of strong beat, for instance, but the British lion's roar at present is like that of Bottom in Shakespeare's *Midsummer Night's Dream*—as gentle as any sucking dove. A virile new Britain cannot continue indefinitely to be traduced in the eyes, or rather ears, of the world by the effete languors of Langham Place, brazenly masquerading as "standard English." When the Voice of Britain is heard at nine o'clock, better far and infinitely less ludicrous to hear aitches honestly dropped than the present priggish, inflated, inhibited, schoolma'amish arch braying of blameless bashful mewing maidens!

Letter in *Tribune*

4   Each of these passages has faults of its own, but, quite apart from avoidable ugliness, two qualities are common to all of them. The first is staleness of imagery; the other is lack of precision. The writer either has a meaning and cannot express it, or he inadvertently says something else, or he is almost indifferent as to whether his words mean anything or not. This mixture of vagueness and sheer incompetence is the most marked characteristic of modern English prose, and especially of any kind of political writing. As soon as certain topics are raised, the concrete melts into the abstract and no one seems able to think of turns of speech that are not hackneyed: prose consists less and less of *words* chosen for the sake of their meaning, and more and more of *phrases* tacked together like the sections of a prefabricated hen-house. I list below, with notes and examples, various of the tricks by means of which the work of prose-construction is habitually dodged:

Dying metaphors. A newly-invented metaphor assists thought by evoking a visual image, while on the other hand a metaphor which is technically "dead" (e.g., *iron resolution*) has in effect reverted to being an ordinary word and can generally be used without loss of vividness. But in between these two classes there is a huge dump of worn-out metaphors which have lost all evocative power and are merely used because they save people the trouble of inventing phrases for themselves. Examples are: *Ring the changes on, take up the cudgels for, toe the line, ride roughshod over, stand shoulder to shoulder with, play into the hands of, an axe to grind, grist to the mill, fishing in troubled waters, on the order of the day, Achilles' heel, swan song, hotbed.* Many of these are used without knowledge of their meaning (what is a "rift," for instance?), and incompatible metaphors are frequently mixed, a sure sign that the writer is not interested in what he is saying. Some metaphors now current have been twisted out of their original meaning without those who use them even being aware of the fact. For example, *toe the line* is sometimes written *tow the line.* Another example is *the hammer and the anvil,* now always used with the implication that the anvil gets the worst of it. In real life it is always the anvil that breaks the hammer, never the other way about: a writer who stopped to think what he was saying would be aware of this, and would avoid perverting the original phrase.

Operators, or *verbal false limbs.* These save the trouble of picking out appropriate verbs and nouns, and at the same time pad each sentence with extra syllables which give it an appearance of symmetry. Characteristic phrases are: *render inoperative, militate against, prove unacceptable, make contact with, be subjected to, give rise to, give grounds for, have the effect of, play a leading part (role) in, make itself felt, take effect, exhibit a tendency to, serve the purpose of,* etc., etc. The keynote is the elimination of simple verbs. Instead of being a single word, such as *break, stop, spoil, mend, kill,* a verb becomes a *phrase,* made up of a noun or adjective tacked on to some general-purposes verb such as *prove, serve, form, play, render.* In addition, the passive voice is wherever possible used in preference to the active, and noun constructions are used instead of gerunds (*by examination of* instead of *by examining*). The range of verbs is further cut down by means of the *-ize* and *de-* formations, and banal statements are given an appearance of profundity by means of the *not un-* formation. Simple conjunctions and prepositions are replaced by such phrases as *with respect to, having regard to, the fact that, by dint of, in*

view of, in the interests of, on the hypothesis that; and the ends
of sentences are saved from anti-climax by such resounding com-
monplaces as *greatly to be desired, cannot be left out of account,
a development to be expected in the near future, deserving of
serious consideration, brought to a satisfactory conclusion,* and so
on and so forth.

Pretentious diction. Words like *phenomenon, element, individual* (as noun), *objective, categorical, effective, virtual, basic,
primary, promote, constitute, exhibit, exploit, utilize, eliminate,
liquidate,* are used to dress up simple statements and give an air
of scientific impartiality to biased judgments. Adjectives like
*epoch-making, epic, historic, unforgettable, triumphant, age-old,
inevitable, inexorable, veritable,* are used to dignify the sordid
processes of international politics, while writing that aims at glori-
fying war usually takes on an archaic color, its characteristic
words being: *realm, throne, chariot, mailed fist, trident, sword,
shield, buckler, banner, jackboot, clarion.* Foreign words and expressions such as *cul de sac, ancien régime, deus ex machina,
mutatis mutandis, status quo, gleichschaltung, weltanschauung,*
are used to give an air of culture and elegance. Except for the
useful abbreviations *i.e., e.g.,* and *etc.,* there is no real need for
any of the hundreds of foreign phrases now current in English.
Bad writers, and especially scientific, political and sociological
writers, are nearly always haunted by the notion that Latin or
Greek words are grander than Saxon ones, and unnecessary words
like *expedite, ameliorate, predict, extraneous, deracinated, clan-
destine, subaqueous* and hundreds of others constantly gain
ground from their Anglo-Saxon opposite numbers.[1] The jargon
peculiar to Marxist writing (*hyena, hangman, cannibal, petty
bourgeois, these gentry, lackey, flunkey, mad dog, White Guard,*
etc.) consists largely of words and phrases translated from Russian, German or French; but the normal way of coining a new
word is to use a Latin or Greek root with the appropriate affix
and, where necessary, the *-ize* formation. It is often easier to make
up words of this kind (*de-regionalize, im-permissible, extramari-*

[1]An interesting illustration of this is the way in which the English flower
names which were in use till very recently are being ousted by Greek ones,
snap-dragon becoming *antirrhinum, forget-me-not* becoming *myosotis,* etc. It
is hard to see any practical reason for this change of fashion: it is probably
due to an instinctive turning-away from the more homely word and a vague
feeling that the Greek word is scientific.

tal, non-fragmentary and so forth) than to think up the English words that will cover one's meaning. The result, in general, is an increase in slovenliness and vagueness.

Meaningless words. In certain kinds of writing, particularly in art criticism and literary criticism, it is normal to come across long passages which are almost completely lacking in meaning.[2] Words like *romantic, plastic, values, human, dead, sentimental, natural, vitality,* as used in art criticism, are strictly meaning-less, in the sense that they not only do not point to any dis-coverable object, but are hardly even expected to do so by the reader. When one critic writes, "The outstanding feature of Mr. X's work is its living quality," while another writes, "The im-mediately striking thing about Mr. X's work is its peculiar dead-ness," the reader accepts this as a simple difference of opinion. If words like *black* and *white* were involved, instead of the jargon words *dead* and *living,* he would see at once that language was being used in an improper way. Many political words are simi-larly abused. The word *Fascism* has now no meaning except in so far as it signifies "something not desirable." The words *democ-racy, socialism, freedom, patriotic, realistic, justice,* have each of them several different meanings which cannot be reconciled with one another. In the case of a word like *democracy,* not only is there no agreed definition, but the attempt to make one is re-sisted from all sides. It is almost universally felt that when we call a country democratic we are praising it: consequently the defenders of every kind of régime claim that it is a democracy, and fear that they might have to stop using the word if it were tied down to any one meaning. Words of this kind are often used in a consciously dishonest way. That is, the person who uses them has his own private definition, but allows his hearer to think he means something quite different. Statements like *Mar-shal Pétain was a true patriot, The Soviet Press is the freest in the world, The Catholic Church is opposed to persecution,* are almost always made with intent to deceive. Other words used in

[2]Example: "Comfort's catholicity of perception and image, strangely Whit-manesque in range, almost the exact opposite in aesthetic compulsion, con-tinues to evoke that trembling atmospheric accumulative hinting at a cruel, an inexorably serene timelessness. . . . Wrey Gardiner scores by aiming at simple bullseyes with precision. Only they are not so simple, and through this contented sadness runs more than the surface bittersweet of resignation." (*Poetry Quarterly.*)

variable meanings, in most cases more or less dishonestly, are: *class, totalitarian, science, progressive, reactionary, bourgeois, equality.*

5   Now that I have made this catalogue of swindles and perversions, let me give another example of the kind of writing that they lead to. This time it must of its nature be an imaginary one. I am going to translate a passage of good English into modern English of the worst sort. Here is a well-known verse from *Ecclesiastes:*

> I returned, and saw under the sun, that the race is not to the swift, nor the battle to the strong, neither yet bread to the wise, nor yet riches to men of understanding, nor yet favor to men of skill; but time and chance happeneth to them all.

6   Here it is in modern English:

> Objective consideration of contemporary phenomena compels the conclusion that success or failure in competitive activities exhibits no tendency to be commensurate with innate capacity, but that a considerable element of the unpredictable must invariably be taken into account.

7   This is a parody, but not a very gross one. Exhibit (3), above, for instance, contains several patches of the same kind of English. It will be seen that I have not made a full translation. The beginning and ending of the sentence follow the original meaning fairly closely, but in the middle the concrete illustrations—race, battle, bread—dissolve into the vague phrase "success or failure in competitive activities." This had to be so, because no modern writer of the kind I am discussing—no one capable of using phrases like "objective consideration of contemporary phenomena"—would ever tabulate his thoughts in that precise and detailed way. The whole tendency of modern prose is away from concreteness. Now analyze these two sentences a little more closely. The first contains 49 words but only 60 syllables, and all its words are those of everyday life. The second contains 38 words of 90 syllables: 18 of its words are from Latin roots, and one from Greek. The first sentence contains six vivid images, and only one phrase ("time and chance") that could be called vague. The second contains not a single fresh, arresting phrase, and in

spite of its 90 syllables it gives only a shortened version of the meaning contained in the first. Yet without a doubt it is the second kind of sentence that is gaining ground in modern English. I do not want to exaggerate. This kind of writing is not yet universal, and outcrops of simplicity will occur here and there in the worst-written page. Still, if you or I were told to write a few lines on the uncertainty of human fortunes, we should probably come much nearer to my imaginary sentence than to the one from *Ecclesiastes*.

8   As I have tried to show, modern writing at its worst does not consist in picking out words for the sake of their meaning and inventing images in order to make the meaning clearer. It consists in gumming together long strips of words which have already been set in order by someone else, and making the results presentable by sheer humbug. The attraction of this way of writing is that it is easy. It is easier—even quicker, once you have the habit—to say *In my opinion it is a not unjustifiable assumption that* than to say *I think*. If you use ready-made phrases, you not only don't have to hunt about for words; you also don't have to bother with the rhythms of your sentences, since these phrases are generally so arranged as to be more or less euphonious. When you are composing in a hurry—when you are dictating to a stenographer, for instance, or making a public speech —it is natural to fall into a pretentious, Latinized style. Tags like *a consideration which we should do well to bear in mind* or *a conclusion to which all of us would readily assent* will save many a sentence from coming down with a bump. By using stale metaphors, similes and idioms, you save much mental effort, at the cost of leaving your meaning vague, not only for your reader but for yourself. This is the significance of mixed metaphors. The sole aim of a metaphor is to call up a visual image. When these images clash—as in *The Fascist octopus has sung its swan song, the jackboot is thrown into the melting pot*—it can be taken as certain that the writer is not seeing a mental image of the objects he is naming; in other words he is not really thinking. Look again at the examples I gave at the beginning of this essay. Professor Laski (1) uses five negatives in 53 words. One of these is superfluous, making nonsense of the whole passage, and in addition there is the slip *alien* for *akin*, making further

nonsense, and several avoidable pieces of clumsiness which increase the general vagueness. Professor Hogben (2) plays ducks
and drakes with a battery which is able to write prescriptions,
and, while disapproving of the everyday phrase *put up with,* is
unwilling to look *egregious* up in the dictionary and see what it
means; (3), if one takes an uncharitable attitude towards it, is
simply meaningless: probably one could work out its intended
meaning by reading the whole of the article in which it occurs.
In (4), the writer knows more or less what he wants to say, but
an accumulation of stale phrases chokes him like tea leaves block-
ing a sink. In (5), words and meaning have almost parted company. People who write in this manner usually have a general
emotional meaning—they dislike one thing and want to express
solidarity with another—but they are not interested in the detail
of what they are saying. A scrupulous writer, in every sentence
that he writes, will ask himself at least four questions, thus:
What am I trying to say? What words will express it? What
image or idiom will make it clearer? Is this image fresh enough
to have an effect? And he will probably ask himself two more:
Could I put it more shortly? Have I said anything that is avoid-
ably ugly? But you are not obliged to go to all this trouble.
You can shirk it by simply throwing your mind open and letting the ready-made phrases come crowding in. They will construct your sentences for you—even think your thoughts for you,
to a certain extent—and at need they will perform the important
service of partially concealing your meaning even from yourself.
It is at this point that the special connection between politics
and the debasement of language becomes clear.

9   In our time it is broadly true that political writing is bad
writing. Where it is not true, it will generally be found that the
writer is some kind of rebel, expressing his private opinions and
not a "party line." Orthodoxy, of whatever color, seems to demand a lifeless, imitative style. The political dialects to be found
in pamphlets, leading articles, manifestoes, White Papers and
the speeches of under-secretaries do, of course, vary from party
to party, but they are all alike in that one almost never finds in
them a fresh, vivid, home-made turn of speech. When one
watches some tired hack on the platform mechanically repeating
the familiar phrases—*bestial atrocities, iron heel, bloodstained*

tyranny, free peoples of the world, stand shoulder to shoulder—
one often has a curious feeling that one is not watching a live
human being but some kind of dummy: a feeling which suddenly becomes stronger at moments when the light catches the
speaker's spectacles and turns them into blank discs which seem
to have no eyes behind them. And this is not altogether fanciful.
A speaker who uses that kind of phraseology has gone some distance towards turning himself into a machine. The appropriate
noises are coming out of his larynx, but his brain is not involved
as it would be if he were choosing his words for himself. If the
speech he is making is one that he is accustomed to make over
and over again, he may be almost unconscious of what he is saying, as one is when one utters the responses in church. And this
reduced state of consciousness, if not indispensable, is at any
rate favorable to political conformity.

10   In our time, political speech and writing are largely the defense of the indefensible. Things like the continuance of British
rule in India, the Russian purges and deportations, the dropping
of the atom bombs on Japan, can indeed be defended, but only
by arguments which are too brutal for most people to face, and
which do not square with the professed aims of political parties.
Thus political language has to consist largely of euphemism,
question-begging and sheer cloudy vagueness. Defenseless villages
are bombarded from the air, the inhabitants driven out into the
countryside, the cattle machine-gunned, the huts set on fire with
incendiary bullets: this is called *pacification*. Millions of peasants are robbed of their farms and sent trudging along the roads
with no more than they can carry: this is called *transfer of population* or *rectification of frontiers*. People are imprisoned for
years without trial, or shot in the back of the neck or sent to
die of scurvy in Arctic lumber camps: this is called *elimination
of unreliable elements*. Such phraseology is needed if one wants
to name things without calling up mental pictures of them. Consider for instance some comfortable English professor defending
Russian totalitarianism. He cannot say outright, "I believe in
killing off your opponents when you can get good results by doing
so." Probably, therefore, he will say something like this:

> While freely conceding that the Soviet régime exhibits certain
> features which the humanitarian may be inclined to deplore, we

must, I think, agree that a certain curtailment of the right to
political opposition is an unavoidable concomitant of transitional
periods, and that the rigors which the Russian people have been
called upon to undergo have been amply justified in the sphere
of concrete achievement.

11   The inflated style is itself a kind of euphemism. A mass of
Latin words falls upon the facts like soft snow, blurring the outlines and covering up all the details. The great enemy of clear
language is insincerity. When there is a gap between one's real
and one's declared aims, one turns, as it were instinctively, to
long words and exhausted idioms, like a cuttlefish squirting out
ink. In our age there is no such thing as "keeping out of politics."
All issues are political issues, and politics itself is a mass of lies,
evasions, folly, hatred and schizophrenia. When the general atmosphere is bad, language must suffer. I should expect to find—
this is a guess which I have not sufficient knowledge to verify—
that the German, Russian and Italian languages have all deteri-
orated in the last ten or fifteen years, as a result of dictatorship.

12   But if thought corrupts language, language can also corrupt
thought. A bad usage can spread by tradition and imitation, even
among people who should and do know better. The debased
language that I have been discussing is in some ways very convenient. Phrases like *a not unjustifiable assumption, leaves much
to be desired, would serve no good purpose, a consideration
which we should do well to bear in mind,* are a continuous
temptation, a packet of aspirins always at one's elbow. Look back
through this essay, and for certain you will find that I have again
and again committed the very faults I am protesting against. By
this morning's post I have received a pamphlet dealing with
conditions in Germany. The author tells me that he "felt impelled" to write it. I open it at random, and here is almost the
first sentence that I see: "[The Allies] have an opportunity not
only of achieving a radical transformation of Germany's social
and political structure in such a way as to avoid a nationalistic
reaction in Germany itself, but at the same time of laying the
foundations of a cooperative and unified Europe." You see, he
"feels impelled" to write—feels, presumably, that he has something new to say—and yet his words, like cavalry horses answering the bugle, group themselves automatically into the familiar

dreary pattern. This invasion of one's mind by ready-made phrases (*lay the foundations, achieve a radical transformation*) can only be prevented if one is constantly on guard against them, and every such phrase anesthetizes a portion of one's brain.

13 I said earlier that the decadence of our language is probably curable. Those who deny this would argue, if they produced an argument at all, that language merely reflects existing social conditions, and that we cannot influence its development by any direct tinkering with words and constructions. So far as the general tone or spirit of a language goes, this may be true, but it is not true in detail. Silly words and expressions have often disappeared, not through any evolutionary process but owing to the conscious action of a minority. Two recent examples were *explore every avenue* and *leave no stone unturned*, which were killed by the jeers of a few journalists. There is a long list of fly-blown metaphors which could similarly be got rid of if enough people would interest themselves in the job; and it should also be possible to laugh the *not un-* formation out of existence,[3] to reduce the amount of Latin and Greek in the average sentence, to drive out foreign phrases and strayed scientific words, and, in general, to make pretentiousness unfashionable. But all these are minor points. The defense of the English language implies more than this, and perhaps it is best to start by saying what it does *not* imply.

14 To begin with, it has nothing to do with archaism, with the salvaging of obsolete words and turns of speech, or with the setting-up of a "standard English" which must never be departed from. On the contrary, it is especially concerned with the scrapping of every word or idiom which has outworn its usefulness. It has nothing to do with correct grammar and syntax, which are of no importance so long as one makes one's meaning clear, or with the avoidance of Americanisms, or with having what is called a "good prose style." On the other hand it is not concerned with fake simplicity and the attempt to make written English colloquial. Nor does it even imply in every case preferring the Saxon

[3]One can cure oneself of the *not un-* formation by memorizing this sentence: *A not unblack dog was chasing a not unsmall rabbit across c. not ungreen field.*

word to the Latin one, though it does imply using the fewest and shortest words that will cover one's meaning. What is above all needed is to let the meaning choose the word, and not the other way about. In prose, the worst thing one can do with words is to surrender to them. When you think of a concrete object, you think wordlessly, and then, if you want to describe the thing you have been visualizing, you probably hunt about till you find the exact words that seem to fit it. When you think of something abstract you are more inclined to use words from the start, and unless you make a conscious effort to prevent it, the existing dialect will come rushing in and do the job for you, at the expense of blurring or even changing your meaning. Probably it is better to put off using words as long as possible and get one's meaning as clear as one can through pictures or sensations. Afterwards one can choose—not simply *accept*—the phrases that will best cover the meaning, and then switch round and decide what impressions one's words are likely to make on another person. This last effort of the mind cuts out all stale or mixed images, all prefabricated phrases, needless repetitions, and humbug and vagueness generally. But one can often be in doubt about the effect of a word or a phrase, and one needs rules that one can rely on when instinct fails. I think the following rules will cover most cases:

(i) Never use a metaphor, simile or other figure of speech which you are used to seeing in print.

(ii) Never use a long word where a short one will do.

(iii) If it is possible to cut a word out, always cut it out.

(iv) Never use the passive where you can use the active.

(v) Never use a foreign phrase, a scientific word or a jargon word if you can think of an everyday English equivalent.

(vi) Break any of these rules sooner than say anything outright barbarous.

These rules sound elementary, and so they are, but they demand a deep change of attitude in anyone who has grown used to writing in the style now fashionable. One could keep all of them and still write bad English, but one could not write the kind of stuff that I quoted in these five specimens at the beginning of this article.

15   I have not here been considering the literary use of language, but merely language as an instrument for expressing and not for

concealing or preventing thought. Stuart Chase and others have come near to claiming that all abstract words are meaningless, and have used this as a pretext for advocating a kind of political quietism. Since you don't know what Fascism is, how can you struggle against Fascism? One need not swallow such absurdities as this, but one ought to recognize that the present political chaos is connected with the decay of language, and that one can probably bring about some improvement by starting at the verbal end. If you simplify your English, you are freed from the worst follies of orthodoxy. You cannot speak any of the necessary dialects, and when you make a stupid remark its stupidity will be obvious, even to yourself. Political language—and with variations this is true of all political parties, from Conservatives to Anarchists—is designed to make lies sound truthful and murder respectable, and to give an appearance of solidity to pure wind. One cannot change this all in a moment, but one can at least change one's own habits, and from time to time one can even, if one jeers loudly enough, send some worn-out and useless phrase —some *jackboot, Achilles' heel, hotbed, melting pot, acid test, veritable inferno* or other lump of verbal refuse—into the dustbin where it belongs.

the medium is the message
MARSHALL McLUHAN

1 In a culture like ours, long accustomed to splitting and dividing all things as a means of control, it is sometimes a bit of a shock to be reminded that, in operational and practical fact, the medium is the message. This is merely to say that the personal and social consequences of any medium—that is, of any extension of ourselves—result from the new scale that is introduced into our affairs by each extension of ourselves, or by any new technology. Thus, with automation, for example, the new patterns of human association tend to eliminate jobs, it is true. That is the negative result. Positively, automation creates roles for people, which is to say depth of involvement in their work and human association that our preceding mechanical technology had destroyed. Many people would be disposed to say that it was not the machine, but what one did with the machine, that was its meaning or message. In terms of the ways in which the machine altered our relations to one another and to ourselves, it mattered not in the least whether it turned out cornflakes or Cadillacs. The restructuring of human work and association was shaped by the technique of fragmentation that is the essence of machine technology. The essence of automation technology is the opposite. It is integral and decentralist in depth, just as the machine was

Reprinted with permission of McGraw-Hill Book Company, from *Understanding Media: The Extension of Man*, by Marshall McLuhan. © 1964 by Marshall McLuhan.

fragmentary, centralist, and superficial in its patterning of human relationships.

2   The instance of the electric light may prove illuminating in this connection. The electric light is pure information. It is a medium without a message, as it were, unless it is used to spell out some verbal ad or name. This fact, characteristic of all media, means that the "content" of any medium is always another medium. The content of writing is speech, just as the written word is the content of print, and print is the content of the telegraph. If it is asked, "What is the content of speech?," it is necessary to say, "It is an actual process of thought, which is in itself nonverbal." An abstract painting represents direct manifestation of creative thought processes as they might appear in computer designs. What we are considering here, however, are the psychic and social consequences of the designs or patterns as they amplify or accelerate existing processes. For the "message" of any medium or technology is the change of scale or pace or pattern that it introduces into human affairs. The railway did not introduce movement or transportation or wheel or road into human society, but it accelerated and enlarged the scale of previous human functions, creating totally new kinds of cities and new kinds of work and leisure. This happened whether the railway functioned in a tropical or a northern environment, and is quite independent of the freight or content of the railway medium. The airplane, on the other hand, by accelerating the rate of transportation, tends to dissolve the railway form of city, politics, and association, quite independently of what the airplane is used for.

3   Let us return to the electric light. Whether the light is being used for brain surgery or night baseball is a matter of indifference. It could be argued that these activities are in some way the "content" of the electric light, since they could not exist without the electric light. This fact merely underlines the point that "the medium is the message" because it is the medium that shapes and controls the scale and form of human association and action. The content or uses of such media are as diverse as they are ineffectual in shaping the form of human association. Indeed, it is only too typical that the "content" of any medium blinds us to the character of the medium. It is only today that industries have become aware of the various kinds of business in which they are engaged.

When IBM discovered that it was not in the business of making office equipment or business machines, but that it was in the business of processing information, then it began to navigate with clear vision. The General Electric Company makes a considerable portion of its profits from electric light bulbs and lighting systems. It has not yet discovered that, quite as much as A.T. & T., it is in the business of moving information.

4   The electric light escapes attention as a communication medium just because it has no "content." And this makes it an invaluable instance of how people fail to study media at all. For it is not till the electric light is used to spell out some brand name that it is noticed as a medium. Then it is not the light but the "content" (or what is really another medium) that is noticed. The message of the electric light is like the message of electric power in industry, totally radical, pervasive, and decentralized. For electric light and power are separate from their uses, yet they eliminate time and space factors in human association exactly as do radio, telegraph, telephone, and TV, creating involvement in depth.

5   A fairly complete handbook for studying the extensions of man could be made up from selections from Shakespeare. Some might quibble about whether or not he was referring to TV in these familiar lines from *Romeo and Juliet:*

> But soft! what light through yonder window breaks? . . .
> It speaks, and yet says nothing.

In *Othello*, which, as much as *King Lear*, is concerned with the torment of people transformed by illusions, there are these lines that bespeak Shakespeare's intuition of the transforming powers of new media:

>   Is there not charms
> By which the property of youth and maidhood
> May be abus'd? Have you not read, Roderigo,
> Of some such thing?

In Shakespeare's *Troilus and Cressida*, which is almost completely devoted to both a psychic and social study of communication, Shakespeare states his awareness that true social and political navigation depend upon anticipating the consequences of innovation:

> The providence that's in a watchful state
> Knows almost every grain of Plutus' gold,
> Finds bottom in the uncomprehensive deeps,
> Keeps place with thought and almost, like the gods,
> Does thoughts unveil in their dumb cradles.

6 The increasing awareness of the action of media, quite independently of their "content" or programming, was indicated in the annoyed and anonymous stanza:

> In modern thought (if not in fact),
> Nothing is that doesn't act,
> So that is reckoned wisdom which
> Describes the scratch but not the itch.

The same kind of total, configurational awareness that reveals why the medium is socially the message has occurred in the most recent and radical medical theories. In his *Stress of Life*, Hans Selye tells of the dismay of a research colleague on hearing of Selye's theory:

> When he saw me thus launched on yet another enraptured description of what I had observed in animals treated with this or that impure, toxic material, he looked at me with desperately sad eyes and said in obvious despair: "But Selye, try to realize what you are doing before it is too late! You have now decided to spend your entire life studying the pharmacology of dirt!"
>
> HANS SELYE, *The Stress of Life*

As Selye deals with the total environmental situation in his "stress" theory of disease, so the latest approach to media study considers not only the "content" but the medium and the cultural matrix within which the particular medium operates. The older unawareness of the psychic and social effects of media can be illustrated from almost any of the conventional pronouncements.

7 In accepting an honorary degree from the University of Notre Dame a few years ago, General David Sarnoff made this statement: "We are too prone to make technological instruments the scapegoats for the sins of those who wield them. The products of modern science are not in themselves good or bad; it is the way they are used that determines their value." That is the voice of the current somnambulism. Suppose we were to say, "Apple pie

is in itself neither good nor bad; it is the way it is used that determines its value." Or, "The smallpox virus is in itself neither good nor bad; it is the way that it is used that determines its value." Again, "Firearms are in themselves neither good nor bad; it is the way they are used that determines their value." That is, if the slugs reach the right people firearms are good. If the TV tube fires the right ammunition at the right people it is good. I am not being perverse. There is simply nothing in the Sarnoff statement that will bear scrutiny, for it ignores the nature of the medium, of any and all media, in the true Narcissus style of one hypnotized by the amputation and extension of his own being in a new technical form. General Sarnoff went on to explain his attitude to the technology of print, saying that it was true that print caused much trash to circulate, but it had also disseminated the Bible and the thoughts of seers and philosophers. It has never occurred to General Sarnoff that any technology could do anything but *add* itself on to what we already are.

8   Such economists as Robert Theobald, W. W. Rostow, and John Kenneth Galbraith have been explaining for years how it is that "classical economics" cannot explain change or growth. And the paradox of mechanization is that although it is itself the cause of maximal growth and change, the principle of mechanization excludes the very possibility of growth or the understanding of change. For mechanization is achieved by fragmentation of any process and by putting the fragmented parts in a series. Yet, as David Hume showed in the eighteenth century, there is no principle of causality in a mere sequence. That one thing follows another accounts for nothing. Nothing follows from following, except change. So the greatest of all reversals occurred with electricity, that ended sequence by making things instant. With instant speed the causes of things began to emerge to awareness again, as they had not done with things in sequence and in concatenation accordingly. Instead of asking which came first, the chicken or the egg, it suddenly seemed that a chicken was an egg's idea for getting more eggs.

9   Just before an airplane breaks the sound barrier, sound waves become visible on the wings of the plane. The sudden visibility of sound just as sound ends is an apt instance of that great pattern of being that reveals new and opposite forms just as the earlier forms reach their peak performance. Mechanization was

never so vividly fragmented or sequential as in the birth of the movies, the moment that translated us beyond mechanism into the world of growth and organic interrelation. The movie, by sheer speeding up the mechanical, carried us from the world of sequence and connections into the world of creative configuration and structure. The message of the movie medium is that of transition from lineal connections to configurations. It is the transition that produced the now quite correct observation: "If it works, it's obsolete." When electric speed further takes over from mechanical movie sequences, then the lines of force in structures and in media become loud and clear. We return to the inclusive form of the icon.

10   To a highly literate and mechanized culture the movie appeared as a world of triumphant illusions and dreams that money could buy. It was at this moment of the movie that cubism occurred, and it has been described by E. H. Gombrich (*Art and Illusion*) as "the most radical attempt to stamp out ambiguity and to enforce one reading of the picture—that of a man-made construction, a colored canvas." For cubism substitutes all facets of an object simultaneously for the "point of view" or facet of perspective illusion. Instead of the specialized illusion of the third dimension on canvas, cubism sets up an interplay of planes and contradiction or dramatic conflict of patterns, lights, textures that "drives home the message" by involvement. This is held by many to be an exercise in painting, not in illusion.

11   In other words, cubism, by giving the inside and outside, the top, bottom, back, and front and the rest, in two dimensions, drops the illusion of perspective in favor of instant sensory awareness of the whole. Cubism, by seizing on instant total awareness, suddenly announced that *the medium is the message*. Is it not evident that the moment that sequence yields to the simultaneous, one is in the world of the structure and of configuration? Is that not what has happened in physics as in painting, poetry, and in communication? Specialized segments of attention have shifted to total field, and we can now say, "The medium is the message" quite naturally. Before the electric speed and total field, it was not obvious that the medium is the message. The message, it seemed, was the "content," as people used to ask what a painting was *about*. Yet they never thought to ask what a melody was about, nor what a house or a dress was about. In such matters,

people retained some sense of the whole pattern, of form and function as a unity. But in the electric age this integral idea of structure and configuration has become so prevalent that educational theory has taken up the matter. Instead of working with specialized "problems" in arithmetic, the structural approach now follows the linea of force in the field of number and has small children meditating about number theory and "sets."

12   Cardinal Newman said of Napoleon, "He understood the grammar of gunpowder." Napoleon had paid some attention to other media as well, especially the semaphore telegraph that gave him a great advantage over his enemies. He is on record for saying that "Three hostile newspapers are more to be feared than a thousand bayonets."

13   Alexis de Tocqueville was the first to master the grammar of print and typography. He was thus able to read off the message of coming change in France and America as if he were reading aloud from a text that had been handed to him. In fact, the nineteenth century in France and in America was just such an open book to de Tocqueville because he had learned the grammar of print. So he, also, knew when that grammar did not apply. He was asked why he did not write a book on England, since he knew and admired England. He replied:

> One would have to have an unusual degree of philosophical folly to believe oneself able to judge England in six months. A year always seemed to me too short a time in which to appreciate the United States properly, and it is much easier to acquire clear and precise notions about the American Union than about Great Britain. In America all laws derive in a sense from the same line of thought. The whole of society, so to speak, is founded upon a single fact; everything springs from a simple principle. One could compare America to a forest pierced by a multitude of straight roads all converging on the same point. One has only to find the center and everything is revealed at a glance. But in England the paths run criss-cross, and it is only by travelling down each one of them that one can build up a picture of the whole.

De Tocqueville, in earlier work on the French Revolution, had explained how it was the printed word that, achieving cultural saturation in the eighteenth century, had homogenized the French nation. Frenchmen were the same kind of people from north to south. The typographic principles of uniformity, continuity, and lineality had overlaid the complexities of ancient feudal and oral society. The Revolution was carried out by the new literati and lawyers.

14　In England, however, such was the power of the ancient oral traditions of common law, backed by the medieval institution of Parliament, that no uniformity or continuity of the new visual print culture could take complete hold. The result was that the most important event in English history has never taken place; namely, the English Revolution on the lines of the French Revolution. The American Revolution had no medieval legal institutions to discard or to root out, apart from monarchy. And many have held that the American Presidency has become very much more personal and monarchical than any European monarch ever could be.

15　De Tocqueville's contrast between England and America is clearly based on the fact of typography and of print culture creating uniformity and continuity. England, he says, has rejected this principle and clung to the dynamic or oral common-law tradition. Hence the discontinuity and unpredictable quality of English culture. The grammar of print cannot help to construe the message of oral and nonwritten culture and institutions. The English aristocracy was properly classified as barbarian by Matthew Arnold because its power and status had nothing to do with literacy or with the cultural forms of typography. Said the Duke of Gloucester to Edward Gibbon upon the publication of his *Decline and Fall:* "Another damned fat book, eh, Mr. Gibbon? Scribble, scribble, scribble, eh, Mr. Gibbon?" De Tocqueville was a highly literate aristocrat who was quite able to be detached from the values and assumptions of typography. That is why he alone understood the grammar of typography. And it is only on those terms, standing aside from any structure or medium, that its principles and lines of force can be discerned. For any medium has the power of imposing its own assumption on the unwary. Prediction and control consist in avoiding this subliminal state of Narcissus trance. But the greatest aid to this end is simply in knowing that the spell can occur immediately upon contact, as in the first bars of a melody.

16　*A Passage to India* by E. M. Forster is a dramatic study of the inability of oral and intuitive oriental culture to meet with the rational, visual European patterns of experience. "Rational," of course, has for the West long meant "uniform and continuous and sequential." In other words, we have confused reason with literacy, and rationalism with a single technology. Thus in the electric age man seems to the conventional West to become irrational. In Forster's novel the moment of truth and dislocation from the typographic trance of the West comes in the Marabar Caves. Adela Quested's reasoning powers cannot cope with the total inclusive field of resonance that is India. After the Caves: "Life went on as usual, but had no consequences, that is to say, sounds did not echo nor thought develop. Everything seemed cut off at its root and therefore infected with illusion."

17   *A Passage to India* (the phrase is from Whitman, who saw America headed Eastward) is a parable of Western man in the electric age, and is only incidentally related to Europe or the Orient. The ultimate conflict between sight and sound, between written and oral kinds of perception and organization of existence is upon us. Since understanding stops action, as Nietzsche observed, we can moderate the fierceness of this conflict by understanding the media that extend us and raise these wars within and without us.

18   Detribalization by literacy and its traumatic effects on tribal man is the theme of a book by the psychiatrist J. C. Carothers, *The African Mind in Health and Disease* (World Health Organization, Geneva, 1953). Much of his material appeared in an article in *Psychiatry* magazine, November, 1959: "The Culture, Psychiatry, and the Written Word." Again, it is electric speed that has revealed the lines of force operating from Western technology in the remotest areas of bush, savannah, and desert. One example is the Bedouin with his battery radio on board the camel. Submerging natives with floods of concepts for which nothing has prepared them is the normal action of all of our technology. But with electric media Western man himself experiences exactly the same inundation as the remote native. We are no more prepared to encounter radio and TV in our literate milieu than the native of Ghana is able to cope with the literacy that takes him out of his collective tribal world and beaches him

in individual isolation. We are as numb in our new electric world as the native involved in our literate and mechanical culture.

19   Electric speed mingles the cultures of prehistory with the dregs of industrial marketeers, the nonliterate with the semiliterate and the postliterate. Mental breakdown of varying degrees is the very common result of uprooting and inundation with new information and endless new patterns of information. Wyndham Lewis made this a theme of his group of novels called *The Human Age*. The first of these, *The Childermass*, is concerned precisely with accelerated media change as a kind of massacre of the innocents. In our own world as we become more aware of the effects of technology on psychic formation and manifestation, we are losing all confidence in our right to assign guilt. Ancient prehistoric societies regard violent crime as pathetic. The killer is regarded as we do a cancer victim. "How terrible it must be to feel like that," they say. J. M. Synge took up this idea very effectively in his *Playboy of the Western World*.

20   If the criminal appears as a nonconformist who is unable to meet the demand of technology that we behave in uniform and continuous patterns, literate man is quite inclined to see others who cannot conform as somewhat pathetic. Especially the child, the cripple, the woman, and the colored person appear in a world of visual and typographic technology as victims of injustice. On the other hand, in a culture that assigns roles instead of jobs to people—the dwarf, the skew, the child create their own spaces. They are not expected to fit into some uniform and repeatable niche that is not their size anyway. Consider the phrase "It's a man's world." As a quantitative observation endlessly repeated from within a homogenized culture, this phrase refers to the men in such a culture who have to be homogenized Dagwoods in order to belong at all. It is in our I.Q. testing that we have produced the greatest flood of misbegotten standards. Unaware of our typographic cultural bias, our testers assume that uniform and continuous habits are a sign of intelligence, thus eliminating the ear man and the tactile man.

21   C. P. Snow, reviewing a book of A. L. Rowse (*The New York Times Book Review*, December 24, 1961) on *Appeasement and the road to Munich*, describes the top level of British brains and

experience in the 1930s. "Their I.Q.'s were much higher than usual among political bosses. Why were they such a disaster?" The view of Rowse, Snow approves: "They would not listen to warnings because they did not wish to hear." Being anti-Red made it impossible for them to read the message of Hitler. But their failure was as nothing compared to our present one. The American stake in literacy as a technology or uniformity applied to every level of education, government, industry, and social life is totally threatened by the electric technology. The threat of Stalin or Hitler was external. The electric technology is within the gates, and we are numb, deaf, blind, and mute about its encounter with the Gutenberg technology, on and through which the American way of life was formed. It is, however, no time to suggest strategies when the threat has not even been acknowledged to exist. I am in the position of Louis Pasteur telling doctors that their greatest enemy was quite invisible, and quite unrecognized by them. Our conventional response to all media, namely that it is how they are used that counts, is the numb stance of the technological idiot. For the "content" of a medium is like the juicy piece of meat carried by the burglar to distract the watchdog of the mind. The effect of the medium is made strong and intense just because it is given another medium as "content." The content of a movie is a novel or a play or an opera. The effect of the movie form is not related to its program content. The "content" of writing or print is speech, but the reader is almost entirely unaware either of print or of speech.

22   Arnold Toynbee is innocent of any understanding of media as they have shaped history, but he is full of examples that the student of media can use. At one moment he can seriously suggest that adult education, such as the Workers Educational Association in Britain, is a useful counterforce to the popular press. Toynbee considers that although all of the oriental societies have in our time accepted the industrial technology and its political consequences: "On the cultural plane, however, there is no uniform corresponding tendency." Somervell, I. 267) This is like the voice of the literate man, floundering in a milieu of ads, who boasts, "Personally, I pay no attention to ads." The spiritual and cultural reservations that the oriental peoples may have toward our technology will avail them not at all. The

effects of technology do not occur at the level of opinions or concepts, but alter sense ratios or patterns of perception steadily and without any resistance. The serious artist is the only person able to encounter technology with impunity, just because he is an expert aware of the changes in sense perception.

23 The operation of the money medium in seventeenth-century Japan had effects not unlike the operation of typography in the West. The penetration of the money economy, wrote G. B. Sansom (in *Japan,* Cresset Press, London, 1931) "caused a slow but irresistible revolution, culminating in the breakdown of feudal government and the resumption of intercourse with foreign countries after more than two hundred years of seclusion." Money has reorganized the sense life of peoples just because it is an *extension* of our sense lives. This change does not depend upon approval or disapproval of those living in the society.

24 Arnold Toynbee made one approach to the transforming power of media in his concept of "etherialization," which he holds to be the principle of progressive simplification and efficiency in any organization or technology. Typically, he is ignoring the *effect* of the challenge of these forms upon the response of our senses. He imagines that it is the response of our opinions that is relevant to the effect of media and technology in society, a "point of view" that is plainly the result of the typographic spell. For the man in a literate and homogenized society ceases to be sensitive to the diverse and discontinuous life of forms. He acquires the illusion of the third dimension and the "private point of view" as part of his Narcissus fixation, and is quite shut off from Blake's awareness or that of the Psalmist, that we become what we behold.

25 Today when we want to get our bearings in our own culture, and have need to stand aside from the bias and pressure exerted by any technical form of human expression, we have only to visit a society where that particular form has not been felt, or a historical period in which it was unknown. Professor Wilbur Schramm made such a tactical move in studying *Television in the Lives of Our Children*. He found areas where TV had not penetrated at all and ran some tests. Since he had made no study of the peculiar nature of the TV image, his tests were of "content" preferences, viewing time, and vocabulary counts. In a word,

his approach to the problem was a literary one, albeit unconsciously so. Consequently, he had nothing to report. Had his methods been employed in 1500 A.D. to discover the effects of the printed book in the lives of children or adults, he could have found out nothing of the changes in human and social psychology resulting from typography. Print created individualism and nationalism in the sixteenth century. Program and "content" analysis offer no clues to the magic of these media or to their subliminal charge.

26   Leonard Doob, in his report *Communication in Africa,* tells of one African who took great pains to listen each evening to the BBC news, even though he could understand nothing of it. Just to be in the presence of those sounds at 7 P.M. each day was important for him. His attitude to speech was like ours to melody —the resonant intonation was meaning enough. In the seventeenth century our ancestors still shared this native's attitude to the forms of media, as is plain in the following sentiment of the Frenchman Bernard Lam expressed in *The Art of Speaking* (London, 1696):

> 'Tis an effect of the Wisdom of God, who created Man to be happy, that whatever is useful to his conversation (way of life) is agreeable to him . . . because all victual that conduces to nourishment is relishable, whereas other things that cannot be assimulated and be turned into our substance are insipid. A Discourse cannot be pleasant to the Hearer that is not easie to the Speaker; nor can it be easily pronounced unless it be heard with delight.

Here is an equilibrium theory of human diet and expression such as even now we are only striving to work out again for media after centuries of fragmentation and specialism.

27   Pope Pius XII was deeply concerned that there be serious study of the media today. On February 17, 1950, he said:

> It is not an exaggeration to say that the future of modern society and the stability of its inner life depend in large part on the maintenance of an equilibrium between the strength of the techniques of communication and the capacity of the individual's own reaction.

28   Failure in this respect has for centuries been typical and total for mankind. Subliminal and docile acceptance of media impact

has made them prisons without walls for their human users. As A. J. Liebling remarked in his book, *The Press,* a man is not free if he cannot see where he is going, even if he has a gun to help him get there. For each of the media is also a powerful weapon with which to clobber other media and other groups. The result is that the present age has been one of multiple civil wars that are not limited to the world of art and entertainment. In *War and Human Progress,* Professor J. U. Nef declared: "The total wars of our time have been the result of a series of intellectual mistakes. . . ."

29   If the formative power in the media are the media themselves, that raises a host of large matters that can only be mentioned here, although they deserve volumes. Namely, that technological media are staples or natural resources, exactly as are coal and cotton and oil. Anybody will concede that society whose economy is dependent upon one or two major staples like cotton, or grain, or lumber, or fish, or cattle is going to have some obvious social patterns of organization as a result. Stress on a few major staples creates extreme instability in the economy but great endurance in the population. The pathos and humor of the American South are embedded in such an economy of limited staples. For a society configured by reliance on a few commodities accepts them as a social bond quite as much as the metropolis does the press. Cotton and oil, like radio and TV, become "fixed charges" on the entire psychic life of the community. And this pervasive fact creates the unique cultural flavor of any society. It pays through the nose and all its other senses for each staple that shapes its life.

30   That our human senses, of which all media are extensions, are also fixed charges on our personal energies, and that they also configure the awareness and experience of each one of us, may be perceived in another connection mentioned by the psychologist C. G. Jung:

> Every Roman was surrounded by slaves. The slave and his psychology flooded ancient Italy, and every Roman became inwardly, and of course unwittingly, a slave. Because living constantly in the atmosphere of slaves, he became infected through the unconscious with their psychology. No one can shield himself from such an influence.
>
> *Contributions to Analytical Psychology,* London, 1928

an explication of dickinson's
"after great pain"

FRANCIS MANLEY

1   Between 1860 and 1862 Emily Dickinson is commonly believed
to have experienced a psychic catastrophe, which drove her into
poetry instead of out of her mind. According to her explanation,
she was haunted by some mysterious fright, and her fear, or
whatever it was, opened the floodgates of her poetry.[1] But despite
their overwhelming number, the poems she produced under
these conditions are not an amorphous overflow from a distraught
mind; they are informed and well-wrought, the creations of
controlled artistry—especially about twenty-five or thirty poems
which, unlike the rest, treat specifically the intense subtleties of
mental anguish, anatomizing them with awesome precision. And
since all of the poems in this small cluster deal with varied aspects
of that one subject, all of them follow a certain basic pattern
dictated by the abstract nature of pain.

2   In each of these poems Dickinson was faced with this initial
problem: somehow she had to describe a formless, internal entity
which could never be revealed to others except in terms of its outward signs and manifestations. Moreover, these externalizations

---

[1]*The Letters of Emily Dickinson*, ed. Thomas H. Johnson (Cambridge,
Mass., 1958), ii, letters 248a, 261.

Reprinted with permission of The Johns Hopkins Press, from *MLN*, April
1958, pages 260–264. © The Johns Hopkins Press.

did not always correspond to the internal condition but at times, in fact, represented the exact opposite. Yet in poetry if such signs were completely misleading, they would obviously defeat their own purpose by communicating the wrong thing. Consequently, they must offer some oblique means for the reader to penetrate appearances to the reality beneath. In solving this problem Dickinson created some of her most interesting and complex poetry. Generally speaking, irony was her weapon as well as her strategy. First, she usually set up for her *persona* some sort of external ritual or drama which contains various levels of calm objectivity. Then, through a series of ironic involutions generated in the course of this symbolic action, she eventually led the reader from appearances to the reality of a silent anguish made more terrifying by its ironic presentation, as here:

> After great pain, a formal feeling comes—
> The Nerves sit ceremonious, like Tombs—
> The stiff Heart questions was it He, that bore,
> And Yesterday, or Centuries before?
>
> The Feet, mechanical, go round—
> Of Ground, or Air, or Ought—
> A Wooden way
> Regardless grown,
> A Quartz contentment, like a stone—
>
> This is the Hour of Lead—
> Remembered, if outlived,
> As Freezing persons, recollect the Snow—
> First—chill—then Stupor—then the letting go.[2]

3   In a literal sense, this poem has neither *persona* nor ritual, and since it describes a state of mind, neither would seem to be necessary. In such a case attention should be centered on the feeling itself and secondarily on its location. Consequently Dickinson personified various parts of the body so as to demonstrate the action of numbness on them—*the* nerves, *the* heart, *the*

[2]Reprinted by permission of the publishers and the Trustees of Amherst College, from *The Poems of Emily Dickinson*, edited by Thomas H. Johnson. Cambridge, Massachusetts: The Belknap Press of Harvard University Press. Copyright 1951, 1955 by The President and Fellows of Harvard College.

feet—generalized entities belonging to no one. Yet that is precisely the formal feeling benumbed contentment produces in a
person, especially one who has lost the sense of time and his own
identity (lines 3–4). All the parts of his body seem to be autonomous beings moving in mysterious ways. If that constitutes a
persona, it is necessarily an unobtrusive one that must be recon-
structed from *disjecta membra.* Similarly, the various actions
performed in this poem are disjunctive, and though vaguely related to a chaotic travesty of a funeral, they are not patterned
by any consistent, overall ceremony. Since they are all external
manifestations or metaphors for numbness, however, they are all
as they should be, lifeless forms enacted in a trance as though
they were part of some meaningless rite.

4   The first stanza, for instance, is held rigid by the ceremonious
formality of the chamber of death when, after the great pain of
its passing, the corpse lies tranquil and composed, surrounded by
mourners hushed in awe so silent that time seems to have gone
off into eternity "Yesterday, or Centuries before." In one respect
this metaphor is particularly suitable since the nerves are situated
round about the body or the "stiff Heart" like mourners about
the bed of death. But if the metaphor is extended further, it
seems to become ludicrously unsuitable. These nerves, for example, are not neighbors lamenting with their silent presence
the death of a friend. They are sensation itself, but here they are
dead, as ceremonious and lifeless as tombs. Consequently, the
formal feeling that comes after great pain is, ironically, no feeling
at all, only benumbed rigidness. Conversely, if the "stiff Heart"
is the corpse, he nevertheless has life or consciousness enough to
question whether it was "He, that bore,/And Yesterday or
Centuries before." Obviously, this is moving toward artistic
chaos since metaphors should be more and more applicable the
further they are extended, but this one apparently became
progressively worse. Curiously, however, by breaking all the rules
Dickinson achieved the exact effect she needed. Her problem was
to describe an essentially paradoxical state of mind in which
one is alive but yet numb to life, both a living organism and a
frozen form. Consequently she took both terms of this paradox
and made each a reversed reflection of the other. Although the
mourners, the nerves, appear to be the living, they are in actuality the dead, and conversely the stiff heart, the metaphoric

corpse, has ironically at least a semblance of consciousness. In their totality, both these forms of living death define the "stop sensation" that comes after great pain.

5   Since the metaphoric nightmare of the first stanza could hardly be extended any further, Dickinson is obviously not concerned with elaborating a conceit. In the second stanza, then, the cataleptically formal rites of the dead are replaced by a different sort of action ceremoniously performed in a trance, an extension not of the previous metaphor, but of the paradox which informed it. For although movement usually indicates vitality, there is no life in the aimless circles of the walking dead. Whether numb feet go on the hardness of ground or on the softness of air, their way is wooden because paralysis is within them. Since they cannot feel nor know nor even care where they are going ("Regardless grown"), they wander in circles ("go round") on an insane tread-mill as though lost, suspended between life and death and sharing the attributes of both.

6   The third stanza is, in one respect, an imagistic repetition of the second. Benumbed, aimless movements through a world of waste, the motions of the living dead are similar to the trance-like, enchanted steps of persons freezing in a blank and silent world of muffling snow. But at the same time that this metaphor refers particularly to the preceding stanza, it also summarizes the entire poem since the ambiguous antecedent of *This* in line 10 is, in one respect, everything that went before. Consequently, this final image should somehow fuse all the essential elements of the poem. Not only that, it should present them in sharp focus.

7   Certainly the chill and subsequent stupor of freezing, a gradual numbing of the senses, incorporates many of the attributes of death itself: a loss of vital warmth, of locomotion, of a sense of identity in time and space conjoined with an increasing coolness, rigidness, and apathy. Since freezing, however, is neither life nor death but both simultaneously, it is an excellent, expansive meta-phor for the living death which comes after great pain. But in addition to extending the basic paradox which informs the poem, this final figure serves a more important function by drawing to the surface and presenting in full ambivalence a certain ironic ambiguity which in the first two stanzas remains somewhat below the threshold of conscious awareness.

8   In its furthest extent great pain produces internal paralysis,

but, ironically, this numbness is not itself a pain. It is no feeling, "an element of blank," which gradually emerges from the poem until at the end it almost engulfs it in white helplessness. In the first stanza it lurks just below the surface, unstated, but ironically present in the situation itself. For although the nerves represent metaphorically the formal feeling which comes after great pain by being silent, ceremonious mourners, they are simultaneously dead sensation, no feeling, formal or otherwise, not pain, but nothing. In the second stanza this implication is no longer subliminal, but even though it is at the surface, it is not developed, merely stated: "A Quartz contentment, like a stone." According to Webster's *American Dictionary* (1851), the lexicon Dickinson used, *contentment* was a "Rest or quietness of mind in the present condition; satisfaction which holds the mind in peace, restraining complaint, opposition, or further desire, and often implying a moderate degree of happiness." Apparently, then, by the second stanza anguish has resolved itself into its impossible opposite, a hard, cold, quartz-like peaceful satisfaction of the mind. In the third stanza, this inert irony fully emerges to modify response and ultimately to qualify it to such an extent that the poem ends in tense, unresolved ambivalence. According to the superficial movement of the poem, the time after great pain will later be remembered as a period of living death similar to the sensation of freezing. Yet the qualifications attached to that statement drain it of its assertiveness and curiously force it to imply its own negative. For there is not only a doubt that this hour of crisis may not be outlived (line 11), but even the positive statement (that it will be remembered) is made fully ambivalent by being modified by its own negative (that it will be remembered just as freezing persons recollect the snow). Ironically, freezing persons can never remember the snow since they die in it, destroyed by a warm, contented numbness in which they sleep and perish in entranced delusion. Because there is no solution to this ambivalence, the poem ends unresolved, suspended between life and death in a quartz contentment, the most deadly anguish of all, the very essence of pain, which is not pain, but a blank peace, just as the essence of sound is silence.

ode on a grecian urn

JOHN KEATS

1

Thou still unravished bride of quietness,
   Thou foster-child of Silence and slow Time,
Sylvan historian, who canst thus express
   A flowery tale more sweetly than our rhyme:
What leaf-fringed legend haunts about thy shape
    Of deities or mortals, or of both,
      In Tempe or the dales of Arcady?
    What men or gods are these? What maidens loth?
What mad pursuit? What struggle to escape?
      What pipes and timbrels? What wild ecstasy?

2

Heard melodies are sweet, but those unheard
   Are sweeter; therefore, ye soft pipes, play on;
Not to the sensual ear, but, more endeared,
   Pipe to the spirit ditties of no tone:
Fair youth, beneath the trees, thou canst not leave
    Thy song, nor ever can those trees be bare;
      Bold Lover, never, never canst thou kiss,
Though winning near the goal—yet, do not grieve;

She cannot fade, though thou has not thy bliss,
For ever wilt thou love, and she be fair!

3

Ah, happy, happy boughs! that cannot shed
　　Your leaves, nor ever bid the Spring adieu;
And, happy melodist, unwearied,
　　For ever piping songs for ever new.
More happy love! more happy, happy love!
　　For ever warm and still to be enjoyed,
　　　　For ever panting, and for ever young;
All breathing human passion far above,
　　That leaves a heart high-sorrowful and cloyed,
　　　　A burning forehead, and a parching tongue.

4

Who are these coming to the sacrifice?
　　To what green altar, O mysterious priest,
Lead'st thou that heifer lowing at the skies,
　　And all her silken flanks with garlands drest?
What little town by river or sea shore,
　　Or mountain-built with peaceful citadel,
　　　　Is emptied of this folk, this pious morn?
And, little town, thy streets for evermore
　　Will silent be; and not a soul to tell
　　　　Why thou art desolate, can e'er return.

5

O Attic shape! Fair attitude! with brede
　　Of marble men and maidens overwrought,
With forest branches and the trodden weed;
　　Thou, silent form! dost tease us out of thought
As doth eternity: Cold Pastoral!

When old age shall this generation waste,
  Thou shalt remain, in midst of other woe
Than ours, a friend to man, to whom thou say'st,
"Beauty is truth, truth beauty,"—that is all
  Ye know on earth, and all ye need to know.

DISCUSSION AND WRITING MATERIAL

"The Best-Known Monument of American Prose" and "Politics and the English Language"

Using all of the criteria suggested by Gilbert Highet and George Orwell, analyze the following address by John F. Kennedy for some of its stylistic features (sentence structure, word choice, imagery and metaphor, use of sound).

Inaugural Address

Vice President Johnson, Mr. Speaker, Mr. Chief Justice, President Eisenhower, Vice President Nixon, President Truman, Reverend Clergy, Fellow Citizens:

We observe today not a victory of party but a celebration of freedom—symbolizing an end as well as a beginning—signifying renewal as well as change. For I have sworn before you and Almighty God the same solemn oath our forebears prescribed nearly a century and three quarters ago.

The world is very different now. For man holds in his mortal hands the power to abolish all forms of human poverty and all forms of human life. And yet the same revolutionary beliefs for which our forebears fought are still at issue around the globe— the belief that the rights of man come not from the generosity of the state but from the hand of God.

We dare not forget today that we are the heirs of that first revolution. Let the word go forth from this time and place, to friend and foe alike, that the torch has been passed to a new generation of Americans—born in this century, tempered by war, disciplined by a hard and bitter peace, proud of our ancient heritage —and unwilling to witness or permit the slow undoing of those human rights to which this Nation has always been committed, and to which we are committed today at home and around the world.

Let every nation know, whether it wishes us well or ill, that we shall pay any price, bear any burden, meet any hardship, support any friend, oppose any foe to assure the survival and the success of liberty.

This much we pledge—and more.

To those old allies whose cultural and spiritual origins we

share, we pledge the loyalty of faithful friends. United, there is little we cannot do in a host of cooperative ventures. Divided, there is little we can do—for we dare not meet a powerful challenge at odds and split asunder.

To those new states whom we welcome to the ranks of the free, we pledge our word that one form of colonial control shall not have passed away merely to be replaced by a far more iron tyranny. We shall not always expect to find them supporting our view. But we shall always hope to find them strongly supporting their own freedom—and to remember that, in the past, those who foolishly sought power by riding the back of the tiger ended up inside.

To those peoples in the huts and villages of half the globe struggling to break the bonds of mass misery, we pledge our best efforts to help them help themselves, for whatever period is required—not because the Communists may be doing it, not because we seek their votes, but because it is right. If a free society cannot help the many who are poor, it cannot save the few who are rich.

To our sister republics south of our border, we offer a special pledge—to convert our good words into good deeds—in a new alliance for progress—to assist free men and free governments in casting off the chains of poverty. But this peaceful revolution of hope cannot become the prey of hostile powers. Let all our neighbors know that we shall join with them to oppose aggression or subversion anywhere in the Americas. And let every other power know that this hemisphere intends to remain the master of its own house.

To that world assembly of sovereign states, the United Nations, our last best hope in an age where the instruments of war have far outpaced the instruments of peace, we renew our pledge of support—to prevent it from becoming merely a forum for invective—to strengthen its shield of the new and the weak—and to enlarge the area in which its writ may run.

Finally, to those nations who would make themselves our adversary, we offer not a pledge but a request: that both sides begin anew the quest for peace, before the dark powers of destruction unleashed by science engulf all humanity in planned or accidental self-destruction.

We dare not tempt them with weakness. For only when our arms are sufficient beyond doubt can we be certain beyond doubt that they will never be employed.

But neither can two great and powerful groups of nations take comfort from our present course—both sides overburdened by the cost of modern weapons, both rightly alarmed by the steady spread of the deadly atom, yet both racing to alter that uncertain balance of terror that stays the hand of mankind's final war.

So let us begin anew—remembering on both sides that civility is not a sign of weakness, and sincerity is always subject to proof. Let us never negotiate out of fear. But let us never fear to negotiate.

Let both sides explore what problems unite us instead of belaboring those problems which divide us.

Let both sides, for the first time, formulate serious and precise proposals for the inspection and control of arms—and bring the absolute power to destroy other nations under the absolute control of all nations.

Let both sides seek to invoke the wonders of science instead of its terrors. Together let us explore the stars, conquer the deserts, eradicate disease, tap the ocean depths, and encourage the arts and commerce.

Let both sides unite to heed in all corners of the earth the command of Isaiah—to "undo the heavy burdens and to let the oppressed go free."

And if a beachhead of cooperation may push back the jungle of suspicion, let both sides join in creating a new endeavor, not a new balance of power, but a new world of law, where the strong are just and the weak secure and the peace preserved.

All this will not be finished in the first 100 days. Nor will it be finished in the first 1,000 days, nor in the life of this administration, nor even perhaps in our lifetime on this planet. But let us begin.

In your hands, my fellow citizens, more than in mine, will rest the final success or failure of our course. Since this country was founded, each generation of Americans has been summoned to give testimony to its national loyalty. The graves of young Americans who answered the call to service are found around the globe.

Now the trumpet summons us again—not as a call to bear arms, though arms we need; not as a call to battle, though embattled we are; but a call to bear the burden of a long twilight struggle, year in, and year out, "rejoicing in hope, patient in tribulation"—a struggle against the common enemies of man: tyranny, poverty, disease, and war itself.

Can we forge against these enemies a grand and global alliance, North and South, East and West, that can assure a more fruitful life for all mankind? Will you join in that historic effort?

In the long history of the world, only a few generations have been granted the role of defending freedom in its hour of maximum danger. I do not shrink from this responsibility—I welcome it. I do not believe that any of us would exchange places with any other people or any other generation. The energy, the faith, the devotion which we bring to this endeavor will light our country and all who serve it—and the glow from that fire can truly light the world.

And so, my fellow Americans, ask not what your country can do for you: Ask what you can do for your country.

My fellow citizens of the world: Ask not what America will do for you, but what together we can do for the freedom of man.

Finally, whether you are citizens of America or citizens of the world, ask of us the same high standards of strength and sacrifice which we ask of you. With a good conscience our only sure reward, with history the final judge of our deeds, let us go forth to lead the land we love, asking His blessing and His help, but knowing that here on earth God's work must truly be our own.

"The Medium Is the Message"

What effect does McLuhan's style have on his communication process? How important is the use of analogy and metaphor to his style? What kinds of literary and mythic allusions does he make? Discuss the relationship of McLuhan's understanding of education to today's student. Consider the following: the "lineal-sequential" form of communication and the "mosaic, impressionistic form"; where education really takes place; the necessity for participation in the learning process.

"An Explication of Dickinson's 'After Great Pain'"

Using the analytical approach employed by Francis Manley, analyze the following poem by Emily Dickinson and explain as best you can its meaning.

Because I Could Not Stop for Death (712)

Because I could not stop for Death—
He kindly stopped for me—
The Carriage held but just Ourselves—
And Immortality.

We slowly drove—He knew no haste   5
And I had put away
My labor and my leisure too,
For His Civility—

We passed the School, where Children strove   9
At Recess—in the Ring—
We passed the Fields of Gazing Grain—
We passed the Setting Sun—

Or rather—He passed Us—   13
The Dews drew quivering and chill—
For only Gossamer, my Gown—
My Tippet—only Tulle—

We paused before a House that seemed   17
A Swelling of the Ground—
The Roof was scarcely visible—
The Cornice—in the Ground—

Since then—'tis Centuries—and yet   21
Feels shorter than the Day
I first surmised the Horses Heads
Were toward Eternity—[1]

"Ode on a Grecian Urn"

Since the ode is on (not "to") the ancient work of art, explain
the process of analysis that the poet uses as he explores and
selects the various characteristics of the urn. What role does
the imagination play in the poem?

[1]Reprinted by permission of the publishers and the Trustees of Amherst
College, from *The Poems of Emily Dickinson*, edited by Thomas H. Johnson,
Cambridge, Massachusetts: The Belknap Press of Harvard University Press.
Copyright 1951, 1955 by The President and Fellows of Harvard College.

ANALOGY

To understand properly the concept of analogy as a means of rhetorical development, it is first necessary to understand the idea of *imagery* in writing. In its broadest sense, imagery is the appeal through language to any one (or any combination of) the five senses. It is a linguistic device which can be used for ornament, emphasis, or clarification; and it includes such variant devices as simile, metaphor, pun, personification, onomatopeia, and many others. For our more limited purposes here we will consider only simile and metaphor.

The simile, as you perhaps recall from your courses in poetry, is an explicit comparison employing either of the words "like" or "as"; the metaphor is an implicit comparison in which neither of those words are used. The sentence, "The sun poised like a golden ball in the sky," is a simile comparing the appearance of the sun to a golden ball. By altering the same sentence slightly, "The golden ball of the sun poised in the sky," we change the simile into a metaphor; and though the comparison is still the same, in the first instance it is explicit, in the second implicit.

A good share of language has evolved by imagery, and indeed much of our commonplace phraseology is fundamentally imagistic. Slang, jargon, and colloquial language are replete with images used, for the most part, unconsciously and as a matter of course. When we observe that someone "eats like a pig" or is "thin as a rail" we are, perhaps, being rather trite, but we are most certainly depending on images to help express our meaning.

A skillful writer will often employ imagery deliberately for one of two effects: clarity and emotional persuasion. In expository writing it is the former, clarity, we are most concerned with, for generally it is best in this sort of writing to avoid appeals to the emotions. When one does use images in exposition they are called analogies and their purpose is to make clear to the reader one idea or object by close reference to another. For example, the physical workings of the human heart may be explained to a layman audience by likening it to a pump. The several functions of a pump are similar enough to the action of the heart to make such an analogy valid and to clarify in the reader's mind some of the mysteries of the latter. Another common illustration is the analogy drawn between a current of electricity flowing through a wire and water flowing through a pipe. The expansion of this analogy can shed light on a difficult physical process through simple comparison with a more familiar one, one the reader can visually reconstruct by means of the verbal image.

Imagery that appeals to the emotions is doubtless much more common than analogy used for the purposes of clarification, and because of its popularity it deserves a special word. Many essayists, novelists, and poets are given to the use of this sort of imagery because of its effectiveness in ordering the reader's response. Consider, for example, the effect achieved by the writer who describes a building as a "grey smudge on the horizon." Clearly, such an image is intended to evoke a particular—and negative—response in the mind of the reader, an effect that can be reversed by picturing the same building as "framed like a towering cathedral by the brilliant sky." The point is that in both of these illustrations imagistic language is used to stimulate an emotional response to the material, a purpose considerably different from that of analogy.

Regardless of how imagery is employed, whether for analogy or emotional appeal, it serves an important role in rhetoric. Effectively employed, it helps us to understand by recognizing patterns and to communicate by assembling those patterns in coherent fashion. The following selections all deal essentially with obscure ideas or notions which the writers attempt to elucidate through analogy. In some cases their use of analogy extends beyond the goal of mere clarification and moves into the realm of emotional appeal. It will be helpful to examine carefully all of the images and to determine the writer's special purpose and the effectiveness of his imagery in achieving that purpose.

the battle of the ants

HENRY DAVID THOREAU

1 One day when I went out to my wood-pile, or rather my pile of stumps, I observed two large ants, the one red, the other much larger, nearly half an inch long, and black, fiercely contending with one another. Having once got hold they never let go, but struggled and wrestled and rolled on the chips incessantly. Looking farther, I was surprised to find that the chips were covered with such combatants, that it was not a *duellum*, but a *bellum*, a war between two races of ants, the red always pitted against the black, and frequently two red ones to one black. The legions of these Myrmidons covered all the hills and vales in my wood-yard, and the ground was already strewn with the dead and dying, both red and black. It was the only battle which I have ever witnessed, the only battle-field I ever trod while the battle was raging; internecine war; the red republicans on the one hand, and the black imperialists on the other. On every side they were engaged in deadly combat, yet without any noise that I could hear, and human soldiers never fought so resolutely. I watched a couple that were fast locked in each other's embraces, in a little sunny valley amid the chips, now at noonday prepared to fight till the sun went down, or life went out. The smaller red champion had fastened himself like a vice to his adversary's front, and through all the tumblings on that field never for an instant ceased to gnaw at one of his feelers near the root, having already caused the other to go by the board; while the stronger black one dashed him from side to side, and,

as I saw on looking nearer, had already divested him of several of his members. They fought with more pertinacity than bull-dogs. Neither manifested the least disposition to retreat. It was evident that their battle-cry was "Conquer or die." In the mean-while there came along a single red ant on the hillside of this valley, evidently full of excitement, who either had despatched his foe, or had not yet taken part in the battle; probably the latter, for he had lost none of his limbs; whose mother had charged him to return with his shield or upon it. Or perchance he was some Achilles, who had nourished his wrath apart, and had now come to avenge or rescue his Patroclus. He saw this unequal combat from afar—for the blacks were nearly twice the size of the red—he drew near with rapid pace till he stood on his guard within half an inch of the combatants; then, watching his opportunity, he sprang upon the black warrior, and com-menced his operations near the root of his right fore leg, leaving the foe to select among his own members; and so there were three united for life, as if a new kind of attraction had been invented which put all other locks and cements to shame. I should not have wondered by this time to find that they had their respective musical bands stationed on some eminent chip, and playing their national airs the while, to excite the slow and cheer the dying combatants. I was myself excited somewhat even as if they had been men. The more you think of it, the less the difference. And certainly there is not the fight recorded in Concord history, at least, if in the history of America, that will bear a moment's comparison with this, whether for the numbers engaged in it, or for the patriotism and heroism displayed. For numbers and for carnage it was an Austerlitz or Dresden. Con-cord Fight! Two killed on the patriots' side, and Luther Blanchard wounded! Why here every ant was a Buttrick—"Fire! for God's sake fire!"—and thousands shared the fate of Davis and Hosmer. There was not one hireling there. I have no doubt that it was a principle they fought for, as much as our ancestors, and not to avoid a three-penny tax on their tea; and the results of this battle will be as important and memorable to those whom it concerns as those of the battle of Bunker Hill, at least.

2　　I took up the chip on which the three I have particularly described were struggling, carried into my house, and placed it under a tumbler on my window-sill, in order to see the issue. Holding a microscope to the first-mentioned red ant, I saw that, though he was assiduously gnawing at the near fore leg of his enemy, having severed his remaining feeler, his own breast was all torn away, exposing what vitals he had there to the jaws of the black warrior, whose breastplate was apparently too thick for him to pierce; and the dark carbuncles of the sufferer's eyes shone with ferocity such as war only could excite. They struggled half an hour longer under the tumbler, and when I looked again the black soldier had severed the heads of his foes from their bodies, and the still living heads were hanging on either side of him like ghastly trophies at his saddle-bow, still apparently as firmly fastened as ever, and he was endeavoring with feeble struggles, being without feelers, and with only the remnant of a leg, and I know not how many other wounds, to divest himself of them; which at length, after half an hour more, he accomplished. I raised the glass, and he went off over the window-sill in that crippled state. Whether he finally survived that combat, and spent the remainder of his days in some Hôtel des Invalides, I do not know; but I thought that his industry would not be worth much thereafter. I never learned which party was victorious, nor the cause of the war, but I felt for the rest of that day as if I had my feelings excited and harrowed by witnessing the struggle, the ferocity and carnage, of a human battle before my door.

3   Kirby and Spence tell us that the battles of ants have long been celebrated and the date of them recorded, though they say that Huber is the only modern author who appears to have witnessed them. "Aeneas Sylvius," say they, "after giving a very circumstantial account of one contested with great obstinacy by a great and small species on the trunk of a pear tree," adds that " 'this action was fought in the pontificate of Eugenius the Fourth, in the presence of Nicholas Pistoriensis, an eminent lawyer, who related the whole history of the battle with the greatest fidelity.' A similar engagement between great and small ants is recorded by Olaus Magnus, in which the small ones, being victorious, are said to have buried the bodies of their own soldiers, but left those of their giant enemies a prey to the birds.

This event happened previous to the expulsion of the tyrant Christiern the Second from Sweden." The battle which I witnessed took place in the Presidency of Polk, five years before the passage of Webster's Fugitive-Slave Bill.

from *troilus and cressida*[1]
WILLIAM SHAKESPEARE

The specialty of rule hath been neglected.
And, look, how many Grecian tents do stand
Hollow upon this plain, so many hollow factions.
When that the general is not like the hive
To whom the foragers shall all repair,
What honey is expected? Degree being vizarded,
The unworthiest shows as fairly in the mask.
The heavens themselves, the planets and this centre,
Observe degree, priority and place,
Insisture, course, proportion, season, form,   10
Office, and custom, in all line of order:
And therefore is the glorious planet Sol
In noble eminence enthroned and sphered
Amidst the other; whose medicinable eye
Corrects the ill aspects of planets evil,
And posts like the commandment of a king,
Sans check to good and bad: but when the planets
In evil mixture to disorder wander,
What plagues and what portents, what mutiny,
What raging of the sea, shaking of earth,   20
Commotion in the winds, frights, changes, horrors,
Divert and crack, rend and deracinate

[1]Ulysses speaking to the Greek Army giving reasons for their failure to capture Troy.

The unity and married calm of states
Quite from their fixture! O, when degree is shaked,
Which is the ladder to all high designs,
The enterprise is sick! How could communities,
Degrees in schools and brotherhoods in cities,
Peaceful commerce from dividable shores,
The primogenitive and due of birth,
Prerogative of age, crowns, sceptres, laurels,   30
But by degree, stand in authentic place?
Take but degree away, untune that string,
And, hark, what discord follows! each thing meets
In mere oppugnancy: the bounded waters
Should lift their bosoms higher than the shores,
And make a sop of all this solid globe:
Strength should be lord of imbecility,
And the rude son should strike his father dead:
Force should be right; or rather, right and wrong,
Between whose endless jar justice resides,   40
Should lose their names, and so should justice too.
Then every thing includes itself in power,
Power into will, will into appetite;
And appetite, an universal wolf,
So doubly seconded with will and power,
Must make perforce an universal prey,
And last eat up himself. Great Agamemnon,
This chaos, when degree is suffocate,
Follows the choking.
And this neglection of degree it is   50
That by a pace goes backward, with a purpose
It hath to climb. The general's disdain'd
By him one step below; he by the next;
That next by him beneath: so every step,
Exampled by the first pace that is sick
Of his superior, grows to an envious fever
Of pale and bloodless emulation:
And 'tis this fever that keeps Troy on foot,
Not her own sinews.

nirvana now

DANIEL P. MOYNIHAN

1 One of the defining qualities of the period of current history that began, roughly, with the assassination of President Kennedy has been the emergence of widespread, radical protest on the part of American youth. As it happens, this development has been congruent, and in some measure associated, with even wider protest against the current course of American foreign policy, but there is a distinction between those who differ with decisions made by the existing system, and those who reject the system itself. There is at this moment a high level of both kinds of protest, but the latter is the more singular, and almost certainly the more significant.

2 Following a period when college youth in particular were repeatedly accused of quiescent conformism, this development has taken the World War II generation rather by surprise. More than one college president given to deploring "the silent generation" appears in retrospect not half so bold, and considerably less prescient than he would have had his charges suppose. Never to trust anyone under thirty has become almost a first principle of prudence for academic administrators, and not a bad rule for politicians. It is yet to be seen, however, what if anything we shall learn from this surprising and unexpected development.

Reprinted with permission of the publishers, from *The American Scholar*, Volume 36, Number 4, Autumn, 1967. © 1967 by the United Chapters of Phi Beta Kappa.

3   Of necessity, we tend to interpret present events in terms of past experience, there being, despite the efforts of the American Academy of Arts and Sciences, as yet but little future experience to guide us. I would, however, argue that we have so far been looking to misleading analogues. We have been seeing in the flamboyance of the hippies, the bitterness of the alienated college youth, the outrageousness of the New Left, little more than mutants of the old bohemianism, the never-ending conflict of generations, and perhaps the persistence of neo-Marxist radicalism. We may be wrong. Just possibly, something more important is abroad. We may be witnessing the first heresies of liberalism.

4   In its familiar setting heresy refers to religious views contrary to the established dogma of a church. It will seem odd to use it to describe such assertively nonreligious phenomena as the Students for a Democratic Society. Some also will object that inasmuch as the doctrines of liberalism are derived from experience, rather than right reason, there can be no final liberal view about anything, and therefore no finally heretical dissent from such views. I suggest, however, that the phenomenon of protest we observe today is more psychological than doctrinal in origin, and that to the youth of this time secular liberalism presents itself as every bit as much a system of "established and commonly received doctrine" as did Christianity, for example, when it was the legally prescribed belief of the Holy Roman Empire, or the Massachusetts Bay Colony. To be sure, the doctrines of liberalism can be elusive. It is a conviction, Learned Hand might say, that is not too sure of itself—save on the point that it is vastly to be preferred to any creed that is. Liberals are not without tracts—hardly—but tend more to look to institutions as repositories of their beliefs, liberalism being in every sense as much a *way* of doing things, as it is a set of propositions as to what is to be done. It is not without its schisms and assuredly not without its confusions. But in all its essentials of an optimistic belief in progress, in toleration, in equality, in the rule of law, and in the possibility of attaining a high and sustained measure of human happiness here on earth, liberalism is the nigh universally accepted creed of the ruling elites of the Western world. Religious faith persists, even grows. But it does so as a private matter: supernatural beliefs have almost no influence

on the course of events. Secular liberalism is triumphant. Not surprisingly, then, given especially the great value liberalism places on skepticism and inquiry, liberalism itself is beginning to be questioned.

5   It is notorious, of course, that among the most eminent of the literary men of this century the liberal values of the larger society have been viewed with a detachment ranging from indifference to detestation. But these were men born in the nineteenth century, and raised in a world that still had, or thought it had, some options with respect to forsaking the traditionalist, hierarchical, Christan past and embracing the new creed. To these writers it had been a mistake to do so; they withheld their own assent. Thus it may have been incongruous, even perhaps unpatriotic, for a St. Louis boy such as Mr. Eliot to show such enthusiasm for the Church of England and the Royal Family, but it was not absurd. American youth today have no such option. The liberal present is the only world they know, and if it is not to their liking, as for many it is not, their only alternative is to consider how it might evolve into something new, there being no possibility of reverting to something old. What follows is very like a spiritual crisis, and in the manner of individuals and communities that have confronted such in the past, some lapse into indifference and quietism, others escape into varied forms of stabilized hysteria, while still others turn to confront doctrine itself, and in a mood of intensely felt revelation reject the very foundations of orthodoxy.

6   What indeed is most striking about the current surge of protest is the degree to which it reenacts in matters of style and structure the great heresies that have assailed the religious establishments of other ages. "The sun shone," Samuel Beckett writes in the opening passage of *Murphy,* "having no alternative, on the nothing new."

7   The forms of youthful protest at this time are many, and not all, of course, visible. But there are three clusters of behavior that are sufficiently coherent as to suggest a central tendency in each, and to offer the possibility of analogies with earlier phenomena.

8   The most familiar-seeming, and for that reason possibly the most deceptive of the new tendencies, is that of the New Left

itself. It is familiar because it has taken a familiar form: the
organization of a group defined by political objectives. Yet in
truth something profoundly new may be present here, for the
object of the New Left is not to capture the system but to
transform it. The older radicalisms were inextricably involved
with things-as-they-are, and, owing especially to Marx's view of
economic determinism, they largely deprived the radical challenge to liberal capitalism of any *moral* basis: the system had a
destiny that was working itself out regardless of any intentions,
good or evil, on the part of mortals so innocent of the laws of
economics as to suppose they, rather than things, were in the
saddle. The Old Left was so utterly "materialistic" and "realistic"
as to use those very terms to describe one of its defining dogmas.
As Richard Blumenthal, of the Harvard Class of 1967, recently
observed in the *Nation,* it is precisely this "crass materialism"
that the Students for a Democratic Society reject. It is precisely
the "dehumanizing" of modern society that they resent. Society's
"main and transcending" concern, Tom Hayden writes, "must
be the unfolding and refinement of the moral, aesthetic and
logical capacities of men in a manner that creates genuine independence." However that is to be achieved, Blumenthal adds,
it is not likely to be by way of "a house in the country and a
two-car garage." The movement is purposely "anti-ideological,
even anti-intellectual." It is precisely that rational commitment
to logic and consistency—of the kind that can lead from game
theory at the RAND Corporation to the use of napalm in
Vietnam—that these young persons abhor.

9   Of late they have set about building things called "independent power bases" among the poor (a concept one fears may
have been borrowed from the Strategic Air Command), but the
striking fact about the famous Port Huron Statement adopted
by S.D.S. in 1962 is that it barely, and then only indirectly,
touches on problems such as poverty. It is addressed exclusively
to middle-class intellectuals and college students: the "people of
this generation, bred in at least modest comfort, housed now
in universities, looking uncomfortably to the world we inherit."
The world about them was so content with material affluence as
to suppose it had attained stability, where in truth there was only
stagnation. The theme of the Port Huron Statement is that

men must *live,* not simply exist. "Some would have us believe
that Americans feel contentment amidst prosperity—but might
it not better be called a glaze above deeply felt anxieties about
their role in the new world?" Man, they declared, had acquired
a role of consumer rather than creator. His capacity for love,
for creativity, for meaningful relations with others was being
lost amidst the machinery of government. S.D.S. proclaimed a
social system in which men would not only share one another's
fate, but participate, each one, in shaping that destiny: "We
believe in generosity of a kind that imprints one's unique individual qualities in the relation to other men, and to all human
activity." For such a goal the Gross National Product is indeed
a crude indicator of success.

10   Who are these outrageous young people? I suggest to you
they are Christians arrived on the scene of Second Century Rome.
The quality of life of that time remains difficult to assess, not
least because triumphant Christianity did so much to put an
end to it. James Anthony Froude, however, in his great Victorian
essay "Origen and Celsus," gives us a glimpse of that world in
his reconstruction of the mind of the Epicurean Celsus, a contemporary of Marcus Aurelius, who composed a tract concerning
the illogicalities and misstatements of fact in Christian doctrine
of such apparent force that Origen himself undertook to refute
him. The second century was not unlike the twentieth, and,
leaving aside the somewhat gratuitous assumptions of Europeans
that they are the Greeks of this age, let there be no doubt that
we are the Romans. It was a world, Froude writes, in which
"Moral good and moral evil were played with as fancies in the
lecture rooms; but they were fancies merely, with no bearing on
life. The one practical belief was that pleasure was pleasant.
The very memory disappeared that there was any evil except
bodily pain. . . ." It was a tolerant world that knew too much
about itself to expect words and deeds invariably to conform.
"Into the midst of this strange scene of imposture, profligacy,
enthusiasm and craving for light," Froude continues, "Christianity emerged out of Palestine with its message of lofty humility."

11   Who were these Christians? They were first of all outrageous.
They were "bad citizens, refusing public employment and avoiding service in the army; and while . . . they claimed toleration for

their own creed, they had no toleration for others; every god but their own they openly called a devil. . . ." They had no temples, no altars, no images, and boasted just that. "Fathers and tutors, they say, are mad or blind, unable to understand or do any good thing, given over to vain imaginations. The weavers and cobblers only are wise, they only have the secret of life, they only can show the way to peace and happiness." Of learning they had little and cared less. Nor had they any great interest in respectable people who observed the rules of society and tried to keep it running; they cared only for the outcast and miserable. To be a sinner, they seemed to say, was the one sure way to be saved. They were altogether of a seditious and revolutionary character.

12   Such people were a bafflement to Celsus. If he spoke bitterly about them, he observed, it was because he was bitter. One can imagine him thinking, if not quite putting to paper: "Do they not see how precarious is the balance of things; how readily it might all be brought down?" He was every bit an admirable, reasonable man. "He considered," Froude writes, "that human affairs could be best ordered by attention and obedience to the teaching of observed facts, and that superstition, however accredited by honorable objects or apparent good effects, could only be mischievous in the long run. Sorcerers, charlatans, enthusiasts were rising thick on all sides, pretending a mission from the invisible world. Of such men and such messages Celsus and his friends were inexorable antagonists." His is the tone of the sensitive, and in ways holy, Inquisitor speaking before the trial of the Maid in Shaw's *Saint Joan:* "If you have seen what I have seen of heresy, you would not think it a light thing even in the most apparently harmless and even lovable and pious origins. Heresy begins with people who are to all appearances better than their neighbors. A gentle and pious girl, or a young man who has obeyed the command of our Lord by giving all his riches to the poor, and putting on the garb of poverty, the life of austerity, and the rule of humility and charity, may be the founder of a heresy that will wreck both Church and Empire if not ruthlessly stamped out in time." The Christians, Celsus declared, were welcome to stay and become part of the commonwealth, but if that was to be their choice, they must live by its

rules. Otherwise be gone. Nothing was required that a reasonable
man need find objectionable: to salute the sun, or to sing a hymm
to Athene did no harm to anyone. Whatever private views one
might have on the subject were one's own affair. But society
had a right to allegiance.

13   Point by point Celsus took on Christianity. Point by point he
won the intellectual argument, and lost the moral and spiritual
one. For he was thinking about the world, and Christians were
thinking about the soul. "Most persons," Froude notes, "would
now admit that Celsus spoke with wise diffidence when he hesitated at the assumption that the universe and all that it contained was created solely for the sake of man. Origen is perfectly
certain that God had no other object. Sun, moon, and stars, and
earth and everything living upon it were subordinated to man.
In man alone, or in reference to man, the creation had its purpose
and meaning." God commanded that the world provide that
which is needed by man: as he is weak there must be compassion;
as he is sinful there must be the forgiveness of sins; and above
all, as he is Godlike, his life must be seen as sacred. If that condition has never been achieved, neither has the Western world
ever been the same since first embracing the belief that it should
be. Can there be any mistaking that the New Left speaks to the
rational, tolerant, reasonable society of the present with the same
irrationality, intolerance and unreasonableness, but possibly also
the same truth with which the absurd Christians spoke to
Imperial Rome? Even Froude, professed and militant Christian,
was not less a product of Imperial Britain, and in his grasp of
Celsus' arguments, a certain affinity shows through. One recalls
the curious moral judgments on display in his own essay, "The
English in Ireland in the Eighteenth Century."

> Among reasonable beings right is forever tending to make
> might. Inferiority of numbers is compensated by superior co-
> hesiveness, intelligence, and daring. The better sort of men sub-
> mit willingly to be governed by those who are nobler and wiser
> than themselves; organization creates superiority of force; and the
> ignorant and the selfish may be and are justly compelled for their
> own advantage to obey a rule which rescues them from their
> natural weakness. . . . And the right of a people to self-government
> consists and can consist in nothing but their power to defend

themselves. No other definition is possible. . . . When resistance
has been tried and failed—when the inequality has been proved
beyond dispute by long and painful experience—the wisdom, and
ultimately the duty, of the weaker party is to accept the benefits
which are offered in exchange for submission.

In truth, is there not a touch of this in the liberal doctrines of
the American Empire, with its panoply of technical assistance,
constitutional conventions, mutual assistance treaties and development loans, accompanied as it seems to be by the un-
troubled, or at least willing, use of astonishing degrees of violence to help others perceive the value of going along?

14   The young people of the New Left know what they want; a
larger, more diffuse group can best be described as knowing
what they do not want, which is what they have. These are so-
called alienated students of the present generation. The psychiatrist Seymour L. Halleck recently described them as "existing in
a state of chronic identity crisis. . . . [their] constant cries of
'Who am I, I don't know what I believe, I have no self' are
accompanied by anxiety which while subdued is nevertheless
pervasive and relentless." Affluence means nothing and the increase in personal freedom that comes with growing up is as
much as anything a threat to which the individual responds with
"a peculiar kind of apathy and withdrawal. . . . Having failed
to develop an internalized value system which allows him to
determine his direction in life, he is paralyzed when the external
world removes its guidelines and restraints." Such persons, Dr.
Halleck reports, will occasionally involve themselves in campus
protest movements and sustain the interest for a short while,
but not long, which is perhaps just as well as "When he does
become involved with the activist groups he can be characterized
as the most angry and irrational member of that group." Sex
and drugs are outlets, but joyless ones. They have everything,
but nothing works.

15   Have we not seen this person through history, turning away
from a religion that was failing him, rejecting its laws and
opting instead for standards of conduct derived wholly from
internal personal resources? The object of a liberal secular society
being to induce human happiness, it more or less follows that
those who reject it will choose to be unhappy and evoke their

spirituality in despair more than ecstasy, but *mutatis mutandis,*[1]
are we not witnessing the emergence of secular antinomianism?
16   Not a precise, but an interesting parallel is to be seen in
Sabbatianism, the mystical Jewish heresy that sprang up in the
Holy Land in the seventeenth century and spread through large
sections of Sephardic and then Ashkenazic Jewry. Gershom G.
Scholem described this heresy in the Hilda Stich Stroock Lectures
delivered in New York in 1938. Judaism faced a series of crises
at that time: persecution, apostasy and, for some reason, a sudden
impatience with the Lord: how long were the Jews to wander
in exile? Scholem writes: "Doctrines arose which had one thing
in common: That they tried to bridge the gap between the inner
experience and the external reality which had ceased to function
as its symbol." Sabbatai Zevi, a Cabalistic ascetic, and almost
certainly a manic depressive, proclaimed himself the Messiah in
Gaza in 1665, and eventually won a great following even though
—and seemingly because—he went on to become an apostate! A
singular quality of the man was that under the influence of his
manic enthusiasms he would commit acts counter to religious
law. Harmless enough at first, this practice developed among his
radical followers into full-fledged antinomianism. "The Torah,"
the radical Sabbatians were fond of declaring, "is the seed-corn
of Salvation, and just as the seed-corn must rot in the earth in
order to sprout and bear fruit, the Torah must be subverted in
order to appear in its true Messianic glory." This developed in
time into a doctrine of the holiness of sin when committed by
an elect who are fundamentally different from the crowd. It was
of course a profound affront to Rabbinical Judaism, and in its
extreme forms acquired a sinister cast indeed, but Scholem
writes, "The religious . . . and moral nihilism of the radicals is
after all only the confused and mistaken expression of their
urge towards a fundamental regeneration of Jewish life, which
under the historic conditions of those times could not find a
normal expression." The heresy plagued Jewry for a century or
more, and seems to have some influence in the rise of the openly
antireligious doctrines of the French Revolution. Nathan M.
Pusey has voiced his own serious doubts about "the idea that

[1]"The necessary changes being made."

the way to advance civilization is to start over," but one cannot deny the attraction of just this view for persons who find themselves inexplicably not getting from society exactly those satisfactions society most confidently promises them.

17 Of course, far the most visible of the new protestants are those who do not protest at all, who simply smile, wave daffodils, cover the walls of their *quartiers* with graffiti suggesting we "Legalize Living," and wear their own variety of campaign buttons the quintessential of which demands with purest obstinacy, "Nirvana Now." These are the hippies. Lilies of the field. Bearded and sandaled, they live on air, and love and, alas, drugs. They seek not to change our society, but simply to have nothing to do with it. They are in quest of experiences wholly mystical and internal on the one hand, and tribal on the other. The modern American style of the effective individual functioning in a coherent but competitive society is not for them. Hunter S. Thompson in *The New York Times Sunday Magazine* recently reported an interview with such a young woman living in the Haight-Ashbury section of San Francisco: "I love the whole world," she said, "I am the divine mother, part of Buddha, part of God, part of everything." How did she live? "From meal to meal. I have no money, no possessions, money is beautiful only when it's flowing; when it piles up it's a hang-up. We take care of each other." Did she use drugs? Yes: "When I find myself becoming confused I drop out and take a dose of acid. It's a shortcut to reality; it throws you right into it." Did she pray? "Oh yes, I pray in the morning sun. It nourishes me with its energy so I can spread love and beauty and nourish others. I never pray *for* anything; I don't need anything. Whatever turns me on is a sacrament: LSD, sex, my bells, my colors . . . that is the holy communion, you dig?"

18 Perhaps not. Yet those assertions would have seemed perfectly clear and altogether admirable to a member of the Brethren of the Free Spirit (or the Spiritual Libertines), a mystical Christian heresy that permeated vast areas of medieval Europe, notably the teeming cities of Flanders and the lowlands, from the twelfth century onward almost to our time. Perhaps because its adepts lived in communities within larger polities, and never took over regions for themselves, and also, being clearly heretical, tended

at most times to be more or less underground, little attention has been given the Brethren. But they appear to have significantly influenced the political, if not the religious, development of Europe.

19   In their mystical craving for an immediate experience of God, their antinomianism, and emphasis on ecstasy, the Brethren of the Free Spirit were not unlike the Jewish Sabbatians, or for that matter the early Christians. Indeed a certain correspondence obtains among all these movements. When they took matters to an extreme of public display, the Brethren, like those before and after them, both fascinated and horrified the orthodox. "The core of the heresy," Norman Cohn writes in *The Pursuit of the Millenium,* ". . . lay in the adept's attitude towards himself: he believed that he had attained a perfection so absolute that he was incapable of sin." Sexual promiscuity became a matter of principle, and marriage was denounced as an impure state. Eroticism and ecstasy were valued beyond all things as symbols of having achieved what was in truth a state of self-deification. In an age when wealth suddenly appeared in Europe, these heretics characteristically preached a communism of property, and chose to be utterly penniless: in Cohn's words, an elite of amoral supermen.

20   As with Celsus, we are forced to learn most about the views of the Brethren from denunciations by their enemies. Documents from Cromwell's England, a time when the Brethren, known as Ranters, were flourishing, leave no doubt, again in Cohn's words, that the " 'Free Spirit' really was exactly what it was said to be: a system of self-exaltation often amounting to self-deification; a pursuit of total emancipation which in practice could result in antinomianism and particularly in anarchic eroticism; often also a revolutionary social doctrine which denounced the institution of private property; and aimed at its abolition." The Quakers at first saw them as kindred spirits—and the two were often lumped together by others—but efforts at rapprochement were unavailing. The saintly George Fox came upon a group of them as fellow prisoners at Charing Cross. He proposed, we cannot doubt, that they meditate together on the love of God. They called instead for beer and tobacco. A comedy of 1651 by Samuel Sheppard describes the "Character of the roaring Ranters of these Times" in terms that are familiar to say the least:

> . . . our women are all in common.
> We drink quite drunk together, share our Oaths,
> If one man's cloak be rent, all their Cloaths.

A chorus goes:

> Come away, make no delay, of mirth we are no scanters,
> Dance and sing all in a Ring, for we are Jovial Ranters.

And the verses fearfully so:

> All lie down, as in a swown,
> To have a pleasing vision.
> And then rise with bared thighs,
> Who'd fear such sweet incision?
>
> About, about, ye Joviall rout,
> Dance antick like Hob-goblins;
> Drink and roar, and swear and whore,
> But yet no brawls or squoblings.

21   It is said the youth of Haight-Ashbury are not much addicted to scholarship, and they may be pardoned for giving to their service corps the name of "Diggers," after the primitivist community established near Cobham in Surrey in 1649–50. (Such folk have an instinct for agreeable settings.) But they are nonetheless mistaken. Hippies are Ranters.

22   Supposing all this to be so, does it matter? I believe it does. In the first place these persons matter: they number some of the fine spirits of the age. A liberal must regret the loss of belief in another as much as a decent churchman would. In the second place, these youths are trying to tell us something. It was Chesterton, surely, who described heresy as truth gone astray.

23   Seen in large terms, it is clear that these protests have been generated by at least three problems facing our society, each one of which can be said to arise from tendencies that are distinctively those of secular liberalism.

24   The first tendency is that our optimism, belief in progress, and the possibility of achieving human happiness on earth, combined with our considerable achievement in this respect at home, have led us to an increasingly dangerous and costly effort to extend our system abroad. We are in the grip of what Reinhold Niebuhr has called "The Myth of Democratic University," the idea that democracy is a "universal option for all nations." The irony, of

course, is that it is just because our own history has been so unique that we are led to suppose that the system that has emerged from it can be made worldwide. It is an effort doomed to fail.

25   No civilization has ever succeeded in doing anything of the kind, and surely none whose qualities are as historically conditioned as ours should even try. But it is not just that we shall fail: something more serious is involved. In his inaugural lecture at the London School of Economics and Political Science, Michael Oakeshott, succeeding Harold Laski, made a remark of some significance here. ". . . To try to do something which is inherently impossible," he said, "is always a corrupting enterprise." That, in a word, is what I believe has happened to us overseas. As our efforts repeatedly fall short of their pronounced goals, we begin covering up, taking shortcuts, and in desperation end up doing things we would never conceivably start out to do. Princes of the Church, modest sons of small-town grocers, begin proclaiming holy wars in Asia, while the man in the street acquires an appallingly troubled vision of those who protest. In the words of a Columbia student, describing the mood of a crowd watching a peace march: "War is virility; love of peace is bohemianism and quite probably a sexual perversion."

26   Liberals have simply got to restrain their enthusiasm for civilizing others. It is their greatest weakness and ultimate arrogance. Bertrand Russell suggests that the great Albigensian heresy, with its quest for personal holiness and cult of poverty, was due at least in part to "disappointment of the failure of the crusades." Very likely it will be the success rather than the failure of *our* crusades that will most repel youth. Nathan Glazer has suggested that this generation is already marked by the belief that its government is capable of performing abhorrent deeds.

27   Not the least reason the American commitment to the diffusion of liberal democracy abroad has become a corrupting enterprise is that those values are not yet genuinely secure at home. This is an ugly fact we somehow never finally confront. At just those moments when we seem about to do so, something, somehow, comes along to distract us. Yet there persists in American opinion a powerful component that is illiberal, irrational, intolerant, anti-intellectual, and capable if unleashed of

doing the most grievous damage to the fabric of our own society. A century of universal education has not destroyed this tendency, it has only made it more articulate. And it can drive the liberal elite to astonishing distortions. During this past year we have had to begin admitting that during the height of the cold war the United States government began secretly using intelligence funds to support organizations of liberal and even left-leaning students and intellectuals. This was done out of a sincere and almost certainly sound conviction that the activities of these groups would aid in the struggle against totalitarianism. Observe the irony: the liberals running American foreign policy were forced to resort, in effect, to corrupt practices—to totalitarian practices if you will—in order to advance liberal causes—*because the popularly elected Congress would never dream of doing so.* The man most commonly blamed, of course, is a decent enough Irish Democrat from Brooklyn: his voting record is impeccably progressive, but neither he nor his constituents share the elite enthusiasm for intellectuals. In the explanations of it all a note even of poignancy enters: can you imagine, writes one former member of the intelligence establishment, trying to get the F.B.I. to grant security clearances to the Boston Symphony Orchestra? The problem goes beyond an affinity for Culture. We have not been able to get rid of racism, or to secure an equal place for Negroes in our society. (An effort in which liberals themselves have not been unfailingly helpful: Woodrow Wilson restored segregation to federal employment policies.) And we begin to perceive that Negroes are not immune to some of the less attractive qualities of their persecutors. We have not been able to get rid of poverty, and begin to perceive that some of our more treasured liberal reforms may have had unanticipated consequences that may even make it more difficult to do so. (Thus, having destroyed the power of the working class political party organization in our cities, we now pour millions of dollars of federal funds into projects designed to overcome the psychic effects of "powerlessness" among the poor.) And we have not rid ourselves of a brutal streak of violence. If the Administration has escalated the conflict in Vietnam, remember that the largest body of opinion in the United States would bomb the yellow bastards into the stone age, and a solid quarter specifically favors using the atom bomb. Cohn reports that the Ranters really began to flourish after the execution of Charles I.

28   A third problem that has contributed to the rise of youthful protest is, I would suggest, that as the life of the educated elite in America becomes more rational, more dogged of inquiry and fearless of result, the wellsprings of emotion *do* dry up, and in particular the primal sense of community begins to fade. As much for the successful as for the failed, society becomes, in Durkheim's phrase, "a dust of individuals." But to the rational liberal, the tribal attachments of blood and soil appear somehow unseemly and primitive. They repress or conceal them, much as others might a particularly lurid sexual interest. It is for this reason, I would suggest, that the nation has had such difficulties accepting the persistence of ethnicity and group cohesion as a fact both of domestic and of world politics.

29   Thus it is possible not only to sympathize with the new protest, but to see much that is valid in it. At the same time we are required to note that which is dangerous. The protest movement is likely to grow rather than otherwise, for the educated middle class from which it draws its strength is growing, and will soon be the dominant American social group. Moreover, the forms of protest are likely to have a striking impact for the very reason that their object is not to redirect the system, but to disrupt it, and this is never a difficult thing to do. It is entirely possible that this disruption could bring to power the forces of the right, and this is indeed an avowed strategy. *Nach Hitler uns.*[2] As the traditional radical Tom Kahn wrote recently in *Partisan Review,* it would be silly to blame the 1966 liberal defeat in California on the New Left and the advocates of Black Power, but "it is enough to say that what they could do, they did." In some forms the rejection of existing society is merely confused, and essentially sophomoric. This winter at Harvard, for example, a document was distributed by a left group that brought to light the fact that in certain regions of Alaska community affairs are under the control of "local politicians, a control that in practice has often been responsive to local interests." At another level, it is anything but. This year, also at Harvard,

2"Hitler's way for us."

when a member of the Cabinet came as an invited guest, but under arrangements that did not suit them, the students of the New Left took possession of his person. Such tactics in the early days of Fascist Italy appalled civilization. They are not less objectionable on the Harvard campus. Kahn has described the New Left as "panic disguised as moral superiority" and others have noted how that panic subtly induces a fascination with violence—the most grievous of all possible liberal heresies.

30   To see history as an earnest evolution from the peat bogs to John Stuart Mill, or to the 1964 Democratic platform, is a simplicity that will not much commend itself to anyone any longer. Having read Mill and having helped draft that platform, I am for one aware of greater shortcomings than, say, the former's need to read Wordsworth at the onset of middle age. But neither would I reject the theme of J. H. Plumb's new series, *The History of Human Society,* "that the condition of man now is superior to what it was." Things are better, and where they are best is in the liberal industrial democracies of the North Atlantic world. I hold these regimes to be the best accommodation to the human condition yet devised, and will demand to know of those who reject it, just what they have in mind as a replacement. By and large the central religious and philosophical traditions of the West have led us to where we are now. Some of the heresies against that tradition have helped, and some indeed have been incorporated into it. But just as many have evidenced ugly and dangerous tendencies, of which a terrible certainty about things is surely the foremost.

31   The ancient Gnostics were a charming people, and there is much to be learned from their contact between the hidden, benevolent God, and the Old Testament, law-giving one. But as Scholem writes, "The term *Jewish God,* or *God of Israel,* is abusive and meant to be so. The Gnostics regarded the confusion between the two Gods, the higher, loving one, and the lower who is merely just, as a misfortune for religion. It is metaphysical antisemitism in its profoundest and most effective form which has found expression in these ideas and continues to do so." The Brethren of the Free Sprit are nothing if not a lovable folk, but Cohn notes, "They were in fact gnostics intent upon their own individual salvation; but the gnosis at which

they arrived was a quasi-mystical anarchism—an affirmation of freedom so reckless and unqualified that it amounted to a total denial of every kind of restraint and limitation." They were in fact the "remote precursers" of Bakunin and of Nietzsche: "Nietzsche's Superman, in however vulgarized a form, certainly obsessed the imagination of many of the 'armed bohemians' who made the National-Socialist revolution; and many a Communist intellectual, whether he knows it or not, owes more to Bakunin than to Marx."

32 To protect dissent, no matter how noxious, is one thing. To be indifferent to its growth is another. Men who would undo the system may speak: but they must be answered. The less than soul stirring belief of the liberal in due process, in restraint, in the rule of law is something more than a bourgeois *apparat*.[3] It involves, I argue, the most profound perception of the nature of human society that has yet been achieved, and, precisely in its acknowledgment of the frailty of man and the persistence of sin and failure, it is in the deepest harmony with the central tradition of Judeo-Christian theology. It is not a belief to be frittered away in deference to a mystique of youth.

33 What we must do first of all is listen. Young people are trying to tell us something. They are probably right in much of what they say, however wrong their prescriptions for righting matters. Then we must respond. American liberalism needs to bring its commitments in balance with its resources—overseas and at home. Some years ago Robert Warshaw noted that "So much of 'official' American culture has been cheaply optimistic that we are likely almost by reflex to take pessimism as a measure of seriousness." It is just this unthinking encouragement of bloated expectation that leads young persons to compare forecast with outcome and to conclude that hypocrisy and duplicity are at work. What is asked of us is honesty: and what that requires is a great deal more rigor is matching our performance to our standards. It is now the only way to maintain the credibility of those standards.

3"Affectation."

symbolic language of dreams

ERICH FROMM

1 One of the current definitions of a symbol is that it is "something that stands for something else." The definition is too
general to be useful, unless we can be more specific with regard
to the crucial question concerning the nature of the connection
between symbol and that which it symbolizes. While there are
many approaches to this question, I want to suggest the following differentiation between kinds of symbol as one most suited
to guide us in our understanding of symbolic language as used in
dreams.

2　We can differentiate between three kinds of symbols: the
conventional, the *accidental,* and the *universal* symbol.

3　The *conventional* symbol is the best known of the three, since
we employ it in everyday language. If we see the word "table" or
hear the sound "table," the letters *t-a-b-l-e* stand for something
else. They stand for the thing "table" that we see, touch, and
use. What is the connection between the *word* "table" and the
thing "table"? Is there any inherent relationship between them?
Obviously not. The *thing* table has nothing to do with the *sound*
table, and the only reason the word symbolizes the thing is the
convention of calling this particular thing by a name. We learn
this connection as children by the repeated experience of hearing

Reprinted with permission of Harper & Row, Publishers, Inc., from *Language: An Enquiry into Its Meaning and Function,* by Erich Fromm, edited
by Ruth N. Anshen. © 1957 by Harper & Row, Publishers, Inc.

the word in reference to the thing until a lasting association is formd so that we don't have to think to find the right word.

4   There are some words, however, in which the association is not only conventional. When we say "phooey," for instance, we make with our lips a movement of dispelling the air quickly. It is an expression of disgust in which our mouths participate. By this quick expulsion of air we imitate and thus express our intention to expel something, to get it out of our system. In this case, as in some others, the symbol has an inherent connection with the feeling it symbolizes. But even if we assume that originally many or even all words had their origins in some inherent connection between symbol and the symbolized, most words no longer have this meaning for us when we learn a language.

5   Words are not the only illustration for conventional symbols, although they are the most frequent and best-known ones. Pictures also can be conventional symbols. A flag, for instance, may stand for a specific country, and yet there is no intrinsic connection between the specific colors and the country for which they stand. They have been accepted as denoting that particular country, and we translate the visual impression of the flag into the concept of that country, again on conventional grounds. Some pictorial symbols are not entirely conventional; for example, the cross. The cross can be merely a conventional symbol of the Christian Church and in that respect no different from a flag. But the specific content of the cross referring to Jesus' death or, beyond that, to the interpenetration of the material and spiritual planes, puts the connection between the symbol and what it symbolizes beyond the level of mere conventional symbols.

6   The opposite to the conventional symbol is the *accidental* symbol, although they have one thing in common: there is no intrinsic relationship between the symbol and that which it symbolizes. Let us assume that someone has had a saddening experience in a certain city; when he hears the name of that city, he will easily connect the name with a mood of sadness, just as he would connect it with a mood of joy had his experience been a happy one. Quite obviously there is nothing in the nature of the city that is either sad or joyful. It is the individual ex-

perience connected with the city that makes it a symbol of a mood.

7   The same reaction could occur in connection with a house, a street, a certain dress, certain scenery, or anything once connected with a specific mood. We might find ourselves dreaming that we are in a certain city. In fact, there may be no particular mood connected with it in the dream; all we see is a street or even simply the name of the city. We ask ourselves why we happened to think of that city in our sleep and may discover that we had fallen asleep in a mood similar to the one symbolized by the city. The picture in the dream represents this mood, the city "stands for" the mood once experienced in it. The connection between the symbol and the experience symbolized is entirely accidental.

8   In contrast to the conventional symbol, the accidental symbol cannot be shared by anyone else except as we relate the events connected with the symbol. For this reason accidental symbols are rarely used in myths, fairy tales, or works of art written in symbolic language because they are not communicable unless the writer adds a lengthy comment to each symbol he uses. In dreams, however, accidental symbols are frequent, and Freud by his method of free association devised a method for understanding their meaning.

9   The *universal* symbol is one in which there is an intrinsic relationship between the symbol and that which it represents. Take, for instance, the symbol of fire. We are fascinated by certain qualities of fire in a fireplace. First of all, by its aliveness. It changes continuously, it moves all the time, and yet there is constancy in it. It remains the same without being the same. It gives the impression of power, of energy, of grace and lightness. It is as if it were dancing, and had an inexhaustible source of energy. When we use fire as a symbol, we describe the *inner experience* characterized by the same elements which we notice in the sensory experience of fire—the mood of energy, lightness, movement, grace, gaiety, sometimes one, sometimes another of these elements being predominant in the feeling.

10   Similar in some ways and different in others is the symbol of water—of the ocean or of the stream. Here, too, we find the

blending of change and constant movement and yet of permanence. We also feel the quality of aliveness, continuity, and energy.
But there is a difference; where fire is adventurous, quick, exciting, water is quiet, slow, and steady. Fire has an element of
surprise; water an element of predictability. Water symbolizes
the mood of aliveness, too, but one which is "heavier," "slower,"
and more comforting than exciting.

11   That a phenomenon of the physical world can be the adequate
expression of an inner experience, that the world of things can
be a symbol of the world of the mind, is not surprising. We all
know that our body expresses our mind. Blood rushes to our
head when we are furious, it rushes from it when we are afraid;
our heart beats more quickly when we are angry, and the whole
body has a different tonus if we are happy from the one it has
when we are sad. We express our mood by our facial expression
and our attitudes and feelings by movements and gestures so
precise that others recognize them more accurately from our
gestures than from our words. Indeed, the body is a symbol—
and not an allegory—of the mind. Deeply and genuinely felt
emotion, and even any genuinely felt thought, is expressed in our
whole organism. In the case of the universal symbol, we find the
same connection between mental and physical experience.
Certain physical phenomena suggest by their very nature certain
emotional and mental experiences, and we express emotional
experiences in the language of physical experiences, that is to
say, symbolically.

12   The universal symbol is the only one in which the relationship
between the symbol and that which is symbolized is not coincidental but intrinsic. It is rooted in the experience of the affinity
between an emotion or thought, on the one hand, and a sensory
experience, on the other. It can be called universal because it is
shared by all men, in contrast not only to the accidental symbol,
which is by its very nature entirely personal, but also to the
conventional symbol, which is restricted to a group of people
sharing the same convention. The universal symbol is rooted in
the properties of our body, our senses, and our mind, which
are common to all men and, therefore, not restricted to individuals or to specific groups. Indeed, *the language of the
universal symbol is the one common tongue developed by the*

human race, a language which it forgot before it succeeded in developing a universal conventional language.

13   There is no need to speak of a racial inheritance in order to explain the universal character of symbols. Every human being sharing the essential features of bodily and mental equipment with the rest of mankind is capable of speaking and understanding the symbolic language that is based upon these common properties. Just as we do not need to learn to cry when we are sad or to get red in the face when we are angry, and just as these reactions are not restricted to any particular race or group of people, symbolic language does not have to be learned and is not restricted to any segment of the human race. Evidence for this is to be found in the fact that symbolic language as it is employed in myths and dreams is found in all cultures, in the so-called primitive as well as such developed cultures as those of Egypt and Greece. Furthermore, the symbols used in these various cultures are strikingly similar since they all go back to the basic sensory as well as emotional experiences shared by men of all cultures. Dreams of people living in the United States, India, or China today, as well as those which are reported to us from Greece, Palestine, or Egypt 3000 years ago, are essentially the same in contents and structure.

14   The foregoing statement needs qualification, however. Some symbols differ in meaning according to the difference in their realistic significance in various cultures. For instance, the function and consequently the meaning of the sun is different in northern countries and in tropical countries. In northern countries, where water is plentiful, all growth depends on sufficient sunshine. The sun is the warm, life-giving, protecting, loving power. In the Near East, where the heat of the sun is much more powerful, the sun is a dangerous and even threatening power from which man must protect himself, while water is felt to be the source of all life and the main condition for growth. We may speak of *dialects of universal symbolic language,* which are determined by those differences in natural conditions which cause certain symbols to have a different meaning in different regions of the earth.

15   Different from these "symbolic dialects" is the fact that many symbols have more than one meaning in accordance with various

kinds of experiences which can be connected with one and the same natural phenomenon. Let us take the symbol of fire again. If we watch fire in the fireplace, which is a source of pleasure and comfort, it is expressive of a mood of aliveness, warmth, and pleasure. But if we see a building or forest on fire, it conveys to us an experience of threat and terror, of the powerlessness of man against the elements of nature. Fire, then, can be the symbolic representation of inner aliveness and happiness as well as of fear, powerlessness, or of one's own destructive tendencies. The same holds true of the symbol water. Water can be a most destructive force when it is whipped up by a storm or when a swollen river floods its banks. Therefore, it can be the symbolic expression of horror and chaos as well as of comfort and peace.

16   Another illustration of the same principle is a symbol of a valley. The valley enclosed between mountains can arouse in us the feeling of security and comfort, of protection against all dangers from the outside. But the protecting mountains can also mean isolating walls which do not permit us to get out of the valley and thus the valley can become a symbol of imprisonment. The particular meaning of the symbol in any given place can only be determined from the whole context in which the symbol appears, and in terms of the predominant experiences of the person using the symbol.

17   Accidental and universal symbols constitute the language which the dream employs. And almost all attempts to understand the nature of dreams were based on the common assumption that symbolic language gave expression to inner experiences in the form of sensory experiences happening in the physical world. There was also agreement in all great cultures throughout history that all dreams are meaningful and significant. Meaningful, because they contain a message which can be understood if one has the key for its translation. Significant, because we do not dream of anything that is trifling, even though the significant message might be hidden behind a seemingly trifling façade. But while there is agreement with regard to these main principles, we find a great deal of disagreement running through the centuries with regard to the essential meaning of dreams.

18   One school of thought, of which Plato and Freud are outstand-

ing representatives, holds that dreams are expressions of the lowest and animal-like part of our soul, and that our irrational and evil strivings appear in our dreams, when the control of reason and conscience has gone to sleep. The opposite view, that dreams reveal our highest and most rational faculties, and even gifts of prediction which we do not have in our waking life, was held by many others from Biblical times to thinkers like Goethe and Emerson and psychoanalysts like C. G. Jung. From my own experiences in trying to understand dreams, I have come to the conclusion that dreams are not necessarily the expression either of our higher or of our lower self, but that there is no kind of mental activity, feeling, or thought which does not appear in dreams expressed in symbolic language. I believe that the only description of the nature of dreams which does not distort our interpretation by too narrow an expectation of the meaning of dreams is the broad definition that *dreaming is a meaningful and significant expression of any kind of mental activity under the condition of sleep.*

19   Obviously this definition is too broad to be of much help for the understanding of the nature of dreams unless we can say something more definite about the "condition of sleep" and the particular effect of this condition on our mental activity. If we can find out what the specific effect of sleeping is on our mental activity, we may discover a good deal more about the nature of dreaming.

20   Physiologically, sleep is a condition of chemical regeneration of the organism; energy is restored while no action takes place and even sensory perception is almost entirely shut off. Psychologically, sleep suspends the main function characteristic of waking life: man's reacting toward reality by perception and action. This difference between the biological functions of waking and of sleeping is, in fact, a difference between two states of existence.

21   The difference between the functions of sleeping and waking is more fundamental than any difference between various other kinds of activity, and accordingly the difference between the conceptual systems accompanying the two states is incomparably greater. In the waking state thoughts and feelings respond pri-

marily to challenge—the task of mastering our environment, changing it, defending ourselves against it. Survival is the task of waking man; he is subject to the laws that govern reality. This means that he has to think in terms of time and space and that his thoughts are subject to the laws of time and space logic.

22   While we sleep we are not concerned with bending the outside world to our purposes. We are helpless, and sleep, therefore, has rightly been called the "brother of death." But we are also free, freer than when awake. We are free from the burden of work, from the task of attack or defense, from watching and mastering reality. We need not look at the outside world; we look at our inner world, are concerned exclusively with ourselves. When asleep we may be likened to angels, who are not subject to the laws of "reality." In sleep the realm of necessity has given way to the realm of freedom in which "I am" is the only system to which thoughts and feelings refer.

23   Mental activity during sleep has a logic different from that of waking existence. Sleep experience need not pay any attention to qualities that matter only when one copes with reality. If I feel, for instance, that a person is a coward, I may dream that he changed from a man into a chicken. This change is logical in terms of what I feel about the person, absurd only in terms of my orientation to outside reality (in terms of what I could *do*, realistically, to or with the person). Sleep experience is not lacking in logic but is subject to different logical rules, which are valid in that particular experiential state.

24   Sleep and waking life are the two poles of human existence. Waking life is taken up with the function of action, sleep is freed from it. Sleep is taken up with the function of self-experience. When we wake from our sleep, we move into the realm of action. We are then oriented in terms of this system, and our memory operates within it: we remember what can be recalled in space-time concepts. The sleep world has disappeared. Experiences we had in it—our dreams—are remembered with the greatest difficulty.[1] The situation has been represented sym-

---

[1]Cf. to the problem of memory function in its relation to dream activity the stimulating article by Dr. Ernest G. Schachtel, "On Memory and Childhood Amnesia," *Psychiatry*, February, 1947.

bolically in many a tale: at night ghosts and spirits, good and evil, occupy the scene, but when dawn arrives, they disappear, and nothing is left of all the intense experience.

25 From these considerations certain conclusions about the nature of the unconscious follow:

26 It is neither Jung's mythical realm of racially inherited experience nor Freud's seat of irrational libidinal forces. It is inner experience produced and molded by the specific conditions of sleep as against those of waking life. It must be understood in terms of the principle: "What we think and feel is influenced by what we do."

27 *Consciousness* is the mental activity in our state of being preoccupied with external reality—with acting. The *unconscious* is mental experience in a state of existence in which we have shut off communications with the outer world, are no longer preoccupied with action but with our self-experience. The unconscious is related to a special mode of life—that of nonactivity; and the characteristics of the unconscious follow from the nature of this mode of existence. The qualities of consciousness, on the other hand, are determined by the nature of action and by the survival function of the waking state of existence.

28 The "unconscious" is the unconscious only in relation to the "normal" state of activity. When we speak of "unconscious" we really say only that an experience is alien to that frame of mind which exists while and as we act; it is then felt as a ghostlike, intrusive element, hard to get hold of and hard to remember. But the day world is as unconscious in our sleep experience as the night world is in our waking experience. The term "unconscious" is customarily used solely from the standpoint of day experience; and thus it fails to denote that both conscious and unconscious are only different states of mind referring to different states of existence. This dilemma has been beautifully expressed by the old Chinese poet who said: "Last night I dreamed that I was a butterfly. I do not know now, am I a man who dreamed that he was a butterfly, or am I a butterfly who dreams now that I am a man?"

29 It will be argued that in the waking state of existence, too, thinking and feeling are not entirely subject to the limitations of time and space; that our creative imagination permits us to think

about past and future objects as if they were present, and of distant objects as if they were before our eyes; that our waking feeling is not dependent on the physical presence of the object nor on its coexistence in time; that, therefore, the absence of the space-time system is not characteristic of sleep existence in contradistinction to waking existence, but of thinking and feeling in contradistinction to acting. This welcome objection permits me to clarify an essential point in my argument.

30   We must differentiate between the *contents* of thought processes and the *logical categories* employed in thinking. While it is true that the contents of our waking thoughts are not subject to limitations of space and time, the categories of local thinking are those of the space-time nature. I can, for instance, think of my father and state that his attitude in a certain situation is identical with mine. This statement is logically correct. On the other hand, if I state "I am my father," the statement is "illogical" because it is not conceived in reference to the physical world. The sentence is logical, however, in a purely experimental realm: it expresses the experience of identity with my father. Logical thought processes in the waking state are subject to categories which are rooted in a special form of existence—the one in which we relate ourselves to reality in terms of action. In sleep existence, which is characterized by lack of even potential action, logical categories are employed which have reference only to my self-experience. The same holds true of feeling. When I feel, in the waking state, with regard to a person whom I have not seen for twenty years, I remain aware of the fact that the person is not present. If I dream about the person, my feeling deals with the person as if he or she were present. But to say "as if he were present" is to express the feeling in logical "waking life" concepts. In sleep existence there is no "as if"; the person *is* present.

31   In the foregoing pages the attempt has been made to describe the conditions of sleep and to draw from this description certain conclusions concerning the quality of dream activity. We must now proceed to study one specific element among the conditions of sleep which will prove to be of great significance to the understanding of dream processes. We have said that while we are asleep we are not occupied with managing outer reality. We do

not perceive it and we do not influence it, nor are we subject to the influences of the outside world on us. From this it follows that the *effect of this separation from reality depends on the quality of reality itself.* If the influence from the outside world is essentially beneficial, the absence of this influence during sleep would tend to lower the value of our dream activity, so that it would be inferior to our mental activities during the daytime, when we are exposed to the beneficial influence of outside reality.

32   But are we right in assuming that the influence of reality is exclusively a beneficial one? May it not be that it is also harmful and that, therefore, the absence of its influence tends to bring forth qualities superior to those we have when we are awake?

33   In speaking of the reality outside ourselves, reference is not made primarily to the world of nature. Nature as such is neither good nor bad. It may be helpful to us or dangerous, and the absence of our perception of it relieves us, indeed, from our task of trying to master it or of defending ourselves against it; but it does not make us either more stupid or wiser, better or worse. It is different with the man-made world around us, with the culture in which we live. Its effect upon us is ambiguous, although we are prone to assume that it is entirely to our benefit.

34   Indeed, the evidence that cultural influences are beneficial to us seems almost overwhelming. The progress of the human race is based on the cooperation with all men, which was possible only in a social context, and by man's ability to communicate his ideas and practical achievements to his fellow men, and future generations. Man is what he is by his capacity for social organization, and the creation of culture, and this capacity differentiates him from the animal.

35   Is then the man-made reality outside ourselves not the most significant factor for the development of the best in us, and must we not expect that, when deprived of contact with the outside world, we regress temporarily to a primitive, animal-like, unreasonable state of mind? Much can be said in favor of such an assumption, and the view that such a regression is the essential feature of the state of sleep, and thus of dream activity, has been held by many students of dreaming from Plato to Freud. From this viewpoint dreams are expected to be expressions of the irrational, primitive strivings in us, and the fact that we

forget our dreams so easily is amply explained by our being ashamed of those irrational and criminal impulses which we express when we were not under the control of society. Undoubtedly this interpretation of dreams is true, but the question is whether it is exclusively true or whether the negative elements in the influence of society do not account for the paradoxical fact that *we are not only less reasonable and less decent in our dreams but also more intelligent, wiser, and capable of better judgment when we are asleep than when we are awake.*

36   Indeed, culture has not only a beneficial but also a detrimental influence on our intellectual and moral functions. Human beings are dependent on each other, they need each other. But human history up to now has been influenced by one fact: material production was not sufficient to satisfy the legitimate needs of all men. The table was set for only a few of the many who wanted to sit down and eat. Those who were stronger tried to secure places for themselves, which meant that they had to prevent others from getting seats. Moreover, they used their power not only to secure their own positions but also to make use of and to exploit their fellow men, for their own material or psychic needs. Aside from a number of primitive communities, the history of mankind up to now is a history of the use of man by man. The power used to achieve these ends was often the power of the conquerer, the physical power that forced the majority to be satisfied with their lot. But physical power was not always available or sufficient. One had to have power over the minds of people in order to make them refrain from using their fists. This control over mind and feeling was a necessary element in retaining the privileges of the few. In this process, however, the minds of the few became as distorted as the minds of the many. The guard who watches a prisoner becomes almost as much a prisoner as the prisoner himself. The "elite" who have to control those who are not "chosen" become the prisoners of their own restrictive tendencies. Thus the human mind, of both rulers and ruled, becomes deflected from its essential human purpose, which is to feel and to think humanly, to use and to develop the powers of reason and love that are inherent in man and without the full development of which he is crippled.

37   In this process man's character becomes distorted and his

heart hardens. Aims which are in contrast to the interests of his real human self become paramount. His powers of love are impoverished, and he is driven to want power over others. His inner security is lessened, and he is driven to seek compensation by passionate cravings for fame and prestige. He loses the sense of dignity and integrity and is forced to turn himself into a commodity, deriving his self-respect from his salability, from his success. All this makes for the fact that the man-made world of ideas is a mixture of his very best with all the lies and deceptions which are to hide and rationalize his inhumanity.

38   This holds true for a primitive tribe in which strict laws and customs influence the mind, but it is true also for modern society with its alleged freedom from rigid ritualism. In many ways the spread of literacy and of the media of mass communication has made the influence of cultural clichés as effective as it is in a small, highly restricted tribal culture. Modern man is exposed to an almost unceasing "noise," the noise of the radio, television, headlines, advertising, the movies, most of which do not enlighten our minds but stultify them. We are exposed to rationalizing lies which masquerade as truths, to plain nonsense which masquerades as common sense or as the higher wisdom of the specialist, to double talk, intellectual laziness, or to dishonesty which speaks in the name of "honor" or "realism," as the case may be. We feel superior to the superstitions of former generations and so-called primitive cultures, and we are constantly hammered at by the same kind of superstitious beliefs that set themselves up as the latest discoveries of "science." Is it surprising, then, that to be awake is not exclusively a blessing but also a curse? Is it surprising that in a state of sleep, when we are alone with ourselves, when we can look into ourselves without being bothered by the noise and nonsense that surround us in the daytime, we are better able to feel and to think our truest and most valuable feelings and thoughts?

39   This, then, is the conclusion at which we arrive: the state of sleep has an ambiguous function. In it the lack of contact with culture makes for the appearance both of our worst *and* of our best; therefore, in our dreaming, *we may be less intelligent, less wise, and less decent, but we may also be better and wiser than in our waking life.*

40   To conclude, it must be stressed again that the study of dreams
is by no means primarily a tool to be used in psychotherapy for
the understanding of neurotic phenomena. Dreams represent a
language *sui generis,* a language with its own syntax and grammar, as it were, and the one universal language which the human
race possesses. The study of dream language cannot be omitted
if we wish to arrive at an understanding of language in its most
general and universal aspects.

the tyger

WILLIAM BLAKE

Tyger! Tyger! burning bright
In the forests of the night,
What immortal hand or eye
Could frame thy fearful symmetry?

In what distant deeps or skies   5
Burnt the fire of thine eyes?
On what wings dare he aspire?
What the hand dare seize the fire?

And what shoulder, & what art,   9
Could twist the sinews of thy heart?
And when thy heart began to beat,
What dread hand? & what dread feet?

What the hammer? what the chain?   13
In what furnace was thy brain
What the anvil? what dread grasp
Dare its deadly terrors clasp?

When the stars threw down their spears,   17
And water'd heaven with their tears,
Did he smile his work to see?
Did he who made the Lamb make thee?

Tyger! Tyger! burning bright   21
In the forests of the night,
What immortal hand or eye
Dare frame thy fearful symmetry?

DISCUSSION AND WRITING MATERIAL

"The Battle of the Ants"

How do the references to literary and historical figures contribute to the overall analogy? What relationship does the sentence structure in paragraph 2 have to the meaning? Cite some of the similes and metaphors in the description and comment on their effectiveness.

"Troilus and Cressida"

Trace the importance of analogy in Ulysses' argument. According to Ulysses, why are not the Greeks winning the war?

"Nirvana Now"

The author suggests that the SDS and Hippie movements are analogous to certain historical religious heresies. Define the heresies and analogies he constructs. What validity does he offer for these analogies? What is his reason for presenting them? How effective is the essay's conclusion? Is Moynihan's concept of liberalism similar to Sears' ("Liberals and Conservatives")? Is the essay intended as a defense of liberalism?

"Symbolic Language of Dreams"

How does analogy operate in our dreams? Analyze the following poem using the classification of symbols suggested by Fromm.

> Western wind, when wilt thou blow?
>   The small rain down can rain.
> Christ, that my love were in my arms,
>   And I in my bed again!

In light of your own experiences, discuss Fromm's belief that culture may be a negative force in the moral and intellectual development of an individual (reread paragraph 36).

"Tyger"

Explain the analogy in the fourth stanza. Is it extended to any of the other stanzas? How does the imagery of fire which permeates the poem contribute to the analogy? What is the function of the various questions? What is the effect of the almost identical repetition of the last stanza to the first? How does the poet achieve his rhythm in the poem?

Discuss the effectiveness of the following analogies.

> Nothing in progression (i.e., nothing changing, growing) can rest on its original plan. We may as well think of rocking a grown man in the cradle of an infant.
>
> EDMUND BURKE

> Genuine vital integrity does not consist in satisfaction, in attainment, in arrival. As Cervantes said long since: "The road is always better than the inn."
>
> JOSE ORTEGA Y GASSET

> The empirics (those who rely only on practical experience) are like ants heaping up a collection of data. The natural philosophers (those who rely only on rules, principles, or theories) are like spiders spinning their webs out of their own interior. Scientists ought to take up an intermediate position, like that of bees, whch extract matter from flowers and then refashion it by their own efforts.
>
> FRANCIS BACON

> This is one of the basic troubles of our nation today: We are running the country by committee. Every decision is a compromise, attuned to the lowest common denominator, designed only to keep everybody satisfied. We cannot afford compromises. We must commit whatever industrial capacity and manpower we possess to a decisive force operating in a decisive medium.
>
> We can afford only *one* strategic plan. We cannot obtain the correct answer to our problems today by averaging opposing viewpoints any more than surgeons who fail to agree on a diagnosis can settle the issue by operating on some in-between part of the anatomy. A strategy is either right or wrong, and we cannot risk being wrong.
>
> ALEXANDER DESEVERSKY

Civilization becomes more complex and difficult in proportion as it advances. The problems which it sets before us today are of the most intricate. The number of people whose minds are equal to those problems becomes increasingly smaller. This disproportion between the complex subtlety of the problems and the minds that should study them will become greater if a remedy be not found, and it constitutes the basic tragedy of our civilization. All previous civilizations have died through the insufficiency of their principles.

It is painful to hear even relatively cultured people speak concerning the most elementary problems of the day. They seem like rough farmhands trying with thick, clumsy fingers to pick up a needle lying on a table.

JOSE ORTEGA Y GASSET

The process of communication, like a great river, is continually shaping and changing our lives. Like a river, the process of communication can be dammed only momentarily. Television is the most powerful medium of mass communication man has ever toyed with. In its brief years, we have only begun to explore its vast social force. In denying people access to this medium, just as in damming a river, these forces can spill over and inundate a society. We see these forces today on our campuses, and have seen them in our ghettos.

TOMMY SMOTHERS

Woodstock was to 1969 what the McCarthy campaign was to 1968—a romantic splurge of earnest spontaneity, demonstrating unity, strength and beauty.

Getting arrested for pot is like getting arrested for sex.

You can't turn the clock back.

Man landing on the moon is like the first fish that flopped upon the solid earth.

Consider the effectiveness of the following argument for reduction of armaments by the United States in the hope that the Soviet Union would do likewise.

Imagine two husky men standing facing each other near the middle, but on opposite sides, of a long and rigid seesaw balanced over an abyss. As either man takes a step outward, the other must compensate with a nearly equal step outward on his side or the balance will be destroyed. The farther out they move, the greater the unbalancing effect of each step, and the more agile and quick to react both men must become in order to maintain the precarious equilibrium. To make the situation even worse, both of these husky men realize that this teetering board has some limit to its tensile strength—at some point it is certain to crack, dropping them both to destruction. So both men are frightened, but neither is willing to admit it for fear the other might take advantage of him.

How are these two men to escape from this dangerous situation, a situation in which the fate of each is bound up with that of the other? One reasonable solution immediately presents itself: let them agree to walk slowly and carefully toward the center of the teetering board in unison. To do this they must trust each other. But these men do not trust each other, and each imagines the other to be irrational enough to destroy them both unless he (Ego) preserves the balance. But now let us suppose that it occurs to one of these men that perhaps the other is just as frightened as he is and would also welcome some way of escaping from this intolerable situation. So this man decides to gamble on his new insight and calls out loudly, "I am taking a small step *toward* you!" The other man, rather than have the precarious balance upset, also takes a tentative step forward, whereupon the first takes another, larger step. Thus they work their ways back to safety by a series of unilateral, yet reciprocal steps—very much as they originally moved out against each other.

CAUSE AND EFFECT

The concept of cause and effect is accepted and applied by all of us—unconsciously, for the most part—every day of our lives. When we insert the ignition key in our auto we assume that turning it will *cause* the engine to start. We strike a match across a rough surface and we trust that the effect will be flame. Through training and repetition such acts become all but instinctive. Equally, in our discussion of a variety of topics, the principle of cause and effect becomes a sort of built-in "logical" tool. Why did the Packers fail to win the league title this year (effect)? Most assuredly, we argue, because of their coaching staff (cause). Clearly, the Republican party was responsible for the depression of the thirties; they were in office, weren't they? Surely we must all starve in the near future; the world is becoming grossly overpopulated.

While the principle of the cause-and-effect relationship is important—even necessary—for the establishment of a modicum of order in one's life, it is unfortunately true that this principle gets vastly oversimplified in actual practice (as our illustrations would indicate). Apparently so simple, the principle has been the subject of philosophical analysis and inquiry for centuries past; and recent scientific advances in both microcosm and macrocosm suggest that its validity and meaning will continue to intrigue thinkers in the future. We are not, of course, concerned here with such involved, technical discussions; but we cannot avoid certain fundamental issues of the cause-and-effect concept as they pertain to expository writing. Indeed, it would appear that anyone undertaking this form of organizational pattern for writing should first be warned of a number of potential fallacies and hazards inherent in the pattern. Thus, what follows amounts to a set of strictures intended as guidelines for the writer who would employ cause-and-effect reasoning as the basis for his essay.

The seventeenth century English philosopher John Locke defined *cause* as "that which makes any other thing . . . begin to be." But Locke was fully aware of the fact that when we claim or imply that something makes something else "begin to be" we inevitably simplify a complex relationship; that is, we point to but one of a series of factors which often work in conjunction to create the effect. It would release us from a considerable burden of reason and proof if causes and effects occurred in isolation; but, sad to say, this is seldom the case. More often than not, surrounding conditions and circumstances influence the relationship. If a match were struck in a vacuum, naturally it could not ignite, which is to say that one contributing factor (or cause) for fire is oxygen. And when we suggest that the Packers' football fortunes can be traced to their coaching staff, we ignore such significant considerations as draft choices, retirements, strengths and weaknesses of competitors, team morale, and a host of other conditions. The point is that even the most predictable relationships are not always as obvious as they seem, and the astute writer will take care to discuss as many of those contributing factors and conditions as are necessary to establish firmly his principle of cause and effect.

Another problem arises when we understand that point of view can frequently influence our identification of a cause. Let us consider again our earlier example of the Republican party and the depression. A Democrat might very well be tempted to lay the blame for those trying times squarely in the lap of the Republican administration. An economist, on the other hand, might sidestep the political issues and attribute cause to rampant speculation on the stock market. An ecologist could see in the dust bowls of the midwest contributing cause, and a temperance man might suggest moral bankruptcy growing out of flagrant disregard for the law. The list of possible points of view, then, is endless; and it indicates that the cause of an effect can quite easily be defined in a number of ways. What the writer must do is take into account the most salient of those points of view; he must also be constantly aware of the extent to which his own particular stance influences his view of the cause he postulates for a given effect.

Another common fallacy (designated *post hoc ergo propter hoc*—"after this therefore because of this") is the assumption that a sequence of events implies a necessary causal relationship. An easy illustration of this fallacy can be taken from superstition: We walk under a ladder and a personal misfortune does indeed strike us. All the same, only the most credulous would fix the blame on the ladder. Obvious enough, one might say, and in the next breath urge that inflation is patently the fault of the administration in office.

Similarly, hasty generalization in causal analysis may lead us to overlook all the potential contributing factors. If on a given day thirty diners at the Hi-Way Eats come down with ptomaine poisoning, it may give us pause before taking our dinner there; but in all fairness we must not neglect noting the ninety other diners who left that establishment well-fed, happy, and in perfect health. Once again, our point is that the writer must be wary of leaping to the most obvious casual conclusion, regardless of the topic.

Finally, once the writer has (hopefully) skirted these several dangers in reasoning, he must offer his reader one thing more, and that is evidence for his contention that a stated cause produces a stated effect. It is not enough, for example, to merely claim that a poet's tangled love life affected his work. Surely it is reasonable to expect some proof for that claim: cross-reference between the poet's biography and certain elements of his poetry, letters and notes which irrefutably establish such a relationship, and possibly close analysis of relevant lines in his poems.

The writers in this section are a heterogeneous lot—mathematician, philosopher, biologist, poet, and novelist—but all of them work with some form of the principle of cause and effect. In some instances that principle is employed in very oblique fashion, and it will be challenging for the student to follow the line of reasoning and to weigh it against the fallacies cited in this introduction. Through judging the skill and effectiveness with which professional writers use this principle, he will hopefully be better equipped to apply it in his own work.

the crisis of american masculinity
ARTHUR SCHLESINGER, JR.

1   What has happened to the American male? For a long time, he
seemed utterly confident in his manhood, sure of his masculine
role in society, easy and definite in his sense of sexual identity.
The frontiersmen of James Fenimore Cooper, for example, never
had any concern about masculinity; they were men, and it did
not occur to them to think twice about it. Even well into the
twentieth century, the heroes of Dreiser, of Fitzgerald, of Hemingway remain men. But one begins to detect a new theme
emerging in some of these authors, especially in Hemingway:
the theme of the male hero increasingly preoccupied with proving
his virility to himself. And by mid-century, the male role had
plainly lost its rugged clarity of outline. Today men are more
and more conscious of maleness not as a fact but as a problem.
The ways by which American men affirm their masculinity are
uncertain and obscure. There are multiplying signs, indeed, that
something has gone badly wrong with the American male's
conception of himself.

2   On the most superficial level, the roles of male and female are
increasingly merged in the American household. The American
man is found as never before as a substitute for wife and mother
—changing diapers, washing dishes, cooking meals and performing a whole series of what once were considered female duties.

Reprinted with permission of Houghton Mifflin Company, from *The Politics of Hope*, by Arthur Schlesinger, Jr. © 1962 by Arthur M. Schlesinger, Jr.

The American woman meanwhile takes over more and more of the big decisions, controlling them indirectly when she cannot do so directly. Outside the home, one sees a similar blurring of function. While men design dresses and brew up cosmetics, women become doctors, lawyers, bank cashiers and executives. "Woman now fill many 'masculine' roles," writes the psychologist, Dr. Bruno Bettelheim, "and expect their husbands to assume many of the tasks once reserved for their own sex." Women seem an expanding, aggressive force, seizing new domains like a conquering army, while men, more and more on the defensive, are hardly able to hold their own and gratefully accept assignments from their new rulers. A recent book bears the stark and melancholy title *The Decline of the American Male.*

3   Some of this evidence, it should be quickly said, has been pushed too far. The willingness of a man to help his wife around the house may as well be evidence of confidence in masculinity as the opposite; such a man obviously does not have to cling to masculine symbols in order to keep demonstrating his maleness to himself. But there is more impressive evidence than the helpful husband that this is an age of sexual ambiguity. It appears no accident, for example, that the changing of sex—the Christine Jorgensen phenomenon—so fascinates our newspaper editors and readers; or that homosexuality, that incarnation of sexual ambiguity, should be enjoying a cultural boom new in our history. Such developments surely express a deeper tension about the problem of sexual identity.

4   Consider the theatre, that faithful mirror of a society's preoccupations. There have been, of course, popular overt inquiries into sexual ambiguities, like *Compulsion* or *Tea and Sympathy.* But in a sense these plays prove the case too easily. Let us take rather two uncommonly successful plays by the most discussed young playwrights of the United States and Great Britain—Tennessee Williams's *Cat On A Hot Tin Roof* and John Osborne's *Look Back in Anger.* Both deal with the young male in a singular state of confusion and desperation. In *Cat On A Hot Tin Roof,* Brick Pollitt, the professional football player, refuses to sleep with his wife because of guilty memories of his relations with a dead team mate. In *Look Back in Anger,* Jimmy Porter, the embittered young intellectual who can sustain a relationship

with his wife only by pretending they are furry animals together, explodes with hatred of women and finds his moments of happiness rough-housing around the stage with a male pal.

5   Brick Pollitt and Jimmy Porter are all too characteristic modern heroes. They are, in a sense, castrated; one is stymied by fear of homosexuality, the other is an unconscious homosexual. Neither is capable of dealing with the woman in his life: Brick surrenders to a strong woman, Jimmy destroys a weak one. Both reject the normal female desire for full and reciprocal love as an unconscionable demand and an intolerable burden. Now not many American males have been reduced to quite the Pollitt-Porter condition. Still the intentness with which audiences have watched these plays suggests that exposed nerves are being plucked—that the Pollitt-Porter dilemma expresses in vivid and heightened form something that many spectators themselves feel or fear.

6   Or consider the movies. In some ways, the most brilliant and influential American film since the war is *High Noon*. That remarkable movie, which invested the Western with the classic economy of myth, can be viewed in several ways: as an existentialist drama, for example, or as a parable of McCarthyism. It can also be viewed as a mordant comment on the effort of the American woman to emasculate the American man. The sheriff plainly did not suffer from Brick Pollitt's disease. But a large part of the story dealt with the attempt of his girl to persuade him not to use force—to deny him the use of his pistol. The pistol is an obvious masculine symbol, and, in the end, it was the girl herself, in the modern American manner, who used the pistol and killed a villain. (In this connection, one can pause and note why the Gary Coopers, Cary Grants, Clark Gables and Spencer Tracys continue to play romantic leads opposite girls young enough to be their daughters; it is obviously because so few of the younger male stars can project a convincing sense of masculinity.)

7   Psychoanalysis backs up the theatre and the movies in emphasizing the obsession of the American male with his manhood. "Every psychoanalyst knows," writes one of them, "how many emotional difficulties are due to those fears and insecurities of neurotic men who are unconsciously doubting their masculinity."

"In our civilization," Dr. Theodor Reik says, "men are afraid
that they will not be men enough." Reik adds significantly: "And
women are afraid that they might be considered only women."
Why is it that women worry, not over whether they can fill the
feminine role, but whether filling that role is enough, while men
worry whether they can fill the masculine role at all? How to
account for this rising tide of male anxiety? What has unmanned
the American man?

8   There is currently a fashionable answer to this question. Male
anxiety, many observers have declared, is simply the result of
female aggression: what has unmanned the American man is the
American woman. The present male confusion and desperation,
it is contended, are the inevitable consequence of the threatened
feminization of American society. The victory of women is the
culmination of a long process of masculine retreat, beginning
when Puritanism made men feel guilty about sex and the frontier
gave women the added value of scarcity. Fleeing from the reality
of femininity, the American man, while denying the American
women juridical equality, transformed her into an ideal of
remote and transcendent purity with overriding authority over
the family, the home, the school and culture. This habit of
obeisance left the male psychologically disarmed and vulnerable
when the goddess stepped off the pedestal and demanded in addition equal economic, political and legal rights. In the last part
of the nineteenth century, women won their battle for equality.
They gained the right of entry into one occupation after another
previously reserved for males. Today they hold the key positions
of personal power in our society and use this power relentlessly
to consolidate their mastery. As mothers, they undermine masculinity through the use of love as a technique of reward and
punishment. As teachers, they prepare male children for their
role of submission in an increasingly feminine world. As wives,
they complete the work of subjugation. Their strategy of conquest is deliberately to emasculate men—to turn them into Brick
Pollitts and Jimmy Porters.

9   Or so a standard indictment runs; and no doubt there is something in it. American women have unquestionably gained
through the years a place in our society which American men
have not been psychologically prepared to accept. Whether be-

cause of Puritanism or the frontier, there has been something immature in the traditional American male attitude toward women—a sense of alarm, at times amounting to panic. Almost none of the classic American novels, for example, presents the theme of mature and passionate love. Our nineteenth-century novelists saw women either as unassailable virgins or abandoned temptresses—never simply as women. One looks in vain through *Moby Dick* and *The Adventures of Huckleberry Finn*, through Cooper and Poe and Whitman, for an adult portrayal of relations between men and women. "Where," Leslie Fiedler has asked, "is the American *Madame Bovary, Anna Karenina, Wuthering Heights,* or *Vanity Fair?*"

10 Yet the implication of the argument that the American man has been unmanned by the emancipation of the American woman is that the American man was incapable of growing up. For the nineteenth-century sense of masculinity was based on the psychological idealization and the legal subjection of women; masculinity so spuriously derived could never—and should never—have endured. The male had to learn to live at some point with the free and equal female. Current attempts to blame "the decline of the American male" on the aggressiveness of the American female amount to a confession that, under conditions of free competition, the female was bound to win. Simple observation refutes this supposition. In a world of equal rights, some women rise; so too do some men; and no pat generalization is possible about the sexual future of society. Women have gained power in certain ways; in others, they have made little progress. It is safe to predict, for example, that we will have a Roman Catholic, perhaps even a Jew, for President before we have a woman. Those amiable prophets of an impending American matriarchy (all men, by the way) are too pessimistic.

11 Something more fundamental is involved in the unmanning of American men than simply the onward rush of American women. Why is the American man so unsure today about his masculine identity? The basic answer to this is surely because he is so unsure about his identity in general. Nothing is harder in the whole human condition than to achieve a full sense of identity—than to know who you are, where you are going, and what you mean to live and die for. From the most primitive myths of the most

contemporary novels—from Oedipus making the horrified discovery that he had married his mother, to Leopold Bloom and Stephen Dedalus searching their souls in Joyce's Dublin and the haunted characters of Kafka trying to make desperate sense out of an incomprehensible universe—the search for identity has been the most compelling human problem. That search has always been ridden with trouble and terror. And it can be plausibly argued that the conditions of modern life make the quest for identity more difficult than it has ever been before.

12   The pre-democratic world was characteristically a world of status in which people were provided with ready-made identities. But modern western society—free, equalitarian, democratic—has swept away all the old niches in which people for so many centuries found safe refuge. Only a few people at any time in human history have enjoyed the challenge of "making" themselves; most have fled from the unendurable burden of freedom into the womblike security of the group. The new age of social mobility may be fine for those strong enough to discover and develop their own roles. But for the timid and the frightened, who constitute the majority in any age, the great vacant spaces of equalitarian society can become a nightmare filled with nameless horrors. Thus mass democracy, in the very act of offering the individual new freedom and opportunity, offers new moral authority to the group and thereby sets off a new assault on individual identity. Over a century ago Alexis de Tocqueville, the perceptive Frenchman who ruminated on the contradictions of equality as he toured the United States in the Eighteen Thirties, pointed to the "tyranny of the majority" as a central problem of democracy. John Stuart Mill, lamenting the decline of individualism in Great Britain, wrote: "That so few now dare to be eccentric marks the chief danger of the time." How much greater that danger seems a century later!

13   For our own time has aggravated the assault on identity by adding economic and technological pressures to the political and social pressures of the 19th century. Modern science has brought about the growing centralization of the economy. We work and think and live and even dream in larger and larger units. William H. Whyte, Jr., has described the rise of "the organization man," working by day in immense business concerns, sleeping by

night in immense suburban developments, deriving his fantasy life from mass-produced entertainments, spending his existence, not as an individual, but as a member of a group and coming in the end to feel guilty and lost when he deviates from his fellows. Adjustment rather than achievement becomes the social ideal. Men no longer fulfill an inner sense of what they *must* be; indeed, with the cult of the group, that inner sense itself begins to evaporate. Identity consists, not of self-realization, but of smooth absorption into the group. Nor is this just a matter of passive acquiescence. The group is aggressive, imperialistic, even vengeful, forever developing new weapons with which to overwhelm and crush the recalcitrant individual. Not content with disciplining the conscious mind, the group today is even experimenting with means of violating the subconscious. The subliminal invasion represents the climax of the assault on individual identity.

14   It may seem a long way from the loss of the sense of self to the question of masculinity. But if people do not know *who* they are, it is hardly surprising that they are no longer sure what sex they are. Nigel Dennis's exuberant novel, *Cards of Identity*, consists of a series of brilliant variations on the quest for identity in contemporary life. It reaches one of its climaxes in the tale of a person who was brought up by enlightened parents to believe that there was no such thing as pure male or female— everyone had elements of both—and who accepted this proposition so rigorously that he (she) could not decide what his (her) own sex was. "In what identity do you intend to face the future?" someone asks. "It seems that nowadays," comes the plaintive reply, "one must choose between being a woman who behaves like a man, and a man who behaves like a woman. In short, I must choose to be one in order to behave like the other." If most of us have not yet quite reached that condition of sexual chaos, yet the loss of a sense of identity is obviously a fundamental step in the decay of masculinity. And the gratification with which some American males contemplate their own decline should not obscure the fact that women, for all their recent legal and economic triumphs, are suffering from a loss of identity too. It is not accidental that the authors of one recent book described modern woman as the "lost sex."

15   If this is true, then the key to the recovery of masculinity does not lie in any wistful hope of humiliating the aggressive female and restoring the old masculine supremacy. Masculine supremacy, like white supremacy, was the neurosis of an immature society. It is good for men as well as for women that women have been set free. In any case, the process is irreversible; that particular genie can never be put back into the bottle. The key to the recovery of masculinity lies rather in the problem of identity. When a person begins to find out *who* he is, he is likely to find out rather soon what sex he is.

16   For men to become men again, in short, their first task is to recover a sense of individual spontaneity. And to do this a man must visualize himself as an individual apart from the group, whatever it is, which defines his values and commands his loyalty. There is no reason to suppose that the group is always wrong: to oppose the group automatically is nearly as conformist as to surrender to it automatically. But there is every necessity to recognize that the group is one thing and the individual —oneself—is another. One of the most sinister of present-day doctrines is that of *togetherness*. The recovery of identity means, first of all, a new belief in apartness. It means a determination to resist the overpowering conspiracy of blandness, which seeks to conceal all tension and conflict in American life under a blanket of locker-room affability. And the rebirth of spontaneity depends, at bottom, on changes of attitude *within* people—changes which can perhaps be described, without undue solemnity, as moral changes. These changes will no doubt come about in as many ways as there are individuals involved. But there are some general suggestions that can be made about the techniques of liberation. I should like to mention three such techniques: satire, art, and politics.

17   Satire means essentially the belief that nothing is sacred—that there is no person or institution or idea which cannot but benefit from the exposure of comedy. Our nation in the past has reveled in satire; it is, after all, the nation of Abraham Lincoln, of Mark Twain, of Finley Peter Dunne, of H. L. Mencken, of Ring Lardner. Indeed, the whole spirit of democracy is that of satire; as Montaigne succinctly summed up the democratic faith: "Sit he on ever so high a throne, a man still sits on his own

bottom." Yet today American society can only be described as a pompous society, at least in its official manifestations. Early in 1958 Mort Sahl, the night-club comedian, made headlines in New York because he dared make a joke about J. Edgar Hoover! It was not an especially good joke, but the fact that he made it at all was an encouraging sign. One begins to feel that the American people can only stand so much reverence—that in the end our native skepticism will break through, sweep aside the stuffed shirts and the stuffed heads and insist that platitudes are platitudinous and the great are made, among other things, to be laughed at. Irony is good for our rulers; and it is even better for ourselves because it is a means of dissolving the pomposity of society and giving the individual a chance to emerge.

18   If irony is one source of spontaneity, art is another. Very little can so refresh our vision and develop our vision and develop our values as the liberating experience of art. The mass media have cast a spell on us: the popular addiction to prefabricated emotional clichés threatens to erode our capacity for fresh and direct aesthetic experience. Individual identity vanishes in the welter of machine-made reactions. But thoughtful exposure to music, to painting, to poetry, to the beauties of nature, can do much to restore the inwardness, and thereby the identity, of man. There is thus great hope in the immense cultural underground of our age —the paperbound books, the long-playing records, the drama societies, the art festivals, the new interest in painting and sculpture. All this represents a disdain for existing values and goals, a reaching out for something more exacting and more personal, an intensified questing for identity.

19   And politics in a true sense can be a means of liberation—not the banal politics of rhetoric and self-congratulation, which aims at burying all real issues under a mass of piety and platitude; but the politics of responsibility, which tries to define the real issues and present them to the people for decision. Our national politics have become boring in recent years because our leaders have offered neither candid and clear-cut formulations of the problems nor the facts necessary for intelligent choice. A virile political life will be definite and hard-hitting, respecting debate and dissent, seeking clarity and decision.

20   As the American male develops himself by developing his

comic sense, his aesthetic sense and his moral and political sense,
the lineaments of personality will at last begin to emerge. The
achievement of identity, the conquest of a sense of self—these will
do infinitely more to restore American masculinity than all the
hormones in the test tubes of our scientists. "Whoso would be a
man," said Emerson, "must be a nonconformist"; and, if it is the
present writer who adds the italics, nonetheless one feels that no
injustice is done to Emerson's intention. How can masculinity,
femininity, or anything else survive in a homogenized society,
which seeks steadily and benignly to eradicate all differences between the individuals who compose it? If we want to have *men*
again in our theatres and our films and our novels—not to speak
of in our classrooms, our business offices and our homes—we must
first have a society which encourages each of its members to have
a distinct identity.

man against darkness
WALTER T. STACE

1

1 The Catholic bishops of America recently issued a statement in which they said that the chaotic and bewildered state of the modern world is due to man's loss of faith, his abandonment of God and religion. For my part I believe in no religion at all. Yet I entirely agree with the bishops. It is no doubt an oversimplification to speak of *the* cause of so complex a state of affairs as the tortured condition of the world today. Its causes are doubtless multitudinous. Yet allowing for some element of oversimplification, I say that the bishops' assertion is substantially true.

2 M. Jean-Paul Sartre, the French existentialist philosopher, labels himself an atheist. Yet his views seem to me plainly to support the statement of the bishops. So long as there was believed to be a God in the sky, he says, men could regard him as the source of their moral ideals. The universe, created and governed by a fatherly God, was a friendly habitation for man. We could be sure that, however great the evil in the world, good in the end would triumph and the forces of evil would be routed. With the disappearance of God from the sky all this has changed. Since the world is not ruled by a spiritual being, but rather by blind forces, there cannot be any ideals, moral or otherwise, in the uni-

Reprinted with permission of The Atlantic Monthly Company. © 1948 by The Atlantic Monthly Company, Boston, Massachusetts.

verse outside us. Our ideals, therefore, must proceed only from our own minds; they are our own inventions. Thus the world which surrounds us is nothing but an immense spiritual emptiness. It is a dead universe. We do not live in a universe which is on the side of our values. It is completely indifferent to them.

3   Years ago Mr. Bertrand Russell, in his essay *Free Man's Worship*, said much the same thing.

> Such in outline, but even more purposeless, more void of meaning, is the world which Science presents for our belief. Amid such a world, if anywhere, our ideals henceforward must find a home. . . . Blind to good and evil, reckless of destruction, omnipotent matter rolls on its relentless way; for man, condemned today to lose his dearest, tomorrow himself to pass through the gate of darkness, it remains only to cherish, ere yet the blow falls, the lofty thoughts that ennoble his little day; . . . to worship at the shrine his own hands have built; . . . to sustain alone, a weary but unyielding Atlas, the world that his own ideals have fashioned despite the trampling march of unconscious power.

4   It is true that Mr. Russell's personal attitude to the disappearance of religion is quite different from either that of M. Sartre or the bishops or myself. The bishops think it a calamity. So do I. M. Sartre finds it "very distressing." And he berates as shallow the attitude of those who think that without God the world can go on just the same as before, as if nothing had happened. This creates for mankind, he thinks, a terrible crisis. And in this I agree with him. Mr. Russell, on the other hand, seems to believe that religion has done more harm than good in the world, and that its disappearance will be a blessing. But his picture of the world, and of the modern mind, is the same as that of M. Sartre. He stresses the *purposelessness* of the universe, the facts that man's ideals are his own creations, that the universe outside him in no way supports them, that man is alone and friendless in the world.

5   Mr. Russell notes that it is science which has produced this situation. There is no doubt that this is correct. But the way in which it has come about is not generally understood. There is a popular belief that some particular scientific discoveries or theories, such as the Darwinian theory of evolution, or the views of

geologists about the age of the earth, or a series of such discoveries, have done the damage. It would be foolish to deny that these discoveries have had a great effect in undermining religious dogmas. But this account does not at all go to the root of the matter. Religion can probably outlive any scientific discoveries which could be made. It can accommodate itself to them. The root cause of the decay of faith has not been any particular discovery of science, but rather the general spirit of science and certain basic assumptions upon which modern science, from the seventeenth century onwards, has proceeded.

2

6   It was Galileo and Newton—notwithstanding that Newton himself was a deeply religious man—who destroyed the old comfortable picture of a friendly universe governed by spiritual values. And this was effected, not by Newton's discovery of the law of gravitation nor by any of Galileo's brilliant investigations, but by the general picture of the world which these men and others of their time made the basis of the science, not only of their own day, but of all succeeding generations down to the present. That is why the century immediately following Newton, the eighteenth century, was notoriously an age of religious skepticism. Skepticism did not have to wait for the discoveries of Darwin and the geologists in the nineteenth century. It flooded the world immediately after the age of the rise of science.

7   Neither the Copernican hypothesis nor any of Newton's or Galileo's particular discoveries were the real causes. Religious faith might well have accommodated itself to the new astronomy. The real turning point between the medieval age of faith and the modern age of unfaith came when the scientists of the seventeenth century turned their backs upon what used to be called "final causes." The final cause of a thing or event meant the purpose which it was supposed to serve in the universe, its cosmic purpose. What lay back of this was the presupposition that there is a cosmic order or plan and that everything which exists could in the last analysis be explained in terms of its place in this cosmic plan, that is, in terms of its purpose.

8   Plato and Aristotle believed this, and so did the whole medieval Christian world. For instance, if it were true that the sun
and the moon were created and exist for the purpose of giving
light to man, then this fact would explain why the sun and the
moon exist. We might not be able to discover the purpose of
everything, but everything must have a purpose. Belief in final
causes thus amounted to a belief that the world is governed by
purposes, presumably the purposes of some overruling mind. This
belief was not the invention of Christianity. It was basic to the
whole of Western civilization, whether in the ancient pagan
world or in Christendom, from the time of Socrates to the rise of
science in the seventeenth century.

9   The founders of modern science—for instance, Galileo, Kepler,
and Newton—were mostly pious men who did not doubt God's
purposes. Nevertheless they took the revolutionary step of consciously and deliberately expelling the idea of purpose as controlling nature from their new science of nature. They did this
on the ground that inquiry into purposes is useless for what science aims at: namely, the prediction and control of events. To
predict an eclipse, what you have to know is not its purpose but
its causes. Hence science from the seventeenth century onwards
became exclusively an inquiry into causes. The conception of
purpose in the world was ignored and frowned on. This, though
silent and almost unnoticed, was the greatest revolution in human history, far outweighing in importance any of the political
revolutions whose thunder has reverberated through the world.

10   For it came about in this way that for the past three hundred
years there has been growing up in men's minds, dominated as
they are by science, a new imaginative picture of the world. The
world, according to this new picture, is purposeless, senseless,
meaningless. Nature is nothing but matter in motion. The motions of matter are governed, not by any purpose, but by blind
forces and laws. Nature on this view, says Whitehead—to whose
writings I am indebted in this part of my paper—is "merely the
hurrying of material, endlessly, meaninglessly." You can draw a
sharp line across the history of Europe dividing it into two
epochs of very unequal length. The line passes through the lifetime of Galileo. European man before Galileo—whether ancient

pagan or more recent Christian—thought of the world as controlled by plan and purpose. After Galileo European man thinks of it as utterly purposeless. This is the great revolution of which I spoke.

11   It is this which has killed religion. Religion could survive the discoveries that the sun, not the earth, is the center; that men are descended from simian ancestors; that the earth is hundreds of millions of years old. These discoveries may render out of date some of the details of older theological dogmas, may force their restatement in new intellectual frameworks. But they do not touch the essence of the religious vision itself, which is the faith that there is plan and purpose in the world, that the world is a moral order, that in the end all things are for the best. This faith may express itself through many different intellectual dogmas, those of Christianity, of Hinduism, of Islam. All and any of these intellectual dogmas may be destroyed without destroying the essential religious spirit. But that spirit cannot survive destruction of belief in a plan and purpose of the world, for that is the very heart of it. Religion can get on with any sort of astronomy, geology, biology, physics. But it cannot get on with a purposeless and meaningless universe.

12   If the scheme of things is purposeless and meaningless, then the life of man is purposeless and meaningless too. Everything is futile, all effort is in the end worthless. A man may, of course, still pursue disconnected ends, money, fame, art, science, and may gain pleasure from them. But his life is hollow at the center. Hence the dissatisfied, disillusioned, restless, spirit of modern man.

13   The picture of a meaningless world, and a meaningless human life, is, I think, the basic theme of much modern art and literature. Certainly it is the basic theme of modern philosophy. According to the most characteristic philosophies of the modern period from Hume in the eighteenth century to the so-called positivists of today, the world is just what it is, and that is the end of all inquiry. There is no reason for its being what it is. Everything might just as well have been quite different, and there would have been no reason for that either. When you have stated what things are, what things the world contains, there is nothing

more which could be said, even by an omniscient being. To ask any question about *why* things are thus, or what purpose their being serves, is to ask a senseless question, because they serve no purpose at all. For instance, there is for modern philosophy no such thing as the ancient problem of evil. For this once fa-mous question presupposes that pain and misery, though they seem so inexplicable and irrational to us, must ultimately sub-serve some rational purpose, must have their places in the cosmic plan. But this is nonsense. There is no such overruling rational-ity in the universe. Belief in the ultimate irrationality of every-thing is the quintessence of what is called the modern mind.

14   It is true that, parallel with these philosophies which are typi-cal of the modern mind, preaching the meaninglessness of the world, there has run a line of idealistic philosophies whose con-tention is that the world is after all spiritual in nature and that moral ideals and values are inherent in its structure. But most of these idealisms were simply philosophical expressions of ro-manticism, which was itself no more than an unsuccessful coun-terattack of the religious against the scientific view of things. They perished, along with romanticism in literature and art, about the beginning of the present century, though of course they still have a few adherents.

15   At the bottom these idealistic systems of thought were ration-alizations of man's wishful thinking. They were born of the refusal of men to admit the cosmic darkness. They were comfort-ing illusions within the warm glow of which the more tender-minded intellectuals sought to shelter themselves from the icy winds of the universe. They lasted a little while. But they are shattered now, and we return once more to the vision of a pur-poseless world.

3

16   Along with the ruin of the religious vision there went the ruin of moral principles and indeed of all values. If there is a cosmic purpose, if there is in the nature of things a drive towards good-ness, then our moral systems will derive their validity from this.

But if our moral rules do not proceed from something outside us in the nature of the universe—whether we say it is God or simply the universe itself—then they must be our own inventions. Thus it came to be believed that moral rules must be merely an expression of our own likes and dislikes. But likes and dislikes are notoriously variable. What pleases one man, people, or culture displeases another. Therefore morals are wholly relative.

17   This obvious conclusion from the idea of a purposeless world made its appearance in Europe immediately after the rise of science, for instance in the philosophy of Hobbes. Hobbes saw at once that if there is no purpose in the world there are no values either. "Good and evil," he writes, "are names that signify our appetites and aversions; which in different tempers, customs, and doctrines of men are different. . . . Every man calleth that which pleaseth him, good; and that which displeaseth him, evil."

18   This doctrine of the relativity of morals, though it has recently received an impetus from the studies of anthropologists, was thus really implicit in the whole scientific mentality. It is disastrous for morals because it destroys their entire traditional foundation. That is why philosophers who see the danger signals, from the time at least of Kant, have been trying to give to morals a new foundation, that is, a secular or nonreligious foundation. This attempt may very well be intellectually successful. Such a foundation, independent of the religious view of the world, might well be found. But the question is whether it can ever be a *practical* success, that is, whether apart from its logical validity and its influence with intellectuals, it can ever replace among the masses of men the lost religious foundation. On that question hangs perhaps the future of civilization. But meanwhile disaster is overtaking us.

19   The widespread belief in "ethical relativity" among philosophers, psychologists, ethnologists, and sociologists is the theoretical counterpart of the repudiation of principle which we see all around us, especially in international affairs, the field in which morals have always had the weakest foothold. No one any longer effectively believes in moral principles except as the private prejudices either of individual men or of nations or cultures. This is the inevitable consequence of the doctrine of ethical relativity,

which in turn is the inevitable consequence of believing in a purposeless world.

20 Another characteristic of our spiritual state is loss of belief in the freedom of the will. This also is a fruit of the scientific spirit, though not of any particular scientific discovery. Science has been built up on the basis of determinism, which is the belief that every event is completely determined by a chain of causes and is therefore theoretically predictable beforehand. It is true that recent physics seems to challenge this. But so far as its practical consequences are concerned, the damage has long ago been done. A man's actions, it was argued, are as much events in the natural world as is an eclipse of the sun. It follows that men's actions are as theoretically predictable as an eclipse. But if it is certain now that John Smith will murder Joseph Jones at 2.15 P.M. on January 1, 1963, what possible meaning can it have to say that when that time comes John Smith will be *free* to choose whether he will commit the murder or not? And if he is not free, how can he be held responsible?

21 It is true that the whole of this argument can be shown by a competent philosopher to be a tissue of fallacies—or at least I claim that it can. But the point is that the analysis required to show this is much too subtle to be understood by the average entirely unphilosophical man. Because of this, the argument against free will is generally swallowed whole by the unphilosophical. Hence the thought that man is not free, that he is the helpless plaything of forces over which he has no control, has deeply penetrated the modern mind. We hear of economic determinism, cultural determinism, historical determinism. We are not responsible for what we do because our glands control us, or because we are the products of environment or heredity. Not moral self-control, but the doctor, the psychiatrist, the educationist, must save us from doing evil. Pills and injections in the future are to do what Christ and the prophets have failed to do. Of course I do not mean to deny that doctors and educationists can and must help. And I do not mean in any way to belittle their efforts. But I do wish to draw attention to the weakening of moral controls, the greater or less repudiation of personal responsibility which, in the popular thinking of the day, result from these tendencies of thought.

4

22 What, then, is to be done? Where are we to look for salvation from the evils of our time? All the remedies I have seen suggested so far are, in my opinion, useless. Let us look at some of them.

23 Philosophers and intellectuals generally can, I believe, genuinely do something to help. But it is extremely little. What philosophers can do is to show that neither the relativity of morals nor the denial of free will really follows from the grounds which have been supposed to support them. They can also try to discover a genuine secular basis for morals to replace the religious basis which has disappeared. Some of us are trying to do these things. But in the first place philosophers unfortunately are not agreed about these matters, and their disputes are utterly confusing to the nonphilosophers. And in the second place their influence is practically negligible because their analyses necessarily take place on a level on which the masses are totally unable to follow them.

24 The bishops, of course, propose as remedy a return to belief in God and in the doctrines of the Christian religion. Others think that a new religion is what is needed. Those who make these proposals fail to realize that the crisis in man's spiritual condition is something unique in history for which there is no sort of analogy in the past. They are thinking perhaps of the collapse of the ancient Greek and Roman religions. The vacuum then created was easily filled by Christianity, and it might have been filled by Mithraism if Christianity had not appeared. By analogy they think that Christianity might now be replaced by a new religion, or even that Christianity itself, if revivified, might bring back health to men's lives.

25 But I believe that there is no analogy at all between our present state and that of the European peoples at the time of the fall of paganism. Men had at that time lost their belief only in particular dogmas, particular embodiments of the religious view of the world. It had no doubt become incredible that Zeus and the other gods were living on the top of Mount Olympus. You could go to

the top and find no trace of them. But the imaginative picture of a world governed by purpose, a world driving towards the good —which is the inner spirit of religion—had at that time received no serious shock. It had merely to re-embody itself in new dogmas, those of Christianity or some other religion. Religion itself was not dead in the world, only a particular form of it.

26   But now the situation is quite different. It is not merely that particular dogmas, like that of the virgin birth, are unacceptable to the modern mind. That is true, but it constitutes a very superficial diagnosis of the present situation of religion. Modern skepticism is of a wholly different order from that of the intellectuals of the ancient world. It has attacked and destroyed not merely the outward forms of the religious spirit, its particularized dogmas, but the very essence of that spirit itself, belief in a meaningful and purposeful world. For the founding of a new religion a new Jesus Christ or Buddha would have to appear, in itself a most unlikely event and one for which in any case we cannot afford to sit and wait. But even if a new prophet and a new religion did appear, we may predict that they would fail in the modern world. No one for long would believe in them, for modern men have lost the vision, basic to all religion, of an ordered plan and purpose of the world. They have before their minds the picture of a purposeless universe, and such a world-picture must be fatal to any religion at all, not merely to Christianity.

27   We must not be misled by occasional appearances of a revival of the religious spirit. Men, we are told, in their disgust and disillusionment at the emptiness of their lives, are turning once more to religion, or are searching for a new message. It may be so. We must expect such wistful yearnings of the spirit. We must expect men to wish back again the light that is gone, and to try to bring it back. But however they may wish and try, the light will not shine again,—not at least in the civilization to which we belong.

28   Another remedy commonly proposed is that we should turn to science itself, or the scientific spirit, for our salvation. Mr. Russell and Professor Dewey both make this proposal, though in somewhat different ways. Professor Dewey seems to believe that discoveries in sociology, the application of scientific method to social and political problems will rescue us. This seems to me to be utterly naïve. It is not likely that science, which is basically the

cause of our spiritual troubles, is likely also to produce the cure for them. Also it lies in the nature of science that, though it can teach us the best means for achieving our ends, it can never tell us what ends to pursue. It cannot give us any ideals. And our trouble is about ideals and ends, not about the means for reaching them.

5

29   No civilization can live without ideals, or to put it in another way, without a firm faith in moral ideas. Our ideals and moral ideas have in the past been rooted in religion. But the religious basis of our ideals has been undermined, and the superstructure of ideals is plainly tottering. None of the commonly suggested remedies on examination seems likely to succeed. It would therefore look as if the early death of our civilization were inevitable.

30   Of course we know that it is perfectly possible for individual men, very highly educated men, philosophers, scientists, intellectuals in general, to live moral lives without any religious convictions. But the question is whether a whole civilization, a whole family of peoples, composed almost entirely of relatively uneducated men and women, can do this.

31   It follows, of course, that if we could make the vast majority of men as highly educated as the very few are now, we might save the situation. And we are already moving slowly in that direction through the techniques of mass education. But the critical question seems to concern the time-lag. Perhaps in a few hundred years most of the population will, at the present rate, be sufficiently highly educated and civilized to combine high ideals with an absence of religion. But long before we reach any such stage, the collapse of our civilization may have come about. How are we to live through the intervening period?

32   I am sure that the first thing we have to do is to face the truth, however bleak it may be, and then next we have to learn to live with it. Let me say a word about each of these two points. What I am urging as regards the first is complete honesty. Those who wish to resurrect Christian dogmas are not, of course, consciously dishonest. But they have that kind of unconscious

dishonesty which consists in lulling oneself with opiates and dreams. Those who talk of a new religion are merely hoping for a new opiate. Both alike refuse to face the truth that there is, in the universe outside man, no spirituality, no regard for values, no friend in the sky, no help or comfort for man of any sort. To be perfectly honest in the admission of this fact, not to seek shelter in new or old illusions, not to indulge in wishful dreams about this matter, this is the first thing we shall have to do.

33   I do not urge this course out of any special regard for the sanctity of truth in the abstract. It is not self-evident to me that truth is the supreme value to which all else must be sacrificed. Might not the discoverer of a truth which would be fatal to mankind be justified in suppressing it, even in teaching men a falsehood? Is truth more valuable than goodness and beauty and happiness? To think so is to invent yet another absolute, another religious delusion in which Truth with a capital T is substituted for God. The reason why we must now boldly and honestly face the truth that the universe is non-spiritual and indifferent to goodness, beauty, happiness, or truth is not that it would be wicked to suppress it, but simply that it is too late to do so, so that in the end we cannot do anything else but face it. Yet we stand on the brink, dreading the icy plunge. We need courage. We need honesty.

34   Now about the other point, the necessity of learning to live with the truth. This means learning to live virtuously and happily, or at least contentedly, without illusions. And this is going to be extremely difficult because what we have now begun dimly to perceive is that human life in the past, or at least human happiness, has almost wholly depended upon illusions. It has been said that man lives by truth, and that the truth will make us free. Nearly the opposite seems to me to be the case. Mankind has managed to live only by means of lies, and the truth may very well destroy us. If one were a Bergsonian one might believe that nature deliberately puts illusions into our souls in order to induce us to go on living.

35   The illusions by which men have lived seem to be of two kinds. First, there is what one may perhaps call the Great Illusion—I mean the religious illusion that the universe is moral and good, that it follows a wise and noble plan, that it is gradually generating some supreme value, that goodness is bound to triumph in it.

Secondly, there is a whole host of minor illusions on which human happiness nourishes itself. How much of human happiness notoriously comes from the illusions of the lover about his beloved? Then again we work and strive because of the illusions connected with fame, glory, power, or money. Banners of all kinds, flags, emblems, insignia, ceremonials, and rituals are invariably symbols of some illusion or other. The British Empire, the connection between mother country and dominions, is partly kept going by illusions surrounding the notion of kingship. Or think of the vast amount of human happiness which is derived from the illusion of supposing that if some nonsense syllable, such as "sir" or "count" or "lord" is pronounced in conjunction with our names, we belong to a superior order of people.

36 There is plenty of evidence that human happiness is almost wholly based upon illusions of one kind or another. But the scientific spirit, or the spirit of truth, is the enemy of illusions and therefore the enemy of human happiness. That is why it is going to be so difficult to live with the truth.

37 There is no reason why we should have to give up the host of minor illusions which render life supportable. There is no reason why the lover should be scientific about the loved one. Even the illusions of fame and glory may persist. But without the Great Illusion, the illusion of a good, kindly, and purposeful universe, we shall *have* to learn to live. And to ask this is really no more than to ask that we become genuinely civilized beings and not merely sham civilized beings.

38 I can best explain the difference by a reminiscence. I remember a fellow student in my college days, an ardent Christian, who told me that if he did not believe in a future life, in heaven and hell, he would rape, murder, steal, and be a drunkard. That is what I call being a sham civilized being. On the other hand, not only could a Huxley, a John Stuart Mill, a David Hume, live great and fine lives without any religion, but a great many others of us, quite obscure persons, can at least live decent lives without it.

39 To be genuinely civilized means to be able to walk straightly and to live honorably without the props and crutches of one or another of the childish dreams which have so far supported men. That such a life is likely to be ecstatically happy I will not claim.

But that it can be lived in quiet content, accepting resignedly what cannot be helped, not expecting the impossible, and thankful for small mercies, this I would maintain. That it will be difficult for men in general to learn this lesson I do not deny. But that it will be impossible I would not admit since so many have learned it already.

40 Man has not yet grown up. He is not adult. Like a child he cries for the moon and lives in a world of fantasies. And the race as a whole has perhaps reached the great crisis of its life. Can it grow up as a race in the same sense as individual men grow up? Can man put away childish things and adolescent dreams? Can he grasp the real world as it actually is, stark and bleak, without its romantic or religious halo, and still retain his ideals, striving for great ends and noble achievements? If he can, all may yet be well. If he cannot, he will probably sink back into the savagery and brutality from which he came, taking a humble place once more among the lower animals.

war as a biological phenomenon
JULIAN HUXLEY

1   Whenever we tend to become completely absorbed in an enterprise or an idea, it is a good thing to stand off from it now and
again and look at it from the most dispassionate point of view
possible. War is no exception. Quite rightly, all our major efforts
must to-day be devoted to the urgent business of making sure
that we win the war and win it as quickly as possible. We are for
most purposes immersed in the war; however, it will not merely
do no harm, but will actually be of service, if no wand again we
try to get outside it and to look at it as objectively as we can in
long perspective.

2   The longest possible perspective is that of the biologist, to
whom man is a single animal species among hundreds of thousands of others, merely one of the products (albeit the latest and
the most successful) of millions of years of evolution.

3   How does war look when pinned out in the biologist's collection? In the first place, he is able to say with assurance that war
is not a general law of life, but an exceedingly rare biological
phenomenon. War is not the same thing as conflict or bloodshed.
It means something quite definite: an organized physical conflict
between groups of one and the same species. Individual disputes
between members of the same species are not war, even if they
involve bloodshed and death. Two stags fighting for a harem of

Reprinted with permission of Harper & Row, Publishers, Inc., from *On
Living in a Revolution*, by Julian Huxley. © 1942 by Julian Huxley.

hinds, or a man murdering another man, or a dozen dogs fighting over a bone, are not engaged in war. Competition between two different species, even if it involves physical conflict, is not war. When the brown rat was accidentally brought to Europe and proceeded to oust the black rat from most of its haunts, that was not war between the two species of rat; nor is it war in any but a purely metaphorical sense when we speak of making war on the malaria mosquito or the boll-weevil. Still less is it war when one species preys upon another, even when the preying is done by an organized group. A pack of wolves attacking a flock of sheep or deer, or a peregrine killing a duck, is not war. Much of nature, as Tennyson correctly said, is "red in tooth and claw"; but this only means what it says, that there is a great deal of killing in the animal world, not that war is the rule of life.

4   In point of fact, there are only two kinds of animals that habitually make war—man and ants. Even among ants war is mainly practised by one group, comprising only a few species among the tens of thousands that are known to science. They are the harvester ants, inhabitants of arid regions where there is little to pick up during the dry months. Accordingly they collect the seeds of various grasses at the end of the growing season and store them in special underground granaries in their nests. It is these reserve supplies which are the object of ant warfare. The inhabitants of one nest set out deliberately to raid the supplies of another group. According to Forel and other students of ant life, they may employ quite elaborate military tactics, and the battles generally result in heavy casualties. If the attackers win, they remove the stores grain by grain to their own nest. Ant wars never last nearly so long as human wars. One campaign observed by the American myrmecologist McCook in Penn Square in the centre of Philadelphia, lasted almost 3 weeks. The longest on record is 6½ weeks.

5   Harvesters are the only kind of ants to go in for accumulating property, as well as the chief kind to practise war. This association of property with war is interesting, as various anthropologists believe that in the human species war, or at any rate habitual and organized war, did not arise in human evolution until man had reached the stage of settled civilization, when he began to accumulate stores of grain and other forms of wealth.

6   Less deliberate wars may also occur in some other species, between communities whose nests are so close that they compete for the same food-territory. When similarly provoked conflicts occur between closely related species, the term war may perhaps be extended to them. On the other hand, the raids of the slave-making ants are not true war, but a curious combination of predation and parasitism.

7   There is another group of ants called army ants, which suggests military activity; but the phrase is really a mis-nomer, for these army ants are in reality simply predatory species which happen to hunt in packs: they are the wolves of the insect world, not the war-mongers.

8   So much then for war as a biological phenomenon. The facts speak for themselves. War, far from being a universal law of nature, or even a common occurrence, is a very rare exception among living creatures; and where it occurs, it is either associated with another phenomenon, almost equally rare, the amassing of property, or with territorial rights.

9   Biology can help put war in its proper perspective in another way. War has often been justified on biological grounds. The program of life, say war's apologists, depends on the struggle for existence. This struggle is universal and results in what Darwin called "Natural Selection," and this in its turn results in the "Survival of the Fittest." Natural Selection, of course, works only in a mass way, so that those which survive in the struggle will merely have an average of fitness a little above those which perish or fail to reproduce themselves. But some of the qualities which make for success in the struggle, and so for a greater chance of survival, will certainly be inherited; and since the process continues generation after generation not merely for thousands but for millions of years, the average fitness and efficiency of the race will steadily and continuously be raised until it can be pushed no higher. In any case, say the believers in this doctrine, struggle is necessary to maintain fitness; if the pressure of competition and conflict is removed, biological efficiency will suffer, and degeneration will set in.

10   Darwin's principle of Natural Selection, based as it is on constant pressure of competition or struggle, has been invoked to justify various policies in human affairs. For instance, it was used,

especially by politicians in late Victorian England, to justify the principles of *laissez-faire* and free competition in business and economic affairs. And it was used, especially by German writers and politicians from the late nineteenth century onwards, to justify militarism. War, so ran this particular version of the argument, is the form which is taken by Natural Selection and the Struggle for Existence in the affairs of the nations. Without war, the heroic virtues degenerate; without war, no nation can possibly become great or successful.

11   It turns out, however, that both the *laissez-faire* economists and the militarists were wrong in appealing to biology for justification of their policies. War is a rather special aspect of competition between members of the same species—what biologists call "intra-specific competition." It is a special case because it involves physical conflict and often the death of those who undertake it, and also because it is physical conflict not between individuals but between organized groups; yet it shares certain properties in common with all other forms of intra-specific struggle or competition. And recent studies of the way in which Natural Selection works and how the Struggle for Existence operates in different conditions have resulted in this rather surprising but very important conclusion—that intra-specific competition need not, and usually does not, produce results of any advantage to the species as a whole.

12   A couple of examples will show what I mean. In birds like the peacock or the argus pheasant, the males are polygamous—if they can secure a harem. They show off their gorgeous plumage before the hen birds in an elaborate and very striking display, at definite assembly grounds where males and females go for the purpose of finding mates. The old idea that the hen deliberately selects the male she thinks the most beautiful is putting the matter in human terms which certainly do not apply to a bird's mind; but it seems certain that the brilliant and exciting display does have an effect on the hen bird, stimulating her to greater readiness to mate. Individual male birds meet with different degrees of success in this polygamous love business: some secure quite a number of mates, others only one or a few, and some get none at all. This puts an enormous biological premium on success: the really successful male leaves many times more descendants than the

unsuccessful. Here, then, is Natural Selection working at an exceedingly high pitch of intensity to make their display plumage and display actions more effective in their business of stimulating the hens. Accordingly, in polygamous birds of this kind, we often find the display plumage developed to a fantastic extent, even so far as to be a handicap to the species as a whole. Thus the display organ of the peacock, his train of enormously over-grown tail-covert feathers, is so long and cumbersome that it is a real handicap in flight. In the argus pheasant the chief display organs are the beautifully adorned wings which the male throws up and forward in display so that he looks like a gigantic bell-shaped flower. The business of display has been so important that it has overridden the business of flying, and now the male argus pheasant can fly only with difficulty, a few feet at a time.

13   Here are two good examples of how a purely intra-specific struggle, in this case between individual rival males, can produce results which are not merely useless, but harmful to the species as a whole in its struggle for existence against its enemies and the forces of nature. In general, selection for success in reproduction reaches greater intensities than selection for individual survival, for the simple reason that reproduction implies multiplication: the individual is a single unit, but, as we have just seen for polygamous birds, success in reproduction may give the individual's characteristics a multiple representation in later generations.

14   In flowering plants, the intra-specific struggle for reproduction between different individuals often produces results which, if not directly harmful to the species, are at least incredibly wasteful. We need only think of the fantastic profusion of bloom on flowering trees like dogwood or hawthorn or catalpa, or the still more fantastic profusion of pollen in trees which rely on fertilization by the wind, like pine and fir. The individual trees are competing for the privilege of surviving in their descendants; the species could certainly perpetuate itself with a much more modest expenditure of living material.

15   One final example. Naturalists have often noted the almost unbelievable perfection of the protective resemblance of certain insects to their surroundings. The most extraordinary cases are the resemblances of various butterflies, like the Kallima, to dead leaves. Not only do the folded wings perfectly resemble a dead

leaf in shape and colour, not only do they have a projection to imitate the stalk, and dark lines which perfectly simulate the veins, but some even go so far as to be marked with imitation mould-spots and holes!

16   Now, in all butterflies the survival of the species depends to a preponderant degree on the capacity of the defenceless and juicy caterpillar and chrysalis to survive. Selection presses with much greater intensity on the larval and pupal stages than on the adult. Furthermore, there is some sort of balance between the number of adults which survive to reproduce themselves and the intensity of selection which presses on the next generation of caterpillars. If more adults reproduce, there will be many more caterpillars, and they will be more easily found by their enemies, especially the tiny parasitic wasps which lay eggs inside the caterpillars, the eggs growing into grubs which devour the unfortunate animals from within. Conversely, if fewer adults reproduce, there are many fewer caterpillars, but each of them has a better chance of surviving to the butterfly stage. Accordingly, the protection of the adults is, from the point of view of the species, a secondary matter. Of course they must be protected sufficiently well for a reasonable number to survive and reproduce, but after this it is quite unimportant—for the species—if a slightly higher or a slightly lower proportion survives.

17   It is unimportant for the species but it remains important for the individual. If one kind of adult is better protected than another, it will automatically leave a higher average number of offspring; and so the intra-specific struggle for reproduction among the individual adult butterflies will continue to push any protective devices they possess on toward ever greater efficiency, even though this may be quite immaterial to the survival of the species. The perfection of the Kallima's resemblance to a dead leaf is one of the marvels of nature; not the least marvelous part of it is that it is of no value to the species as a whole.

18   On the other hand, intra-specific competition and struggle need not always lead to results which are useless to the species. The competition between individuals may concern qualities which are also useful in the struggle of the species against its enemies, as in deer or zebra or antelope—the same extra turn of speed which gives one individual an advantage over another in escap-

ing from wolf or lion or cheetah will also stand the whole species in good stead. Or it may concern qualities which help the species in surviving in a difficult environment; an extra capacity for resisting drought in an individual cactus or yucca will help the species in colonizing new and more arid regions. It will not be useless or harmful to the species unless the competition is directed solely or mainly against other individuals like itself.

19   Furthermore, the results will differ according to conditions. When there is competition for mates among male birds, it will become really intense only when polygamy prevails and the advantage of success is therefore multiplied. Monogamous birds also stimulate their mates with a display of bright plumage, but in this case the display plumage is never developed to a pitch at which it is actually harmful in the general struggle for existence; the balance is struck at a different level.

20   All these considerations apply to war. In the first place it is obvious that war is an example of intra-specific competition—it is a physical conflict between groups within the same species. As such, it might be not merely useless but harmful to the species as a whole—a drag on the evolutionary progress of humanity. But, further, it might turn out to be harmful in some conditions and not in others. This indeed seems to be the truth. Those who say that war is always and inevitably harmful to humanity are indulging in an unjustified generalization (though not nearly so unjustified as the opposite generalization of the militarists who say that war is both necessary and beneficial to humanity). Warfare between peoples living on the tribal level of early barbarism may quite possibly have been on balance a good thing for the species—by encouraging the manly virtues, by mixing the heritage of otherwise closed communities through the capture of women, by keeping down excessive population-pressure, and in other ways. War waged by small professional armies according to a professional code was at least not a serious handicap to general progress. But long-continued war in which the civilian population is starved, oppressed, and murdered and whole countries are laid waste, as in the Thirty Years War—that is harmful to the species; and so is total war in the modern German sense in which entire populations may be enslaved and brutalized, as with Poland or Greece to-day, whole cities smashed,

like Rotterdam, the resources of large regions deliberately destroyed, as in the Ukraine. The more total war becomes, both
intensively, as diverting more of the energies of the population
from construction to destruction, and extensively, as involving
more and more of the countries of the globe, the more of a threat
does it become to the progress of the human species. As H. G.
Wells and many others have urged, it might even turn back the
clock of civilization and force the world into another Dark Age.
War of this type is an intra-specific struggle from which nobody,
neither humanity at large nor any of the groups engaged in the
conflict, can really reap any balance of advantage, though of
course we may snatch particular advantages out of the results of
war.

21   But it is one thing to demonstrate that modern war is harmful
to the species, another thing to do something about abolishing
it. What has the biologist to say to those who assert that war is
inevitable, since, they say, it is a natural outcome of human
nature and human nature cannot possibly be changed?

22   To this the biologist can give a reassuring answer. War is not
an inevitable phenomenon of human life; and when objectors of
this type talk of human nature they really mean the expression
of human nature, and this can be most thoroughly changed.

23   As a matter of observable fact, war occurs in certain conditions,
not in others. There is no evidence of prehistoric man's having
made war, for all his flint implements seem to have been designed
for hunting, for digging, or for scraping hides; and we can be
pretty sure that even if he did, any wars between groups in the
hunting stage of human life would have been both rare and
mild. Organized warfare is most unlikely to have begun before
the stage of settled civilization. In man, as in ants, war in any
serious sense is bound up with the existence of accumulations of
property to fight about.

24   However, even after man had learned to live in cities and
amass property, war does not seem to have been inevitable. The
early Indus civilization, dating from about 3000 B.C., reveals no
traces of war. There seem to have been periods in early Chinese
history, as well as in the Inca civilization in Peru, in which war
was quite or almost absent.

25   As for human nature, it contains no specific war instinct, as

does the nature of harvester ants. There is in man's make-up a general aggressive tendency, but this, like all other human urges, is not a specific and unvarying instinct; it can be moulded into the most varied forms. It can be canalized into competitive sport, as in our own society, or as when certain Filipino tribes were induced to substitute football for head-hunting. It can be sublimated into non-competitive sport, like mountain-climbing, or into higher types of activity altogether, like exploration or research or social crusades.

26   There is no theoretical obstacle to the abolition of war. But do not let us delude ourselves with the idea that this will be easy. The first step needed is the right kind of international machinery. To invent that will not be particularly simple: sanctions against aggressors, the peaceful reconciliation of national interests in a co-operative international system, an international police force—we can see in principle that these and other necessary bits of anti-war machinery are possible, but it will take a great deal of hard thinking to design them so that they will really work.

27   The second step is a good deal more difficult. It is to find what William James called a "moral equivalent for war," while at the same time reducing the reservoir of potential aggressiveness which now exists in every powerful nation. This is a psychological problem. Thanks to Freud and modern psychology in general, we are now beginning to understand how the self-assertive impulses of the child may be frustrated and repressed in such a way as to drive them underground. There in the subconscious they may persist in the form of crude urges to aggression and cruelty, which are all the more dangerous for not being consciously recognized.

28   To prevent the accumulation of this store of psychological dynamite and to find ways in which our self-assertive impulses can issue along conscious and constructive channels is a big job. It means a better structure of social and family life, one which does not inflict such frustrations on the growing human personality; it means a new approach to education; it means providing outlets in the form of physical or mental adventure for the impulses which would otherwise be unused even if not repressed. It is a difficult task; but by no means an impossible one.

29 Thus in the perspective of biology war first dwindles to the status of a rare curiosity. Further probing, however, makes it loom larger again. For one thing, it is a form of intra-specific struggle, and as such may be useless or even harmful to the species as a whole. Then we find that one of the very few animal species which make war is man; and man is to-day not merely the highest product of evolution, but the only type still capable of real evolutionary progress. And, war, though it need not always be harmful to the human species and its progress, indubitably is so when conducted in the total fashion which is necessary in this technological age. Thus war is not merely a human problem; it is a biological problem of the broadest scope, for on its abolition may depend life's ability to continue the progress which it has slowly but steadily achieved through more than a thousand million years.

30 But the biologist can end on a note of tempered hope. War is not inevitable for man. His aggressive impulses *can* be canalized into other outlets; his political machinery *can* be designed to make war less likely. These things *can* be done: but to do them will require a great deal of hard thinking and hard work. While waging this particular war with all our might, we have a duty to keep a corner of our minds open, engaged on the job of thinking out ways and means of preventing war in general in the future.

meditation

JOHN DONNE

Nunc lento sonitu dicunt, Morieris.

*Now, this bell tolling softly for another says
to me, Thou must die.*

1 Perchance he for whom this bell tolls may be so ill, as that
he knows not it tolls for him. And perchance I may think myself
so much better than I am, as that they who are about me and
see my state may have caused it to toll for me, and I know not
that. The church is catholic, universal; so are all her actions.
All that she does belongs to all. When she baptizes a child, that
action concerns me. For that child is thereby connected to that
head which is my head too and engraffed into that body whereof
I am a member. And when she buries a man, that action concerns
me. All mankind is of one author and is one volume. When one
man dies, one chapter is not torn out of the book, but translated
into a better language. And every chapter must be so translated.
God employs several translators: some pieces are translated by
age, some by sickness, some by war, some by justice. But God's
hand is in every translation, and his hand shall bind up all our
scattered leaves again for that library where every book shall
lie open to one another.

2   As, therefore, the bell that rings to a sermon calls not upon
the preacher only, but upon the congregation to come, so this
bell calls us all. But how much more me, who am brought so
near the door by this sickness. There was a contention as far as

a suit (in which both piety and dignity, religion, and estimation were mingled) which of the religious orders should ring to prayers first in the morning, and it was determined that they should ring first that rose earliest. If we understand aright the dignity of this bell that tolls for our evening prayer, we would be glad to make it ours by rising early in that application, that it might be ours, as well as his whose indeed it is. The bell doth toll for him that thinks it doth. And though it intermit again, yet from that minute that that occasion wrought upon him, he is united to God.

3   Who casts not up his eye to the sun when it rises? But who takes off his eye from a comet when that breaks out? Who bends not his ear to any bell, which upon any occasion rings? But who can remove it from that bell which is passing a piece of himself out of this world? No man is an island, entire of itself. Every man is a piece of the continent, a part of the main. If a clod be washed away by the sea, Europe is the less, as well as if a promontory were, as well as if a manor of thy friend's or of thine own were. Any man's death diminishes me, because I am involved in mankind. And therefore never send to know for whom the bell tolls: it tolls for thee.

4   Neither can we call this a begging of misery or a borrowing of misery, as though we were not miserable enough of ourselves but must fetch in more from the next house in taking upon us the misery of our neighbors. Truly, it were an excusable covetousness if we did. For affliction is a treasure, and scarce any man hath enough of it. No man hath affliction enough that is not matured and ripened by it, and made fit for God by that affliction. If a man carry treasure in bullion or in a wedge of gold and have none coined into current moneys, his treasure will not defray him as he travels. Tribulation is treasure in the nature of it, but it is not current money in the use of it, except we get nearer and nearer our home, heaven, by it. Another man may be sick too, and sick to death, and this affliction may lie in his bowels as gold in a mine and be of no use to him. But this bell that tells me of his affliction, digs out and applies that gold to me, if by this consideration of another's danger, I take mine own into contemplation and so secure myself by making my recourse to my God, who is our only security.

counterparts

JAMES JOYCE

The bell rang furiously and, when Miss Parker went to the tube, a furious voice called out in a piercing North of Ireland accent:

"Send Farrington here!"

Miss Parker returned to her machine, saying to a man who was writing at a desk:

"Mr. Alleyne wants you upstairs."

The man muttered "*Blast* him!" under his breath and pushed back his chair to stand up. When he stood up he was tall and of great bulk. He had a hanging face, dark wine-coloured, with fair eyebrows and moustache: his eyes bulged forward slightly and the whites of them were dirty. He lifted up the counter and, passing by the clients, went out of the office with a heavy step.

He went heavily upstairs until he came to the second landing, where a door bore a brass plate with the inscription *Mr. Alleyne.* Here he halted, puffing with labour and vexation, and knocked. The shrill voice cried:

"Come in!"

The man entered Mr. Alleyne's room. Simultaneously Mr. Alleyne, a little man wearing gold-rimmed glasses on a clean-shaven face, shot his head up over a pile of documents. The head

Reprinted with permission of The Viking Press, Inc., from *Dubliners*, by James Joyce. Originally published by B. W. Huebsch, Inc. in 1916. © 1967 by the Estate of James Joyce. All rights reserved.

itself was so pink and hairless it seemed like a large egg reposing on the papers. Mr. Alleyne did not lose a moment:

"Farrington? What is the meaning of this? Why have I always to complain of you? May I ask you why you haven't made a copy of that contract between Bodley and Kirwan? I told you it must be ready by four o'clock."

"But Mr. Shelley said, sir——"

"*Mr. Shelley said, sir.* . . . Kindly attend to what I say and not to what *Mr. Shelley says, sir.* You have always some excuse or another for shirking work. Let me tell you that if the contract is not copied before this evening I'll lay the matter before Mr. Crosbie. . . . Do you hear me now?"

"Yes, sir."

"Do you hear me now? . . . Ay and another little matter! I might as well be talking to the wall as talking to you. Understand once for all that you get a half an hour for your lunch and not an hour and a half. How many courses do you want, I'd like to know. . . . Do you mind me now?"

"Yes, sir."

Mr. Alleyne bent his head again upon his pile of papers. The man stared fixedly at the polished skull which directed the affairs of Crosbie & Alleyne, gauging its fragility. A spasm of rage gripped his throat for a few moments and then passed, leaving after it a sharp sensation of thirst. The man recognized the sensation and felt that he must have a good night's drinking. The middle of the month was passed and, if he could get the copy done in time, Mr. Alleyne might give him an order on the cashier. He stood still, gazing fixedly at the head upon the pile of papers. Suddenly Mr. Alleyne began to upset all the papers, searching for something. Then, as if he had been unaware of the man's presence till that moment, he shot up his head again, saying:

"Eh? Are you going to stand there all day? Upon my word, Farrington, you take things easy!"

"I was waiting to see . . ."

"Very good, you needn't wait to see. Go downstairs and do your work."

The man walked heavily towards the door and, as he went out of the room, he heard Mr. Alleyne cry after him that if the contract was not copied by evening Mr. Crosbie would hear of the matter.

He returned to his desk in the lower office and counted the sheets which remained to be copied. He took up his pen and dipped it in the ink but he continued to stare stupidly at the last words he had written: *In no case shall the said Bernard Bodley be . . .* The evening was falling and in a few minutes they would be lighting the gas: then he could write. He felt that he must slake the thirst in his throat. He stood up from his desk and, lifting the counter as before, passed out of the office. As he was passing out the chief clerk looked at him inquiringly.

"It's all right, Mr. Shelley," said the man, pointing with his finger to indicate the objective of his journey.

The chief clerk glanced at the hat-rack, but, seeing the row complete, offered no remark. As soon as he was on the landing the man pulled a shepherd's plaid cap out of his pocket, put it on his head and ran quickly down the rickety stairs. From the street door he walked on furtively on the inner side of the path towards the corner and all at once dived into a doorway. He was now safe in the dark snug of O'Neill's shop, and, filling up the little window that looked into the bar with his inflamed face, the colour of dark wine or dark meat, he called out:

"Here, Pat, give us a g.p., like a good fellow."

The curate brought him a glass of plain porter. The man drank it at a gulp and asked for a caraway seed. He put his penny on the counter and, leaving the curate to grope for it in the gloom, retreated out of the snug as furtively as he had entered it.

Darkness, accompanied by a thick fog, was gaining upon the dusk of February and the lamps in Eustace Street had been lit. The man went up by the houses until he reached the door of the office, wondering whether he could finish his copy in time. On the stairs a moist pungent odour of perfumes saluted his nose: evidently Miss Delacour had come while he was out in O'Neill's. He crammed his cap back again into his pocket and re-entered the office, assuming an air of absent-mindedness.

"Mr. Alleyne has been calling for you," said the chief clerk severely. "Where were you?"

The man glanced at the two clients who were standing at the counter as if to intimate that their presence prevented him from answering. As the clients were both male the chief clerk allowed himself a laugh.

"I know that game," he said. "Five times in one day is a little bit. . . . Well, you better look sharp and get a copy of our correspondence in the Delacour case for Mr. Alleyne."

This address in the presence of the public, his run upstairs and the porter he had gulped down so hastily confused the man and, as he sat down at his desk to get what was required, he realised how hopeless was the task of finishing his copy of the contract before half past five. The dark damp night was coming and he longed to spend it in the bars, drinking with his friends amid the glare of gas and the clatter of glasses. He got out the Delacour correspondence and passed out of the office. He hoped Mr. Alleyne would not discover that the last two letters were missing.

The moist pungent perfume lay all the way up to Mr. Alleyne's room. Miss Delacour was a middle-aged woman of Jewish appearance. Mr. Alleyne was said to be sweet on her or on her money. She came to the office often and stayed a long time when she came. She was sitting beside his desk now in an aroma of perfumes, smoothing the handle of her umbrella and nodding the great black feather in her hat. Mr. Alleyne had swivelled his chair round to face her and thrown his right foot jauntily upon his left knee. The man put the correspondence on the desk and bowed respectfully but neither Mr. Alleyne nor Miss Delacour took any notice of his bow. Mr. Alleyne tapped a finger on the correspondence and then flicked it towards him as if to say: *"That's all right: you can go."*

The man returned to the lower office and sat down again at his desk. He stared intently at the incomplete phrase: *In no case shall the said Bernard Bodley be* . . . and thought how strange it was that the last three words began with the same letter. The chief clerk began to hurry Miss Parker, saying she would never have the letters typed in time for post. The man listened to the clicking of the machine for a few minutes and then set to work to finish his copy. But his head was not clear and his mind wandered away to the glare and rattle of the public-house. It was a night for hot punches. He struggled on with his copy, but when the clock struck five he had still fourteen pages to write.

Blast it! He couldn't finish it in time. He longed to execrate aloud, to bring his fist down on something violently. He was so enraged that he wrote *Bernard Bernard* instead of *Bernard Bodley* and had to begin again on a clean sheet.

He felt strong enough to clear out the whole office single-handed. His body ached to do something, to rush out and revel in violence. All the indignities of his life enraged him. . . . Could he ask the cashier privately for an advance? No, the cashier was no good, no damn good: he wouldn't give an advance. . . . He knew where he would meet the boys: Leonard and O'Halloran and Nosey Flynn. The barometer of his emotional nature was set for a spell of riot.

His imagination had so abstracted him that his name was called twice before he answered. Mr. Alleyne and Miss Delacour were standing outside the counter and all the clerks had turned round in anticipation of something. The man got up from his desk. Mr. Alleyne began a tirade of abuse, saying that two letters were missing. The man answered that he knew nothing about them, that he had made a faithful copy. The tirade continued: it was so bitter and violent that the man could hardly restrain his fist from descending upon the head of the manikin before him.

"I know nothing about any other two letters," he said stupidly.

"*You—know—nothing*. Of course you know nothing," said Mr. Alleyne. "Tell me," he added, glancing first for approval to the lady beside him, "do you take me for a fool? Do you think me an utter fool?"

The man glanced from the lady's face to the little egg-shaped head and back again; and, almost before he was aware of it, his tongue had found a felicitous moment:

"I don't think, sir," he said, "that that's a fair question to put to me."

There was a pause in the very breathing of the clerks. Everyone was astounded (the author of the witticism no less than his neighbours) and Miss Delacour, who was a stout amiable person, began to smile broadly. Mr. Alleyne flushed to the hue of a wild rose and his mouth twitched with a dwarf's passion. He shook his fist in the man's face till it seemed to vibrate like the knob of some electric machine:

"You impertinent ruffian! You impertinent ruffian! I'll make short work of you! Wait till you see! You'll apologise to me for your impertinence or you'll quit the office instanter! You'll quit this, I'm telling you, or you'll apologise to me!"

.   .   .

He stood in a doorway opposite the office watching to see if the cashier would come out alone. All the clerks passed out and finally the cashier came out with the chief clerk. It was no use trying to say a word to him when he was with the chief clerk. The man felt that his position was bad enough. He had been obliged to offer an abject apology to Mr. Alleyne for his impertinence but he knew what a hornet's nest the office would be for him. He could remember the way in which Mr. Alleyne had hounded little Peake out of the office in order to make room for his own nephew. He felt savage and thirsty and revengful, annoyed with himself and with everyone else. Mr. Alleyne would never give him an hour's rest; his life would be a hell to him. He had made a proper fool of himself this time. Could he not keep his tongue in his cheek? But they had never pulled together from the first, he and Mr. Alleyne, ever since the day Mr. Alleyne had overheard him mimicking his North of Ireland accent to amuse Higgins and Miss Parker: that had been the beginning of it. He might have tried Higgins for the money, but sure Higgins never had anything for himself. A man with two establishments to keep up, of course he couldn't. . . .

He felt his great body again aching for the comfort of the public-house. The fog had begun to chill him and he wondered could he touch Pat in O'Neill's. He could not touch him for more than a bob—and a bob was no use. Yet he must get money somewhere or other: he had spent his last penny for the g.p. and soon it would be too late for getting money anywhere. Suddenly, as he was fingering his watchchain, he thought of Terry Kelly's pawn-office in Fleet Street. That was the dart! Why didn't he think of it sooner?

He went through the narrow alley of Temple Bar quickly, muttering to himself that they could all go to hell because he was going to have a good night of it. The clerk in Terry Kelly's said *A crown!* but the consignor held out for six shillings; and in the end the six shillings was allowed him literally. He came out of the pawn-office joyfully, making a little cylinder of the coins between his thumb and fingers. In Westmoreland Street the footpaths were crowded with young men and women return- ing from business and ragged urchins ran here and there yelling out the names of the evening editions. The man passed through the crowd, looking on the spectacle generally with proud satisfac- tion and staring masterfully at the office-girls. His head was full of the noises of tram-gongs and swishing trolleys and his nose already sniffed the curling fumes of punch. As he walked on he preconsidered the terms in which he would narrate the incident to the boys:

"So, I just looked at him—coolly, you know, and looked at her. Then I looked back at him again—taking my time, you know. 'I don't think that that's a fair question to put to me,' says I."

Nosey Flynn was sitting up in his usual corner of Davy Byrne's and, when he heard the story, he stood Farrington a half-one, saying it was as smart a thing as ever he heard. Farring- ton stood a drink in his turn. After a while O'Halloran and Paddy Leonard came in and the story was repeated to them. O'Halloran stood tailors of malt, hot, all round and told the story of the retort he had made to the chief clerk when he was in Callan's of Frownes's Street; but, as the retort was after the man- ner of the liberal shepherds in the eclogues, he had to admit that it was not as clever as Farrington's retort. At this Farrington told the boys to polish off that and have another.

Just as they were naming their poisons who should come in but Higgins! Of course he had to join in with the others. The men asked him to give his version of it, and he did so with great vivacity for the sight of five small hot whiskies was very exhilarat- ing. Everyone roared laughing when he showed the way in which Mr. Alleyne shook his fist in Farrington's face. Then he imitated Farrington, saying, *"And here was my nabs, as cool as you please,"* while Farrington looked at the company out of his heavy dirty eyes, smiling and at times drawing forth stray drops of liquor from his moustache with the aid of his lower lip.

When that round was over there was a pause. O'Halloran had money but neither of the other two seemed to have any; so the whole party left the shop somewhat regretfully. At the corner of

Duke Street Higgins and Nosey Flynn bevelled off to the left
while the other three turned back towards the city. Rain was
drizzling down on the cold streets and, when they reached the
Ballast Office, Farrington suggested the Scotch House. The bar
was full of men and loud with the noise of tongues and glasses.
The three men pushed past the whining match-sellers at the
door and formed a little party at the corner of the counter. They
began to exchange stories. Leonard introduced them to a young
fellow named Weathers who was performing at the Tivoli as an
acrobat and knockabout *artiste*. Farrington stood a drink all
round. Weathers said he would take a small Irish and Apollinaris. Farrington, who had definite notions of what was what,
asked the boys would they have an Apollinaris too; but the boys
told Tim to make theirs hot. The talk became theatrical.
O'Halloran stood a round and then Farrington stood another
round, Weathers protesting that the hospitality was too Irish.
He promised to get them in behind the scenes and introduce
them to some nice girls. O'Halloran said that he and Leonard
would go, but that Farrington wouldn't go because he was a
married man; and Farrington's heavy dirty eyes leered at the
company in token that he understood he was being chaffed.
Weathers made them all have just one little tincture at his expense and promised to meet them later on at Mulligan's in
Poolbeg Street.

When the Scotch House closed they went round to Mulligan's.
They went into the parlour at the back and O'Halloran ordered
small hot specials all round. They were all beginning to feel
mellow. Farrington was just standing another round when
Weathers came back. Much to Farrington's relief he drank a
glass of bitter this time. Funds were getting low but they had
enough to keep them going. Presently two young women with
big hats and a young man in a check suit came in and sat at a
table close by. Weathers saluted them and told the company
that they were out of the Tivoli. Farrington's eyes wandered at
every moment in the direction of one of the young women.
There was something striking in her appearance. An immense
scarf of peacock-blue muslin was wound round her hat and
knotted in a great bow under her chin; and she wore bright
yellow gloves, reaching to the elbow. Farrington gazed admiringly

at the plump arm which she moved very often and with much grace; and when, after a little time, she answered his gaze he admired still more her large dark brown eyes. The oblique staring expression in them fascinated him. She glanced at him once or twice and, when the party was leaving the room, she brushed against his chair and said "*O, pardon!*" in a London accent. He watched her leave the room in the hope that she would look back at him, but he was disappointed. He cursed his want of money and cursed all the rounds he had stood, particularly all the whiskies and Apollinaris which he had stood to Weathers. If there was one thing that he hated it was a sponge. He was so angry that he lost count of the conversation of his friends.

When Paddy Leonard called him he found that they were talking about feats of strength. Weathers was showing his biceps muscle to the company and boasting so much that the other two had called on Farrington to uphold the national honour. Farrington pulled up his sleeve accordingly and showed his biceps muscle to the company. The two arms were examined and compared and finally it was agreed to have a trial of strength. The table was cleared and the two men rested their elbows on it, clasping hands. When Paddy Leonard said "*Go!*" each was to try to bring down the other's hand on to the table. Farrington looked very serious and determined.

The trial began. After thirty seconds Weathers brought his opponent's hand slowly down on to the table. Farrington's dark wine-coloured face flushed darker still with anger and humiliation at having been defeated by such a stripling.

"You're not to put the weight of your body behind it. Play fair," he said.

"Who's not playing fair?" said the other.

"Come on again. The two best out of three."

The trial began again. The veins stood out on Farrington's forehead, and the pallor of Weathers' complexion changed to peony. Their hands and arms trembled under the stress. After a long struggle Weathers again brought his opponent's hand slowly on to the table. There was a murmur of applause from the spectators. The curate, who was standing beside the table, nodded his red head towards the victor and said with stupid familiarity:

"Ah! that's the knack!"

"What the hell do you know about it?" said Farrington fiercely, turning on the man. "What do you put in your gab for?"

"Sh, sh!" O'Halloran, observing the violent expression of Farrington's face. "Pony up, boys. We'll have just one little smahan more and then we'll be off."

A very sullen-faced man stood at the corner of O'Connell Bridge waiting for the little Sandymount tram to take him home. He was full of smouldering anger and revengefulness. He felt humiliated and discontented; he did not even feel drunk; and he had only twopence in his pocket. He cursed everything. He had done for himself in the office, pawned his watch, spent all his money; and he had not even got drunk. He began to feel thirsty again and he longed to be back again in the hot reeking public-house. He had lost his reputation as a strong man, having been defeated twice by a mere boy. His heart swelled with fury and, when he thought of the woman in the big hat who had brushed against him and said *Pardon!* his fury nearly choked him.

His tram let him down at Shelbourne Road and he steered his great body along in the shadow of the wall of the barracks. He loathed returning to his home. When he went in by the side-door he found the kitchen empty and the kitchen fire nearly out. He bawled upstairs:

"Ada! Ada!"

His wife was a little sharp-faced woman who bullied her husband when he was sober and was bullied by him when he was drunk. They had five children. A little boy came running down the stairs.

"Who is that?" said the man peering through the darkness.

"Me, pa."

"Who are you? Charlie?"

"No, pa. Tom."

"Where's your mother?"

"She's out at the chapel."

"That's right. . . . Did she think of leaving any dinner for me?"

"Yes, pa. I ——"

"Light the lamp. What do you mean by having the place in darkness? Are the other children in bed?"

The man sat down heavily on one of the chairs while the little boy lit the lamp. He began to mimic his son's flat accent, saying half to himself: *"At the chapel. At the chapel, if you please!"* When the lamp was lit he banged his fist on the table and shouted:

"What's for my dinner?"

"I'm going . . . to cook it, pa," said the little boy.

The man jumped up furiously and pointed to the fire.

"On that fire! You let the fire out! By God, I'll teach you to do that again!"

He took a step to the door and seized the walking-stick which was standing behind it.

"I'll teach you to let the fire out!" he said, rolling up his sleeve in order to give his arm free play.

The little boy cried *"O, pa!"* and ran whimpering round the table, but the man followed him and caught him by the coat. The little boy looked about him wildly but, seeing no way of escape, fell upon his knees.

"Now, you'll let the fire out the next time!" said the man, striking at him vigorously with the stick. "Take that, you little whelp!"

The boy uttered a squeal of pain as the stick cut his thigh. He clasped his hands together in the air and his voice shook with fright.

"O pa!" he cried. "Don't beat me, pa! And I'll . . . I'll say a *Hail Mary* for you. . . . I'll say a *Hail Mary* for you, pa, if you don't beat me. . . . I'll say a *Hail Mary*. . . ."

DISCUSSION AND WRITING MATERIAL

"The Crisis of American Masculinity"

Fill in the partially completed outline with subheadings and paragraph numbers.

Introduction ( )
I. Effects of the masculine crisis ( )
II. Causes for the problem ( )
III. The remedies ( )
Conclusion ( )

What is the basis of proof for Schlesinger's assertions? Does he take anything for granted? Is there any evidence in the course of the essay to indicate that the author is trained in the field of history? What is it in our modern society that is assaulting our identity? What does "the group" hold for man today?

"Man Against Darkness"

Stace points out that science is the major cause for man's attitude toward his existence in the modern world. Point out specifically what it is in science that has led to this attitude. Analyze paragraphs 2, 11, 13, and 28 for their methods of development. Reconstruct the argument in paragraph 16 in the form of a deductive syllogism.

"War as a Biological Phenomenon"

How satisfactory is Huxley's definition of war? Trace the basis of the cause-and-effect relationship claimed by those who defend war on biological grounds. Describe Huxley's analysis of the biological causes of war. Does the following quote from *African Genesis* by Robert Ardrey contribute to or detract from Huxley's argument?

Man's original nature is peaceable and good. His social environment must therefore be the cause of hostility and vice. The nature of man's society is determined by the ownership of land

and the means of production. The nature of man himself is therefore determined by the ownership of capital. So long as ownership remains in private hands, humankind will remain divided
between the exploiters and the exploited, and states will exist to
protect the exploiters. All history, in consequence, must be interpreted in terms of the struggle between the two classes; all wars
in terms solely of the exploiting class's efforts to gain or defend
economic advantage. But if the exploited can gain control of the
state, then private ownership will be ended. The exploiting class
will be ended. The class struggle will be ended. War, misery, vice,
hostility, and at last the need for the state itself will be ended,
since man is naturally peaceable and good.

"Meditation"

The structural basis of the sermon is fashioned on a cause-
to-effect pattern. Explain how each of the paragraphs contributes
to that pattern. What characteristics of Donne's style help
to facilitate the structural intent? How effective are the
metaphors?

"Counterparts"

What is the significance of the title? Discuss the reasons for
Farrington's beating his son by tracing the chain of cause
and effect which leads to this act.

Discuss the basis for the argument in the following poem by
Andrew Marvell:

To His Coy Mistress

Had we but world enough, and time,
This coyness, lady, were no crime.
We would sit down, and think which way
To walk, and pass our long love's day.
Thou by the Indian Ganges' side   5
Should'st rubies find: I by the tide

Of Humber would complain. I would
Love you ten years before the Flood,
And you should, if you please, refuse

Till the conversion of the Jews.   10
My vegetable love should grow
Vaster than empires and more slow:
An hundred years should go to praise
Thine eyes, and on thy forehead gaze.
Two hundred to adore each breast: 15
But thirty thousand to the rest.
An age at least to every part,
And the last age should show your heart.
For, lady, you deserve this state,
Nor would I love at lower rate.

But at my back I always hear   21
Time's winged chariot hurrying near:
And yonder all before us lie
Deserts of vast eternity.
Thy beauty shall no more be found,
Nor, in thy marble vault, shall sound   26
My echoing song: then worms shall try
That long-preserv'd virginity:
And your quaint honour turn to dust;
And into ashes all my lust.
The grave's a fine and private place,   31
But none I think do there embrace.

Now, therefore, while the youthful hue   33
Sits on thy skin like morning dew,
And while thy willing soul transpires
At every pore with instant fires,
Now let us sport us while we may;
And now, like am'rous birds of prey,   38
Rather at once our time devour,
Than languish in his slow-chappt pow'r.
Let us roll all our strength, and all
Our sweetness, up into one ball:
And tear our pleasures with rough strife,   43
Thorough the iron gates of life:
Thus, though we cannot make our sun
Stand still, yet we will make him run.

COMPARISON AND CONTRAST

Comparison and contrast, as a rhetorical technique, always implies the treatment of one subject through reference to one or more other subjects; thus X may be juxtaposed with Y to establish likenesses and differences between the two. Comparison, of course, deals with the former, the likenesses, and contrast with the latter, the differences. Like the principle of cause and effect discussed in the preceding section, comparison and contrast seems to be built-in to our thinking processes; we use it regularly to make distinctions and render judgments on a multitude of subjects. Is the National Football League superior to the American League? Are foreign cars less expensive to operate than the Detroit models? Is China a greater Communist threat than Russia? Our responses (which will not necessarily be "answers") to questions of this sort must inevitably grow out of our judgments of likenesses and differences, out of comparison and contrast.

Comparison and contrast has two fundamental roles in the rhetorical process: to clarify a hazy or obscure subject through reference to a more familiar one and to examine equally two subjects by setting up lines of similarities and differences. In the first instance our presupposition is that the unfamiliar can often be explained in light of the familiar. Thus one might explain the sport of soccer by comparing and contrasting it with football. Both are team sports played on an outdoor field, both employ a ball, and both involve body contact. On the other hand, the lengths of those fields differ, the number of men per team differs, and the personal equipment, shape of the balls, types of body contact and scoring system all differ. As we said, in an example such as this the reader's knowledge of football is presumed and used as a reference base for the explanation of soccer. The second role of comparison and contrast is useful for the analysis and appraisal of two subjects which, it must now be presumed, are equally well known too and understood by the reader. Two writers, for example, could be compared and contrasted for their styles and social views; but in such a case the reader's familiarity with both authors will doubtless be assumed.

Because unity and coherence are more difficult to maintain in a comparison and contrast essay, the organizational pattern is particularly important and deserves a special word. First, the comparison and contrast of two subjects must be developed along clearly defined lines; that is, a random listing of the characteristics of the subjects is by itself not enough. A set of traits pertinent to both should be selected and expanded according to some pattern discernible to the reader. In comparing and contrasting two universities, for example, one might establish four criteria or traits to serve as the basis for the essay: admission requirements, tuition costs, library holdings, and success of athletic teams (this is not to suggest that other, perhaps more relevant traits are not available to the writer). These four criteria then become the unifying set of principles around which the comparing and contrasting may proceed, and they provide a coherent structure for the essay.

The second factor in organization is the manner of developing the essay *after* these principles have been established. There are two means open to the writer, and his choice will depend upon the complexity of his material and the particular focus he desires. In comparing and contrasting our two universities we might first examine one school completely in relation to the four criteria noted; this done, we would proceed to consider the second school in similar fashion. On the other hand, we might discuss both universities on the basis of the first characteristic, admission requirements, then move to the second, third, and fourth characteristics in order, alternating from one school to the other relative to the trait under consideration. While neither method is inherently superior, the first is most effective when the subject matter is quite simple, for the obvious assumption here is that the reader will be able to recall all the pertinent facts on one school when he reads about the other. The second method works best on subjects of greater complexity and difficulty, subjects treated in more detail. In the case of comparison and contrast, the reader is required to remember fewer specific details as he moves from one characteristic to the next. It is worth repeating that neither method is preferable in itself; the writer's decision on which to employ will be based on his assessment of the difficulty of his material.

Many subjects can be treated effectively through comparison and contrast, but it is well to keep in mind two general suggestions, regardless of one's topic. For one thing, we should be certain that our subjects have enough in common to make comparison and contrast relevant. Robert Burns compares his love to a rose; and though such a comparison is vivid and imaginative, it is usually best for the novice writer to leave such figurative comparisons to the poet. Thus political systems are better compared with other political systems, and ideologies with ideologies. Further, it should be remembered that effective comparison and contrast assumes the use of *both;* that is, unless the writer's purpose is to present only similarities or differences, the exclusion of either comparison or contrast will doubtless result in a distortion of the relationship between the two subjects under consideration. To describe football and soccer as two team sports played on an outdoor field with a ball would be to ignore several real differences between them, and would leave the reader with a false impression of their similarity.

In reading the selections that follow, the student should first judge the adaptability of the topics to the technique of comparison and contrast. Next, he should attempt to follow (perhaps in outline form) the organizational pattern each author chooses for the development of his subject. Having done this, he will be in a better position to determine the effectiveness of that development and to learn from these examples the best means of applying comparison and contrast in his own writing.

a note on style
and the limits of language
WALKER GIBSON

1   Questions about style can most usefully be approached if we
think of a style as the expression of a personality. I do not mean
at all that our words necessarily reveal what we are "really like."
I do mean that every writer and talker, more or less consciously,
chooses a role which he thinks appropriate to express for a given
time and situation. The personality I am expressing in this
written sentence is not the same as the one I orally express to
my three-year-old who at this moment is bent on climbing onto
my typewriter. For each of these two situations, I choose a
different "voice," a different mask, in order to accomplish what I
want accomplished. There is no point in asking here which of
these voices is closer to the Real Me. What may be worth asking
is this: what kinds of voices, in written prose, may be said to
respond most sensitively and efficiently to the sort of contemporary world that this book has been describing?

2   First, let's be logical about it. Given the kind of dilemma with
respect to knowledge and language that this book defines, what
sort of style might we *expect* in our own time? What sort of
speaking voice adopted by the writer, what mask, would be
appropriate in a world where, as we have seen, the very nature

Reprinted with permission of Hill & Wang, Inc., from *The Limits of Language*, edited by Walker Gibson. © 1962 by Walker Gibson.

of nature may be inexpressible? If we live in a pluralistic and fluxlike universe, what manner of word-man should we become in order to talk about it? Well, we might at least expect a man who knows his limits, who admits the inevitably subjective character of his wisdom. We might expect a man who knows that he has no right in a final sense to consider himself any wiser than the next fellow, including the one he is talking to. The appropriate tone, therefore, might be informal, a little tense and self-conscious perhaps, but genial as between equals. With our modern relativistic ideas about the impossibility of determining any "standard dialect" for expressing Truth in all its forms, we might expect the cautious writer to employ many dialects, to shift from formal to colloquial diction, to avoid the slightest hint of authoritarianism. The rhythm of his words will be an irregular, conversational rhythm—not the symmetrical periods of formal Victorian prose. Short sentences alternating erratically with longer sentences. Occasional sentence fragments. In sum we might expect a style rather like *this!*[1]

3   This style, indeed, is easily recognizable and can be discovered all around us in modern prose. Thirty years ago in a book called *Modern Prose Style,* Bonamy Dobrée described it much as we have done here. "Most of us have ceased to believe, except provisionally, in truths," he wrote, "and we feel that what is important is not so much truth as the way our minds move toward truth." The consequence is a kind of self-searching need for frankness and humility on the part of the writer. "The modern prose-writer, in returning to the rhythms of everyday speech, is trying to be more honest with himself than if he used, as is too wreckingly easy, the forms and terms already published as the expression of other people's minds." Finally, in a touching sen-

[1] A few of the writer's obvious attempts to echo a conversational tone in that paragraph can be quickly summarized. Contractions (let's). Colloquialisms (well . . . , the next fellow). Some very short sentences. Capitalization in an effort to place an ironical turn on a Big Fat Abstraction (Truth)—an effort that is of course much easier to accomplish with the actual voice. Italics (*except*, like *this!*), again in mimicry of the way one speaks in conversation. And so on. The purpose of such devices, to compensate for the loss of oral intonation, is strictly speaking impossible to achieve. If only you were here I could *say* all this to you [Gibson's note].

tence, "In our present confusion our only hope is to be scrupulously honest with ourselves." That was written in 1933:
since then the confusion has multiplied spectacularly, while our
hopes of ever being "scrupulously honest" about anything look
pretty dim. Still, the relation Dobrée made, between an intellectual difficulty and a style, is essentially the relation we are
making here.

4   The trouble with it—and a reminder of the awful complexity
of our subject—is that sometimes this proposition simply doesn't
work. Some contemporary writers, sensitively aware of the limits
of language, indeed conceding them explicitly, nevertheless write
in a *style* that sounds like the wisdom of Moses, or like Winston
Churchill. Far from echoing the rhythms of ordinary speech, they
pontificate or chant in authoritarian rhythms the assertion that
one cannot be authoritarian. We have a fine example of this
paradox in the paragraph by Oppenheimer that I have so much
admired.[2] Oppenheimer uses a vocabulary, sentence structure,
tone, and rhythm all highly structured and formalized; there is
no unbending there. The theme of his discourse—that style is
"the deference that action pays to uncertainty"—seems at odds
with the *personality* we hear uttering this theme. That personality, because of the way the words are chosen and arranged,
appears curiously self-confident, even dictatorial, with echoes
perhaps of Johnsonian prose, or Macaulay's elegant sentences.
Thus the first sentence is built around a handsome triplet of
alliterative abstractions ("the implicit, the imponderable, and
the unknown"); the second sentence is built out of another
triplet of nicely balanced clauses. The extraordinary final sen-

[2]The paragraph to which Gibson refers is as follows: "The problem of
doing justice to the implicit, the imponderable, and the unknown is of course
not unique to politics. It is always with us in science, it is with us in the
most trivial of personal affairs, and it is one of the great problems of writing
and of all forms of art. The means by which it is solved is sometimes called
style. It is style which complements affirmation with limitation and with
humility; it is style which makes it possible to act effectively, but not absolutely; it is style which, in the domain of foreign policy, enables us to find a
harmony between the pursuit of ends essential to us and the regard for the
views, the sensibilities, the aspirations of those to whom the problem may
appear in another light; it is style which is the deference that action pays to
uncertainty; it is above all style through which power defers to reason."

tence approaches incantation in its parallel repetitions of structure. The "voice" we hear, remote indeed from ordinary conversation, seems to *know* even as it asserts its own humility. Different readers will explain all this in different ways: some will argue that the traditional manner lends sincerity and persuasiveness to the message, while others will be set off by what they consider a real discrepancy between matter and manner. We recall that the passage was taken from an address delivered at a formal occasion. I have heard Mr. Oppenheimer's platform manner described as "arrogant"; our stylistic observations might well account in part for such an impression. In any case it is clear that no easy formula —Dobrée's or anyone else's—is going to account for all the vagaries of modern prose.

5   Other writers . . . will illustrate Dobrée's thesis with less embarrassment—that is, will show clear evidence of a "conversational" voice. Thus Muller:

> Emerson remarked that it is a good thing, now and then, to take a look at the landscape from between one's legs. Although this stunt might seem pointless when things are already topsy-turvy, it can be the more helpful then. One may say that what this chaotic world needs first of all is *dis*-sociation; by breaking up factitious alliances and oppositions, one may get at the deep uniformities. Or . . .

The simplicity of the diction in that first sentence, and the absurdity of the described action, support a familiar relation of equality between the speaking voice and the reader. There is no talking down; we all know who Emerson is. (Not "That great American Transcendentalist, Ralph Waldo Emerson. . . .") "Now and then," "stunt," "topsy-turvy" contribute the colloquial touch. The slightly awkward "then" at the end of the second sentence suggests that in this particular communication formal grace would be inappropriate. But with the third sentence the writer boldly shifts his tone as his diction becomes more polysyllabic and his sentence structure more complex. "Enough of geniality," he seems to say, "you must now follow me into a serious tangle." With this abruptness, Muller is perhaps "breaking up factitious alliances" *in his style,* so that his own prose both expresses and dramatizes the point he is making.

6   The trick, if that is what it is, of mingling formal and colloquial vocabulary can convey a kind of ironical thrust by the
writer at his own pretensions. Thus he can have it both ways—
make his great assertion and kid himself for his own gall. It is a
device much employed in circles that are verbally sophisticated,
including academic circles. Consider an extreme example, from a
professor of law at Chicago, here discussing a flexible approach to
problems of judicial interpretation:

> But it leads to *good* rules of law and in the main toward flex-
> ible ones, so that most cases of a given type can come to be
> handled not only well but easily, and so that the odd case can
> normally come in also for a smidgeon of relief. The whole setup
> leads above all—a recognition of imperfection in language and in
> officer—to *on-going and unceasing judicial review of prior judi-
> cial decision* on the side of rule, tool, and technique. That, plus
> freedom and duty to do justice *with* the rules but *within* both
> them and their whole temper, that is the freedom, the leeway for
> own-contribution, the scope for the person, which the system
> offers.[3]

7   Here style and message work with a degree of co-operation: a
call for unceasing flexibility in the operations of judicial review
is expressed in an idiom that is itself almost wildly flexible. The
speaker in this passage betrays the strains of an impassioned con-
versationalist, with his heavy reliance on italics and his inter-
rupted sentence structures. We are buttonholed. This is a technical discussion, and most of the vocabulary has to be fairly heavy,
but we have "smidgeon" and "whole setup" to cut across the
formality. We have even a jazzy bit of alliteration and rhyme—
"rule, tool, and technique." The "recognition of imperfection in
language," therefore, which is explicitly granted by the text, is
implicitly conveyed as well by the unorthodox scramblings of
language. Nobody has to like this style (many are simply irri-
tated), but at least one can see what is going on, and why.

8   Or consider another extreme example, from a professor of
English at Wisconsin, here discussing problems of usage:

[3]From Karl N. Llewellyn, *The Common Law Tradition: Deciding Appeals,*
Little, Brown, 1960 [Gibson's note].

Bad, fair, good, better, best. Only the best is Correct. No busy man can be Correct. But his wife can. That's what women are for. That's why we have women to teach English and type our letters and go to church for us and discover for us that the English say "Aren't I?" while we sinfully hunt golf-balls in the rough on Sunday and, when our partner finds two of them, ask "Which is me?" (Webster: *colloq.*—Professor K of Harvard: I speak colloq myself, and sometimes I write it.) . . . Only a few of us today are aware of the other scales of English usage. It is our business to consciously know about their social utility.[4]

These sentences from a treatise on language admirably demonstrate that self-consciously unbuttoned informality which the subject nowadays seems to demand. To some, again, it will appear offensively "cute," idiosyncratic. Short sentences, some without predicates, surround one almost endless rambling sentence. The ironical capital in Correct (cf. Truth *supra*). Indifference to the rule that pronouns should have specific antecedents ("That's what women are for. That's why . . ."). Muddled number in using personal pronouns (we hunt golf balls, our partner [sing.] finds, [we] ask 'Which is me?'). Deliberately split infinitive in the last sentence quoted, at a point in the utterance when a conventionally formal tone has begun to enter. We may anticipate, I am sure, a time when writers will endeavor to carefully split their infinitives, at whatever cost in awkwardness, just as writers of a former generation endeavored so elaborately to avoid the "error." All this should prove to at least be amusing.

9   To many readers, the style displayed by a Professor Llewellyn or a Professor Joos will seem undisciplined, vulgar, and chaotic. A sign of academic deterioration. A result of wild "permissiveness" in education and in society generally. But such readers will be missing the point. There is nothing indiscriminately permissive in this style, but the writers do accept and reject different kinds of language from those accepted and rejected by traditional stylists. They express different personalities. Without insisting on the merits of these particular passages, which are certainly debatable, it ought nevertheless to be clear that you do not write in

[4]From Martin Joos, *The Five Clocks.* Copyright 1961 by Martin Joos [Gibson's note].

this way simply by saying anything that occurs to you. The process of selection can be, indeed, *more* discriminating because the
available supply of language and experience is larger. As this is
being written, in the autumn of 1961, a mild flurry about such
extensions of language is going on in the press, relating to the
publication of a new edition of Webster's *New International Dictionary*. The New York *Times* has editorialized as follows:

> A passel of double-domes at the G. & C Merriam Company joint
> in Springfield, Mass., have been confabbing and yakking for
> twenty-seven years—which is not intended to infer that they have
> not been doing plenty work—and now they have finalized Web-
> ster's Third New International Dictionary, Unabridged, a new
> edition of that swell and esteemed word book.
>
> Those who regard the foregoing paragraph as acceptable Eng-
> lish prose will find that the new Webster's is just the dictionary
> for them. The words in that paragraph all are listed in the new
> work with no suggestion that they are anything but standard.
>
> Webster's has, it is apparent, surrendered to the permissive
> school that has been busily extending its beachhead on English
> instruction in the schools. This development is disastrous. . . .

10   The *Times* goes on to acknowledge "the lexical explosion that
has showered us with so many words in recent years," and to
congratulate the Dictionary for including 100,000 new words or
new definitions. "These are improvements, but they cannot out-
weigh the fundamental fault." Webster's has always been a "peerless authority on American English," and therefore its editors
have "to some degree a public responsibility." "A new start is
needed."

11   There is, I think, something wrong about all this. If you are
acknowledging a "lexical explosion," a language changing with
accelerating rapidity, then it seems rather difficult to insist at the
same time on a "peerless authority." The editors of the Dictionary may have fulfilled their public responsibility by taking
the only wise course—by including as many new words and
definitions as they could without making "authoritative" judgments about "standard," "colloquial," and "slang." This is not to
say that the modern writer ignores such distinctions; on the contrary he is sensitively aware of them as never before. But he
knows, and the dictionary editors know, that no such label is

good for long in a culture as volatile as this one. Yesterday's slang is today's standard, and the writer who remains resonant to these shifts has at his disposal a huge and varicolored vocabulary for his art.

12 The reason we call that opening paragraph in the *Times* editorial "unacceptable English" is not that it contains slang. The reason is that it contains too many kinds of slang at once, without any awareness of their differences. You do not say "passel of double-domes" unless you have some good reason for juxtaposing terms from utterly distinct language worlds. "Passel" is presumably of western-frontier origin and now has a kind of weary whimsy about it, while "double-domes" is recent, cheaply anti-intellectual, with a history something like "egghead" but without the popular acceptance of "egghead." It is conceivable that these words could be included in one sentence, but/it would take more skill than the *Times* man has employed. Of course the appearance of clumsiness was just what served his purpose.

13 Meanwhile the writer who looks backward to "authority," who takes a static view of Standard Language, is likely to sound like the "straight" paragraphs of that editorial. The voice there is closer to a chiding or dictatorial professor than were the voices of the actual professors quoted. And when such a writer uses "modern" terms, he uses them in ways that are long overused before he gets to them—ways like "extending its beachhead on English instruction" or "lexical explosion that has showered us with so many words." It is this sort of thing that is the true vulgarity in our time.

14 Nevertheless our society remains generous with half-conscious concessions to the imperfections of its language. It may be, for example, that the language of the beatniks, especially their oral conventions, could be looked at in the light of such concessions. Consider just one curious symptom of jive-talk (now dated)—the suffix-plus-prefix *like*. "We came to this big town like and all the streets were like crazy, man." This attempt at rendering beat dialect is doubtless inaccurate but it should serve to make the point. That point is that the beats have (deliberately?) modified or qualified their nouns and adjectives by suggesting that they are not quite accurate, not quite the way things are. "This big town like"—it is a one-ended metaphor. Like what? We have a tenor

but no vehicle, or is it a vehicle without a tenor? I have been told that many beats are determinedly antiverbal, preferring to listen to jazz while lying on beaches in Zenlike silence. It fits. The skepticism about the validity of words that "like" implies is a peculiarly twentieth-century skepticism, it seems to me, though there may be analogies with other ages such as the seventeenth century, when scientific developments encouraged similar self-scrutinies and self-doubts. In any event the beats, in their crude and sloppy way of course, have surrounded much of their language with a metaphorical blur by using (among other things) the simple device of "like." They suggest, with this blur, their conviction of the impossibility of anybody else's doing any better with words. Only squares believe you can speak "precisely."

15   The complexities of experience do occasionally get faced one way or another—if not with the beats' pose of inarticulateness, then with some other pose that will serve to avoid the charge of *really knowing*. Modern novelists adopt a "point of view" which is often no point of view at all, but several points of view from which to indicate various inadequate interpretations of various fictitious characters. It is a technique that will show how two novels as apparently unlike as *The Waves* * * * and Faulkner's *As I Lay Dying* belong after all to the same age. There is no narrator, no one of whom the reader might conceivably say, "There! That's the author talking." The technique is not new; there is *The Ring and the Book,* to mention one example. But the difference is that when you read *The Ring and the Book,* you feel how firmly and finally Browning is on Pompilia's "side," in spite of his wonderful multiplicity throughout that great poem. Whereas in many modern novels you scarcely know who is on anybody's side—you must simply flow in the flux. Sometimes it is so lifelike you can hardly stand it.

16   And of course that road—the road of chaos chaotically expressing chaos—is a dead end of imitative form where we end with a grunt, or maybe a whimper. The very point is that language will never say our experience "as is," and recognizing this truth, we have immense freedom of possibility to make, create, form what we can out of words or out of anything else. The most elaborate of villanelles is not much further removed from Real Life than the latest Allen Ginsberg poem, or a slice of Mr.

Bloom's day. So write a villanelle if that will meet your need. But whatever it is, there remains this simple blasphemy to be avoided, and that is the blasphemy of ignoring the limits, of assuming that one's words do indeed tell the reader what is going on. There is an important sense in which nobody knows what he is talking about.

17   I hope I do not except myself and everything uttered here.

bluspels and flalansferes

C. S. LEWIS

1 Philologists often tell us that our language is full of dead metaphors. In this sentence, the word 'dead' and the word 'metaphors' may turn out to be ambiguous; but the fact, or group of facts, referred to, is one about which there is no great disagreement. We all know in a rough and ready way, and all admit, these things which are being called 'dead metaphors,' and for the moment I do not propose to debate the propriety of the name. But while their existence is not disputed, their nature, and their relation to thought, gives rise to a great deal of controversy. For the benefit of any who happen to have avoided this controversy hitherto, I had better make plain what it is, by a concrete example. Bréal in his *Semantics* often spoke in metaphorical, that is consciously, rhetorically, metaphorical language, of language itself. Messrs. Ogden and Richards in *The Meaning of Meaning* took Bréal to task on the ground that 'it is impossible thus to handle a scientific subject in metaphorical terms.' Barfield in his *Poetic Diction* retorted that Ogden and Richards were, as a matter of fact, just as metaphorical as Bréal. They had forgotten, he complained, that all language has a figurative origin and that the 'scientific' terms on which they piqued themselves—words like *organism, stimulus, reference*—were not miraculously exempt. On the contrary, he maintained, 'these authors who pro-

Reprinted with permission of Curtis Brown Ltd., from *Rehabilitation and Other Essays*, by C. S. Lewis.

fessed to eschew figurative expressions were really confining themselves to one very old kind of figure; they were rigid under the
spell of those verbal ghosts of the physical sciences which to-day
make up practically the whole meaning-system of so many European minds.'[1] Whether Ogden and Richards will see fit, or have
seen fit, to reply to this, I do not know; but the lines on which
any reply would run are already traditional. In fact the whole
debate may be represented by a very simple dialogue.

2   A. You are being metaphorical.

3   B. You are just as metaphorical as I am, but you don't know it.

4   A. No, I'm not. Of course I know all about *attending* once
having meant *stretching,* and the rest of it. But that is not what
it means now. It may have been a metaphor to Adam—but I am
not using it metaphorically. What I *mean* is a pure concept with
no metaphor about it at all. The fact that it *was* a metaphor is
no more relevant than the fact that my pen is made of wood.
You are simply confusing derivation with meaning.

5   There is clearly a great deal to be said for both sides. On the
one hand it seems odd to suppose that what we *mean* is conditioned by a dead metaphor of which we may be quite ignorant.
On the other hand, we see from day to day, that when a man
uses a current and admitted metaphor without knowing it, he
usually gets led into nonsense; and when, we are tempted to ask,
does a metaphor become so old that we can ignore it with impunity? It seems harsh to rule that a man must know the whole
semantic history of every word he uses—a history usually undis-
coverable—or else talk without thinking. And yet, on the other
hand, an obstinate suspicion creeps in that we cannot entirely
jump off our own shadows, and that we deceive ourselves if we
suppose that a new and purely conceptual notion of *attention* has
replaced and superseded the old metaphor of stretching. Here,
then, is the problem which I want to consider. How far, if at all,
is thinking limited by these dead metaphors? Is Anatole France
in any sense right when he reduces 'The soul possesses God' to
'the breath sits on the bright sky'? Or is the other party right
when it urges 'Derivations are one thing. Meanings are another'?
Or is the truth somewhere between them?

[1]A. O. Barfield, *Poetic Diction*, 1928, pp. 139, 140.

6   The first and easiest case to study is that in which we ourselves
invent a new metaphor. This may happen in one of two ways. It
may be that when we are trying to express clearly to ourselves or
to others a conception which we have never perfectly understood,
a new metaphor simply starts forth, under the pressure of composition or argument. When this happens, the result is often as
surprising and illuminating to us as to our audience; and I am
inclined to think that this is what happens with the great, new
metaphors of the poets. And when it does happen, it is plain that
our new understanding is bound up with the new metaphor. In
fact, the situation is for our purpose indistinguishable from that
which arises when we hear a new metaphor from others; and for
that reason, it need not be separately discussed. One of the ways,
then, in which we invent a new metaphor, is by *finding* it, as un-
expectedly as we might find it in the pages of a book; and whatever is true of the new metaphors that we find in books will also
be true of those which we reach by a kind of lucky chance, or inspiration. But, of course, there is another way in which we invent
new metaphors. When we are trying to explain, to some one
younger or less instructed than ourselves, a matter which is already perfectly clear in our own minds, we may deliberately, and
even painfully, pitch about for the metaphor that is likely to
help him. Now when this happens, it is quite plain that our
thought, our power of meaning, is not much helped or hindered
by the metaphor that we use. On the contrary, we are often
acutely aware of the discrepancy between our meaning and our
image. We know that our metaphor is in some respects misleading; and probably, if we have acquired the tutorial shuffle, we
warn our audience that it is 'not to be pressed.' It is apparently
possible, in this case at least, to use metaphor and yet to keep our
thinking independent of it. But we must observe that it is possible, only because we have other methods of expressing the same
idea. We have already our own way of expressing the thing: we
could say it, or we suppose that we could say it, literally instead.
This clear conception we owe to other sources—to our previous
studies. We can adopt the new metaphor as a temporary tool
which we dominate and by which we are not dominated ourselves, only because we have other tools in our box.

7   Let us now take the opposite situation—that in which it is we

ourselves who are being instructed. I am no mathematician; and some one is trying to explain to me the theory that space is finite. Stated thus, the new doctrine is, to me, meaningless. But suppose he proceeds as follows.

8 'You,' he may say, 'can intuit only three dimensions; you therefore cannot conceive how space should be limited. But I think I can show you how that which must appear infinite in three dimensions, might nevertheless be finite in four. Look at it this way. Imagine a race of people who knew only two dimensions —like the Flatlanders. And suppose they were living on a globe. They would have no conception, of course, that the globe was curved—for it is curved round in that third dimension of which they have no inkling. They will therefore imagine that they are living on a plane; but they will soon find out that it is a plane which nowhere comes to an end; there are no edges to it. Nor would they be able even to imagine an edge. For an edge would mean that, after a certain point, there would be nothing to walk on; nothing below their feet. But that *below* and *above* dimension is just what their minds have not got; they have only backwards and forwards, and left and right. They would thus be forced to assert that their globe, which they could not see as a globe, was infinite. You can see perfectly well that it is finite. And now, can you not conceive that as these Flatlanders are to you, so you might be to a creature that intuited four dimensions? Can you not conceive how that which seems necessarily infinite to your three-dimensional consciousness might none the less be really finite?' The result of such a metaphor on my mind would be—in fact, has been—that something which before was sheerly meaningless acquires at least a faint hint of meaning. And if the particular example does not appeal to every one, yet every one has had experiences of the same sort. For all of us there are things which we cannot fully understand at all, but of which we can get a faint inkling by means of metaphor. And in such cases the relation between the thought and the metaphor is precisely the opposite of the relation which arises when it is we ourselves who understand and then invent the metaphors to help others. We are here entirely at the mercy of the metaphor. If our instructor has chosen it badly, we shall be thinking nonsense. If we have not got the imagery clearly before us, we shall be thinking

nonsense. If we have it before us without knowing that it is metaphor—if we forget that our Flatlanders on their globe are a copy of the thing and mistake for the thing itself—then again we shall be thinking nonsense. What truth we can attain in such a situation depends rigidly on three conditions. First, that the imagery should be originally well chosen; secondly, that we should apprehend the exact imagery; and thirdly, that we should know that the metaphor is a metaphor. (That metaphors, mis-read as statements of fact, are the source of monstrous errors, need hardly be pointed out.)

9   I have now attempted to show two different kinds of meta-phorical situation as they are at their birth. They are the two extremes, and furnish the limits within which our inquiry must work. On the one hand, there is the metaphor which we invent to teach by; on the other, the metaphor from which we learn. They might be called the Master's metaphor, and the Pupil's metaphor. The first is freely chosen; it is one among many possible modes of expression; it does not at all hinder, and only very slightly helps, the thought of its maker. The second is not chosen at all; it is the unique expression of a meaning that we cannot have on any other terms; it dominates completely the thought of the recipient; his truth cannot rise above the truth of the original metaphor. And between the Master's metaphor and the Pupil's there comes, of course, an endless number of types, dotted about in every kind of intermediate position. Indeed, these Pupil-Teachers' metaphors are the ordinary stuff of our conversation. To divide them into a series of classes and sub-classes and to attempt to discuss these separately would be very laborious, and, I trust, un-necessary. If we can find a true doctrine about the two extremes, we shall not be at a loss to give an account of what falls between them. To find the truth about any given metaphorical situation will merely be to plot its position. In so far as it inclines to the 'magistral' extreme, so far our thought will be independent of it; in so far as it has a 'pupillary' element, so far it will be the unique expression, and therefore the iron limit of our thinking. To fill in this framework would be, as Aristotle used to say, 'anybody's business.'

10   Our problem, it will be remembered, was the problem of 'dead' or 'forgotten' metaphors. We have now gained some light on the

relation between thought and metaphor as it is at the outset, when the metaphor is first made; and we have seen that this relation varies greatly according to what I have called the 'metaphorical situation.' There is, in fact, one relation in the case of the Master's metaphor, and an almost opposite relation in that of the Pupil's metaphor. The next step must clearly be to see what becomes of these two relations as the metaphors in question progress to the state of death or fossilization.

11   The question of the Master's metaphor need not detain us long. I may attempt to explain the Kantian philosophy to a pupil by the following metaphor. 'Kant answered the question "How do I know that whatever comes round the corner will be blue?" by the supposition "I am wearing blue spectacles." ' In time I may come to use 'the blue spectacles' as a kind of shorthand for the whole Kantian machinery of the categories and forms of perception. And let us suppose, for the sake of analogy with the real history of language, that I continue to use this expression long after I have forgotten the metaphor which originally gave rise to it. And perhaps by this time the form of the word will have changed. Instead of the 'blue spectacles' I may now talk of the *bloospel* or even the *bluspel*. If I live long enough to reach my dotage I may even enter on a philological period in which I attempt to find the derivation of this mysterious word. I may suppose that the second element is derived from the word *spell* and look back with interest on the supposed period when Kant appeared to be magical; or else, arguing that the whole word is clearly formed on the analogy of *gospel,* may indulge in unhistorical reminiscences of the days when the *Critique* seemed to me irrefragably true. But how far, if at all, will my thinking about Kant be affected by all this linguistic process? In practice, no doubt, there will be some subtle influence; the mere continued use of the word *bluspel* may have led me to attribute to it a unity and substantiality which I should have hesitated to attribute to "the whole Kantian machinery of the categories and forms of perception.' But that is a result rather of the noun-making than of the death of the metaphor. It is an interesting fact, but hardly relevant to our present inquiry. For the rest, the mere forgetting of the metaphor does not seem to alter my thinking about Kant, just as the original metaphor did not limit my

thinking about Kant; provided always—and this is of the last importance—that it was, to begin with, a genuine Master's metaphor. I had my conception of Kant's philosophy before I ever thought of the blue spectacles. If I have continued philosophical studies I have it still. The 'blue spectacles' phrase was from the first a temporary dress assumed by my thought for a special purpose, and ready to be laid aside at my pleasure; it did not penetrate the thinking itself, and its subsequent history is irrelevant. To any one who attempts to refute my later views on Kant by telling me that I don't know the real meaning of *bluspel,* I may confidently retort 'Derivations aren't meanings.' To be sure, if there was any *pupillary* element in its original use, if I received, as well as gave, new understanding when I used it, then the whole situation will be different. And it is fair to admit that in practice very few metaphors can be purely magistral; only that which to some degree enlightens ourselves is likely to enlighten others. It is hardly possible that when I first used the metaphor of the blue spectacles I did not gain some new awareness of the Kantian philosophy; and, so far, it was not purely magistral. But I am deliberately idealizing for the sake of clarity. Purely magistral metaphor may never occur. What is important for us is to grasp that *just in so far* as any metaphor began by being magistral, so far I can continue to use it long after I have forgotten its metaphorical nature, and my thinking will be neither helped nor hindered by the fact that it was originally a metaphor, nor yet by my forgetfulness of that fact. It is a mere accident. Here, derivations are irrelevant to meanings.

12   Let us now turn to the opposite situation, that of the Pupil's metaphor. And let us continue to use our old example of the unmathematical man who has had the finitude of space suggested to him (we can hardly say 'explained') by the metaphor of the Flatlanders on their sphere. The question here is rather more complicated. In the case of the Master's metaphor, by hypothesis, the master knew, and would continue to know, what he meant, independently of the metaphor. In the present instance, however, the fossilization of the metaphor may take place in two different ways. The pupil may himself become a mathematician, or he may remain as ignorant of mathematics as he was before; and in either case, he may continue to use the metaphor of the Flat-

landers while forgetting its real content and its metaphorical nature.

13 I will take the second possibility first. From the imagery of the Flatlanders' sphere I have got my first inkling of the new meaning. My thought is entirely conditioned by this imagery. I do not apprehend the thing at all, except by seeing 'it could be something like this.' Let us suppose that in my anxiety to docket this new experience, I label the inkling or vague notion, 'the Flatlanders' sphere.' When I next hear the fourth dimension spoken of, I shall say, 'Ah yes—the Flatlanders' sphere and all that.' In a few years (to continue our artificial parallel) I may be talking glibly of the *Flalansfere* and may even have forgotten the whole of the imagery which this word once represented. And I am still, according to the hypothesis, profoundly ignorant of mathematics. My situation will then surely be most ridiculous. The meaning of *Flalansfere* I never knew except through the imagery. I could get beyond the imagery, to that whereof the imagery was a copy, only by learning mathematics; but this I have neglected to do. Yet I have lost the imagery. Nothing remains, then, but the conclusion that the word *Flalansfere* is now really meaningless. My thinking, which could never get beyond the imagery, at once its boundary and its support, has now lost that support. I mean strictly nothing when I speak of the *Flalansfere*. I am only talking, not thinking, when I use the word. But this fact will be long concealed from me, because *Flalansfere,* being a noun, can be endlessly fitted into various contexts, so as to conform to syntactical usage and to give an appearance of meaning. It will even conform to the logical rules; and I can make many judgments about the *Flalansfere;* such as *it is what it is,* and has *attributes* (for otherwise of course it wouldn't be a thing, and if it wasn't a thing, how could I be talking about it?), and is a *substance* (for it can be the subject of a sentence). And what *affective* overtones the word may have taken on by that time, it is dangerous to predict. It had an air of mystery from the first: before the end I shall probably be building temples to it, and exhorting my countrymen to fight and die for the *Flalansfere*. But the *Flalansfere,* when once we have forgotten the metaphor, is only a noise.

14 But how if I proceed, after once having grasped the metaphor of the Flatlanders, to become a mathematician? In this case, too, I

may well continue to use the metaphor, and may corrupt it in form till it becomes a single noun, the *Flalansfere*. But I shall have advanced, by other means, from the original symbolism; and I shall be able to study the thing symbolized without reference to the metaphor that first introduced me to it. It will then be no harm though I should forget that *Flalansfere* had ever been metaphorical. As the metaphor, even if it survived, would no longer limit my thoughts, so its fossilization cannot confuse them.

15   The results which emerge may now be summarized as follows. Our thought is independent of the metaphors we employ, in so far as these metaphors are optional: that is, in so far as we are able to have the same idea without them. For that is the real characteristic both of the magistral metaphors and of those which become optional, as the Flatlanders would become, if the pupil learned mathematics. On the other hand, where the metaphor is our only method of reaching a given idea at all, there our thinking is limited by the metaphor so long as we retain the metaphor; and when the metaphor becomes fossilized, our 'thinking' is not thinking at all, but mere sound or mere incipient movements in the larynx. We are now in a position to reply to the statement that 'Derivations are not meanings,' and to the claim that 'we know what we mean by words without knowing the fossilized metaphors they contain.' We can see that such a statement, as it stands, is neither wholly true nor wholly false. The truth will vary from word to word, and from speaker to speaker. No rule of thumb is possible, we must take every case on its merits. A word can bear a meaning in the mouth of a speaker who has forgotten its hidden metaphor, and a meaning independent of that metaphor, but only on certain conditions. Either the metaphor must have been optional from the beginning, and have remained optional through all the generations of its use, so that the conception has always used and still uses the imagery as a mere tool; or else, at some period subsequent to its creation, we must have gone on to acquire, independently of the metaphor, such new knowledge of the object indicated by it as enables us now, at least, to dispense with it. To put the same thing in another way, meaning is independent of derivation, only if the metaphor was originally 'magistral'; or if, in the case of an originally pupillary metaphor, some quite new kind of apprehension has arisen to

replace the metaphorical apprehension which has been lost. The two conditions may be best illustrated by a concrete example. Let us take the word for *soul* as it exists in the Romance language. How far is a man entitled to say that what he means by the word *âme* or *anima* is quite independent of the image of *breathing*, and that he means just the same (and just as much) whether he happens to know that 'derivation' or not? We can only answer that it depends on a variety of things. I will enumerate all the formal possibilities for the sake of clearness: one of them, of course, is too grotesque to appear for any other purpose.

16 1. The metaphor may originally have been magistral. Primitive men, we are to suppose, were clearly aware, on the one hand, of an entity called *soul;* and, on the other, of a process or object called *breath*. And they used the second figuratively to suggest the first—presumably when revealing their wisdom to primitive women and primitive children. And we may suppose, further, that this magistral relation to the metaphor has never been lost: that all generations, from the probably arboreal to the man saying 'Blast your soul' in a pub this evening, have kept clearly before them these two separate entities, and used the one metaphorically to denote the other, while at the same time being well able to conceive the soul unmetaphorically, and using the metaphor merely as a colour or trope which adorned but did not influence their thought. Now if all this were true, it would unquestionably follow that when a man says *anima* his meaning is not affected by the old image of breath; and also, it does not matter in the least whether he knows that the word once suggested that image or not. But of course all this is not true.

17 2. The metaphor may originally have been pupillary. So far from being a voluntary ornament or pedagogic device, the ideas of *breath* or *something like breath* may have been the only possible inkling that our parents could gain of the soul. But if this was so, how does the modern user of the word stand? Clearly, if he has ceased to be aware of the metaphorical element in *anima,* without replacing the metaphorical apprehension by some new knowledge of the soul, borrowed from other sources, then he will mean nothing by it; we must not, on that account, suppose that he will cease to use it, or even to use it (as we say) intelligibly—i.e. to use it in sentences constructed according to the laws of

grammar, and to insert these sentences into those conversational and literary contexts where usage demands their insertion. If, on the other hand, he has some independent knowledge of the entity which our ancestors indicated by their metaphor of breath, then indeed he may mean something.

18   I take it that it is this last situation in which we commonly suppose ourselves to be. It doesn't matter, we would claim, what the majestic root GNA really stood for; we have learned a great deal about *knowing* since those days, and it is these more recent acquisitions that we use in our thinking. The first name for a thing may easily be determined by some inconsiderable accident. As we learn more, we mean more; the radical meaning of the old syllables does not bind us; what we have learned since has set us free. Assuredly, the accident which led the Romans to call all Hellenes *Graeci* did not continue to limit their power of apprehending Greece. And as long as we are dealing with sensible objects this view is hardly to be disputed. The difficulty begins with objects of thought. It may be stated as follows.

19   Our claim to independence of the metaphor is, as we have seen, a claim to know the object otherwise than through that metaphor. If we can throw the Flatlanders overboard and still think the fourth dimension, then, and not otherwise, we can forget what *Flalansfere* once meant and still think coherently. That was what happened, you will remember, to the man who went on and learned mathematics. He came to apprehend that of which the Flatlanders' sphere was only the image, and consequently was free to think beyond the metaphor and to forget the metaphor altogether. In our previous account of him, however, we carefully omitted to draw attention to one very remarkable fact: namely, that when he deserted metaphor for mathematics, he did not really pass from symbol to symbolized, but only from one set of symbols to another. The equations and what-nots are as unreal, as metaphorical, if you like, as the Flatlanders' sphere. The mathematical problem I need not pursue further; we see at once that it casts a disquieting light on our linguistic problem. We have hitherto been speaking as if we had two methods of thought open to us: the metaphorical, and the literal. We talked as if the creator of a magistral metaphor had it always in his power to think the same concept *literally* if he chose. We talked

as if the present-day user of the word *anima* could prove his right to neglect that word's buried metaphor by turning round and giving us an account of the soul which was not metaphorical at all. That he has power to dispense with the particular metaphor of *breath,* is of course agreed. But we have not yet inquired what he can substitute for it. If we turn to those who are most anxious to tell us about the soul—I mean the psychologists—we shall find that the word *anima* has simply been replaced by complexes, repressions, censors, engrams, and the like. In other words the *breath* has been exchanged for *tyings-up, shovings-back, Roman magistrates,* and *scratchings.* If we inquire what has replaced the metaphorical *bright sky* of primitive theology, we shall only get a *perfect substance,* that is, a *completely made lying-under,* or—which is very much better, but equally metaphorical —a universal Father, or perhaps (in English) a *loaf-carver,* in Latin a *householder,* in Romance *a person older than.* The point need not be laboured. It is abundantly clear that the freedom from a given metaphor which we admittedly enjoy in some cases is often only a freedom to choose between the metaphor and others.

20   Certain reassurances may, indeed, be held out. In the first place, our distinction between the different kinds of metaphorical situation can stand; though it is hardly so important as we had hoped. To have a choice of metaphors (as we have in some cases) is to know more than we know when we are the slaves of a unique metaphor. And, in the second place, all description or identification, all direction of our own thought or another's, is not so metaphorical as definition. If, when challenged on the word *anima,* we proceed to define, we shall only reshuffle the buried metaphors; but if we simply say (or think) 'what I am,' or 'what is going on in here,' we shall have at least something before us which we do not know by metaphor. We shall at least be no worse off than the arboreal psychologists. At the same time, this method will not really carry us far. 'What's going on here' is really the content of *haec anima:* for *anima* we want *'The sort of thing* that is going on here,' and once we are committed to *sorts* and *kinds* we are adrift among metaphors.

21   We have already said that when a man claims to think independently of the buried metaphor in one of his words, his

claim may sometimes be allowed. But it was allowed only in so far as he could really supply the place of that buried metaphor with new and independent apprehension of his own. We now see that this new apprehension will usually turn out to be itself metaphorical; or else, what is very much worse, instead of new apprehension we shall have simply words—each word enshrining one more ignored metaphor. For if he does not know the history of *anima,* how should he know the history of the equally metaphorical words in which he defines it, if challenged? And if he does not know their history and therefore their metaphors, and if he cannot define *them* without yet further metaphors, what can his discourse be but an endless ringing of the changes on such *bluspels* and *Flalansferes* as seem to mean, indeed, but do not mean? In reality, the man has played us a very elementary trick. He claimed that he could think without metaphor, and in ignorance of the metaphors fossilized in his words. He made good the claim by pointing to the knowledge of his object which he possessed independently of the metaphor; and the proof of this knowledge was the definition or description which he could produce. We did not at first observe that where we were promised a freedom from metaphor we were given only a power of changing the metaphors in rapid succession. The things he speaks of he has never apprehended *literally.* Yet only such genuinely literal apprehension could enable him to forget the metaphors which he was actually using and yet to have a meaning. Either literalness, or else metaphor understood: one or other of these we must have; the third alternative is nonsense. But literalness we cannot have. The man who does not consciously use metaphors talks without meaning. We might even formulate a rule: the meaning in any given composition is in inverse ratio to the author's belief in his own literalness.

22   If a man has seen ships and the sea, he may abandon the metaphor of a *sea-stallion* and call a boat a boat. But suppose a man who has never seen the sea, or ships, yet who knows of them just as much as he can glean, say from the following list of *Kenningar* —sea-stallions, winged logs, wave riders, ocean trains. If he keeps all these together in his mind, and knows them for the metaphors they are, he will be able to think of ships, very imperfectly indeed, and under strict limits, but not wholly in vain. But if in-

stead of this he pins his faith on the particular *kenning ocean-trains,* because that *kenning,* with its comfortable air of machinery, seems to him somehow more safely prosaic, less flighty and dangerous than its fellows, and if, contracting that to the form *oshtrans,* he proceeds to forget that it was a metaphor, then, while he talks grammatically, he has ceased to think of anything. It will not avail him to stamp his feet and swear that he is literal; to say 'An *oshtran* is an *oshtran,* and there's an end. I mean what I mean. What I mean is what I say.'

23 The remedy lies, indeed, in the opposite direction. When we pass beyond pointing to individual sensible objects, when we begin to think of causes, relations, of mental states or acts, we become incurably metaphorical. We apprehend none of these things except through metaphor: we know of the ships only what the *Kenningar* will tell us. Our only choice is to use the metaphors and thus to think something, though less than we could wish: or else to be driven by unrecognized metaphors and so think nothing at all. I myself would prefer to embrace the former choice, as far as my ignorance and laziness allow me.

24 To speak more plainly, he who would increase the meaning and decrease the meaningless verbiage in his own speech and writing, must do two things. He must become conscious of the fossilized metaphors in his words; and he must freely use new metaphors, which he creates for himself. The first depends upon knowledge, and therefore on leisure; the second on a certain degree of imaginative ability. The second is perhaps the more important of the two: we are never less the slaves of metaphor than when we are making metaphor, or hearing it new made. When we are thinking hard of the Flatlanders, and at the same time fully aware that they *are* a metaphor, we are in a situation almost infinitely superior to that of the man who talks of the *Flalansfere* and thinks that he is being literal and straightforward.

25 If our argument has been sound, it leads us to certain rather remarkable conclusions. In the first place it would seem that we must be content with a very modest quantity of thinking as the core of all our talking. I do not wish to exaggerate our poverty. Not all our words are equally metaphorical, not all our metaphors are equally forgotten. And even where the old metaphor is lost there is often a hope that we may still restore meaning by

pointing to some sensible object, some sensation, or some concrete memory. But no man can or will confine his cognitive efforts
to this narrow field. At the very humblest we must speak of
things in the plural, we must point not only to isolated sensations, but to groups and classes of sensations; and the universal
latent in every group and every plural inflection cannot be
thought without metaphor. Thus far beyond the security of literal meaning all of us, we may be sure, are going to be driven by
our daily needs; indeed, not to go thus far would be to abandon
reason itself. In practice we all really intend to go much farther.
Why should we not? We have in our hands the key of metaphor,
and it would be pusillanimous to abandon its significant use, because we have come to realize that its meaningless use is necessarily prevalent. We must indeed learn to use it more cautiously;
and one of the chief benefits to be derived from our inquiry is
the new standard of criticism which we must henceforward apply
both to our own apparent thought and to that of others. We
shall find, too, that real meaning, judged by this standard, does
not come always where we have learned to expect. *Flalansferes*
and *bluspels* will clearly be most prevalent in certain types of
writers. The percentage of mere syntax masquerading as meaning
may vary from something like 100 per cent. in political writers,
journalists, psychologists, and economists, to something like forty
per cent. in the writers of children's stories. Some scientists will
fare better than others: the historian, the geographer, and sometimes the biologist will speak significantly more often than their
colleagues; the mathematician, who seldom forgets that his symbols are symbolic, may often rise for short stretches to ninety
per cent. of meaning and ten of verbiage. The philosophers will
differ as widely from one another as any of the other groups differ
among themselves: for a good metaphysical library contains at
once some of the most verbal, and some of the most significant
literature in the world. Those who have prided themselves on
being literal, and who have endeavoured to speak plainly, with
no mystical tomfoolery, about the highest abstractions, will be
found to be among the least significant of writers: I doubt if we
shall find more than a beggarly five per cent. of meaning in the
pages of some celebrated 'tough minded' thinkers, and how the
account of Kant or Spinoza stands, none knows but heaven. But

open your Plato, and you will find yourself among the great creators of metaphor, and therefore among the masters of meaning. If we turn to Theology—or rather to the literature of religion—the result will be more surprising still; for unless our whole argument is wrong, we shall have to admit that a man who says *heaven* and thinks of the visible sky is pretty sure to mean more than a man who tells us that heaven is a state of mind. It may indeed be otherwise; the second man may be a mystic who is remembering and pointing to an actual and concrete experience of his own. But it is long, long odds. Bunyan and Dante stand where they did; the scale of Bishop Butler, and of better men than he, flies up and kicks the beam.

26 It will have escaped no one that in such a scale of writers the poets will take the highest place; and among the poets those who have at once the tenderest care for old words and the surest instinct for the creation of new metaphors. But it must not be supposed that I am in any sense putting forward the imagination as the organ of truth. We are not talking of truth, but of meaning: meaning which is the antecedent condition both of truth and falsehood, whose antithesis is not error but nonsense. I am a rationalist. For me, reason is the natural organ of truth; but imagination is the organ of meaning. Imagination, producing new metaphors or revivifying old, is not the cause of truth, but its condition. It is, I confess, undeniable that such a view indirectly implies a kind of truth or rightness in the imagination itself. I said at the outset that the truth we won by metaphor could not be greater than the truth of the metaphor itself; and we have seen since that all our truth, or all but a few fragments, is won by metaphor. And thence, I confess, it does follow that if our thinking is ever true, then the metaphors by which we think must have been good metaphors. It does follow that if those original equations, between good and light, or evil and dark, between breath and soul and all the others, were from the beginning arbitrary and fanciful—if there is not, in fact, a kind of psycho-physical parallelism (or more) in the universe—then all our thinking is nonsensical. But we cannot, without contradiction, believe it to be nonsensical. And so, admittedly, the view I have taken has metaphysical implications. But so has every view.

new york, the colonial city

JEAN-PAUL SARTRE

1   I really knew I would like New York, but I thought I'd be able
to like it immediately, as I had liked the red·brick of Venice and
London's massive, sombre houses. I didn't know that, for the
newly arrived European, there was a "New York sickness," like
sea-sickness, air-sickness and mountain-sickness.

2   At midnight, an official bus took me from La Guardia field to
the Plaza Hotel. I had pressed my forehead against the window,
but had been able to see only red and green lights and dark
buildings. The next day, without any transition, I found myself
at the corner of 58th Street and Fifth Avenue. I walked for a
long time under the icy sky. It was a Sunday in January, 1945, a
deserted Sunday. I was looking for New York and couldn't find
it. The further I progressed along an avenue that seemed coldly
mediocre and banal, the further the city seemed to retreat before
me, like a ghost town. What I was looking for was probably a
European city.

3   We Europeans live on the myth of the big city that we forged
during the nineteenth century. American myths are not ours, and
the American city is not our city; it has neither the same character nor the same functions. In Spain, Italy, Germany and France
we find circular cities that were originally surrounded by ram-
parts meant not only to protect the inhabitants against enemy

Reprinted by permission of S. G. Phillips, Inc., from *The Literary and
Philosophical Essays*, by Jean-Paul Sartre. © 1955 by S. G. Phillips, Inc.

invasion, but also to conceal the inexorable presence of Nature. These cities are, moreover, divided into sections that are similarly round and closed. The piled-up tangle of houses weighs heavily on the soil. They seem to have a natural tendency to draw together, so much so that now and then we have to clear a way through with an axe, as in a virgin forest. Streets run into other streets. Closed at both ends, they do not look as though they lead outside the city. Inside them, you go around in circles. They are more than mere arteries; each one constitutes a social milieu.

4   You stop along these streets, meet people, drink, eat and linger. On Sundays, you get dressed and take a stroll for the sole pleasure of greeting friends, to see and be seen. These are the streets that inspired Jules Romains' "unanisme." They are filled with a communal spirit that changes from hour to hour.

5   Thus, my near-sighted European eyes, slowly venturing out, on the watch for everything, vainly tried to find something to arrest them. Anything at all—a row of houses suddenly barring the way, a street corner, or some old, time-mellowed house. But it was no use. New York is a city for far-sighted people, a city in which you can only "adjust" to infinity. My glance met nothing but space. It slid over blocks of identical houses, with nothing to arrest it; it was about to lose itself in empty space, at the horizon.

6   Céline has remarked of New York that "it is a vertical city." This is true, but it seemed to me, at first, like a lengthwise city. The traffic that comes to a standstill in the side streets is all-privileged and flows tirelessly down the avenues. How often the taxi-drivers, willing to take passengers from north to south, flatly refuse to take any for the east and west! The side streets have hardly any function other than to mark off the limits of the apartment houses between the avenues. They are cut by the avenues, spread and thrown toward the north. That was why I, a naïve tourist, vainly tried for a long time to find *quartiers*. In France we are surrounded and protected by urban centres; the prosperous districts protect the rich from the poor, and the poor districts protect us from the disdain of the rich, and similarly, the entire city protects us against Nature.

7   In New York, where the major axes are parallel avenues, I was unable to discover *quartiers* except on Lower Broadway. I

could only find filmy atmospheres, longitudinally stretched masses with nothing to mark a beginning or end. I gradually learned to recognize the atmosphere of Third Avenue where, under the shadow of the noisy elevated railway, people meet, smile and chat without even knowing each other; and that Irish bar in which a German, passing by my table, stopped for a minute to say: "Are you French? I'm a Jerry"; the reassuring comfort of the Lexington Avenue shops; the dreary elegance of Park Avenue; the cold luxury and stucco impassiveness of Fifth Avenue; the gay frivolity of Sixth and Seventh Avenues; the food markets on Ninth Avenue; and the No Man's Land of Tenth Avenue. Each avenue wraps its neighbouring streets in its own atmosphere, but one street down, you're suddenly plunged into another world. Not far from the palpitating silence of Park Avenue where glide the cars of the lords and masters, I come to First Avenue where the earth is constantly trembling under the passing of trucks. How am I to feel safe on one of those endless "north-south" highways when, a few steps away to east or west, other lengthwise worlds await me? Behind the Waldorf-Astoria and the blue and white canopies of "smart" buildings, I glimpse the "Elevated," which carries with it something of the Bowery's poverty.

8   All of New York is striped this way with parallel and noncommunicating significances. These long, perfectly straight lines suddenly gave me the feeling of space. Our cities are constructed to protect us against it; the houses cluster like sheep. But space crosses through New York, quickening and expanding it. The space, the great, empty space of the steppes and pampas, flows through New York's arteries like a draught of cold air, separating one side from the other. An American friend who was showing me about the smart sections of Boston pointed to the left side of a boulevard and said, "The 'nice' people live there," and then, pointing to the right side, he added ironically, "No one has ever been able to find out who lives here." The same is true of New York; between the two sides of a given street, you have all of space.

9   New York is half-way between a pedestrian's and a driver's city. You do not go for walks in New York; you fly through it; it is a city in motion. I feel at ease if I walk quickly; if I stop, I get

flustered and wonder, "Why am I in this street rather than in one of the hundreds of others like it?" Why am I standing in front of this drug-store, or this Schrafft's or Woolworth branch, rather than in front of any other of these thousands of identical ones?

10   And suddenly pure space looms into view. I imagine that if a triangle could become conscious of its position in space, it would be terrified at the realization of the rigorousness of its defining co-ordinates, but that it would also be terrified to discover that it is merely any triangle, any place. You never lose your way in New York; one glance is enough for you to get your bearings; you are on the East Side, at the corner of 52nd Street and Lexington Avenue. But this spacial precision is not accompanied by any precision of feeling. In the numerical anonymity of the streets and avenues, I am simply anybody, anywhere. No matter where I may be, my position is marked out in longitude and latitude. But no valid reason justifies my presence in this place rather than in any other, since this one is so like another. You never lose your way, and you are always lost.

11   Is it a city I am lost in, or is it Nature? New York is no protection against Nature's violence. It is an open-skied city. Storms flood its wide streets that take so long to cross when it rains. Hurricanes shake the brick houses and rock the skyscrapers. They are announced formally over the radio, like declarations of war. In summer, the air vibrates between the houses; in winter, the city is flooded, so that you might think yourself in some Parisian suburb flooded by the Seine, but in America, it is only melting snow.

12   Nature weighs so heavily on New York that this most modern of cities is also the dirtiest. From my window I see thick, muddy papers, tossed by the wind, flitting over the pavement. When I go out, I walk in a blackish snow, a sort of puffy crust the same colour as the sidewalk, so that it looks as if the sidewalk is buckling. From the first of May, the heat crashes down on the city like an atomic bomb. The heat is Evil. People go up to one another and say, "It's murder!" The trains carry off millions of fleeing city-dwellers who, on descending from the train, leave damp marks on the seat, like snails. It is not the city they are fleeing, but Nature. Even in the depths of my apartment, I am

open to attack from a mysterious and secretly hostile Nature. I
feel as though I were camping in the heart of a jungle crawling
with insects. There is the wailing of the wind, the electric shocks
I get each time I touch a doorbell or shake a friend's hand, the
cockroaches that scoot across my kitchen, the elevators that make
me nauseous and the inextinguishable thirst that rages in me
from morning till night. New York is a colonial city, an outpost.
All the hostility and cruelity of Nature are present in this city,
the most prodigious monument man has ever erected to himself.
It is a light city; its apparent lack of weight surprises most Europeans. In this immense and malevolent space, in this rocky desert
that will tolerate no vegetation of any kind, millions of brick,
wooden and reinforced concrete houses, that all look as if they
are about to fly away, have been constructed.

13   I like New York. I learned to like it. I become accustomed to
its massive groupings and its long vistas. My eyes no longer linger
over the façades in quest of a house which might, by some remote chance, not be identical with the others. My eyes immediately slip by to the horizon to look for the buildings lost in fog,
mere volumes, merely the sky's austere framework. One is rewarded when one has learned how to look at the two rows of
apartment houses which, like cliffs, line a great artery; their mission is completed down there, at the avenue's end, in simple,
harmonious lines; a scrap of sky floats between them.

14   New York reveals itself only at a certain height, a certain distance, and a certain speed; these are not the pedestrian's height,
distance or speed. This city looks amazingly like the great plains
of Andalusia—monotonous when travelled over on foot, magnifi-
cent and changing when seen from a car.

15   I learned to like New York's sky. In European cities where
roofs are low, the sky crawls close to the earth and seems tamed.
The New York sky is beautiful because the skyscrapers push it
back, very far over our heads. Pure and lonely as a wild beast, it
guards and watches over the city. And it is not only a local protection; one feels that it stretches out into the distance over all
America; it is the whole world's sky.

16   I learned to like Manhattan's avenues. They are not sober little
walks closed in between houses, but national highways. The moment you set foot on one of them, you understand that it has to

go on to Boston or Chicago. It fades away outside the city and the eye can almost follow it into the country. A wild sky over parallel rails, that, more than anything else, is New York. When you are at the heart of this city, you are at the heart of Nature.

17   I had to get used to it, but now that I have, there is no place in which I feel more free than in the New York crowds. This light, ephemeral city that looks every morning and evening, under the sun's inquisitive rays, like a simple juxtaposition of rectangular parallelepipeds, is never oppressing or depressing. You can experience the anguish of solitude here, but never that of oppression.

18   In Europe, we become attached to a neighbourhood, to a cluster of houses or a street-corner, and we are no longer free. But hardly have you plunged into New York than your life is completely cut to New York's size. You can gaze down in the evening from the top of the Queensborough Bridge, in the morning from New Jersey, at noon from the seventy-seventh storey of Rockefeller Centre, but you will never be captivated by any of the city's streets, because none of them has a distinctive beauty of its own. There is beauty in all of them, as all of America's nature and sky is present in them. Nowhere will you ever have a stronger feeling of the simultaneity of human lives.

19   New York moves Europeans in spite of its austerity. Of course, we have learned to love our old cities, but their touching quality for us lies in a Roman wall that forms part of an inn's façade, or a house that Cervantes lived in, or the Place des Vosges, or the town hall at Rouen. We like museum-cities, and all our cities are rather like museums in which we wander about amidst ancestral homes. New York is not a museum-city, yet, for Frenchmen of my generation, it already possesses a melancholy of the past. When we were twenty, around 1925, we heard about the sky-scrapers. For us they symbolized America's fabulous prosperity. We discovered them with amazement in the films. They were the architecture of the future, just as the cinema was the art of the future and jazz the music of the future. Today we know what to think about jazz. We know that it has more of a past than a future. It is a music of popular, Negro inspiration, capable of limited development and in a process of slow decline. Jazz is outliving its day. The talking film has not fulfilled the promise

of the silent one. Hollywood is making no headway in a well-worn rut.

20   The war has certainly taught the Americans that their country was the greatest power in the world. But the period of easy living is over; many economists fear a new depression. Thus, no more skyscrapers are being built. It seems they are too hard to rent.

21   The man who walked about in New York before 1930 saw in the big buildings that dominated the city the first signs of an architecture destined to radiate over the whole country. The skyscrapers were alive then. Today, for a Frenchmen arriving from Europe, they are already mere historical monuments, relics of a bygone age. They still rear up against the sky, but my mind is no longer with them, and the New Yorkers pass by at their feet without even looking. I cannot think of them without a certain sadness; they tell of an age in which we thought that the very last war had just ended and when we believed in peace. They are already a bit rundown; tomorrow, perhaps, they will be torn down. In any case, their construction required a faith we no longer have.

22   I walk between the little brick houses the colour of dried blood. They are younger than Europe's houses, but their fragility makes them look much older. Far away I see the Empire State or the Chrysler Building reaching vainly toward the sky, and suddenly I think that New York is about to acquire a History and that it already possesses its ruins.

23   That is enough to lend a bit of softness to the world's harshest city.

the indispensable opposition
WALTER LIPPMANN

1 Were they pressed hard enough, most men would probably confess that political freedom—that is to say, the right to speak freely and to act in opposition—is a noble ideal rather than a practical necessity. As the case for freedom is generally put today, the argument lends itself to this feeling. It is made to appear that, whereas each man claims his freedom as a matter of right, the freedom he accords to other men is a matter of toleration. Thus, the defense of freedom of opinion tends to rest not on its substantial, beneficial, and indispensable consequences, but on a somewhat eccentric, a rather vaguely benevolent, attachment to an abstraction.

2   It is all very well to say with Voltaire, "I wholly disapprove of what you say, but will defend to the death your right to say it," but as a matter of fact most men will not defend to the death the rights of other men: if they disapprove sufficiently what other men say, they will somehow suppress those men if they can.

3   So, if this is the best that can be said for liberty of opinion, that a man must tolerate his opponents because everyone has a "right" to say what he pleases, then we shall find that liberty of opinion is a luxury, safe only in pleasant times when men can be tolerant because they are not deeply and vitally concerned.

4   Yet actually, as a matter of historic fact, there is a much

Reprinted by permission of The Atlantic Monthly Company. © 1939 by The Atlantic Monthly Company, Boston, Massachusetts.

stronger foundation for the great constitutional right of freedom of speech, and as a matter of practical human experience there is a much more compelling reason for cultivating the habits of free men. We take, it seems to me, a naïvely self-righteous view when we argue as if the right of our opponents to speak were something that we protect because we are magnanimous, noble, and unselfish. The compelling reason why, if liberty of opinion did not exist, we should have to invent it, why it will eventually have to be restored in all civilized countries where it is now suppressed, is that we must protect the right of our opponents to speak because we must hear what they have to say.

5   We miss the whole point when we imagine that we tolerate the freedom of our political opponents as we tolerate a howling baby next door, as we put up with the blasts from our neighbor's radio because we are too peaceable to heave a brick through the window. If this were all there is to freedom of opinion, that we are too good-natured or too timid to do anything about our opponents and our critics except to let them talk, it would be difficult to say whether we are tolerant because we are magnanimous or because we are lazy, because we have strong principles or because we lack serious convictions, whether we have the hospitality of an inquiring mind or the indifference of an empty mind. And so, if we truly wish to understand why freedom is necessary in a civilized society, we must begin by realizing that, because freedom of discussion improves our own opinions, the liberties of other men are our own vital necessity.

6   We are much closer to the essence of the matter, not when we quote Voltaire, but when we go to the doctor and pay him to ask us the most embarrassing questions and to prescribe the most disagreeable diet. When we pay the doctor to exercise complete freedom of speech about the cause and cure of our stomachache, we do not look upon ourselves as tolerant and magnanimous, and worthy to be admired by ourselves. We have enough common sense to know that if we threaten to put the doctor in jail because we do not like the diagnosis and the prescription it will be unpleasant for the doctor, to be sure, but equally unpleasant for our own stomachache. That is why even the most ferocious dictator would rather be treated by a doctor who was free to think and speak the truth than by his own Minister of Prapaganda. For

there is a point, the point at which things really matter, where the freedom of others is no longer a question of their right but of our own need.

7   The point at which we recognize this need is much higher in some men than in others. The totalitarian rulers think they do not need the freedom of an opposition: they exile, imprison, or shoot their opponents. We have concluded on the basis of practical experience, which goes back to Magna Carta and beyond, that we need the opposition. We pay the opposition salaries out of the public treasury.

8   In so far as the usual apology for freedom of speech ignores this experience, it becomes abstract and eccentric rather than concrete and human. The emphasis is generally put on the right to speak, as if all that mattered were that the doctor should be free to go out into the park and explain to the vacant air why I have a stomachache. Surely that is a miserable caricature of the great civic right which men have bled and died for. What really matters is that the doctor should tell *me* what ails me, that I should listen to him; that if I do not like what he says I should be free to call in another doctor; and that then the first doctor should have to listen to the second doctor; and that out of all the speaking and listening, the give-and-take of opinions, the truth should be arrived at.

9   This is the creative principle of freedom of speech, not that it is a system for the tolerating of error, but that it is a system for finding the truth. It may not produce the truth, or the whole truth all the time, or often, or in some cases ever. But if the truth can be found, there is no other system which will normally and habitually find so much truth. Until we have thoroughly understood this principle, we shall not know why we must value our liberty, or how we can protect and develop it.

10   Let us apply this principle to the system of public speech in a totalitarian state. We may, without any serious falsification, picture a condition of affairs in which the mass of the people are being addressed through one broadcasting system by one man and his chosen subordinates. The orators speak. The audience listens but cannot and dare not speak back. It is a system of one-way communication; the opinions of the rulers are broadcast outwardly to the mass of the people. But nothing comes back to

the rulers from the people except the cheers; nothing returns in the way of knowledge of forgotten facts, hidden feelings, neglected truths, and practical suggestions.

11   But even a dictator cannot govern by his own one-way inspiration alone. In practice, therefore, the totalitarian rulers get back the reports of the secret police and of their party henchmen down among the crowd. If these reports are competent, the rulers may manage to remain in touch with public sentiment. Yet that is not enough to know what the audience feels. The rulers have also to make great decisions that have enormous consequences, and here their system provides virtually no help from the give-and-take of opinion in the nation. So they must either rely on their own intuition, which cannot be permanently and continually inspired, or, if they are intelligent despots, encourage their trusted advisers and their technicians to speak and debate freely in their presence.

12   On the walls of the houses of Italian peasants one may see inscribed in large letters the legend. "Mussolini is always right." But if that legend is taken seriously by Italian ambassadors, by the Italian General Staff, and by the Ministry of Finance, then all one can say is heaven help Mussolini, heaven help Italy, and the new Emperor of Ethiopia.

13   For at some point, even in a totalitarian state, it is indispensable that there should exist the freedom of opinion which causes opposing opinions to be debated. As time goes on, that is less and less easy under a despotism; critical discussion disappears as the internal opposition is liquidated in favor of men who think and feel alike. That is why the early successes of despots, of Napoleon I and of Napoleon III, have usually been followed by an irreparable mistake. For in listening only to his yes men—the others being in exile or in concentration camps, or terrified—the despot shuts himself off from the truth that no man can dispense with.

14   We know all this well enough when we contemplate the dictatorships. But when we try to picture our own system, by way of contrast, what picture do we have in our minds? It is, is it not, that anyone may stand up on his own soapbox and say anything he pleases, like the individuals in Kipling's poem[1] who sit each in his separate star and draw the Thing as they see it for the God of

[1]"L'Envoi."

Things as they are. Kipling, perhaps, could do this, since he was a poet. But the ordinary mortal isolated on his separate star will have an hallucination, and a citizenry declaiming from separate soapboxes will poison the air with hot and nonsensical confusion.

15   If the democratic alternative to the totalitarian one-way broadcasts is a row of separate soapboxes, than I submit that the alternative is unworkable, is unreasonable, and is humanly unattractive. It is above all a false alternative. It is not true that liberty has developed among civilized men when anyone is free to set up a soapbox, is free to hire a hall where he may expound his opinions to those who are willing to listen. On the contrary, freedom of speech is established to achieve its essential purpose only when different opinions are expounded in the same hall to the same audience.

16   For, while the right to talk may be the beginning of freedom, the necessity of listening is what makes the right important. Even in Russia and Germany a man may still stand in an open field and speak his mind. What matters is not the utterance of opinions. What matters is the confrontation of opinions in debate. No man can care profoundly that every fool should say what he likes. Nothing has been accomplished if the wisest man proclaims his wisdom in the middle of the Sahara Desert. This is the shadow. We have the substance of liberty when the fool is compelled to listen to the wise man and learn; when the wise man is compelled to take account of the fool, and to instruct him; when the wise man can increase his wisdom by hearing the judgment of his peers.

17   That is why civilized men must cherish liberty—as a means of promoting the discovery of truth. So we must not fix our whole attention on the right of anyone to hire his own hall, to rent his own broadcasting station, to distribute his own pamphlets. These rights are incidental; and though they must be preserved, they can be preserved only by regarding them as incidental, as auxiliary to the substance of liberty that must be cherished and cultivated.

18   Freedom of speech is best conceived, therefore, by having in mind the picture of a place like the American Congress, an assembly where opposing views are represented, where ideas are not merely uttered but debated, or the British Parliament, where

men who are free to speak are also compelled to answer. We may picture the true condition of freedom as existing in a place like a court of law, where witnesses testify and are cross-examined, where the lawyer argues against the opposing lawyer before the same judge and in the presence of one jury. We may picture freedom as existing in a forum where the speaker must respond to questions; in a gathering of scientists where the data, the hypothesis, and the conclusion are submitted to men competent to judge them; in a reputable newspaper which not only will publish the opinions of those who disagree but will re-examine its own opinion in the light of what they say.

19   Thus the essence of freedom of opinion is not in mere toleration as such, but in the debate which toleration provides: it is not in the venting of opinion, but in the confrontation of opinion. That this is the practical substance can readily be understood when we remember how differently we feel and act about the censorship and regulation of opinion purveyed by different media of communication. We find then that, in so far as the medium makes difficult the confrontation of opinion in debate, we are driven towards censorship and regulation.

20   There is, for example, the whispering campaign, the circulation of anonymous rumors by men who cannot be compelled to prove what they say. They put the utmost strain on our tolerance, and there are few who do not rejoice when the anonymous slanderer is caught, exposed, and punished. At a higher level there is the moving picture, a most powerful medium for conveying ideas, but a medium which does not permit debate. A moving picture cannot be answered effectively by another moving picture; in all free countries there is some censorship of the movies, and there would be more if the producers did not recognize their limitations by avoiding political controversy. There is then the radio. Here debate is difficult: it is not easy to make sure that the speaker is being answered in the presence of the same audience. Inevitably, there is some regulation of the radio.

21   When we reach the newspaper press, the opportunity for debate is so considerable that discontent cannot grow to the point where under normal conditions there is any disposition to regulate the press. But when newspapers abuse their power by injuring people who have no means of replying, a disposition to regu-

late the press appears. When we arrive at Congress we find that, because the membership of the House is so large, full debate is impracticable. So there are restrictive rules. On the other hand, in the Senate, where the conditions of full debate exist, there is almost absolute freedom of speech.

22   This shows us that the preservation and development of freedom of opinion are not only a matter of adhering to abstract legal rights, but also, and very urgently, a matter of organizing and arranging sufficient debate. Once we have a firm hold on the central principle, there are many practical conclusions to be drawn. We then realize that the defense of freedom of opinion consists primarily in perfecting the opportunity for an adequate give-and-take of opinion; it consists also in regulating the freedom of those revolutionists who cannot or will not permit or maintain debate when it does not suit their purposes.

23   We must insist that free oratory is only the beginning of free speech; it is not the end, but a means to an end. The end is to find the truth. The practical justification of civil liberty is not that self-expression is one of the rights of man. It is that the examination of opinion is one of the necessities of man. For experience tells us that it is only when freedom of opinion becomes the compulsion to debate that the seed which our fathers planted has produced its fruit. When that is understood, freedom will be cherished not because it is a vent for our opinions but because it is the surest method of correcting them.

24   The unexamined life, said Socrates, is unfit to be lived by man. This is the virtue of liberty, and the ground on which we may best justify our belief in it, that it tolerates error in order to serve the truth. When men are brought face to face with their opponents, forced to listen and learn and mend their ideas, they cease to be children and savages and begin to live like civilized men. Then only is freedom a reality, when men may voice their opinions because they must examine their opinions.

25   The only reason for dwelling on all this is that if we are to preserve democracy we must understand its principles. And the principle which distinguishes it from all other forms of government is that in a democracy the opposition not only is tolerated as constitutional but must be maintained because it is in fact indispensable.

26   The democratic system cannot be operated without effective
opposition. For, in making the great experiment of governing
people by consent rather than by coercion, it is not sufficient that
the party in power should have a majority. It is just as necessary
that the party in power should never outrage the minority. That
means that it must listen to the minority and be moved by the
criticisms of the minority. That means that its measures must
take account of the minority's objections, and that in administer-
ing measures it must remember that the minority may become
the majority.

27   The opposition is indispensable. A good statesman, like any
other sensible human being, always learns more from his opponents than from his fervent supporters. For his supporters will
push him to disaster unless his opponents show him where the
dangers are. So if he is wise he will often pray to be delivered
from his friends, because they will ruin him. But, though it hurts,
he ought also to pray never to be left without opponents; for
they keep him on the path of reason and good sense.

28   The national unity of a free people depends upon a sufficiently
even balance of political power to make it impracticable for the
administration to be arbitrary and for the opposition to be revolutionary and irreconcilable. Where that balance no longer exists,
democracy perishes. For unless all the citizens of a state are
forced by circumstances to compromise, unless they feel that they
can affect policy but that no one can wholly dominate it, unless
by habit and necessity they have to give and take, freedom
cannot be maintained.

spring and fall: to a young child

GERARD MANLEY HOPKINS

Márgarét, are you grieving
Over Goldengrove unleaving?
Leáves, like the things of man, you
With your fresh thoughts care for, can you?
Áh! ás the heart grows older   5
It will come to such sights colder
By and by, nor spare a sigh
Though worlds of wanwood leafmeal lie;
And yet you will weep and know why.
Now no matter, child, the name: 10
Sórrow's springs áre the same.
Nor mouth had, no nor mind, expressed
What heart heard of, ghost guessed:
It ís the blight man was born for,
It is Margaret you mourn for.   15

Reprinted by permission of Oxford University Press, from *Poems of Gerard Manley Hopkins*, third edition, edited by W. H. Gardner. Copyright 1948 by Oxford University Press.

DISCUSSION AND WRITING MATERIAL

"A Note on Style and the Limits of Language"

Explain the difference between a "speaking voice" and a "real" personality. Compare and contrast the speaking voices in each of the following selections.

I have paid no poll-tax for six years. I was put into a jail once on this account, for one night; and, as I stood considering the walls of solid stone, two or three feet thick, the door of wood and iron, a foot thick, and the iron grating which strained the light, I could not help being struck with the foolishness of that institution which treated me as if I were mere flesh and blood and bones, to be locked up. I wondered that it should have concluded at length that this was the best use it could put me to, and had never thought to avail itself of my services in some way. I saw that, if there was a wall of stone between me and my townsmen, there was a still more difficult one to climb or break through before they could get to be as free as I was. I did not for a moment feel confined, and the walls seemed a great waste of stone and mortar. I felt as if I alone of all my townsmen had paid my tax. They plainly did not know how to treat me, but behaved like persons who are underbred. In every threat and in every compliment there was a blunder; for they thought that my chief desire was to stand on the other side of that stone wall. I could not but smile to see how industriously they locked the door on my meditations, which followed them out again without let or hindrance, and they were really all that was dangerous. As they could not reach me, they had resolved to punish my body; just as boys, if they cannot come at some person against whom they have a spite, will abuse his dog. I saw that the State was half-witted, that it was timid as a lone woman with her silver spoons, and that it did not know its friends from its foes, and I lost all my remaining respect for it, and pitied it.

HENRY DAVID THOREAU, from "Civil Disobedience"

Negroes want to be treated like men: a perfectly straightforward statement, containing only seven words. People who have mastered Kant, Hegel, Shakespeare, Marx, Freud, and the Bible find this statement utterly impenetrable. The idea seems to threaten profound, barely conscious assumptions. A kind of panic paralyzes their features, as though they found themselves trapped on the edge of a steep place. I once tried to describe to a very well-known American intellectual the conditions among Negroes in the South. My recital disturbed him and made him indignant; and he asked me in perfect innocence, "Why don't all the Negroes in the South move North?" I tried to explain what *has* happened, unfailingly, whenever a significant body of Negroes move North. They do not escape Jim Crow: they merely encounter another, not-less-deadly variety. They do not move to Chicago, they move to the South Side; they do not move to New York, they move to Harlem. The pressure within the ghetto causes the ghetto walls to expand, and this expansion is always violent. White people hold a line as long as they can, and in as many ways as they can, from verbal intimidation to physical violence. But inevitably the border which has divided the ghetto from the rest of the world falls back bitterly before the black horde; the landlords make a tidy profit by raising the rent, chopping up the rooms, and all but dispensing with the upkeep; and what has once been a neighborhood turns into a "turf." This is precisely what happened when the Puerto Ricans arrived in their thousands—and the bitterness thus caused is, as I write, being fought out all up and down those streets.

JAMES BALDWIN, from "Fifth Avenue, Uptown:
A Letter from Harlem"

Right from the go, let me make one thing absolutely clear: I am not now, nor have I ever been, a white man. Nor, I hasten to add, am I now a Black Muslim—although I used to be. But I *am* an Ofay Watcher, a member of that unchartered, amorphous league which has members on all continents and the islands of the seas. Ofay Watchers Anonymous, we might be called, because we exist concealed in the shadows wherever colored people have known oppression by whites, by white enslavers, colonizers, imperialists, and neo-colonialists.

Did it irritate you, compatriot, for me to string those epithets out like that? Tolerate me. My intention was not necessarily to sprinkle salt over anyone's wounds. I did it primarily to relieve a certain pressure on my brain. Do you cop that? If not, then we're in trouble, because we Ofay Watchers have a pronounced tendency to slip into that mood. If it is bothersome to you, it is quite a task for me because not too long ago it was my way of life to preach, as ardently as I could, that the white race is a race

of devils, created by their maker to do evil, and make evil appear
as good; that the white race is the natural, unchangeable enemy
of the black man, who is the original man, owner, maker, cream
of the planet Earth; that the white race was soon to be destroyed
by Allah, and that the black man would then inherit the earth,
which has always, in fact, been his.

ELDRIDGE CLEAVER, from *Soul on Ice*

"Bluspels and Flalansferes"

Discuss the contrast between the "Master's metaphor'" and
the "Pupil's metaphor." In paragraphs 25 and 26 Lewis
concludes that there is a scale of writers. Which writers does
he place at the top and which at the bottom? Compare
and contrast the following poems for their metaphorical
effectiveness.

Days

Daughters of Time, the hypocritic Days,
Muffled and dumb like barefoot dervishes,
And marching single in an endless file,
Bring diadems and fagots in their hands.
To each they offer gifts after his will,
Bread, kingdoms, stars, and sky that holds them all.
I, in my pleached garden, watched the pomp,
Forgot my morning wishes, hastily
Took a few herbs and apples, and the Day
Turned and departed silent. I, too late,
Under her solemn fillet saw the scorn.

RALPH WALDO EMERSON

Note: Consider the etymology of the word "hypocritic."

When to the Sessions of Sweet Silent Thought

When to the sessions of sweet silent thought
I summon up remembrance of things past,
I sigh the lack of many a thing I sought,
And with old woes new wail my dear time's waste.
Then can I drown an eye, unused to flow,

For precious friends hid in death's dateless night,
And weep afresh love's long since cancelled woe,
And moan the expense of many a vanished sight.
Then can I grieve at grievances foregone,
And heavily from woe to woe tell o'er
The sad account of fore-bemoanéd moan,
Which I new pay as if not paid before.
   But if the while I think on thee, dear friend,
   All losses are restored, and sorrows end.

WILLIAM SHAKESPEARE

"New York, the Colonial City"

Show how Sartre in his first paragraph establishes the contrast that will be the basis for the essay's structure. How do the terms "Nature" and "History" contribute to the contrast between American and European cities? Demonstrate the manner in which the contrast between preconceptions and realities leads to the use of paradox in the essay (paradox is an apparent contradiction, both parts of which are true).

"The Indispensable Opposition"

Through the use of an outline, break the essay into its three parts and discuss the significance or purpose of each. Compare Lippmann's position on protest with Martin Luther King's ("Letter from Birmingham Jail").

"Spring and Fall: To a Young Child"

Consider the possibility of the central idea for this poem as a contrast between a child's sensitivity and an adult's rationality. How are Margaret and the Speaker characterized? How does the title contribute to the contrast?

Argue for comparison and contrast as the structural basis for the following poem.

Dover Beach

The sea is calm tonight.
The tide is full, the moon lies fair

Upon the straits;—on the French coast the light
Gleams and is gone; the cliffs of England stand,
Glimmering and vast, out in the tranquil bay.
Come to the window, sweet is the night-air!
Only, from the long line of spray
Where the sea meets the moon-blanch'd land,
Listen! you hear the grating roar
Of pebbles which the waves draw back, and fling,
At their return, up the high strand,
Begin, and cease, and then again begin,
With tremulous cadence slow, and bring
The eternal note of sadness in.

Sophocles long ago
Heard it on the Aegean, and it brought
Into his mind the turbid ebb and flow
Of human misery; we
Find also in the sound a thought,
Hearing it by this distant northern sea.

The Sea of Faith
Was once, too, at the full, and round earth's shore
Lay like the folds of a bright girdle furl'd.
But now I only hear
Its melancholy, long, withdrawing roar,
Retreating, to the breath
Of the night-wind, down the vast edges drear
And naked shingles of the world.

Ah, love, let us be true
To one another! for the world, which seems
To lie before us like a land of dreams,
So various, so beautiful, so new,
Hath really neither joy, nor love, nor light,
Nor certitude, nor peace, nor help for pain;
And we are here as on a darkling plain
Swept with confused alarms of struggle and flight,
Where ignorant armies clash by night.

MATTHEW ARNOLD

MYTH AND SYMBOL

In his highly influential philosophic study *Language and Myth,*
Ernst Cassirer suggests that *words* are the key to controlling
things. Preceding things in our minds, words are our only means
of knowing and understanding them; thus, it is only after we
designate or name a thing that we control it. Primitive man
tended to confuse the word with the thing and in his confusion
often attributed supernatural power to the word. Hence for him
the power of the actual thing resided in its designation, in its
name, and words became divine. Out of this mystical origin the
word developed into merely a symbol representing the thing and,
for civilized man, lost its magical force.

In a sense, however, the artist hearkens back to the primitive
view. He employs words—the tools of his art—with a kind of
veneration divorced from the supernatural; he uses them as a
bridge of revelation from the imagination to the world of external reality. Many linguistic philosophers insist that all
language is symbolic, and reduced to its lowest terms a symbol
is something that stands for something else. Language, then,
calls to the mind sensory images of that "something else"; the
word *rose,* for example, can conjure images of the blooming
flower but through common convention can extend beyond this
literal correspondence of word and thing to suggest the idea of
beauty. From the basic joining of "word and thing," symbols,

particularly literary symbols, can assume a virtually limitless number of meanings; and it is this sort of symbolic indirection that is behind a good deal of literature.

Myth-making is an extension of the symbolic function of language. A myth is both a means of conceiving the external world and a form of expression of that conception. Since the origin of myth is deeply rooted in mankind's unconscious and is indeed prelogical, the term all but defies definition. The critic William Y. Tindall calls it "a dreamlike narrative in which the individual's central concerns are united wth society, time, and the universe." Ancient myth satisfied deeply religious, ethical, or social needs and strengthened tradition by uniting a community of credulous listeners.

Myth, like language, inevitably became the tool of the artist, for through its offices he could communicate (and expect a reasonable degree of understanding) his own insights into the world about him. As men became more sophisticated, however, their myths became correspondingly more self-conscious, perhaps even more contrived. Societies no longer had common myths, and the individual artist was obliged to construct his own or reconstruct an older myth along modern lines and for modern purposes. The result has been a proliferation of private myths, yet in the work of the finest artists such myths have successfully expressed the temper of an age.

The selections that follow will serve to introduce the student to the literary uses of symbol and myth and to offer examples of both in poetry and fiction. They will lead him from the logical, closely reasoned realm of expository writing to the sometimes more oblique, but equally rewarding, world of literature. The transition may at first seem confusing and difficult, but the end result is well worth the effort.

symbolism and fiction

HARRY LEVIN

1 A few years ago we welcomed to our Department a colleague who had never before taught English literature. As a poet he had practiced it; as a lawyer he had once taught law; and as Assistant Secretary of State he may even have prepared himself to cope with the complexities of academic life. Why should I not mention the honored name of Archibald MacLeish? Mr. MacLeish was anxious to meet the minds of the college generation, and incidentally to test the observation that William Faulkner had supplanted Ernest Hemingway as their literary idol. His first assignment required his class, as a sort of touchstone, to read and report on Mr. Hemingways' "Big Two-Hearted River." They had not read it; but you have, and you remember that it is hardly a story at all; it is simply a sketch about a boy who goes fishing. Its striking quality is the purity of its feeling, its tangible grasp of sensuous immediacy, the physical sensation that Mr. Hemingway is so effective at putting into prose. The students did not seem to feel this quality. They liked the story; they wrote about it at length; but in their protocols, to a man, they allegorized it. Each of those fish that Nick Adams had jerked out of Big Two-Hearted River bore for them a mystical significance, which varied according to its interpreter—Freudian or Jungian, Kierkegaardian or Kafkaesque. May I leave these silvery,

Reprinted with permission of Harvard University Press, from *Contexts of Criticism*, by Harry Levin.

slippery trout dangling there in the water to incarnate the fascination and the elusiveness of our subject?

2   American literature would all be childishness, the innocent
wonderment of the schoolroom—according to one of its most
perceptive interpreters, D. H. Lawrence— if it did not invite us
to look beneath its bland surface and to find a diabolic inner
meaning. The reaction of Professor MacLeish's students might
suggest that we do not enjoy the surfaces enough, that we have
become too morbidly preoccupied with the subliminal. In our
restless search for universals, we may be losing sight of particulars: of the so-called quiddity, that "whatness" which characterizes a work of art, the truth of an object to its peculiar self.
Literature is not a game of charades. Yet Lawrence's reinterpreta-
tion helped to rescue, out of the indiscriminate attic of children's
books, the greatest classic in American literature; and *Moby-
Dick* has plenty of deviltry at its core. When a lightning-rod
man intruded upon Mark Twain, the upshot was a humoristic
sketch. When a lightning-rod man intruded upon Herman
Melville, the consequence became part of his lifelong quarrel
with organized religion. It may now remain for some intrepid
young allegorist to demonstrate, in some little magazine, that
Mark Twain's sketch is nothing less than a crytographic adum-
bration of a Rosicrucian tract.

3   At this juncture it may prove useful to be reminded that
Moby-Dick itself, like "Big Two-Hearted River," is a simple
story about a fishing trip. Basically, it is just another yarn about
the big fish that got away. So is Mr. Hemingway's last book,
The Old Man and the Sea, even though critics have seen themselves symbolized in the sharks that prey on the Old Man's
gigantic catch. *Moby-Dick,* at all events, is a whopper; and, like
all whoppers, it has the capacity to be expanded and elaborated
ad infinitum. In the process of elaboration, Melville has introduced his linked analogies and dark similitudes, sometimes
deliberately and—it would also seem—sometimes intuitively. He
himself seemed scarcely conscious of certain implications which
Nathaniel Hawthorne pointed out, and which thereupon fell
into place—as Melville acknowledged—in "the part-and-parcel
allegoricalness of the whole." (Or did he write "of the whale?"
Melville's handwriting, in his famous letter to Mrs. Hawthorne,

is indeterminate at this crucial point.) One of his chapters, anatomizing the beached skeleton of a whale, tells us that some of its smaller vertebrae have been carried away to make children's rattles. And so, he goes on to moralize, almost anticipating the reception of his book, so the most momentous enterprises can taper off into child's play.

4   Mr. Faulkner, being our contemporary, has not suffered very much from the innocence of his readers. On the contrary, the title of his last novel, A *Fable,* proclaims his own ambition to universalize a message of some sort, impelled perhaps by the sense of international responsibility that seems to go along with the Nobel Prize. But let us revert to a more modest example of his story-telling skill, with which we may feel more at home, *The Bear.* This is another story about a hunting trip; it sticks to his region and it securely belongs, along with *The Adventures of Huckleberry Finn* and *The Red Badge of Courage,* among those wonderful American stories in which a boy reaches manhood through some rite of passage, some baptism of fire, an initiation into experience. We may not have noticed, and we should therefore be grateful for the critical comment that points it out, a possible resemblance between the youthful Ike McCaslin and the epic heroes of Homer and Vergil. But we may be less grateful than puzzled when the same Kenyon Critic informs us that *The Bear* is an allegory of "the transition from pagan to Christian culture, if not from the Old to the New Testament." We may even begin to suspect that the commentator lacks a sense of proportion, if not a sense of humor.

5   Needless to say, these lacks would not be considered serious enough to disqualify him from practicing criticism as it is frequently practiced today. Criticism is a child of the time, and it changes as times change. The catchwords of critics have tended to echo the ideals of their respective periods. Thus a whole epoch is summed up in the term "decorum," and another by the shibboleth "sublime." What is our key word? "Ambiguity" is not my own suggestion; it is an obvious recommendation from our contemporary masters of critical terminology. Their stronghold, be it Axel's castle or Kafka's, is not the old allegorical castle of love or war, of perseverance or indolence; it is a citadel of ambiguity. Since the numerous types of ambiguity presup-

pose as many levels of meaning, it might be more up-to-date to call this castle a skyscraper, and to call our typologists of ambiguity—borrowing a compendious adjective from *Finnegans Wake*—"hierarchitectitiptitoploftical." As in instance of such hierarchitectitiptitoploftical criticism, without pretending to be citing at random, I might cite a recent interpretation of James Joyce's *Portrait of the Artist as a Young Man*. Here at the outset Cranly, the friend of the artist, is said to be not only John the Baptist but likewise Judas and Pilate—a wide and exacting and not exactly compatible range of roles for a secondary character.

6   Part of the difficulty would seem to spring from the critic's addiction to the copula. Some of our literary reviews, in this respect, might just as well be written in Basic English. Suggestive allusions tend to become flat assertions. Something, instead of suggesting some other thing, somehow *is* that other thing; it cannot mean, it must be. Everything must be stated as an equation, without recognizing degrees of relationship or the differences between allusion and fact. Now, as the name of his protagonist indicates, Joyce is fond of alluding to prototypes. Cranly is ironically linked with John the Baptist as a kind of predecessor; and to the extent to which every betrayer of his friend is a Judas and every avoider of moral responsibility is a Pilate, he may be said to have momentarily figured in both of those positions. But what are we then to make of the Artist as a Young Man? A Jesus? There is a sense in which the life of every good Christian is, or should be, an imitation of Christ. But Stephen Dedalus expressly chooses to imitate Satan; *"Non serviam!"* The comment is therefore not an ambiguity nor an ambivalence nor a tension nor an irony nor a paradox. It is a contradiction or— to use a very old-fashioned term—an impertinence; and there are times when reason can do no more than imitate Dr. Johnson and kick the stone.

7   Such interpretations are dismissed as "cabalistics" by the introduction to one of the many current studies of Franz Kafka. But when we turn from this introduction to the study itself, having been all but convinced that its author is uniquely sane and that Kafka's other commentators are uniformly mad, we find that he too has a frenzied glint in his eye and a cabalistic theory of his own: all of Kafka is to be explained by the incidence of the

number two. Two is an important number, of course, when we come to think about it; and when we start to look for it, it appears to be so ubiquitous that it explains not only Kafka but everything else. The only matter it does not explain is the difference between Kafka and everything else. And that, I fear, is the trouble with much that passes for psychoanalytic criticism: it reduces our vocabulary of symbols to a few which are so crudely fundamental and so monotonously recurrent that they cannot help the critic to perform his primary function, which is still— I take it—to discriminate. Nature abounds in protuberances and apertures. Convexities and concavities, like Sir Thomas Browne's quincunxes, are everywhere. The forms they compose are not always enhanced or illuminated by reading our sexual obsessions into them.

8   Isolating text from context in the name of "close reading," we can easily be led astray. So sensible a critic as Edmund Wilson has argued that Henry James's "Turn of the Screw" should be read as a psychological projection of its governess's frustrations. Subsequently it has been shown by Professor Robert L. Wolff—a professional historian on a Jamesian holiday—that the manifest content of the alleged fantasy came from a sentimental illustration in a Christmas annual to which James had also contributed. What is needed today perhaps, what readers and writers might well join together in forming, would be a Society for the Protection of Symbols from Critics. But I do not want to labor a point which is, indeed, that all too many points may have been labored already. Having labored a little in the symbolistic vineyard, I share the curiosities and admire the ingenuities of many of my fellow laborers. If these remarks have the intonation of a caveat, they should also have the overtones of a *mea culpa*. When, however, this hieratic tendency draws back upon itself the leveling criticism of the philistines who are always with us, thereby exacerbating the war of attrition between the quarterlies and the weeklies, we must all be concerned one way or another.

9   A primrose by a river's brim is, obviously, one thing to J. Donald Adams and quite another thing to Kenneth Burke. For the leveling critic the flower in the crannied wall may be simply that and nothing more. A rose itself, the emblem of romance and so much more, the *rosa sempiterna* of Dante, the *rosa mystica*

of Hopkins or Yeats, the garden of T. S. Eliot's agony, the thorn of which Rilke may actually have died in aromatic pain—well, a rose is a rose is a rose. And *Moby-Dick* is a book which exists on a plane of comparison with the novels of Captain Marryat. Without capitulating to that simplistic view, we could well afford to concede that not every literary surface happens to mask a darker meaning. Every work of art may be a form of symbolic action, as Mr. Burke keeps patiently reminding us; and behind the reminder stands Coleridge's conception of the artist as a creator of symbols. When Hamlet could not accuse Claudius directly, he approached him by means of the play-within-the-play —"tropically." So Ernst Jünger, during the Nazi regime, was able to attack it symbolically in his fantastic tale, *From the Marble Cliffs.* But there are symbols and symbols. "My tropes are not tropes," says King Media to the philosopher Babbalanja in Melville's *Mardi,* "but yours are." That is the issue: when is a trope not a trope, and what is it then?

10   It should do us no harm to admit that art continues to have its simpler vehicles, such as love lyrics or works of sculpture, designed to convey feelings rather than ideas. When Mr. MacLeish's students dredged up such grimly subaqueous intimations from the limpid waters of the Big Two-Hearted River, they were essentially engaged in revealing themselves. Furthermore, they were reflecting the outlook of our age—an age which, as it looks back toward the nineteen-twenties from the vantage-point of a full generation afterward—seems to be looking across an enormous gulf. Writing at the end of that fabulous decade, Mr. Wilson terminated his *Axel's Castle* with a kind of farewell to the symbolists: to Yeats and Joyce and Proust and several other supreme individualists, and to those rare artificial worlds of their private creation. But symbolism proved much too deeply rooted to take the hint and retire. In the meanwhile, a call for a "science of symbolism" had been issued by C. K. Ogden and I. A. Richards. Exploring the personal and the collective unconscious, Freud and Jung had shown how primitive myths survive through oneiric fantasies. Furthermore, public events have intervened in our lives to strengthen the authority of symbols. Hence the movement, broadening its base, has been going forward—or is it

backward? For symbolism, in the Hegelian worldview, characterizes the earliest phase of culture.

11   One of the signs of revival has been the popularity of Suzanne
Langer's *Philosophy in a New Key,* with its stimulating argument that modern logic, semantics, metaphysics, and various
schools of thought in the social sciences run parallel to the course
of symbolism among the arts. But the key in which all this is
pitched, by virtue of Mrs. Langer's synesthetic metaphor, is by
no means new. It is so old that we might properly call it a
"mode"; and it leads us back to other modes of thinking which
are rather prelogical than logical, rather magical than scientific,
rather transcendental than empirical. Mrs. Langer's two philosophical masters, Ernst Cassirer and Alfred North Whitehead,
were both profoundly aware that symbolism is inherent in the
very processes of language and thought. So was Quintilian:
"Paene quicquid loquimur figura est." We could hardly speak or
think or vote without symbols; we live and die by them; we
should hesitate to cross the street at a traffic intersection, were it
not for their unambiguous accord. All art, in this sense, is more
or less symbolic. More or less, and whether it is more symbolic or
less may be determined by historical as well as by esthetic considerations.

12   Take an illustration which William Butler Yeats admired because it happened to be "out of nature," because it belonged to
"the artifice of eternity." Take "such a form as Grecian gold-
smiths make"—a Byzantine icon. Such a religious image had to
be stylized and conventionalized along the lines that were sanc-
tioned and prescribed by the Church of the East. Its style could
be considered more symbolic than the painting of the West; for
Western painters, freed from the conventions and prescriptions
and restrictions of Iconoclastic dogma, could come closer and
closer to life—even as material actuality was becoming secular
and realistic. At the eastern extreme, the taboo of the Jewish
and Mohammedan religions against the making of graven images
sponsored an art which was decorative and functional but not
precisely significant, as in a prayer-rug. "In a symbol," wrote
Thomas Carlyle in his handbook for symbolists, *Sartor Resartus,*
"there is both concealment and revelation." But if everything

were revealed, then nothing would be symbolized; and if everything were concealed, then too nothing would be symbolized.
Thus a symbol is a sort of excluded middle between what we
know and what we do not know—or better, as Carlyle put it, a
meeting point between the finite and the infinite.

13   Art is always an imitation, never quite the real thing. It cannot
represent without symbolizing. By its devices of synecdoche or
metonymy, it gives us the part for the whole or the attribute for
the object. It never gives us a perfect replica; on the other hand,
it never gives us a complete abstraction. What has been ineptly
termed "nonobjective painting" proves—if nothing else—that
there is really no such thing as pure design. In the dramatic
moralities, Vanity is a highly feminine creature and the Vice is
full of boyish mischief. Life itself is bound to be mixed up with
any artistic representation of it; yet even the "slice of life" of
the naturalists had to be framed by symbolic conceptions, as in
the fiction of Emile Zola or his American disciple, Frank Norris.
Think of Norris' titles, *The Pit, The Octopus*—not to mention
the monstrous tooth of McTeague. Banish the symbol, and it returns as a simile: the mine-shaft transformed by *Germinal* into a
perpetually crouching beast. The London fog, with its natural
aura of obfuscation, becomes a metaphorical vehicle for Dickens'
critique of the law-courts in *Bleak House*. And Flaubert concentrates with such intensity on the details of materialistic circum-
stance that, in *A Simple Heart,* the stuffed parrot of his old
servant-woman is apotheosized into the Paraclete.

14   Generally speaking, art seems to oscillate between two poles,
the symbolistic and the realistic—or, we might say, the typical
and the individual. In its westward movement it has kept pace
with the development of human individuality. In its eastward
purview it glances backward toward Byzantium, and toward an
order of mind which derives its strength from the opposing
principle of typicality. This polarity is recognized by philosophy
in the habitual problem of the One and the Many, and it has
innumerable repercussions in the political and sociocultural
areas. Through some such oscillation, we have been moving—at
least until lately—in the direction set by the Greeks. A humanistic literature, such as theirs, is not primarily regulated by
symbolism. Homer and Sophocles made use of symbols, yes; but

the *Odyssey* is a story about a man named Odysseus; it is not an ironic commentary upon a day in the life of a man named Leopold Bloom; while Oedipus, since he verily married his mother, was presumably the one recorded man who did not suffer from the frustrations of the Oedipus complex. The world of Odysseus and Oedipus was concrete; it was here and now as long as it lasted. Ages with less pride in the dignity of mankind would preach contempt for this world, along with hope for another and better one hereafter. The visible things of this earth, in the doctrine of Saint Paul, shadow forth the invisible things of God. As Christopher Cranch, the transcendentalist poet, expressed it: "Nature is but a scroll,—God's handwriting thereon." It is held that the artist, like the prophet, should have the insight to read and translate these divine hieroglyphics. Such is the state of mind that makes for symbolism, both in creating and in interpreting a hermetic art.

15   The two points of view, the otherworldly and the humanistic, clashed in the conflict between Christian asceticism and the pagan classics, which Saint Augustine resolved by formulating a masterly distinction between the spirit and the letter. If the letter kills, the spirit brings new life; and if a text is literally profane, it may be read figuratively and endowed retrospectively with a spiritual significance. The Song of Songs reads suspiciously like an erotic poem; yet the Rabbis admitted it to the sacred canon by pronouncing it to be an allegory of God's love for Israel. Similarly the Fathers, for whom the Old Testament prefigured the New, accepted it as an expression of Christ's love for the Church. Following Augustine, through this retroactive procedure known as "figuration," the *Aeneid* could be taken as a pilgrimage of the soul adventuring among divers moral hazards. Thereafter Dante could take Vergil as his guide for a series of literal adventures through the next world. Dante, as he acknowledged, was also following Saint Thomas Aquinas, who—in answering the preliminary questions of his *Summa Theologica*—had sustained the doctrine that although the scriptures were literally true, they could be interpreted as figures on three ascending levels of spiritual meaning.

16   But though the *Divine Comedy* is polysemous, as it is expounded in Dante's dedicatory letter to Can Grande della Scala,

the poem cannot pretend to literal truth; the Florentine poet, after all, was making believe that he himself had journeyed through hell and purgatory and paradise; the "allegory of poets" is not the "allegory of theologians." The next step would be taken by the more worldly Boccaccio, who in his life of Dante supported the validity of poetic truth. Elsewhere he went even farther, with the affirmation that theology is God's poetry. It has remained for latter-day symbolists to round out the cycle by affirming that poetry is man's theology. With the humanism of the Renaissance and the Enlightenment, the other world seems gradually to recede. Nominalistic reality shifts to the foreground; things are valued for themselves, and not for what they may prefigure. The shift from the type to the individual has its protagonist in *Doctor Faustus,* Marlowe's early sketch for Goethe's portrayal of modernism in action. Faustus in one poet who is not content to compare his mistress with famous beauties. Metaphors will not do and symbols are not enough; he must attain the object of his comparison. He must have the one and only Helen of Troy, and he does so *in propria persona;* but the reality proves to be as elusive as the symbol.

17   Poetry with its metaphors, metaphysics with its analogies, bridge a gap between seen and unseen worlds. The breakdown of the bridge is that dissociation of which Mr. Eliot has written so feelingly; and it is more than a "dissociation of sensibility"; it is a break in the whole chain of being. Hume's critique of analogy might be regarded, under this aspect, as a philosophical counterpart of neoclassical poetic diction. A symbol, on the other hand, is a connecting link between two different spheres; for the original word in Greek meant throwing together, a violent fusion, the very act of association. When man stands upon his own feet, proudly conscious of the achievements of his fellow men, he lives most fully and his art embodies the fullness of his life, his basic sense of reality. Then the *Aeneid* is not a *pélérinage de la vie humaine,* but the epic of a hero; the Song of Songs is not an allegory but a chant of love; and Shakespeare's tragedies are dramas of physical action and psychological conflict, not ballets of bloodless images or ceremonials for a dying god. In times which seem to be out of joint, when man is alienated from his environment, the heroic seems less immediately attainable and

love itself may dim to a Platonic vision. A failure of nerve is accompanied by a retreat from reality.

18   Arthur Symons characterized the symbolistic movement of the nineteenth century as a perfervid effort to escape from materialism. It is much easier to comprehend what the symbolists were escaping from than what they were escaping to. Their problem was, and it certainly remains, to establish a viable set of intimate associations with another sphere. Some of them felt they had solved it personally through religious conversion; others frankly used their visionary imaginations, often abetted by stimulants and even by mental disorders. Whereas the traditional symbolist had abstracted objects into ideas, the self-proclaimed *symboliste* —as Jean Moréas announced in his manifesto of 1886—sought to invest the idea in concrete form. Hence his emphasis was on the object itself rather than its conceivable signification, on the denseness of the imagery rather than the pattern of the thought, on concealment rather than revelation in Carlyle's terms. But since the symbol was never clearly acknowledged as the key to any higher plane of existence, poets could not be blamed when it became a fetish cultivated for its own sake. Literature could not be expected to transcend itself by its own bootstraps; and yet, with Mallarmé, the esthetic process became the principal subject for symbolization. So it is with Proust; but when it is manifested in connoisseurship of ecclesiastical architecture, the symbols are already fraught with a transcendence of their own.

19   The unvoiced premise of *symbolisme,* which is not far from that of orthodox mysticism, had been handed on by the German idealists to the New England transcendentalists. For Baudelaire, moving out of the woods of naturalism back toward the church, nature was a temple with trees for pillars. Man walks through this forest of symbols which seem to know him better than he knows them, and the words he hears there are confused. *"Les parfums, les couleurs, et les sons se répondent."* Color and sound and other sensory impressions are linked together through correspondences, associative patterns whose final sanction is not discernible to the senses. Some of these were suggested by Rimbaud in his well-known sonnet on the vowels, but not everyone would accept his linkages. Different sounds would suggest different colors to different readers; and that is the essential dilemma

of *symbolisme*. For all its efforts to reorder the universe, to categorize the diversity of experience, its influence has been unregenerately individualistic. Remy de Gourmont, the critical interpreter of the movement, aptly presents it as—among other things—the ultimate expression of individualism in art.

20   How far it stands apart from its medieval prototype might be measured by consulting the *Rationale* of Durandus, the thirteenth-century manual of Christian symbolism, as embodied in the sacramentalism of the Catholic church. Living tradition was —and is—practiced daily there, through the cruciform structure of the edifice, its orientation, ritual, and liturgy, the relation of the church year to the life of Christ, the reënactment of the last supper in the Eucharist. Through that rite of communion the paschal lamb, originally the sacrifice of the Jewish Passover, had become the commonest symbol for Jesus. The audience at fifteenth-century Wakefield, witnessing their *Second Shepherds' Play*, could not irreverently grasp a serio-comic parallel between the infant in the manger and the stolen sheep of the farcical underplot. This is an authoritative example of the technique of symbolic association. Conversely, we witness the effect of dissociation in *Madame Bovary*, when the great Cathedral of Rouen looks reprovingly down upon the lovers fleeing in their cab, and its disregarded sermons in stones exemplify all the values that Emma and Léon are flouting. It is a far cry from George Herbert's *Temple* to Blaudelaire's.

21   "A symbol remains vital," the late Karl Vossler has written, "only when its representation is accompanied by faith." The number seven was no abstraction for Dante; behind it loomed the power of the Seven Sacraments, the Seven Deadly Sins, the Seven Gifts of the Holy Ghost. But when we turn away from the supernatural, in naturalistic suspension of belief, what—if anything—are we to make of Thomas Mann's conjurations with the same digit in *The Magic Mountain?* The seven chapters of the novel itself, the seven tables in the dining room of the Berghof sanitorium, which has seven letters in its name, as have its seven principal guests in their names, and all the recurrent multiples of seven—these are endowed with no more efficacy than the novelist's deliberate manipulation of coincidence. Whereas, if we now reconsider our fish, we find that it is alpha-

betically associated with the initial letters of the Greek words for "Jesus Christ, Son of God, the Savior," which can be read acrostically as *ichthys*. As such it served in the catacombs, where overt symbols would have been dangerous, to conceal the Christian revelation. In the terms of Durandus, it was a positive rather than a natural symbol, or—as Yeats would say—arbitrary rather than inherent.

22   It is the inherent, the natural symbol that Coleridge seems to have in mind when he asserts that it always partakes of that reality which it renders intelligible. The cross of the lamb, as opposed to the fish, may well be termed an emblem, as distinguished from a sign. But Saint Augustine can transform a sign into an emblem, when he mystically envisions Jesus Christ as a fish swimming through the depths of mortality. This distinction between emblems and signs corresponds with that which has been drawn since Goethe, more broadly and often invidiously, between symbolism and allegory. The symbolic is the only possible expression of some essence, according to Yeats, whereas the allegorical may be one out of many. In the latter case, we are less engaged by the symbol itself than by what is arbitrarily symbolized. Yet when the fish is not a religious acrostic but Captain Ahab's whale, it is emblematic; and then, as W. H. Auden duly warns us, we must not expect a one-to-one correspondence. For what we then encounter is not an allegorical reference to something else in some particular respect, but a multiplicity of potential cross-references to other categories of experience.

23   These formulations could be tested by turning again to *Moby-Dick* and applying the polysemous method, the fourfold scheme of interpretation that Dante invited his readers to follow, which extends the meaning beyond the literal to the three figurative levels—allegorical, moral, and anagogical. Later allegories may not be as multileveled as the *Divine Comedy;* it is hard to discern more than three planes in the *Faerie Queene* or two in the *Pilgrim's Progress.* Under the subsequent impact of realism, the allegorical and the anagogical tend to wither away; the moral blends with the literal or drops out altogether, as writers turn from the Celestial City to Vanity Fair. But the Middle Ages maintained the sharp differentiation formulated in a Latin

distich which can be conveniently paraphrased: the literal tells us what happens, the allegorical what to believe, the moral what to do, and the anagogical whither to strive. Thus, literally Moby-Dick is concerned with the voyage of the *Pequod,* the subject of whaling, the science of cetology; allegorically with society on shipboard, the parable of Ahab's "irresistible dictatorship"; morally with a series of object-lessons, such examples as the monkey-rope, the ligature of brotherhood that binds Ishmael to Queequeg; and anagogically . . . "*Quo tendas?* whither art thou striving?"

24   That is the question, and Melville offers no categorical answer. Dante knew, or believed he knew, the object of his journey; no traveler, to be sure, had returned to map out the topography of the next world; but Dante's account was based on the *terra firma* of assumptions universally shared, while Melville put out to sea in lone pursuit of "the ungraspable phantom of life." He was enough of a transcendentalist to ponder the meaning of this "great allegory, the world," enough of an iconoclast to strike through the pasteboard mask of outer appearances, and enough of a skeptic to respect the uncharted mystery beyond it. But the anagoge, which for Dante is the fulfillment of providential design, for Melville remains an ultimate question mark. His overwhelming whale has been identified with—among other concepts —nature, fate, sex, property, the father-image, God Himself. It has meant various things to varying critics because it is Melville's enigma, like the doubloon nailed by Ahab to the mast, which signifies dollars to the Second Mate, the Zodiac to the First Mate, and the universe to the Captain. Shall we ever identify Moby-Dick? Yes, when we have sprinkled salt on the tail of the Absolute; but not before.

25   In one of his prophetic moments Melville even anticipated atomic fission, describing the tail of the whale as if it were a cyclotron. "Could annihilation occur to matter," Ishmael exclaims, "this were the thing to do it." However, the atomic is just as far beyond our scope as the cosmic; and we cannot necessarily count upon the rock of dogma for that firm foundation on which Durandus constructed his medieval symbology. Are we then at the mercy of sheer subjectivity, of the irresponsible caprice of the overingenious critic, making symbols mean what

he wants them to mean? Or have we still some criteria at our disposal, technical means for determining the relevance—if not the truth—of any given comment? Here I would venture to suggest that students of literature might profitably emulate the researches now being carried on in the plastic arts under the heading of Iconology. Some of us have been collecting images, but not interpreting them very satisfactorily; others have been tracing the history of ideas, without paying much attention to formal context. Could we not hope for a discipline which would bring the tools of critical analysis to bear upon the materials of textual documentation, concentrating upon the thematic relationship between the idea and the image? Shall we ever discover the archetype behind them both except through comparative study of its most impressive manifestations?

26   This is more easily called for than provided. The leaders of the Iconological School are brilliantly conspicuous for their combination of discernment and learning. We shall not have literary iconologists in our Departments of English until our discerners have picked up a little learning and our learners have somehow acquired a little discernment. In the interim, are there not a few reasonable game laws, which we might undertake to observe whenever we go fishing? Or—to state the problem more pragmatically—could we not agree upon a code of fair-trade practices, which might conduce to a closer meeting of critical minds? Granted that divergence of opinion is salutary—indeed necessary —for the evaluation of a work of art, and that the very suggestiveness of some masterworks is most richly attested by the variety of interpretations accruing to them. Yet the work itself is always greater than the sum of its interpretations; and unless these are grounded within some frame of objective reference, we have no basis for differentiating between perception and deception. After all, criticism—in a Baconian phrase—is reason applied to imagination. Doubtless the fourfold method of exegesis, which Dante appealed to and Saint Thomas propounded, would be somewhat hierarchical for our day. Nevertheless, in more democratic terms, the common consent of educated readers might be gained at four descending levels of acceptance.

27   The first, which raises no questions, would be strictly conventional. No one has any doubt what Hawthorne intends by the

accepted symbol of the eagle over the door of the Custom House
in the introductory chapter of *The Scarlet Letter;* and Melville's
eagle soaring over the Catskills, though less official, is a bird of
the same feather. The second use of the symbol is explicit, as
when Melville glosses the monkey-rope or moralizes up and
down the deck in *Moby-Dick;* or, best of all, Hawthorne's scarlet
letter itself—how similar in appearance, how different in connotation, from the "crowned A" of Chaucer's Prioress! Third, and
here we cross an equatorial line, the implicit. "Thou too sail on,
O ship of state!" is highly explicit, not to say conventional. But
the good ship *Pequod*—like the frigate *Neversink* in *White-
jacket, or The World in a Man-of-War*—is a little world in itself;
and when it goes down, what are we to make of the eagle that
goes down with it or that rather sinister emblem, the hand with
a hammer? Melville's "Tartarus of Maids" is explicitly a humani-
tarian sketch of a New England factory, and implicitly an
obstetrical allegory of woman's fate. What is implied, in contrast
to what is explicated by the author himself, can be possibly
gaged by what are known in Shakespearean commentary as
"fervors" and "recurrences."

28   These are patterns of repetition and emphasis, which in some
fortunate cases can be reinforced by the facts of biography and
the insights of psychology. Jay Leyda's *Melville Log* not only
supplements the romances and tales, but fills in some missing
segments of their imaginative configuration. Without such external evidence we could draw no sharp line between the implicit and, fourth, the conjectural level—or, for that matter,
between the conjectural and the inadmissible. But once we admit
degrees of plausibility, we may entertain, for whatever enhance-
ment it may be worth, any conjecture likely to enrich our apprehension of the part-and-parcel allegoricalness of the whole.
Does it enrich our apprehension of the later novels of Henry
James if we construe them as Swedenborgian allegories? There is
one tangential fact in support of this argument: the Sweden-
borgianism of the elder Henry James. And that is outweighed
by the clearest expressions of intention, as well as by the internal
consistency of the author's habits of thinking and writing. Therefore the purported symbolism is not conventional nor explicit
nor implicit; it is, at best, conjectural; and since it obscures

rather more than it illuminates, it should probably be discarded as inadmissible. Let us look for figures in the carpets, and not in the clouds.

29   And let us return, for the last time, to the whale. Surely no other literary symbol has invited and evaded so much conjecture; surely Melville intended to keep us guessing up to the bitter end and afterward. His book does not resemble life the less because it leaves us in a state of suspense. But just as insecurity seeks authority, just as complexity seeks simplification, just as pluralism seeks unity, so our critics long for the archetypal because they are bedeviled by the ambiguous. Groping amid ambiguities, they become increasingly hot for certainties; and symbols, they desperately hope, will provide the keys. So every hero may seem to have a thousand faces; every heroine may be a white goddess *incognita;* and every fishing trip turns out to be another quest for the Holy Grail. However, that boy of Hemingway's, fishing in Big Two-Hearted River, is not a type but an individual. He is not Everyman; he is Nick Adams; and, like every other single human being, he is unique. The river in which he fishes is neither the Nile nor the Liffey; it is a stream which runs through the Upper Peninsula of the state of Michigan. The sun that beats on his back is the same old planet that has generated myths since the world began. But the feeling it evokes is the existential conjunction of the scene, the moment, and human sensibility. Literature can give us many other things; but it gives us, first and last, a taste of reality.

"myth" and the literary scruple
FRANCIS FERGUSSON

1   "Myth" is one of those words which it has become almost impossible to use without apologetic quotation marks. Ill-defined for centuries, it is now used in many senses and for many purposes: to mean nonsense or willful obscurantism in some contexts, the deepest wisdom of man in others. One would like to be able to banish it to that pale Hades where "irony" and "ambiguity" have their impotent but pretentious afterlife. But unfortunately the student of literature cannot get along without "Myth." It is too evident that poetry, to say nothing of religion, philosophy and history, are akin to mythopoeia. Drama, the lyric and fiction live symbolically with myths, nourished by them, and nourishing their flickering lives. Some of the inventions of poets —Kafka's *Metamorphosis,* Plato's tale of the charioteer with his white and his black horse—are modelled on myth. Some poetic works which we like—*Moby Dick,* Lorca's plays—have what we are pleased to call a "mythic" quality. Writers of all kinds use inherited myths in their own work. The student of literature cannot avoid talking about Myth; but how can he use the protean word with any decent rigor?

2   It was the early romantic poets and philosophers who started our modern cult of Myth. They sought in it some alternative to the narrow categories of modern rationalism, some defense of

Reprinted with permission of the publishers, from *The Sewanee Review,* LXIV, No. 2, April 1956, pages 171–185. Copyright by The University of the South.

humane letters in a world created by applied science; often they felt it would replace formal religion. But in our time scientists and pseudo-scientists of every description—psychologists of several persuasions; archeologists, linguists, assorted varieties of anthropologists and sociologists—pronounce upon Myth with an imposing air of authority. And specialists in various fields have filled our books and our museums with countless mythic tales and mythic figures, not only from our own tradition but from every corner of the human time and space. In this welter of facts and theories the student of literature is in danger of losing his bearings altogether. For he cannot simply disregard the labors of countless savants on Myth; he must use them for his own purposes when they strike him as illuminating. On the other hand, he lacks the knowledge and the training to join the debates of specialists on their own terms. What he needs, I think, is a renewed sense of his own stake in Myth, plus a firmer reliance on the evidences in literature and on the methods and the criteria of literary analysis. For the point at which Myth concerns the student of literature is the point at which it is brought to life again in poetry, drama or fiction.

3   From this point of view it is evident that it is not realistic to talk about Myth-in-general, as though we had a generally agreed upon definition which would apply to all the instances of Myth in art and letters. And if one makes the all-important distinction between the second-hand, merely reported or summarized mythic tale, as we find it in Bulfinch or *The Hero with a Thousand Faces,* and the mythic tale as it actually lives in poetry or drama, it appears that we lack an unmistakeable example of even *one* myth. For the myth of Oedipus is one thing in *Oedipus Rex,* and something quite different in the dramas of Seneca or Dryden. Giraudoux, clearly recognizing this point, called his play *Amphytrion 38.* One of the most striking properties of myths is that they generate new forms (like the differing children of one parent) in the imaginations of those who try to grasp them. Until some imagination, that of a poet or only a reader or auditor, is thus fecundated by a myth, the myth would seem to exist only potentially. And if we cannot lay hands on even one myth prior to its imaginative embodiments, how can we hope to pin down myth-in-general in *itself?*

4   We must, I think, adopt an extremely ascetic regimen in our

dealings with Myth. We must abandon hope of reaching any very plausible generalizations, and pay close attention to some of the many ways in which myths actually live in our literature. Of course the evidence, even when thus arbitrarily reduced, is almost endless, and very diverse. How can we rule out any of the living works which the narrative in the Christian Creed at one extreme, the lightest tale of Ovid at the other, have generated in the imaginations of artists in thousands of years? All one could hope to do is to choose rather haphazardly a few examples, as illustrations of what a literary approach to Myth might be.

5   Let us begin with a rough preliminary classification of the kinds of myths to be found in literature. The classification I wish to propose is taken from Malinowski's study of the Trobriand Islanders. He found three types of myth in that culture: Legends, which he defined as stories about the past which were believed to be true of the past, and which served to give the Islanders some significant conception of their history; Folk or Fairy Tales, told only for fun, without reference to truth, on occasions when the tribe was gathered simply for entertainment; and Religious Myths, which represented basic elements in the creed, the morals, and the social structure of that people. Malinowski based this classification on his observations of the Trobrianders, but it looks as though he had understood them by analogy with our own culture, for we can recognize the three types (or the three attitudes to Myth) in our art and literature. Some scientific anthropologists mistrust Malinowski precisely because he feels the kinship between the Trobrianders and us; but for me his value lies in his sympathy and his sense of the humane analogies between cultures. Let us claim him for the Humanities, and see how his classification may help us to understand our own heritage.

6   I think we should have to go back to Dante's Christianized Vergilian Legend of Rome to find a fully developed Historic Legend in Malinowski's sense. But the Fairy Tales, Little Red Riding Hood, the innumerable Greek tales of Arcady, of nymphs and shepherds, charming stories whose truth we never enquire into, have been common since the early Renaissance. Readers of Professor Douglas Bush's studies of literary myths will think of countless examples. It is easy to see why the Fairy Tale conception of Myth is quite at home in times of the most intransigent

rationalism. If the myth makes no claim to truth in itself, but at most serves as pleasing illustration of some moral or political concept, we may enjoy it with a clear conscience. But the romantic and post-romantic cult of Myth is not content with these neo-classic attitudes. It seeks the Religious Myth, or tries to attribute metaphysical meaning to the myths it invokes. Most of the contemporary debates about Myth assume this religious intention on the part of the lovers of Myth, and so we have many interesting attempts (like Wheelwright's in *The Burning Fountain* or Campbell's in *The Hero with a Thousand Faces*) to defend Myth as a mode of knowing.

7 But the most natural view of Myth in the modern world (by which I mean our tradition since Dante defined the "allegory of poets") has been the Fairy Tale conception. And in the hands of Paul Valéry this way with Myth has turned out to have new vitality. No one could accuse Valéry of underestimating Reason, the usual complaint of users of myths in our time. He is the champion of *l'intelligence,* the emancipated but scrupulous mind, Reason at its most ambitious and austere: the ultimate reliance of modernists, from Socrates through Da Vinci to Valéry himself. And at the same time he is the high priest of pure poetry, "the representative poet of the first half of the 20th Century," as Eliot called him. His poetry should therefore be a crucial instance of the life of Myth in literature.

8 The first line of his *Fragments du Narcisse* announces the theme of that poem:

> *Que tu brilles enfin, terme pur de ma course!*

We are to imagine Narcissus bending over the pool, addressing his own shining reflection as the pure goal, now recognized at last, of his life's course. Then come the beautiful music and the Arcadian imagery of the *Fragments:* the reeds, the water, the quiet evening, the echoes and reflections which echo and reflect the inward focus of thought and desire. The poem has the magic suggestiveness, or call it the abstract allusiveness, of the finest *symboliste* achievements, and I do not therefore attempt to analyse it in detail. Suffice it to say that as we let the poem sink in we come to see that the first line is to be understood in more senses than one. It is not only Narcissus' address to his reflection, it is the poet's address to Narcissus, who illustrates the paradoxical goal of pure reason and also of pure poetry. Thus it is also the poet's invocation of his own spirit at that creative center of life where thought and poetic intuition both have their source. When the life of reason attains its highest abstraction its pleasure lies in contemplating itself in the act of contemplation. And when poetry is pure enough—approaching the abstractness of music, freeing itself from all attachment, whether to persons, things, or transcendent moral or religious goals—it becomes its own object. The best poems in Valéry's *symboliste* tradition are based on the sad delectation of poetry's self-love.

9   It is easy to see why Narcissus is addressed by Valéry as the very image of his own goal. Narcissus aptly represents Valéry's lifelong study: the mind's creative or formative power when it turns inward in search of itself. The perversity of the mythic figure, the futility of introversion even when most subtle, is part of the poet's gloomy meaning. And yet the question of the reality of Narcissus himself never arises. The poet is not interested in exploring the mythic narrative itself. He does not present the thwarted nymphs who beseech Narcissus in vain (except in Narcissus' vague fear of their interruption) nor the fight, nor the transformation of Narcissus himself into that pretty specimen of vegetable life, the Narcissus flower, which seems so suggestive in any realistic reading of the story. The figure of Narcissus is perhaps the "inspiration" of the poem, as a metaphor or even a word may be; but its value remains strictly poetic. In all of this Valéry accepts the Fairy Tale notion of Myth, handling it lightly, almost playfully, as though for entertainment only. His use of his myth is basically a more sophisticated version of the neo-classic convention: as a language, closely analogous to the end-lessly worked-over but still iridescent words of French. Hence the deflated exactitude of the Valérian taste, the crystalline hardness one feels beneath the shimmer of his effects.

10   Valéry as *symboliste* represents a culmination of the romantic movement, its "classic" moment of complete self-awareness, as he himself would put it. He is concerned with the unique essence of poetry and its absolute independence; in his hands Myth serves poetry, not vice versa. Though he is the heir of the romantic poets he does not have a trace of their religious attitude to Myth.

This is Malinowski's description of the Religious Myth—the "myth proper" as he calls it—among the Trobrianders:

> A special class of stories, regarded as sacred, embodied in ritual, morals and social organization. . . . These stories live not by idle interest . . . but are to the natives a statement of a primeval, greater and more relevant reality, by which the present life, fates and activities of mankind are determined, the knowledge of which supplies man with the motive for ritual and moral actions, as well as with indications how to perform them.

Valéry could accept none of this without betraying his faith in the independent formative power of the mind. But Malinowski's description applies by analogy to the narrative in the Christian Creed, the basis of European social and cultural order, and of much of European art, for a thousand years. And it applies also to what romantic poets seek vaguely, and more or less in vain, in the myths which they religiously invoke.

11   Wagner's *Tristan und Isolde* is the most perfect example I know of the romantic-religious cult of Myth. Thus Wagner opposes to Valéry's rationalist tradition, in which the mythic tales are told for fun or half-playfully allegorized, the Tristan narrative, in which he finds a "primeval, greater and more relevant reality" than that of reason and common sense. Valéry in *Narcisse* appeals to the individual intellect and its strictly poetic sensibility, but Wagner, basing all on the power of his music, reaches for a primitive, unindividualized mode of awareness in his hypnotized and mob-like audience. Valéry does not take the Narcissus story seriously except as metaphor or illustration, but Wagner makes the course of the Tristan narrative the very form, or "soul" of the opera. Each crucial episode: the drinking of the love-potion, the single night of love, the final *Liebestodt:* has a ritual significance which perhaps reflects (as De Rougemont suggests) the rites of the half-forgotten cult of the Cathars. Valéry expects no result from his poem but the refined pleasures of the mind and the sensibility, but Wagner wants to effect an initiation or change of heart, and the final love-death seems to demand a momentary faith, at least, in a greater, unseen reality. We know that there is, in fact, a Wagnerian cult, which helped to nourish Hitler's attempt to create a German *Volk* by magic. One may even see in

Schopenhauer, in Nietzsche's *Birth of Tragedy,* and in Freud, with his deathwish and his boundless libido, a kind of theology for the gloomy-religious action of *Tristan.*

12   Wagner's treatment of the Tristan myth fulfills the requirements of Malinowski's definition of the Religious Myth. It also agrees with what Maritain has to say of "metaphysical myths" in his *Creative Intuition:* "The metaphysical myths are the organic signs and symbols of some faith actually lived. . . . They are forms through which a conviction of the entire soul nourishes and quickens from within the very power of creative imagination. Such myths have no force except through the faith man has in them." Wagner must, I think, have worked upon *Tristan* with the faith which Maritain describes, for the creative power of the opera is unmistakeable. But unfortunately a faith may be desperate and deluded when one sees in "myth a source of higher teaching and ultra-spiritual insights, converting it into a magic mirror that reflects the heart's desire," as Philip Rahv says of the romantic cult of Myth. Wagner's religious acceptance of the Tristan myth is possible only at too great an expense: the rejection of the contemporary world along with all the achievements of reason, from morality to science. Those who see in the cult of Myth only willful obscurantism would find much in Wagner to support their thesis. And such reflections as these must throw some doubt on the faith which Wagner himself had in the "greater and more relevant reality" symbolized by *Tristan;* we know that he changed his mind about it later in his life.

13   The fact is that we are here in that dim and treacherous realm between firm religious belief on one side and make-believe on the other. Belief and make-believe have similar fertilizing effects upon human creativity. An actor must make-believe his role very deeply and with full concentration if he is to give more than a superficial performance, yet we do not attribute religious faith to him, even when we in the audience "believe" in the character he is presenting. And in our time we are more at home with make-believe than we are with belief—or perhaps we have simply lost the sense of the distinction. Even the truths of science begin to look like partial metaphors: necessary (though sometimes contradictory) hypotheses, which guide and nourish the scientific imagination for a time, not adequate and final truth. Thus the

whole problem of the Religious Myth is on the edge of an even darker mystery: that of the nature, even the possibility, of real faith in our time.

14   That is one important reason why, in our attempt to collect the crucial evidences of poetry as it reincarnates myths, we must at this point remember Dante. For in the *Divine Comedy* we unmistakeably encounter the solidity of real belief. That poem, based on the Christian Creed, celebrates the faith and the moral, philosophic, and liturgical order which regulated Europe from the Dark Ages to the threshold of modern times: that "primeval, greater and more relevant reality" which Malinowski says the Religious Myth, the "myth proper," is supposed to embody. The *Divine Comedy* would, for this reason alone, be required reading for the study of the life of Myth in poetry.

15   Moreover the *Divine Comedy* contains all the kinds of Myth, and all the attitudes to Myth, which Malinowski describes, all in significant relation to each other and to the enlightened Reason of Dante's time. Thus Malinowski's "historic legend" is built into the framework of the poem: Virgil's legendary interpretation of Rome, which Dante combines with the historic drama of the Old Testament and places in the perspective of the Incarnation, wherein both the Hebrew and the Pagan traditions are fulfilled. This historical legend serves exactly the purpose Malinowski describes: based on the known facts of the past, which are accepted as true of the past, it gives Dante's generation its bearings in the historic sequence. What Malinowski calls Fairy Tales—the loot of Ovid and Lucan, more obscure tales from Arabic or Celtic sources —are alive again in every part of the *Comedy*. Dante takes them in a spirit akin to Valéry's: "my not-false errors" he calls them, when they inspire his imagination on the purgatorial stair. They provide much of the great poem's sensuous movement and variety; and when we look more closely we see that each has also its tropological meaning: they are visionary embodiments of the momentary experiences of the pilgrim spirit as the moral life unfolds. The ultimate meaning of the moral life, like that of the life of the race in history, is seen in the Incarnation and Sacrifice of Christ. It is that narrative, of course, which commands Dante's real belief and provides (quite apart from the question of *our* belief) the very pattern of the Religious Myth.

16   A real study of Dante's masterful way with his vast heritage of
myths would require not minutes but years; and it would require
a combination of erudition and tact which is not available. But
one may get some slight sense of his virtuosity from almost any
detail of the poem. Consider, for instance, what he does with the
Siren in the dream which forms the opening sequence of *Purga-
torio* XIX:

> *Nell'ora che non può il calor diurno intiepidar più il freddo
> della luna, vinto da terra o talor da Saturno;*
> *quando i geomanti lor maggior fortuna veggiono in oriente, inanzi
> all'alba, surger per via che poco le sta bruna:*
> *mi venne in sogno una femmina balba, negli occhi guercia e
> sopra i piè distorta, con le man monche, e di colore scialba.*
> *Io la mirava: e come il sol conforta le fredde membra che la
> notte aggrava, così lo sguardo mio le facea scorta*
> *la lingua, e poscia tutta la drizzava in poco d'ora, e lo smarrito
> volto, come amor vuol, così le colorava.*
> *Poi ch'ell'avea il parlar così disciolto, cominciava a cantar sì che
> con pena da lei avrei mio intento rivolto.*
> *"Io son," cantava, 'io son dolce Sirena, che i marinari in mezzo
> mar dismago: tanto son i piacere a sentir piena.*
> *Io volsi Ulisse del suo cammin vago col canto mio; e qual meco
> si ausa rado sen parte, sì tutto l'appago."*
> *Ancor non era sua bocca richiusa, quando una donna apparve
> santa e presta lunghesso me per far colei confusa.*
> *"O Virgilio, o Virgilio, chi è questa?" fieramente diceva; ed ei
> venia con gli occhi fitti pure in quella onesta.*
> *L'altra prendeva, e dinanzi l'apria fendendo i drappi, e mostra-
> vami il ventre; quel mi svegliò col puzzo che n'uscia.*

(At the hour when the heat of the day can no longer warm the
cold of the moon, being overcome by earth or perhaps by Saturn;
When the geomancers see their *fortuna major* in the east, just
before dawn, rising along a path which will not be dark for
long:
There came to me in dream a stuttering woman, squint-eyed,
twisted on her feet, with stunted hands, yellow in color. I gazed
upon her, and as the sun comforts cold limbs which night weighs
down, so my gaze made ready
Her tongue, and then in a short time set her all straight, and her
pale face, just as love wills, it colored.
As soon as her speech was loosened she began to sing, so that with

difficulty I should have turned my attention from her. "I am,"
she sang, "I am that Sweet Siren who bemuses sailors in the
midst of the sea, so full I am of pleasure for them to feel.
"I turned Ulysses from his wandering way to this my song; whoever risks himself with me rarely departs, I satiate him so fully."
Her mouth was hardly closed when there appeared beside me a
woman, alert and holy, to make that one confused.
"O Virgil, Virgil, who is this?" she was saying proudly, and he
was coming, with his eyes fixed only on that honest one. He
seized the other and opened her in front, ripping the clothes, and
showed me the belly, which waked me with the stench that issued
from it.)

17   Dante's treatment of the Siren in this passage is similar in
several ways to Valéry's treatment of Narcissus: it is an exampl
of Dante's "allegory of poets." Thus, like Valéry, he is more i
terested in the mythic figure than in her whole traditional sto
and he uses her to get the sensuous immediacy and the sub
complexity of poetry. But she seems to have more reality t
Valéry's conventional figure: if not a metaphysical entity in
own right, she is at least an ineluctable trope, the embodime
one eternally recurrent human experience. That is becaus
Siren has her place in a vaster vision which includes the p
tives of ethics and faith. Valéry's Narcissus, on the other h
presented as "pure" poetry.

18   Dante establishes the being and the meanings of his S
means of the context in which she appears: a certain poi
Pilgrim's spiritual growth, at a certain place on the M
and toward the end of the second night of the purgato
ney. By showing us the psyche in whose imagination
appears, Dante includes several dimensions of mythop
Valéry omits. We *see* the dreamer see his mythic encl
image which at first says nothing to him. We then s
lieve" the image, and focus his attention and his u
sire upon it. Under that warmth and light the a
"colored as love wills," reveals some of the mea
held only potentially: in short, she is "brought to
night in which she appears also helps us to unders
three nights of the purgatorial journey the P
neither upon his direct perception of the world,

his reason. In the solitude and passivity of sleep he knows the call of many forms of love, including that irrational brute weight of desire which pulls, like gravitation, toward the bottom of the universe. In this passage the nocturnal chill that weighs limbs down presents this pull: the occasion for the Siren's appearance. The direction of love's movement thus indicated (night against reason and the day, the ambiguity of love and death) reminds one strongly of the motivation and the nocturnal imagery of *Tristan*. Dante may have seen at this point the object of Wagner's desperate faith.

19 But this is the *second* night of the purgatorial journey, and the Pilgrim has by this time acquired a certain moral awareness. After the Siren is warmed into beauty and song, at the very moment of pleasurable yielding, Virgil appears by that Grace which hovers over this region, and reveals the Siren's deathly aspect once more. Virgil represents reason and the accumulated wisdom of experience in the real world, and by this time his voice and presence are in a sense *within* the Pilgrim's spirit. In the dream he plays a role like that of the orthodox Freudian "superego," representative of moral truth. At this point in his development the Pilgrim (and the reader) can understand the mythic Siren from a moral point of view, and that suffices for escape.

But because of the sturdy realism which underlies the whole conception of the *Divine Comedy* the Siren, for all her moral meaning, is not reduced to the status of a moral allegory only. She retains some sort of being in her own right; she does not forfeit her status as one of the amoral figures of Myth, and that is characteristic of Dante's way with myths. Their visionary being is established first, their possible philosophical meaning for the Pilgrim, second; and when they disappear we do not feel that they have been rationalized out of all existence. The Siren first looks strange and evil, then she appears as infinitely attractive, then as dismaying and disgusting, but in all of these metamorphoses we never lose the sense that she was somehow *there;* and er power and mystery remain when we leave her.

If Dante can handle the figures of Myth with such subtle and exible realism—that is, with respect both for the reality of the aagination in which they appear, and for the different reality the figures themselves—it is because he understands them, not

in conceptual terms, but by analogy with the Incarnation. The process whereby a myth is brought to life in a human imagination corresponds to that by which Christ lives again in the spirits of the faithful, through belief, concentration, love, and an imitative movement of spirit. The mythic forms which tempt the human spirit may in Dante's scheme be childish or deceptive. But their meaning for us, and the process whereby we reincarnate them in our own beings, are to be understood by analogy with the human figure, and the imitation, of Christ. Even Hell, where Dante endows so many evil forms with his own life and love, was made by Divine Power, Highest Wisdom and Primal Love. It is because Dante believes so completely in the reality of this basic Analogue that he can both share in the lives of many kinds of myths, and yet also pass beyond them, to consider their meaning in other terms and in relation to each other. His belief in the "primeval, greater and more relevant reality" of the Christian Narrative gives him a key to the heritage of Myth, makes him a master (probably *the* master) of the mythic modes of understanding.

21   The view of the world which Dante inherited, formed by the converging and age-long labors of Hebrew and Greek, has dissolved long since. His *modus vivendi* between Reason and Mythopoeia is no longer accessible to us. But if we are to consider the life of Myth in the poetry of our tradition, I do not see how we can continue to neglect the vast lore in the *Divine Comedy*.

22   One can sympathize with those numerous writers who use "Myth" to mean only wishful thinking or Machiavellian obscurantism. It would be nice to get rid of the term and its puzzles so simply. But that recourse is not available to those who stubbornly continue to be interested in Poetry, or indeed in any form of the Humanities. We cannot get rid of "Myth," but we can beware of it. We can remember some of the countless ways in which myths live in our literature from Homer to Faulkner. And we can study some of the forms this life takes with the respect for the unique individuality of play or poem which the masters of literature have taught us.

sweeney among the nightingales

T. S. ELIOT

ὤμοι, πέπληγμαι καιρίαν πληγὴν ἔσω.

Apeneck Sweeney spreads his knees
Letting his arms hang down to laugh,
The zebra stripes along his jaw
Swelling to maculate giraffe.

The circles of the stormy moon   5
Slide westward toward the River Plate,
Death and the Raven drift above
And Sweeney guards the hornèd gate.

Gloomy Orion and the Dog   9
Are veiled; and hushed the shrunken seas;
The person in the Spanish cape
Tries to sit on Sweeney's knees

Slips and pulls the table cloth   13
Overturns a coffee-cup,
Reorganised upon the floor
She yawns and draws a stocking up;

Reprinted with permission of Harcourt, Brace & World, Inc., from *Collected Poems 1909–1962*, by T. S. Eliot. Copyright 1936 by Harcourt, Brace & World, Inc.; © 1963, 1964 by T. S. Eliot.

The silent man in mocha brown   17
Sprawls at the window-sill and gapes;
The waiter brings in oranges
Bananas figs and hothouse grapes;

The silent vertebrate in brown   21
Contracts and concentrates, withdraws;
Rachel *née* Rabinovitch
Tears at the grapes with murderous paws;

She and the lady in the cape   25
Are suspect, thought to be in league;
Therefore the man with heavy eyes
Declines the gambit, shows fatigue,

Leaves the room and reappears   29
Outside the window, leaning in,
Branches of wistaria
Circumscribe a golden grin;

The host with someone indistinct   33
Converses at the door apart,
The nightingales are singing near
The Convent of the Sacred Heart,

And sang within the bloody wood   37
When Agamemnon cried aloud,
And let their liquid siftings fall
To stain the stiff dishonoured shroud.

the horse dealer's daughter

D. H. LAWRENCE

"Well, Mabel, and what are you going to do with yourself?" asked Joe, with foolish flippancy. He felt quite safe himself. Without listening for an answer, he turned aside, worked a grain of tobacco to the tip of his tongue, and spat it out. He did not care about anything, since he felt safe himself.

The three brothers and the sister sat round the desolate breakfast table, attempting some sort of desultory consultation. The morning's post had given the final tap to the family fortune, and all was over. The dreary dining-room itself, with its heavy mahogany furniture, looked as if it were waiting to be done away with.

But the consultation amounted to nothing. There was a strange air of ineffectuality about the three men, as they sprawled at table, smoking and reflecting vaguely on their own condition. The girl was alone, a rather short, sullen-looking young woman of twenty-seven. She did not share the same life as her brothers. She would have been good-looking, save for the impassive fixity of her face, "bull-dog," as her brothers called it.

There was a confused tramping of horses' feet outside. The three men all sprawled round in their chairs to watch. Beyond the dark holly-bushes that separated the strip of lawn from the

Reprinted with permission of The Viking Press, Inc., from *The Complete Short Stories of D. H. Lawrence*, Volume II. Copyright 1922 by Thomas B. Seltzer, Inc.; renewed 1950 by Freida Lawrence.

highroad, they could see a cavalcade of shire horses swinging out of their own yard, being taken for exercise. This was the last time. These were the last horses that would go through their hands. The young men watched with critical, callous look. They were all frightened at the collapse of their lives, and the sense of disaster in which they were involved left them no inner freedom.

Yet they were three fine, well-set fellows enough. Joe, the eldest, was a man of thirty-three, broad and handsome in a hot, flushed way. His face was red, he twisted his black moustache over a thick finger, his eyes were shallow and restless. He had a sensual way of uncovering his teeth when he laughed, and his bearing was stupid. Now he watched the horses with a glazed look of helplessness in his eyes, a certain stupor of downfall.

The great draught-horses swung past. They were tied head to tail, four of them, and they heaved along to where a lane branched off from the highroad, planting their great hoofs floutingly in the fine black mud, swinging their great rounded haunches sumptuously, and trotting a few sudden steps as they were led into the lane, round the corner. Every movement showed a massive, slumbrous strength, and a stupidity which held them in subjection. The groom at the head looked back, jerking the leading rope. And the cavalcade moved out of sight up the lane, the tail of the last horse bobbed up tight and stiff, held out taut from the swinging great haunches as they rocked behind the hedges in a motion like sleep.

Joe watched with glazed hopeless eyes. The horses were almost like his own body to him. He felt he was done for now. Luckily he was engaged to a woman as old as himself, and therefore her father, who was steward of a neighbouring estate, would provide him with a job. He would marry and go into harness. His life was over, he would be a subject animal now.

He turned uneasily aside, the retreating steps of the horses echoing in his ears. Then, with foolish restlessness, he reached for the scraps of bacon-rind from the plates, and making a faint whistling sound, flung them to the terrier that lay against the fender. He watched the dog swallow them, and waited till the creature looked into his eyes. Then a faint grin came on his face, and in a high, foolish voice he said:

"You won't get much more bacon, shall you, you little bitch?"

The dog faintly and dismally wagged its tail, then lowered its haunches, circled round, and lay down again.

There was another helpless silence at the table. Joe sprawled uneasily in his seat, not willing to go till the family conclave was dissolved. Fred Henry, the second brother, was erect, clean-limbed, alert. He had watched the passing of the horses with more sang-froid. If he was an animal, like Joe, he was an animal which controls, not one which is controlled. He was master of any horse, and he carried himself with a well-tempered air of mastery. But he was not master of the situations of life. He pushed his coarse brown moustache upwards, off his lip, and glanced irritably at his sister, who sat impassive and inscrutable.

"You'll go and stop with Lucy for a bit, shan't you?" he asked. The girl did not answer.

"I don't see what else you can do," persisted Fred Henry.

"Go as a skivvy," Joe interpolated laconically.

The girl did not move a muscle.

"If I was her, I should go in for training for a nurse," said Malcolm, the youngest of them all. He was the baby of the family, a young man of twenty-two, with a fresh, jaunty *museau*.

But Mabel did not take any notice of him. They had talked at her and round her for so many years, that she hardly heard them at all.

The marble clock on the mantelpiece softly chimed the half-hour, the dog rose uneasily from the hearthrug and looked at the party at the breakfast table. But still they sat on in ineffectual conclave.

"Oh, all right," said Joe suddenly, apropos of nothing. "I'll get a move on."

He pushed back his chair, straddled his knees with a downward jerk, to get them free, in horsey fashion, and went to the fire. Still he did not go out of the room; he was curious to know what the others would do or say. He began to charge his pipe, looking down at the dog and saying, in a high, affected voice:

"Going wi' me? Going wi' me are ter? Tha'rt goin' further than tha counts on just now, dost hear?"

The dog faintly wagged its tail, the man stuck out his jaw and covered his pipe with his hands, and puffed intently, losing himself in the tobacco, looking down all the while at the dog with an absent brown eye. The dog looked up at him in mournful distrust. Joe stood with his knees stuck out, in real horsey fashion.

"Have you had a letter from Lucy?" Fred Henry asked of his sister.

"Last week," came the neutral reply.

"And what does she say?"

There was no answer.

"Does she *ask* you to go and stop there?" persisted Fred Henry.

"She says I can if I like."

"Well, then, you'd better. Tell her you'll come on Monday."

This was received in silence.

"That's what you'll do then, is it?" said Fred Henry, in some exasperation.

But she made no answer. There was a silence of futility and irritation in the room. Malcolm grinned fatuously.

"You'll have to make up your mind between now and next Wednesday," said Joe loudly, "or else find yourself lodgings on the kerbstone."

The face of the young woman darkened, but she sat on immutable.

"Here's Jack Fergusson!" exclaimed Malcolm, who was looking aimlessly out of the window.

"Where?" exclaimed Joe, loudly.

"Just gone past."

"Coming in?"

Malcolm craned his neck to see the gate.

"Yes," he said.

There was a silence. Mabel sat on like one condemned, at the head of the table. Then a whistle was heard from the kitchen. The dog got up and barked sharply. Joe opened the door and shouted:

"Come on."

After a moment a young man entered. He was muffled up in overcoat and a purple woollen scarf, and his tweed cap, which he did not remove, was pulled down on his head. He was of medium height, his face was rather long and pale, his eyes looked tired.

"Hello, Jack, Well, Jack!" exclaimed Malcolm and Joe. Fred Henry merely said, "Jack."

"What's doing?" asked the newcomer, evidently addressing Fred Henry.

"Same. We've got to be out by Wednesday. Got a cold?"

"I have—got it bad, too."

"Why don't you stop in?"

"*Me* stop in? When I can't stand on my legs, perhaps I shall have a chance." The young man spoke huskily. He had a slight Scotch accent.

"It's a knock-out, isn't it," said Joe, boisterously, "if a doctor goes round croaking with a cold. Looks bad for the patients, doesn't it?"

The young doctor looked at him slowly.

"Anything the matter with *you*, then?" he asked sarcastically.

"Not as I know of. Damn your eyes, I hope not. Why?"

"I thought you were very concerned about the patients, wondered if you might be one yourself."

"Damn it, no, I've never been patient to no flaming doctor, and hope I never shall be," returned Joe.

At this point Mabel rose from the table, and they all seemed to become aware of her existence. She began putting the dishes together. The young doctor looked at her, but did not address her. He had not greeted her. She went out of the room with the tray, her face impassive and unchanged.

"When are you off then, all of you?" asked the doctor.

"I'm catching the eleven-forty," replied Malcolm. "Are you goin' down wi' th' trap, Joe?"

"Yes, I've told you I'm going down wi' th' trap, haven't I?"

"We'd better be getting her in then. So long, Jack, if I don't see you before I go," said Malcolm, shaking hands.

He went out, followed by Joe, who seemed to have his tail between his legs.

"Well, this is the devil's own," exclaimed the doctor, when he was left alone with Fred Henry. "Going before Wednesday, are you?"

"That's the orders," replied the other.

"Where, to Northampton?"

"That's it."

"The devil!" exclaimed Fergusson, with quiet chagrin.

And there was silence between the two.

"All settled up, are you?" asked Fergusson.

"About."

There was another pause.

"Well, I shall miss yer, Freddy, boy," said the young doctor.

"And I shall miss thee, Jack," returned the other.

"Miss you like hell," mused the doctor.

Fred Henry turned aside. There was nothing to say. Mabel came in again, to finish clearing the table.

"What are *you* going to do, then, Miss Pervin?" asked Fergusson. "Going to your sister's, are you?"

Mabel looked at him with her steady, dangerous eyes, that always made him uncomfortable, unsettling his superficial ease.

"No," she said.

"Well, what in the name of fortune are *you* going to do? Say what you mean to do," cried Fred Henry, with futile intensity.

But she only averted her head, and continued her work. She folded the white table-cloth, and put on the chenille cloth.

"The sulkiest bitch that ever trod!" muttered her brother.

But she finished her task with perfectly impassive face, the young doctor watching her interestedly all the while. Then she went out.

Fred Henry stared after her, clenching his lips, his blue eyes fixing in sharp antagonism, as he made a grimace of sour exasperation.

"You could bray her into bits, and that's all you'd get out of her," he said in a small, narrowed tone.

The doctor smiled faintly.

"What's she *going* to do, then?" he asked.

"Strike me if *I* know!" returned the other.

There was a pause. Then the doctor stirred.

"I'll be seeing you to-night, shall I?" he said to his friend.

"Ay—where's it to be? Are we going over to Jessdale?"

"I don't know. I've got such a cold on me. I'll come round to the Moon and Stars, anyway."

"Let Lizzie and May miss their night for once, eh?"

"That's it—if I feel as I do now."

"All's one—"

The two young men went through the passage and down to the back door together. The house was large, but it was servantless now, and desolate. At the back was a small bricked house-yard, and beyond that a big square, gravelled fine and red, and having stables on two sides. Sloping, dank, winter-dark fields stretched away on the open sides.

But the stables were empty. Joseph Pervin, the father of the family, had been a man of no education, who had become a fairly large horse dealer. The stables had been full of horses, there was a great turmoil and come-and-go of horses and of dealers and grooms. Then the kitchen was full of servants. But of late things had declined. The old man had married a second time, to retrieve his fortunes. Now he was dead and everything was gone to the dogs, there was nothing but debt and threatening.

For months, Mabel had been servantless in the big house, keeping the home together in penury for her ineffectual brothers. She had kept house for ten years. But previously it was with unstinted means. Then, however brutal and coarse everything was, the sense of money had kept her proud, confident. The men might be foul-mouthed, the women in the kitchen might have bad reputations, her brothers might have illegitimate children. But so long as there was money, the girl felt herself established, and brutally proud, reserved.

No company came to the house, save dealers and coarse men. Mabel had no associates of her own sex, after her sister went away. But she did not mind. She went regularly to church, she attended to her father. And she lived in the memory of her mother, who had died when she was fourteen, and whom she had loved. She had loved her father, too, in a different way, depending upon him, and feeling secure in him, until at the age of fifty-four he married again. And then she had set hard against him. Now he had died and left them all hopelessly in debt.

She had suffered badly during the period of poverty. Nothing, however, could shake the curious sullen, animal pride that dominated each member of the family. Now, for Mabel, the end had come. Still she would not cast about her. She would follow her own way just the same. She would always hold the keys of her own situation. Mindless and persistent, she endured from day to day. Why should she think? Why should she answer anybody? It was enough that this was the end, and there was no way out. She need not pass any more darkly along the main street of the small town, avoiding every eye. She need not demean herself any more, going into the shops and buying the cheapest food. This was at an end. She thought of nobody, not even of herself. Mindless and persistent, she seemed in a sort of ecstasy to be coming nearer to her fulfillment, her own glorification, approaching her dead mother, who was glorified.

In the afternoon she took a little bag, with shears and sponge and a small scrubbing brush, and went out. It was a grey, wintry day, with saddened, dark green fields and an atmosphere blackened by the smoke of foundries not far off. She went quickly, darkly along the causeway, heeding nobody, through the town to the churchyard.

There she always felt secure, as if no one could see her, although as a matter of fact she was exposed to the stare of every one who passed along under the churchyard wall. Nevertheless, once under the shadow of the great looming church, among the graves, she felt immune from the world, reserved within the thick churchyard wall as in another country.

Carefully she clipped the grass from the grave, and arranged the pinky white, small chrysanthemums in the tin cross. When this was done, she took an empty jar from a neighbouring grave, brought water, and carefully, most scrupulously sponged the marble head-stone and the coping-stone.

It gave her sincere satisfaction to do this. She felt in immediate contact with the world of her mother. She took minute pains, went through the park in a state bordering on pure happiness, as if in performing this task she came into a subtle, intimate connection with her mother. For the life she followed here in the world was far less real than the world of death she inherited from her mother.

The doctor's house was just by the church. Fergusson, being a mere hired assistant, was slave to the countryside. As he hurried now to attend to the out-patients in the surgery, glancing across the graveyard with his quick eye, he saw the girl at her task at the grave. She seemed so intent and remote, it was like looking into another world. Some mystical element was touched in him. He slowed down as he walked, watching her as if spell-bound.

She lifted her eyes, feeling him looking. Their eyes met. And each looked away again at once, each feeling in some way, found out by the other. He lifted his cap and passed on down the road. There remained distinct in his consciousness, like a vision, the memory of her face, lifted from the tombstone in the churchyard, and looking at him with slow, large, portentous eyes. It was portentous, her face. It seemed to mesmerize him. There was a heavy power in her eyes which laid hold of his whole being, as if he had drunk some powerful drug. He had been feeling weak and done before. Now the life came back into him, he felt delivered from his own fretted, daily self.

He finished his duties at the surgery as quickly as might be, hastily filling up the bottle of the waiting people with cheap drugs. Then, in perpetual haste, he set off again to visit several cases in another part of his round, before teatime. At all times he preferred to walk if he could, but particularly when he was not well. He fancied the motion restored him.

The afternoon was falling. It was grey, deadened, and wintry, with a slow, moist, heavy coldness sinking in and deadening all the faculties. But why should he think or notice? He hastily climbed the hill and turned across the dark green fields, following the black cinder-track. In the distance, across a shallow dip in the country, the small town was clustered like smouldering ash, a tower, a spire, a heap of low, raw, extinct houses. And on the nearest fringe of the town, sloping into the dip, was Oldmeadow, the Pervins' house. He could see the stables and the outbuildings distinctly, as they lay towards him on the slope. Well, he would not go there many more times! Another resource would be lost to him, another place gone: the only company he cared for in the alien, ugly little town he was losing. Nothing but work, drudgery, constant hastening from dwelling to dwelling among the colliers and the ironworkers. It wore him out, but at the same time he had a craving for it. It was a stimulant to him to be in the homes of the working people, moving as it were through the innermost body of their life. His nerves were excited and gratified. He could come so near, into the very lives of the rough, inarticulate, powerfully emotional men and women. He grumbled, he said he hated the hellish hole. But as a matter of fact it excited him, the contact with the rough, strongly-feeling people was a stimulant applied direct to his nerves.

Below Oldmeadow, in the green, shallow, soddened hollow of

fields, lay a square, deep pond. Roving across the landscape, the doctor's quick eye detected a figure in black passing through the gate of the field, down towards the pond. He looked again. It would be Mabel Pervin. His mind suddenly became alive and attentive.

Why was she going down there? He pulled up on the path on the slope above, and stood staring. He could just make sure of the small black figure moving in the hollow of the failing day. He seemed to see her in the midst of such obscurity, that he was like a clairvoyant, seeing rather with the mind's eye than with ordinary sight. Yet he could see her positively enough, whilst he kept his eye attentive. He felt, if he looked away from her, in the thick, ugly falling dusk, he would lose her altogether.

He followed her minutely as she moved, direct and intent, like something transmitted rather than stirring in voluntary activity, straight down the field towards the pond. There she stood on the bank for a moment. She never raised her head. Then she waded slowly into the water.

He stood motionless as the small black figure walked slowly and deliberately towards the centre of the pond, very slowly, gradually moving deeper into the motionless water, and still moving forward as the water got up to her breast. Then he could see her no more in the dusk of the dead afternoon.

"There!" he exclaimed. "Would you believe it?"

And he hastened straight down, running over the wet, soddened fields, pushing through the hedges, down into the depression of callous wintry obscurity. It took him several minutes to come to the pond. He stood on the bank, breathing heavily. He could see nothing. His eyes seemed to penetrate the dead water. Yes, perhaps that was the dark shadow of her black clothing beneath the surface of the water.

He slowly ventured into the pond. The bottom was deep, soft clay, he sank in, and the water clasped dead cold round his legs. As he stirred he could smell the cold, rotten clay that fouled up into the water. It was objectionable in his lungs. Still, repelled and yet not heeding, he moved deeper into the pond. The cold water rose over his thighs, over his loins, upon his abdomen. The lower part of his body was all sunk in the hideous cold element. And the bottom was so deeply soft and uncertain, he was afraid of pitching with his mouth underneath. He could not swim, and was afraid.

He crouched a little, spreading his hands under the water and moving them round, trying to feel for her. The dead coid pond swayed upon his chest. He moved again, a little deeper, and again, with his hands underneath, he felt all around under the water. And he touched her clothing. But it evaded his fingers. He made a desperate effort to grasp it.

And so doing he lost his balance and went under, horribly, suffocating in the foul earthy water, struggling madly for a few moments. At last, after what seemed an eternity, he got his footing, rose again into the air and looked around. He gasped, and knew he was in the world. Then he looked at the water. She had risen near him. He grasped her clothing, and drawing nearer, turned to take his way to land again.

He went very slowly, carefully, absorbed in the slow progress. He rose higher, climbing out of the pond. The water was now only about his legs: he was thankful, full of relief to be out of the clutches of the pond. He lifted her and staggered on to the bank, out of the horror of wet, grey clay.

He had her down on the bank. She was quite unconscious and running with water. He made the water come from her mouth, he worked to restore her. He did not have to work very long before he could feel the breathing begin again in her; she was breathing naturally. He worked a little longer. He could feel her live beneath his hands; she was coming back. He wiped her face, wrapped her in his overcoat, looked round into the dim, dark grey world, then lifted her and staggered down the bank and across the fields.

It seemed an unthinkably long way, and his burden so heavy he felt he would never get to the house. But at last he was in the stable-yard, and then in the house-yard. He opened the door and went into the house. In the kitchen he laid her down on the hearthrug, and called. The house was empty. But the fire was burning in the grate.

Then again he kneeled to attend to her. She was breathing regularly, her eyes were wide open and as if conscious, but there seemed something missing in her look. She was conscious in herself, but unconscious of her surroundings.

He ran upstairs, took blankets from a bed, and put them before the fire to warm. Then he removed her saturated, earthy-smelling clothing, rubbed her dry with a towel, and wrapped her naked in the blankets. Then he went into the dining-room, to look for spirits. There was a little whisky. He drank a gulp himself, and put some into her mouth.

The effect was instantaneous. She looked full into his face, as if she had been seeing him for some time, and yet had only just become conscious of him.

"Dr. Fergusson?" she said.

"What?" he answered.

He was divesting himself of his coat, intending to find some dry clothing upstairs. He could not bear the smell of the dead, clayey water, and he was mortally afraid for his own health.

"What did I do?" she asked.

"Walked into the pond," he replied. He had begun to shudder like one sick, and could hardly attend to her. Her eyes remained full on him, he seemed to be going dark in his mind, looking back at her helplessly. The shuddering became quieter in him, his life came back in him, dark and unknowing, but strong again.

"Was I out of my mind?" she asked, while her eyes were fixed on him all the time.

"Maybe, for the moment," he replied. He felt quiet, because his strength had come back. The strange fretful strain had left him.

"Am I out of my mind now?" she asked.

"Are you?" he reflected a moment. "No," he answered truthfully, "I don't see that you are." He turned his face aside. He was afraid now, because he felt dazed, and felt dimly that her power was stronger than his, in this issue. And she continued to look at him fixedly all the time. "Can you tell me where I shall find some dry things to put on?" he asked.

"Did you dive into the pond for me?" she asked.

"No," he answered. "I walked in. But I went in overhead as well."

There was silence for a moment. He hesitated. He very much wanted to go upstairs to get into dry clothing. But there was another desire in him. And she seemed to hold him. His will seemed to have gone to sleep, and left him, standing there slack before her. But he felt warm inside himself. He did not shudder at all, though his clothes were sodden on him.

"Why did you?" she asked.

"Because I didn't want you to do such a foolish thing," he said.

"It wasn't foolish," she said, still gazing at him as she lay on the floor, with a sofa cushion under her head. "It was the right thing to do. *I* knew best, then."

"I'll go and shift these wet things," he said. But still he had not the power to move out of her presence, until she sent him. It was as if she had the life of his body in her hands, and he could not extricate himself. Or perhaps he did not want to.

Suddenly she sat up. Then she became aware of her own immediate condition. She felt the blankets about her, she knew her own limbs. For a moment it seemed as if her reason were going. She looked round, with wild eye, as if seeking something. He stood still with fear. She saw her clothing lying scattered.

"Who undressed me?" she asked, her eyes resting full and inevitable on his face.

"I did," he replied, "to bring you round."

For some moments she sat and gazed at him awfully, her lips parted.

"Do you love me, then?" she asked.

He only stood and stared at her, fascinated. His soul seemed to melt.

She shuffled forward on her knees, and put her arms round him, round his legs, as he stood there, pressing her breasts against his knees and thighs, clutching him with strange, convulsive certainty, pressing his thighs against her, drawing him to her face, her throat, as she looked up at him with flaring, humble eyes of transfiguration, triumphant in first possession.

"You love me," she murmured, in strange transport, yearning and triumphant and confident. "You love me. I know you love me, I know."

And she was passionately kissing his knees, through the wet clothing, passionately and indiscriminately kissing his knees, his legs, as if unaware of everything.

He looked down at the tangled wet hair, the wild, bare, animal shoulders. He was amazed, bewildered, and afraid. He had never thought of loving her. He had never wanted to love her.

When he rescued her and restored her, he was a doctor, and she was a patient. He had had no single personal thought of her. Nay, this introduction of the personal element was very distasteful to him, a violation of his professional honour. It was horrible to have her there embracing his knees. It was horrible. He revolted from it, violently. And yet—and yet—he had not the power to break away.

She looked at him again, with the same supplication of powerful love, and that same transcendent, frightening light of triumph. In view of the delicate flame which seemed to come from her face like a light, he was powerless. And yet he had never intended to love her. He had never intended. And something stubborn in him could not give way.

"You love me," she repeated, in a murmur of deep rhapsodic assurance. "You love me."

Her hands were drawing him, drawing him down to her. He was afraid, even a little horrified. For he had, really, no intention of loving her. Yet her hands were drawing him towards her. He put out his hand quickly to steady himself, and grasped her bare shoulder. A flame seemed to burn the hand that grasped her soft shoulder. He had no intention of loving her: his whole will was against his yielding. It was horrible. And yet wonderful was the touch of her shoulders, beautiful the shining of her face. Was she perhaps mad? He had a horror of yielding to her. Yet something in him ached also.

He had been staring away at the door, away from her. But his hand remained on her shoulder. She had gone suddenly very still. He looked down at her. Her eyes were now wide with fear, with doubt, the light was dying from her face, a shadow of terrible greyness was returning. He could not bear the touch of her eyes' question upon him, and the look of death behind the question.

With an inward groan he gave way, and let his heart yield towards her. A sudden gentle smile came on his face. And her eyes, which never left his face, slowly, slowly filled with tears. He watched the strange water rise in her eyes, like some slow fountain coming up. And his heart seemed to burn and melt away in his breast.

He could not bear to look at her any more. He dropped on his knees, caught her head with his arms and pressed her face against his throat. She was very still. His heart, which seemed to have broken, was burning with a kind of agony in his breast. And he felt her slow, hot tears wetting his throat. But he could not move.

He felt the hot tears wet his neck and the hollows of his neck, and he remained motionless, suspended through one of man's eternities. Only now it had become indispensable to him to have her face pressed close to him, he could never let her go again. He could never let her head go away from the close clutch of his arm. He wanted to remain like that for ever, with his heart hurting him in a pain that was also life to him. Without knowing, he was looking down on her damp, soft brown hair.

Then, as it were suddenly, he smelt the horrid stagnant smell of that water. And at the same moment she drew away from him and looked at him. Her eyes were wistful and unfathomable. He was afraid of them, and he fell to kissing her, not knowing what he was doing. He wanted her eyes not to have that terrible, wistful, unfathomable look.

When she turned her face to him again, a faint delicate flush was glowing, and there was again dawning that terrible shining of joy in her eyes, which really terrified him, and yet which he now wanted to see, because he feared the look of doubt still more.

"You love me?" she said, rather faltering.

"Yes." The word cost him a painful effort. Not because it wasn't true. But because it was too newly true, the *saying* seemed to tear open again his newly-torn heart. And he hardly wanted it to be true, even now.

She lifted her face to him, and he bent forward and kissed her on the mouth, gently, with the one kiss that is an eternal pledge. And as he kissed her his heart strained again in his breast. He never intended to love her. But now it was over. He had crossed over the gulf to her, and all that he had left behind had shrivelled and become void.

After the kiss, her eyes again slowly filled with tears. She sat still, away from him, with her face drooped aside, and her hands folded in her lap. The tears fell very slowly. There was complete silence. He too sat there motionless and silent on the hearthrug. The strange pain of his heart that was broken seemed to consume him. That he should love her? That this was love! That he should be ripped open in this way! Him, a doctor! How they would all jeer if they knew! It was agony to him to think they might know.

In the curious naked pain of the thought he looked again to her. She was sitting there drooped into a muse. He saw a tear fall, and his heart flared hot. He saw for the first time that one of her shoulders was quite uncovered, one arm bare, he could see one of her small breasts; dimly, because it had become almost dark in the room.

"Why are you crying?" he asked, in an altered voice.

She looked up at him, and behind her tears the consciousness of her situation for the first time brought a dark look of shame to her eyes.

"I'm not crying, really," she said, watching him half frightened.

He reached his hand, and softly closed it on her bare arm.

"I love you! I love you!" he said in a soft, low vibrating voice, unlike himself.

She shrank, and dropped her head. The soft, penetrating grip of his hand on her arm distressed her. She looked up at him.

"I want to go," she said. "I want to go and get you some dry things."

"Why?" he said. "I'm all right."

"But I want to go," she said. "And I want you to change your things."

He released her arm, and she wrapped herself in the blanket, looking at him rather frightened. And still she did not rise.

"Kiss me," she said wistfully.

He kissed her, but briefly, half in anger.

Then, after a second, she rose nervously, all mixed up in the blanket. He watched her in her confusion, as she tried to extricate herself and wrap herself up so that she could walk. He watched her relentlessly, as she knew. And as she went, the blanket trailing, and as he saw a glimpse of her feet and her white leg, he tried to remember her as she was when he had wrapped her in the blanket. But then he didn't want to remember, because she had been nothing to him then, and his nature revolted from remembering her as she was when she was nothing to him.

A tumbling, muffled noise from within the dark house startled him. Then he heard her voice:—"There are clothes." He rose and went to the foot of the stairs, and gathered up the garments she had thrown down. Then he came back to the fire, to rub himself down and dress. He grinned at his own appearance when he had finished.

The fire was sinking, so he put on coal. The house was now quite dark, save for the light of a street-lamp that shone in faintly from beyond the holly trees. He lit the gas with matches he found on the mantelpiece. Then he emptied the pockets of his own clothes, and threw all his wet things in a heap into the scullery. After which he gathered up her sodden clothes, gently, and put them in a separate heap on the copper-top in the scullery.

It was six o'clock on the clock. His own watch had stopped. He ought to go back to the surgery. He waited, and still she did not come down. So he went to the foot of the stairs and called:

"I shall have to go."

Almost immediately he heard her coming down. She had on her best dress of black voile, and her hair was tidy, but still damp. She looked at him—and in spite of herself, smiled.

"I don't like you in those clothes," she said.

"Do I look a sight?" he answered.

They were shy of one another.

"I'll make you some tea," she said.

"No, I must go."

"Must you?" And she looked at him again with the wide, strained, doubtful eyes. And again, from the pain of his breast, he knew how he loved her. He went and bent to kiss her, gently, passionately, with his heart's painful kiss.

"And my hair smells so horrible," she murmured in distraction. "And I'm so awful. I'm so awful! Oh, no, I'm too awful." And she broke into bitter, heartbroken sobbing. "You can't want to love me, I'm horrible."

"Don't be silly, don't be silly," he said, trying to comfort her, kissing her, holding her in his arms. "I want you. I want to marry you, we're going to be married, quickly, quickly—tomorrow if I can."

But she only sobbed terribly, and cried:

"I feel awful. I feel awful. I feel I'm horrible to you."

"No, I want you, I want you," was all he answered blindly, with that terrible intonation which frightened her almost more than her horror lest he should *not* want her.

purgatory

WILLIAM BUTLER YEATS

PERSONS IN THE PLAY

A Boy.
An Old Man.

scene: A ruined house and a bare tree in the
background.

Boy.   Half-door, hall door,
   Hither and thither day and night,
   Hill or hollow, shouldering this pack,
   Hearing you talk.
Old Man.   Study that house.
   I think about its jokes and stories;
   I try to remember what the butler
   Said to a drunken gamekeeper
   In mid-October, but I cannot.
   If I cannot, none living can.
   Where are the jokes and stories of a house,
   Its threshold gone to patch a pig-sty?
Boy.   So you have come this path before?

Reprinted with permission of The Macmillan Company, from *The Collected Plays of W. B. Yeats,* by William Butler Yeats. Copyright 1934, 1952
by The Macmillan Company.

Old Man.   The moonlight falls upon the path,
The shadow of a cloud upon the house,
And that's symbolical; study that tree,
What is it like?
Boy.   A silly old man.
Old Man.   It's like—no matter what it's like.
I saw it a year ago stripped bare as now,
So I chose a better trade.
I saw it fifty years ago
Before the thunderbolt had riven it,
Green leaves, ripe leaves, leaves thick as butter,
Fat, greasy life. Stand there and look,
Because there is somebody in that house.
(The Boy *puts down pack and stands in the
doorway.)*
Boy.   There's nobody here.
Old Man.   There's somebody there.
Boy.   The floor is gone, the windows gone,
And where there should be roof there's sky,
And here's a bit of an egg-shell thrown
Out of a jackdaw's nest.
Old Man.   But there are some
That do not care what's gone, what's left:
The souls in Purgatory that come back
To habitations and familiar spots.
Boy.   Your wits are out again.
Old Man.   Re-live
Their transgressions, and that not once
But many times; they know at last
The consequence of those transgressions
Whether upon others or upon themselves;
Upon others, others may bring help,
For when the consequence is at an end
The dream must end; if upon themselves,
There is no help but in themselves
And in the mercy of God.
Boy.   I have had enough!
Talk to the jackdaws, if talk you must.
Old Man.   Stop! Sit there upon that stone.

That is the house where I was born.

Boy. The big old house that was burnt down?

Old Man. My mother that was your grand-dam owned
   it,
   This scenery and this countryside,
   Kennel and stable, horse and hound—
   She had a horse at the Curragh, and there met
   My father, a groom in a training stable,
   Looked at him and married him.
   Her mother never spoke to her again,
   And she did right.

Boy. What's right and wrong?
   My grand-dad got the girl and the money.

Old Man. Looked at him and married him,
   And he squandered everything she had.
   She never knew the worst, because
   She died in giving birth to me,
   But now she knows it all, being dead.
   Great people lived and died in this house;
   Magistrates, colonels, members of Parliament,
   Captains and Governors, and long ago
   Men that had fought at Aughrim and the Boyne.
   Some that had gone on Government work
   To London or to India came home to die;
   Or came from London every spring
   To look at the may-blossom in the park.
   They had loved the trees that he cut down
   To pay what he had lost at cards
   Or spent on horses, drink and women;
   Had loved the house, had loved all
   The intricate passages of the house,
   But he killed the house; to kill a house
   Where great men grew up, married, died,
   I here declare a capital offence.

Boy. My God, but you had luck! Grand clothes,
   And maybe a grand horse to ride.

Old Man. That he might keep me upon his level
   He never sent me to school, but some
   Half-loved me for my half of her:

A gamekeeper's wife taught me to read.
A Catholic curate taught me Latin.
There were old books and books made fine
By eighteenth-century French binding, books
Modern and ancient, books by the ton.

Boy. What education have you given me?

Old Man. I gave the education that befits
A bastard that a pedlar got
Upon a tinker's daughter in a ditch.
When I had come to sixteen years old
My father burned down the house when drunk.

Boy. But that is my age, sixteen years old,
At the Puck Fair.

Old Man. And everything was burnt;
Books, library, all were burnt.

Boy. Is what I have heard upon the road the truth,
That you killed him in the burning house?

Old Man. There's nobody here but our two selves?

Boy. Nobody, Father.

Old Man. I stuck him with a knife,
That knife that cuts my dinner now,
And after that I left him in the fire.
They dragged him out, somebody saw
The knife-wound but could not be certain
Because the body was all black and charred.
Then some that were his drunken friends
Swore they would put me upon trial,
Spoke of quarrels, a threat I had made.
The gamekeeper gave me some old clothes,
I ran away, worked here and there
Till I became a pedlar on the roads,
No good trade, but good enough
Because I am my father's son,
Because of what I did or may do.
Listen to the hoof-beats! Listen, listen!

Boy. I cannot hear a sound.

Old Man.   Beat! Beat!
This night is the anniversary
Of my mother's wedding night,

Or of the night wherein I was begotten.
My father is riding from the public-house,
A whiskey-bottle under his arm.
 (A window is lit showing a young girl.)
Look at the window; she stands there
Listening, the servants are all in bed,
She is alone, he has stayed late
Bragging and drinking in the public-house.

Boy. There's nothing but an empty gap in the wall.
You have made it up. No, you are mad!
You are getting madder every day.

Old Man. It's louder now because he rides
Upon a gravelled avenue
All grass to-day. The hoof-beat stops,
He has gone to the other side of the house,
Gone to the stable, put the horse up.
She has gone down to open the door.
This night she is no better than her man
And does not mind that he is half drunk,
She is mad about him. They mount the stairs,
She brings him into her own chamber.
And that is the marriage-chamber now.
The window is dimly lit again.

Do not let him touch you! It is not true
That drunken men cannot beget,
And if he touch he must beget
And you must bear his murderer.
Deaf! Both deaf! If I should throw
A stick or a stone they would not hear;
And that's a proof my wits are out.
But there's a problem: she must live
Through everything in exact detail,
Driven to it by remorse, and yet
Can she renew the sexual act
And find no pleasure in it, and if not,
If pleasure and remorse must both be there,
Which is the greater?
                    I lack schooling.

Go fetch Tertullian; he and I
Will ravel all that problem out
Whilst those two lie upon the mattress
Begetting me.

                         Come back! Come back!
And so you thought to slip away,
My bag of money between your fingers,
And that I could not talk and see!
You have been rummaging in the pack.

(The light in the window has faded out.)

Boy. You never gave me my right share.

Old Man. And had I given it, young as you are,
You would have spent it upon drink.

Boy. What if I did? I had a right
To get it and spend it as I chose.

Old Man. Give me that bag and no more words.

Boy. I will not.

Old Man. I will break your fingers.

*(They struggle for the bag. In the struggle it drops,
scattering the money.*

The Old Man *staggers but does not fall. They stand
looking at each other. The window is lit up. A man
is seen pouring whiskey into a glass.)*

Boy. What if I killed you? You killed my grand-dad,
Because you were young and he was old.
Now I am young and you are old.

Old Man (staring at window). Better-looking, those sixteen years—

Boy. What are you muttering?

Old Man.   Younger—and yet
She should have known he was not her kind.

Boy. What are you saying? Out with it!

(Old Man points to window.)

My God! The window is lit up
And somebody stands there, although
The floorboards are all burnt away.

Old Man. The window is it up because my father
Has come to find a glass for his whiskey.
He leans there like some tired beast.

Boy. A dead, living, murdered man!
Old Man. 'Then the bride-sleep fell upon Adam':
Where did I read those words?

　　　　　　　　　　　　　　　And yet

There's nothing leaning in the window
But the impression upon my mother's mind;
Being dead she is alone in her remorse.
Boy. A body that was a bundle of old bones
Before I was born. Horrible! Horrible!
　　(He covers his eyes.)
Old Man. That beast there would know nothing, being
nothing,
If I should kill a man under the window
He would not even turn his head. *(He stabs* The Boy.*)*
My father and my son on the same jackknife!
That finishes—there—there—there—
　　(He stabs again and again. The window grows dark.)
'Hush-a-bye baby, thy father's a knight,
Thy mother a lady, lovely and bright.'
No, that is something that I read in a book,
And if I sing it must be to my mother,
And I lack rhyme.
　　(The stage has grown dark except where the tree
　　stands in white light.)
　　　　　　　　　　Study that tree.
It stands there like a purified soul,
All cold, sweet, glistening light.
Dear mother, the window is dark again,
But you are in the light because
I finished all that consequence.
I killed that lad because had he grown up
He would have struck a woman's fancy,
Begot, and passed pollution on.
I am a wretched foul old man
And therefore harmless. When I have stuck
This old jack-knife into a sod
And pulled it out all bright again,
And picked up all the money that he dropped,
I'll to a distant place, and there

Tell my old jokes among new men.
   (*He cleans the knife and begins to pick up money.*)
Hoof-beats! Dear God,
How quickly it returns—beat—beat—!

Her mind cannot hold up that dream.
Twice a murderer and all for nothing,
And she must animate that dead night
Not once but many times!
                                   O God,
Release my mother's soul from its dream!
Mankind can do no more. Appease
The misery of the living and the remorse of the dead.

DISCUSSION AND WRITING MATERIAL

The following propositions can be used as a basis for discussion or writing. Present an argument either for or against the particular proposition using one or several of the developmental devices studied in the course of the book. Further, the essays by Harry Levin ("Symbolism and Fiction") and Francis Fergusson ("Myth and the Literary Scruple") may be helpful as reference material to make your arguments more effective.

"Sweeney Among the Nightingales"

1. The poem is a contrast of the sordid modern world with an ancient splendor.
2. Myth is used in the poem to point out Sweeney's ineffectual relationship with nature, universe, and man.
3. The main significance in the poem is the similarity of the depravity of past and present human activity when compared to the light of eternal beauty and truth.

"The Horse Dealer's Daughter"

1. The story is structured around the central symbol of the pond.
2. The reasons for Mabel's attempted suicide are found in her personal and environmental relationships.
3. The contrasting imagery between the events previous to the attempted suicide and those after reflects the internal emotional states of the characters.

"Purgatory"

1. The play is built upon a series of symbols that encompass not only the objects (tree, house, bird) but the characters themselves.
2. The use of repetition in the play leads one to conclude that the play is a bitter comment on modern Ireland.
3. Since purgatory to Yeats was representative of the imagination, the play is autobiographical in that it represents the dilemma of the poet's imagination.